POLITICS AND ECONOMICS OF THE MIDDLE EAST

IRAN

ECONOMIC, POLITICAL AND NUCLEAR POLICIES

Politics and Economics of the Middle East

Additional books and e-books in this series can be found on Nova's website under the Series tab.

POLITICS AND ECONOMICS OF THE MIDDLE EAST

IRAN

ECONOMIC, POLITICAL AND NUCLEAR POLICIES

EVERETT FOWLER
EDITOR

snova
New York

Library of Congress Cataloging-in-Publication Data

ISBN: 978-1-53614-827-5

Published by Nova Science Publishers, Inc. † New York

CONTENTS

PREFACE

Since the Islamic Revolution in Iran in 1979, the United States and Iran have been estranged and at odds. During the 1980s and 1990s, U.S. officials identified Iran's support for militant Middle East groups as the primary threat posed by Iran to U.S. interests and allies. Iran's nuclear program took precedence in U.S. policy after 2002 as the potential for Iran to develop a nuclear weapon increased. In 2010, the Obama Administration orchestrated broad international economic pressure on Iran to persuade it to agree to strict limits on the program—pressure that contributed to the June 2013 election of the relatively moderate Hassan Rouhani as president of Iran and the negotiation of a nuclear agreement—the "Joint Comprehensive Plan of Action" (JCPOA). The JCPOA exchanged sanctions relief for limits on Iran's nuclear program. The JCPOA reduced the potential threat from Iran's nuclear program, but did not contain strict or binding limits on Iran's ballistic missile program; its regional influence; its conventional military programs; and its human rights abuses. The Trump Administration cited these deficiencies of the JCPOA in its May 8, 2018, announcement that the United States would exit the JCPOA and reimpose all U.S. secondary sanctions by November 4, 2018.

Chapter 1 - With the easing of nuclear-related sanctions on Iran by the United States, European Union and United Nations under the Joint Comprehensive Plan of Action (JCPOA), signed on July 14, 2015, many foreign firms have begun to resume business with Iran. However, on October 13, 2017, President Trump announced he would not issue the certification that sanctions relief is "proportionate" to the measures taken by Iran to terminate its nuclear program. This decision has raised questions over the possible reimposition of U.S. economic sanctions. The EU, which views the JCPOA as a binding international commitment, is threatening to take action to protect its firms from reimposed secondary sanctions. No matter the actions of EU governments, EU companies might base their responses on a calculation of their economic interests in Iran versus risks to their position in U.S. markets.

Chapter 2 - With the easing of nuclear-related sanctions on Iran by the United States, European Union and United Nations under the Joint Comprehensive Plan of Action (JCPOA), signed on July 14, 2015, many foreign firms have begun to resume business with Iran. However, on October 13, 2017, President Trump announced he would not issue the certification that sanctions relief is "proportionate" to the measures taken by Iran to terminate its nuclear program. This decision has raised questions over the possible reimposition of U.S. economic sanctions. The EU, which views the JCPOA as a binding international commitment, is threatening to take action to protect its firms from reimposed secondary sanctions. No matter the actions of EU governments, EU companies might base their responses on a calculation of their economic interests in Iran versus risks to their position in U.S. markets.

Chapter 3 - Since multilateral sanctions on Iran were lifted in January 2016 under the Iran nuclear agreement (Joint Comprehensive Plan of Action, JCPOA), foreign firms have begun to resume business with Iran. Iranian leaders seem to be counting on expanded economic ties with the major East Asian economies to help Iran emerge from the years of international sanctions, diversify its economy away from reliance on hydrocarbon products, and become a regional trading hub. Expanding ties with Asia is politically easy for Iran because the major Asian countries remained engaged in Iran's economy even during the 2010-2016 multilateral sanctions regime.

Chapter 4 - Since the Islamic Revolution in Iran in 1979, the United States and Iran have been estranged and at odds. During the 1980s and 1990s, U.S. officials identified Iran's support for militant Middle East groups as the primary threat posed by Iran to U.S. interests and allies. Iran's nuclear program took precedence in U.S. policy after 2002 as the potential for Iran to develop a nuclear weapon increased. In 2010, the Obama Administration orchestrated broad international economic pressure on Iran to persuade it to agree to strict limits on the program—pressure that contributed to the June 2013 election of the relatively moderate Hassan Rouhani as president of Iran and the negotiation of a nuclear agreement—the "Joint Comprehensive Plan of Action" (JCPOA). The JCPOA exchanged sanctions relief for limits on Iran's nuclear program. The JCPOA reduced the potential threat from Iran's nuclear program, but did not contain strict or binding limits on Iran's ballistic missile program; its regional influence; its conventional military programs; and its human rights abuses. The Trump Administration cited these deficiencies of the JCPOA in its May 8, 2018, announcement that the United States would exit the JCPOA and reimpose all U.S. secondary sanctions by November 4, 2018. The stated intent of Trump Administration policy is to apply maximum economic pressure on Iran to compel it to change its behavior on the various issues of concern to the United States, including its support for regional armed factions. Iran's reaction to the U.S. exit from the JCPOA has raised concerns about the potential for the United States and Iran to come into direct armed conflict. Because of the many facets and issues involved in U.S. policy, on August 16, 2018, Secretary of State Michael Pompeo announced formation of an "Iran Action Group" to coordinate all aspects of State Department activity on Iran. Some experts assert that the threat posed by Iran stems from the nature and ideology of Iran's regime, and that the underlying, if unstated, goal of Trump Administration policy is to bring about regime collapse. A regime change strategy presumably would take advantage of divisions and fissures within Iran, as well as evident popular unrest. Hassan Rouhani, a moderate who seeks to improve Iran's relations with the West, including the United States, won successive presidential elections in 2013 and 2017, and reformist and moderate candidates won overwhelmingly in concurrent municipal council elections in all the major cities. But hardliners continue to control the state institutions that maintain internal security in large part through suppression. In part as a response to repression as well as economic conditions, unrest erupts periodically, most recently during December 2017-January 2018, and more sporadically since then. President Trump has indicated a willingness to meet with Iranian leaders, but his key foreign policy subordinates have set strict conditions for any broader improvement in relations— conditions the regime is highly unlikely to meet. As of mid-2018, Administration officials have been increasingly highlighting Iran's human rights abuses and systemic corruption in an apparent attempt to weaken support for the regime within Iran.

Chapter 5 - Iran's national security policy is the product of many overlapping and sometimes competing factors such as the ideology of Iran's Islamic revolution; perception of threats to the regime and to the country; long-standing Iranian national interests; and the interaction of the Iranian regime's factions and constituencies. Iran's leadership

- seeks to deter or thwart U.S. or other efforts to invade or intimidate Iran or to bring about a change of regime.
- has sought to take advantage of opportunities of regional conflicts to overturn a power structure in the Middle East that it asserts favors the United States, Israel, Saudi Arabia, and other Sunni Muslim Arab regimes.
- seeks to enhance its international prestige and restore a sense of "greatness" reminiscent of ancient Persian empires.
- provides material support to allied governments and armed factions such as the Asad regime in Syria, Lebanese Hezbollah, Houthi rebels in Yemen, Iraqi Shiite militias, and Bahraini militant groups. Iranian officials characterize this support as helping the region's "oppressed" and assert that Saudi Arabia, in particular, is instigating sectarian tensions and trying to exclude Iran from regional affairs.
- has sought to use sanctions relief provided by the July 2015 multilateral nuclear agreement (Joint Comprehensive Plan of Action, JCPOA) to emerge as a regional energy and trade hub and to negotiate future weapons buys.

- sometimes disagrees on tactics and strategies. Supreme Leader Ali Khamene'i and key hardline institutions, such as the Islamic Revolutionary Guard Corps (IRGC), oppose any compromises of Iran's national security core goals, but support the reintegration into regional and international diplomacy that is advocated by Iran's elected president, Hassan Rouhani.
- supports acts of international terrorism, as the "leading" or "most active" state sponsor of terrorism, according to each annual State Department report on international terrorism since the early 1990s.

The Trump Administration has articulated a strategy to counter Iran's "malign activities" and its behavior more broadly, based primarily on reducing Iran's financial resources. The Administration argued that the JCPOA failed to address Iran's regional activities and, partly on these grounds, President Trump withdrew the United States from the JCPOA on May 8, 2018, and announced that all U.S. sanctions would be reimposed. Additional aspects of Administration strategy for countering Iran's malign activities—which include working with partner governments and factions in the region—are enumerated in a report submitted to Congress in late August 2018, a report mandated by the Countering America's Adversaries through Sanctions Act (P.L. 115-44). President Trump and other senior U.S. officials also have indirectly threatened military action against Iranian actions that pose an immediate threat to U.S. regional interests or allies. In late September 2018, the Administration issued a report ("Outlaw Regime: A Chronicle of Iran's Destructive Activities") broadly indicting Iran's malign activities as well as a litany of other activities the Administration termed "Iranian regime's destructive behavior at home and abroad."

Chapter 6 - The exchanges of threats between members of the governments of Iran and the United States, including the presidents of both countries, have again raised the specter of an interruption of shipping through the Strait of Hormuz (the Strait), a key waterway for the transit of oil and natural gas to world markets. In the first half of 2018, approximately 18 million barrels per day (bpd) of crude oil and condensate, almost 4 million bpd of petroleum products, and over 300 million cubic meters per day in liquefied natural gas (LNG) exited the Strait. Iran accounted for about 10% of oil and 0% of the natural gas through the Strait. In a speech on July 22, Iranian President Rouhani stated, "We are the... guarantor of security of the waterway of the region throughout the history. Don't play with the lion's tail; you will regret it." (Western reporting took the reference to the waterway to mean the Strait of Hormuz, which is the narrow waterway that forms the entrance to the Persian Gulf from the Gulf of Oman and ultimately the Arabian Sea.). To which President Trump tweeted, "Never, Ever, Threaten the United States Again or You Will Suffer Consequences the Likes of Which Few Throughout History Have Ever Suffered Before..." Earlier, on July 3, President Rouhani stated, "The Americans have claimed they want to completely stop Iran's oil exports. They don't understand the meaning of this statement, because it has no meaning for Iranian oil not to be exported, while the region's oil is exported." This is not the first time Iran's leaders have threatened to close or hinder shipping through the Strait of Hormuz. Prior to sanctions targeting Iran's oil exports in 2011/12, Iranian leaders threatened to close the Strait of Hormuz. Press reports that Iran is about to begin a large naval exercise in and around the Strait in early August 2018 is likely to inflame tensions further.

Chapter 7 - Iranian voters go to the polls on May 19, 2017, to vote for president and municipal officials countrywide amid tensions between Iran and the United States. On April 19, the Trump Administration certified to Congress, pursuant to the Iran Nuclear Agreement Review Act (INARA, P.L. 114-17), that Iran is complying with the 2015 multilateral nuclear agreement (Joint Comprehensive Plan of Action, JCPOA). Secretary of State Rex Tillerson stated, however, that the JCPOA "only delays [Iran's] goal of becoming a nuclear state" and has failed to curb Iran's objectionable regional behavior. He announced that the United States' Iran policy— including the JCPOA—is under review. In recent weeks, the Trump Administration has imposed sanctions on additional entities allegedly supporting Iran's missile program and has launched strikes on Iran's key regional ally, Syria, for its use of chemical weapons. The Administration reportedly is also contemplating increased support for an effort by a Saudi-led Arab coalition battling Iran-backed Houthi rebels in Yemen.

Chapter 8 - Iran's nuclear program began during the 1950s. The United States has expressed concern since the mid-1970s that Tehran might develop nuclear weapons. Iran's construction of gas centrifuge uranium enrichment facilities is currently the main source of proliferation concern. Gas centrifuges can produce both low-enriched uranium (LEU), which can be used in nuclear power reactors, and weapons-grade highly enriched uranium (HEU), which is one of the two types of fissile material used in nuclear weapons. The United States has assessed that Tehran possesses the technological and industrial capacity to produce nuclear weapons, but has not yet mastered all of the necessary technologies for building such weapons. Whether Iran has a viable design for a nuclear weapon is unclear. A National Intelligence Estimate made public in 2007 assessed that Tehran "halted its nuclear weapons program" in 2003. The estimate, however, also assessed that Tehran is "keeping open the option to develop nuclear weapons" and that any decision to end a nuclear weapons program is "inherently reversible." U.S. intelligence officials have reaffirmed this judgment on several occasions. Obtaining fissile material is widely regarded as the most difficult task in building nuclear weapons. As of January 2014, Iran had produced an amount of LEU containing up to 5% uranium-235 which, if further enriched, could theoretically have produced enough HEU for as many as eight nuclear weapons. Iran had also produced LEU containing nearly 20% uranium-235; the total amount of this LEU would, if it had been in the form of uranium hexafluoride and further enriched, have been sufficient for a nuclear weapon. After the Joint Plan of Action, which Tehran concluded with China,

France, Germany, Russia, the United Kingdom, and the United States (collectively known as the "P5+1"), went into effect in January 2014, Iran either converted much of its LEU containing nearly 20% uranium-235 for use as fuel in a research reactor located in Tehran, or prepared it for that purpose. Iran has diluted the rest of that stockpile so that it contained no more than 5% uranium-235. Although Iran claims that its nuclear program is exclusively for peaceful purposes, the program has generated considerable concern that Tehran is pursuing a nuclear weapons program. The U.N. Security Council responded to Iran's refusal to suspend work on its uranium enrichment program by adopting several resolutions that imposed sanctions on Tehran. Despite evidence that sanctions and other forms of pressure have slowed the program, Iran continued to enrich uranium, install additional centrifuges, and conduct research on new types of centrifuges. Tehran has also worked on a heavy-water reactor, which was a proliferation concern because its spent fuel would have contained plutonium—the other type of fissile material used in nuclear weapons. However, plutonium must be separated from spent fuel—a procedure called "reprocessing." Iran has said that it will not engage in reprocessing. The International Atomic Energy Agency (IAEA) monitors Iran's nuclear facilities and has verified that Tehran's declared nuclear facilities and materials have not been diverted for military purposes. The agency has also verified that Iran has implemented various restrictions on, and provided the IAEA with additional information about, its uranium enrichment program and heavy-water reactor program pursuant to the July 2015 Joint Cooperative Plan of Action (JCPOA), which Tehran concluded with the P5+1. On the JCPOA's Implementation Day, which took place on January 16, 2016, all of the previous Security Council resolutions' requirements were terminated. The nuclear Nonproliferation Treaty (NPT) and U.N. Security Council Resolution 2231, which the Council adopted on July 20, 2015, comprise the current legal framework governing Iran's nuclear program. Iran has continued to comply with the JCPOA and resolution. Iran and the IAEA agreed in 2007 on a work plan to clarify outstanding questions regarding Tehran's nuclear program, most of which concerned possible Iranian procurement activities and research directly applicable to nuclear weapons development. A December 2015, report to the IAEA Board of Governors from agency Director-General Yukiya Amano contains the IAEA's "final assessment on the resolution" of these outstanding issues. Then-Under Secretary of State for Political Affairs Wendy Sherman explained during an October 2013 hearing of the Senate Committee on Foreign Relations that Iran would need as much as one year to produce a nuclear weapon if the government made the decision to do so. At the time, Tehran would have needed two to three months of this time to produce enough weapons-grade HEU for a nuclear weapon. Iran's compliance with the JCPOA has lengthened this time to one year, according to U.S. officials. These estimates apparently assume that Iran would use its declared nuclear facilities to produce fissile material for a weapon. However, Tehran would probably use covert facilities for this purpose; Iranian efforts to produce fissile material for nuclear weapons by using its known nuclear facilities would almost certainly be detected by the IAEA.

Chapter 9 - On July 14, 2015, Iran and the six powers that had negotiated with Tehran about its nuclear program since 2006 (the United States, the United Kingdom, France, Russia, China, and Germany—collectively known as the P5+1) finalized a Joint Comprehensive Plan of Action (JCPOA). The JCPOA required constraints that seek to ensure that Iran's nuclear program can be used for purely peaceful purposes in exchange for a broad lifting of U.S., European Union (EU), and United Nations (U.N.) sanctions on Iran. The agreement replaced the Joint Plan of Action (JPA), an interim nuclear accord in effect from 2014 to 2016. Congress did not enact a resolution of disapproval of the JCPOA by the deadline of September 17, 2015, which was set by the Iran Nuclear Agreement Review Act (P.L. 114-17); the JCPOA formally took effect on "Adoption Day" (October 18, 2015). "Implementation Day" was declared by the P5+1 on January 16, 2016, representing the completion of Iran's nuclear requirements; entry into effect of U.N. Security Council Resolution 2231, which endorsed the JCPOA; and the start of sanctions relief stipulated in the agreement. Officials from both the Barack Obama and Donald Trump Administrations have certified that Iran has abided by its JCPOA commitments. The Obama Administration and other P5+1 leaders asserted that the JCPOA is the most effective means to ensure that Iran cannot obtain a nuclear weapon and that all U.S. options to prevent Iran from developing a nuclear weapon are available indefinitely. The agreement contains provisions for U.N. sanctions to be reimposed if Iran violates its commitments. Top Trump Administration officials have argued that the JCPOA does not adequately serve U.S. interests because the extensive sanctions relief provided under the accord gives Iran additional resources to conduct "malign activities" in the region, and does not restrict Iran's development of ballistic missiles. Resolution 2231, which was adopted in July 2015, prohibits arms transfers to or from Iran, but only for five years, and contains a voluntary restriction on Iran's development of nuclear-capable ballistic missiles for only up to eight years. On May 8, President Trump announced that the United States would no longer participate in the JCPOA and would reimpose sanctions that had been suspended pursuant to the agreement. The other powers that negotiated the accord with Iran—Russia, China, France, Britain, and Germany—opposed the U.S. decision and have been meeting with Iranian officials to continue implementing the JCPOA. Iran's President Hassan Rouhani has pledged to continue implementing the accord, provided Iran continues to receive the economic benefits of the agreement. In the 114th and 115th Congresses, legislation has been introduced with the stated purpose of redressing asserted weaknesses of the deal or preventing any U.S. sanctions relief beyond that explicitly promised in the JCPOA. The Countering America's Adversaries through Sanctions Act (P.L. 115-44) mandates sanctions on Iranian proliferation, human rights abuses, and support for terrorist activities.

Chapter 10 - On July 14, 2015, Iran and the six powers that had negotiated with Tehran about its nuclear program since 2006 (the United States, the United Kingdom, France, Russia, China, and Germany—collectively known as the P5+1) finalized a Joint Comprehensive Plan of Action (JCPOA). The JCPOA required constraints that seek to ensure that Iran's nuclear program can be used for purely peaceful purposes in exchange for a broad lifting of U.S., European Union (EU), and United Nations (U.N.) sanctions on Iran. The agreement replaced the Joint Plan of Action (JPA), an interim nuclear accord in effect from 2014 to 2016. Congress did not enact a resolution of disapproval of the JCPOA by the deadline of September 17, 2015, which was set by the Iran Nuclear Agreement Review Act (P.L. 114-17); the JCPOA formally took effect on "Adoption Day" (October 18, 2015). "Implementation Day" was declared by the P5+1 on January 16, 2016, representing the completion of Iran's nuclear requirements; entry into effect of U.N. Security Council Resolution 2231, which endorsed the JCPOA; and the start of sanctions relief stipulated in the agreement. Officials from both the Barack Obama and Donald Trump Administrations have certified that Iran has abided by its JCPOA commitments. The Obama Administration and other P5+1 leaders asserted that the JCPOA is the most effective means to ensure that Iran cannot obtain a nuclear weapon and that all U.S. options to prevent Iran from developing a nuclear weapon are available indefinitely. The agreement contains provisions for U.N. sanctions to be reimposed if Iran violates its commitments. Top Trump Administration officials have argued that the JCPOA does not adequately serve U.S. interests because the extensive sanctions relief provided under the accord gives Iran additional resources to conduct "malign activities" in the region, and does not restrict Iran's development of ballistic missiles. Resolution 2231, which was adopted in July 2015, prohibits arms transfers to or from Iran, but only for five years, and contains a voluntary restriction on Iran's development of nuclear-capable ballistic missiles for only up to eight years. On May 8, President Trump announced that the United States would no longer participate in the JCPOA and would reimpose sanctions that had been suspended pursuant to the agreement. The other powers that negotiated the accord with Iran—Russia, China, France, Britain, and Germany—opposed the U.S. decision and have been meeting with Iranian officials to continue implementing the JCPOA. Iran's President Hassan Rouhani has pledged to continue implementing the accord, provided Iran continues to receive the economic benefits of the agreement. In the 114th and 115th Congresses, legislation has been introduced with the stated purpose of redressing asserted weaknesses of the deal or preventing any U.S. sanctions relief beyond that explicitly promised in the JCPOA. The Countering America's Adversaries through Sanctions Act (P.L. 115-44) mandates sanctions on Iranian proliferation, human rights abuses, and support for terrorist activities.

Chapter 11 - On February 1, 2017, the Trump Administration announced that it was "officially putting Iran on notice" for recent actions that "threaten U.S. friends and allies in the region," including the January 29 test of a ballistic missile and "weapons transfers [to groups such as Houthi rebels in Yemen], support for terrorism, and other violations of international norms." The July 2015 multilateral nuclear agreement with Iran, the "Joint Comprehensive Plan of Action" (JCPOA), does not restrict Iran's ballistic missile programs. However, U.N. Security Council Resolution 2231, which endorses the JCPOA, prohibits Iran from exporting weaponry and "call[s] upon" Iran "not to undertake any activity related to ballistic missiles designed to be capable of delivering nuclear weapons, including launches." Yet, Iran has conducted several ballistic missile tests since JCPOA Implementation Day on January 16, 2016—the day Resolution 2231 formally took effect.

In: Iran: Economic, Political and Nuclear Policies
Editor: Everett Fowler
ISBN: 978-1-53614-827-5

Chapter 1

DOING BUSINESS WITH IRAN: EU-IRAN TRADE AND INVESTMENT RELATIONS*

Cathleen D. Cimino-Isaacs and Kenneth Katzman

With the easing of nuclear-related sanctions on Iran by the United States, European Union and United Nations under the Joint Comprehensive Plan of Action (JCPOA), signed on July 14, 2015, many foreign firms have begun to resume business with Iran. However, on October 13, 2017, President Trump announced he would not issue the certification that sanctions relief is "proportionate" to the measures taken by Iran to terminate its nuclear program. This decision has raised questions over the possible reimposition of U.S. economic sanctions. The EU, which views the JCPOA as a binding international commitment, is threatening to take action to protect its firms from reimposed secondary sanctions. No matter the actions of EU governments, EU companies might base their responses on a calculation of their economic interests in Iran versus risks to their position in U.S. markets.

EU ECONOMIC ENGAGEMENT IN IRAN

EU sanctions relief, coupled with the lifting of U.S. secondary sanctions under the JCPOA, paved the way for increased trade and foreign direct investment in Iran. The EU lifted its bans on Iranian oil and gas imports and trade in other sectors, and Iran's use of the SWIFT financial messaging services system, among other restrictions. Before the

---

* This is an edited, reformatted and augmented version of Congressional Research Service, Publication No. IN10809, dated October 25, 2017.

escalation of sanctions, in 2010, the EU was Iran's top trading partner, accounting for nearly a quarter of Iran's total goods trade; in 2015, the EU accounted for 8%, replaced by China (25%), the United Arab Emirates (17%), and Turkey (10%), according to International Monetary Fund data. Following adoption of the JCPOA, EU imports from Iran rebounded in 2016 with 347% growth compared to 2015, driven by resumed purchases of fuels and mining products; though trade remains short of pre-sanctions levels (Figure 1). EU exports to Iran expanded by 28%, led by exports in machinery and transport equipment and chemicals.

In early 2017, Iran delivered its largest monthly shipments of crude to Europe since the end of 2011. While Asia has been a top buyer of Iranian energy, National Iranian Oil Company (NIOC) crude sales to Europe are rising as Iran seeks to recapture market share; Europe accounted for 34% of NIOC sales through July 2017, compared to 31% at the end of 2016.

Since the easing of sanctions in January 2016, several EU multinational corporations have announced new investments including in the manufacturing, energy, and auto sectors.

Since the easing of sanctions in January 2016, several EU multinational corporations have announced new investments including in the manufacturing, energy, and auto sectors.

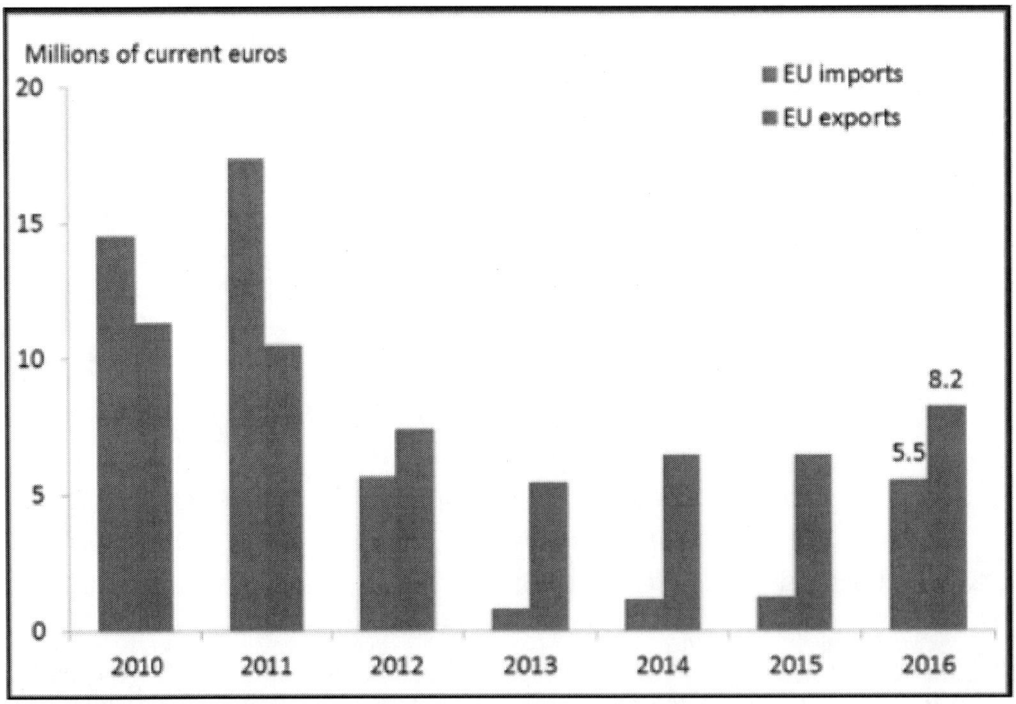

Source: Eurostat, October 2017.

Figure 1. EU-Iran Goods Trade.

- French company Total, China National Petroleum Corporation, and NIOC signed a $4.7 billion deal to develop production in South Pars gas field.
- Auto companies Citroen, Peugeot, Renault, Scania, and Volkswagen announced investments to expand production in Iran.
- German company Siemens signed a contract to modernize Iran's railway network.
- Italian company Danieli signed several contracts to supply heavy machinery for steel production.
- British company Vodafone partnered with Iranian firm HiWeb to modernize Iran's information technology infrastructure.
- British company Quercus announced a €500 million deal to develop Iran's solar energy sector.

At the same time, major European financial institutions and other banks have been cautious about engaging in transactions with Iran. Uncertainty regarding possible reimposition of the waived U.S. sanctions and fear of violating those U.S. sanctions that remain in place are among cited reasons for such reticence. The Treasury Department has taken a number of enforcement actions for sanctions violations and evasion, resulting in hefty civil fines paid by some major European banks.

How risk averse foreign companies will be with regard to expanding activities in Iran given continued uncertainty over the JCPOA is an open question. U.S. sanctions can have a broad chilling effect on economic activity when firms are faced with losing access to the U.S. market. Moreover, some analysts view EU options as increasingly constrained given that "European companies now have far more assets exposed to U.S. regulators, who could retaliate against them, or force them to pick between the Iranian and U.S. markets."

EU Responses to Safeguard Firms

U.S. sanctions that target secondary activities became prominent in U.S. legislation from the early 1990s. The EU has opposed that strategy from the onset and has sometimes resorted to regulatory action and dispute settlement at the World Trade Organization (WTO) to shield its firms.

Blocking Statutes

In response to U.S. sanctions on Cuba, Iran, and Libya, the EU adopted Council Regulation (EC) 2271/96 in 1996 to protect "against the effects of extra-territorial application of legislation adopted by a third country." It remains in force. Key features include: prohibiting compliance (whether directly or through a subsidiary) with specified U.S. laws; prohibiting recognition or compliance with court judgments outside the EU that give effect to U.S. sanctions; and entitlement to recover any damages incurred as a result of noncompliance with U.S. sanctions. An annex lists U.S. laws and regulations subject to the measure (including the Iran [and Libya] Sanctions Act of 1996, P.L. 104-172)—amendments to the annex would be required to include subsequent U.S. laws pertaining to Iran. The regulation also compels EU member states to determine "effective, proportional and dissuasive" sanctions in the event of a breach of the provisions. Member states are responsible for implementation; in practice, there have been few cases of enforcement. In one case, the Austrian government sought to penalize the Austrian Bank Bawag for violating the blocking regulation, after the bank closed accounts of Cuban nationals to comply with the Cuban Liberty and Democratic Solidarity Act of 1996 (P.L. 104-114).

WTO Dispute Settlement

In 1996, the EU also initiated a dispute under WTO procedures to challenge certain provisions of U.S. sanctions against Cuba as inconsistent with U.S. obligations. The United States claimed its policies would be defensible under the broad "national security" exception of the General Agreement on Tariffs and Trade (GATT). The case was ultimately withdrawn in April 1998, after the United States and EU reached a negotiated compromise that effectively exempted the EU from key contested provisions. The EU reserved the right to re-initiate the case if the United States took adverse action against EU firms. The EU could file a complaint in the wake of reimposed sanctions on Iran; however, WTO disputes can take several years to resolve. Moreover, cases involving claims of "national security" have rarely been litigated at the WTO—creating an incentive for a negotiated settlement.

In: Iran: Economic, Political and Nuclear Policies
Editor: Everett Fowler
ISBN: 978-1-53614-827-5

Chapter 2

IRAN POLICY AND THE EUROPEAN UNION*

Derek E. Mix and Kenneth Katzman

POLICY CONTEXT

On October 13, 2017, President Trump announced a new U.S. strategy on Iran. He stated that, under the Iran Nuclear Agreement Review Act (INARA; P.L. 114-17), he would not be certifying that continued Iran sanctions relief is proportionate to the measures taken by Iran to terminate its illicit nuclear program. That and other INARA certification requirements are related to, but separate from, Iran's nuclear obligations under the July 14, 2015, multilateral nuclear agreement (Joint Comprehensive Plan of Action, or JCPOA). The withholding of INARA certification does not automatically end U.S. participation in the JCPOA, which the UK, France, Germany, the United States, Russia, and China negotiated with Iran. But the President linked continued U.S. participation to congressional and allied action to address deficiencies in the JCPOA that he identified in his October 13 statement.

EUROPEAN UNION REACTION

Based on statements by Donald Trump during the 2016 presidential campaign, EU officials have long expressed concern that a Trump Administration might abandon the consensus U.S.-EU policy toward Iran. In February 2017, Trump Administration officials

* This is an edited, reformatted and augmented version of CRS Insight, Publication No. IN10656, dated October 18, 2017.

announced they had begun a "deliberative process" to respond to what officials termed Iran's provocative behavior, including ballistic missile tests and support for armed groups in the Middle East.

President Trump's October 13 announcement raised European fears of a possible U.S. pullout from the JCPOA. EU High Representative Federica Mogherini reiterated the EU's stance, stating, "It is not a bilateral agreement, it does not belong to any single country and it is not up to any single country to terminate it.... There have been no violations of any of the commitments included in the agreement.... The European Union continues to fully support the Iran nuclear deal, and the full and strict implementation of all its provisions by all parties."

A statement released following the October 16, 2017, meeting of EU foreign ministers asserted, "The European Union considers President Trump's decision not to certify Iran's compliance with [JCPOA] as being in the context of an internal U.S. process. The EU encourages the U.S. to maintain its commitment to the JCPOA and to consider the implications for the security of the U.S., its partners and the region before taking further steps."

EU-Iran Policy Background

The JCPOA represented the culmination of years-long coordination between several EU countries and the United States. From the 1979 revolution in Iran until 2012, when EU sanctions on Iran became nearly as strict as those of the United States, the United States and European countries often diverged on the issue of Iran. In 2006, as Iran's nuclear program continued to expand, the United States formally joined an effort by the UK, France, and Germany ("EU-3") to induce Iran to agree to limit the scope of its nuclear program. The EU-3 and the United States, along with Russia and China, formed the "P5+1" group of negotiating states. Between 2006 and 2010, the EU-3 and the United States successfully pushed for United Nations Security Council approval of four rounds of sanctions on Iran. Starting in 2010, the EU demonstrated a willingness to adopt sanctions that were virtually as comprehensive as those imposed on Iran by the United States—exemplified by a 2012 EU ban on importation of Iranian oil.

On JPCOA "Implementation Day" (January 16, 2016), the EU suspended its economic and financial sanctions related to Iran's nuclear program, which are to terminate formally on "Transition Day" of the JCPOA (October 18, 2023). In case of unresolvable "significant non-performance" of Iran's JCPOA commitments, the EU—in concert with a U.N. Security Council decision—could reimpose all suspended sanctions.

The EU continues to maintain sanctions against Iran in response to what it deems human rights violations, and Iranians designated under sanctions related to terrorism and Syria also continue to be listed.

Meanwhile, as evidenced by a stream of European ministers and businesspeople visiting Tehran over the past year, European businesses have sought to reengage Iran following the JCPOA's implementation. EU trade with Iran nearly doubled in 2016, and oil imports from Iran have returned to near pre-embargo levels. European companies—particularly those involved in auto and other manufacturing and the energy sector—have announced investments in Iran worth billions of euros, and European banks and credit agencies have begun to facilitate transactions. Iranian banks have rejoined EU-based electronic payments systems, such as SWIFT.

OUTLOOK

Apparently seeking to head off U.S. action to leave the JCPOA, EU officials have expressed a willingness to work with the Trump Administration to try to engage Iran in new talks on Iranian behavior not covered under the JCPOA, particularly on limits to its ballistic missile program. But EU officials stress that missiles and other non-nuclear concerns identified by President Trump be addressed outside the JCPOA. Should the Trump Administration or Congress decide to cease implementing the JCPOA, the EU will likely seek to continue implementing it by keeping EU sanctions relief in place.

The U.S. sanctions that have had the most effect on Iran are secondary sanctions that were placed on foreign companies doing business with Iran. Were the U.S. Administration to leave the JCPOA and reimpose such sanctions, doing so would likely heighten transatlantic tensions significantly. EU officials have indicated they will take action to protect EU companies from reimposed U.S. sanctions. The EU might initiate a dispute through the World Trade Organization, seeking to secure exemptions from the U.S. measures. The EU and the United States have clashed before over "extraterritorial" sanctions when the United States adopted such measures in relation to Libya, Iran, and Cuba in 1996. The EU responded with the adoption of Council Regulation (EC) No. 2271/96 in an attempt to protect citizens and companies within the EU against the application of sanctions by the United States. In past cases, however, the United States and the EU reached a negotiated compromise before mutual imposition of any penalties.

In: Iran: Economic, Political and Nuclear Policies
Editor: Everett Fowler
ISBN: 978-1-53614-827-5

Chapter 3

IRAN'S EXPANDING ECONOMIC RELATIONS WITH ASIA*

Cathleen D. Cimino-Isaacs and Kenneth Katzman

OVERVIEW

Since multilateral sanctions on Iran were lifted in January 2016 under the Iran nuclear agreement (Joint Comprehensive Plan of Action, JCPOA), foreign firms have begun to resume business with Iran. Iranian leaders seem to be counting on expanded economic ties with the major East Asian economies to help Iran emerge from the years of international sanctions, diversify its economy away from reliance on hydrocarbon products, and become a regional trading hub. Expanding ties with Asia is politically easy for Iran because the major Asian countries remained engaged in Iran's economy even during the 2010-2016 multilateral sanctions regime.

East Asian Economic Engagement with Iran

As top Iranian oil customers, China, Japan and South Korea played a key role in escalating energy sanctions against Iran. Their reductions of Iranian oil purchases (to earn a U.S. sanctions exemption for "significantly reducing" purchases of oil), combined with the EU's oil embargo, led to a significant contraction of Iranian exports after 2011. From 2011-2012, Chinese imports of Iranian crude fell by nearly a quarter; Japanese and South

---

* This is an edited, reformatted and augmented version of Congressional Research Service, Publication No. IN10829, dated November 29, 2017.

Korean imports fell about 40% and further by 2015. Japan and South Korea also banned energy-invested projects in Iran and restricted trade financing.

Iran has worked to regain market share in Asia since sanctions were eased. China and South Korea's oil imports have reached or surpassed pre-sanction levels; purchases by Japan and other Asian countries have been slower to rebound (Figure 1). Iran also regained access to some $115 billion in hard currency held abroad, whose repatriation was restricted by foreign banks, particularly those in Japan and South Korea, to comply with U.S. sanctions.

Tightened sanctions increased Iran's reliance on Chinese trade; China's share of Iran's global trade expanded from 20% in 2010 to 31% in 2016. Due to missing data reported for Iran, the trade shares are based only on the data of Iran's trading partners. Although China cut oil imports it did not fully ban energy trade, allowing China to surpass the EU in 2011 as the top buyer of Iranian oil. While energy remains China's largest import from Iran, plastics, ores, and organic chemicals account for a growing share, some 30% in 2016. This in part reflects Iran's attempt to diversify toward non-oil sectors.

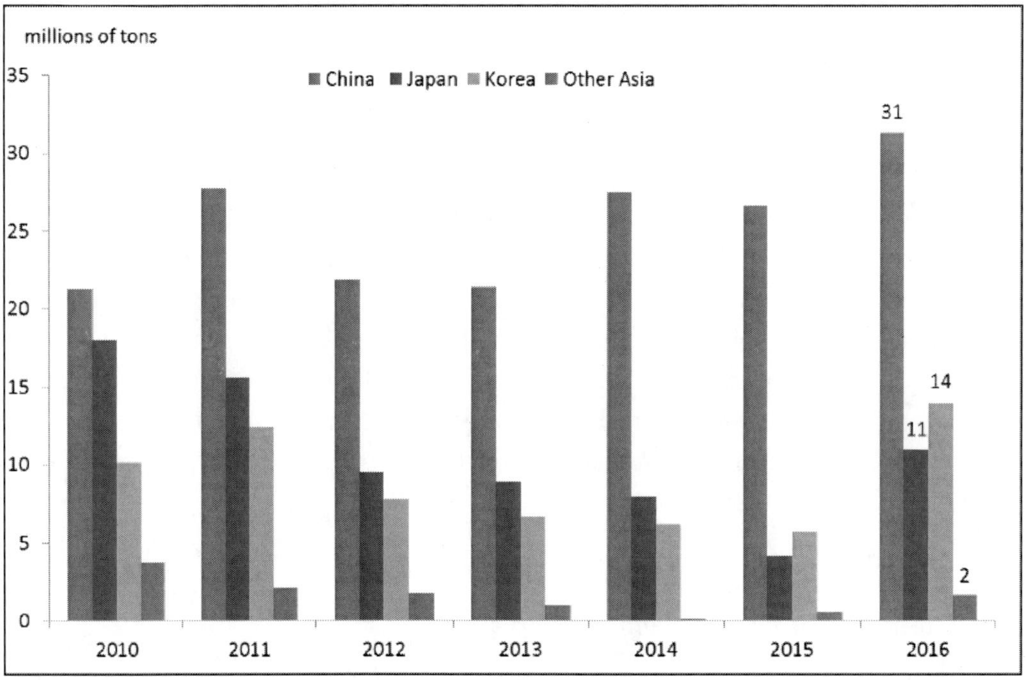

Source: International Trade Centre.

Notes: Crude oil based on HS product code 2709. "Other Asia" includes Malaysia, Singapore, and Taiwan.

Figure 1. Major Asian Crude Oil Importers from Iran.

Blocked from accessing foreign exchange at the height of U.S. sanctions, Iran settled its trade balance with its oil customers, particularly China, in goods rather than hard currency. Chinese exports to Iran doubled from 2010 to 2014. China supplies about one-third of Iran's overall imports, and accounts for as much as 50% to 100% of Iran's imports of such products as textiles, rail locomotives, ships, and iron and steel. South Korea accounts for less than 10% of Iran's imports but remains a key source of certain inputs, such as auto parts. China and South Korea have become Iran's top auto parts suppliers, accounting for 29% and 22% of Iranian imports, respectively. Iran has prioritized its auto industry, the largest industry after energy, after production fell 55% from 2011 to 2013. Iran moved to limit auto imports to incentivize foreign direct investment (FDI) in domestic production.

FDI in Iran has increased since sanctions were eased. In 2016, total announced investment projects in Iran were valued at $12.2 billion, compared to $2.5 billion in 2015. East Asian countries have taken steps to facilitate new investment. In February 2016, Japan and Iran signed an investment agreement, and in May 2016, South Korea and Iran signed memorandums of understanding for 30 joint projects in energy and infrastructure. Among new Asian investments in Iran are:

- *Oil.* Chinese firms CNPC and Sinopec are in talks for phase two development of Yadavaran and Azadegan oil fields. Japanese firm Inpex, which divested its 10% stake in Azadegan in 2010, is reportedly also considering re-joining that project.
- *Oil and gas refineries.* Hyundai, Daelim, Daewoo and SK E&C signed several agreements. In July 2017, Korean and Japanese firms signed a $3 billion agreement for development of Siraf refineries. Sinopec has contracted to renovate the Abadan refinery.
- *Natural gas.* CNPC joined French company Total in a contract to develop the South Pars gas field. In May 2016, KOGAS signed an MOU to explore development of Balal gas field.
- *Shipbuilding.* In December 2016, Hyundai Heavy Industries announced a $700 million deal to build 10 ships for Iran's state-owned shipping company. Daewoo and DSME announced a joint venture for shipyard construction.
- *Autos.* In March 2017, Hyundai signed a joint venture production agreement with Kerman Motor, and Kia Motors resumed selling production kits to Saipa.

China views Iran as an important player in its "Belt and Road" initiative (BRI), which aims to boost economic connectivity across continents, including through financing massive infrastructure and energy projects. BRI is also viewed as an outlet to deal with China's industrial overcapacity in steel, cement, and other commodities. Chinese state-owned enterprises and private businesses are involved in several projects, backed by state financing, to modernize Iran's transportation infrastructure, including the Tehran subway. Chinese automaker, Chery, is the largest foreign automaker in Iran and operates an auto industrial park. In December 2014, Iran, Kazakhstan, and Turkmenistan inaugurated a railway connecting China to Tehran, and in February 2016 the first rail cargo arrived in Iran. BRI may facilitate increased bilateral trade with China, but could also expand Iran's role as a hub linking Central Asia to Europe.

IMPLICATIONS

Iran's expanding economic ties with the countries in East Asia, especially China, are likely to give Tehran additional allies in its efforts to counter pressure by the Trump Administration and Congress to renegotiate the JCPOA or to impose additional sanctions on Iran through legislation. In particular, China, which appears to see Iran as a lynchpin of its regional economic strategy, holds a seat on the U.N. Security Council, and is positioned to slow U.S. efforts to isolate Iran. Yet, the relative lack of East Asian political or military involvement in the region ensures that U.S. and European leverage on Iran remains significant.

In: Iran: Economic, Political and Nuclear Policies
Editor: Everett Fowler

ISBN: 978-1-53614-827-5

Chapter 4

IRAN: INTERNAL POLITICS AND U.S. POLICY AND OPTIONS*

Kenneth Katzman

ABSTRACT

Since the Islamic Revolution in Iran in 1979, the United States and Iran have been estranged and at odds. During the 1980s and 1990s, U.S. officials identified Iran's support for militant Middle East groups as the primary threat posed by Iran to U.S. interests and allies. Iran's nuclear program took precedence in U.S. policy after 2002 as the potential for Iran to develop a nuclear weapon increased. In 2010, the Obama Administration orchestrated broad international economic pressure on Iran to persuade it to agree to strict limits on the program—pressure that contributed to the June 2013 election of the relatively moderate Hassan Rouhani as president of Iran and the negotiation of a nuclear agreement—the "Joint Comprehensive Plan of Action" (JCPOA). The JCPOA exchanged sanctions relief for limits on Iran's nuclear program. The JCPOA reduced the potential threat from Iran's nuclear program, but did not contain strict or binding limits on Iran's ballistic missile program; its regional influence; its conventional military programs; and its human rights abuses.

The Trump Administration cited these deficiencies of the JCPOA in its May 8, 2018, announcement that the United States would exit the JCPOA and reimpose all U.S. secondary sanctions by November 4, 2018. The stated intent of Trump Administration policy is to apply maximum economic pressure on Iran to compel it to change its behavior on the various issues of concern to the United States, including its support for regional armed factions. Iran's reaction to the U.S. exit from the JCPOA has raised concerns about the potential for the United States and Iran to come into direct armed conflict. Because of the many facets and issues involved in U.S. policy, on August 16,

* This is an edited, reformatted and augmented version of Congressional Research Service, Publication No. RL32048, dated August 23, 2018.

2018, Secretary of State Michael Pompeo announced formation of an "Iran Action Group" to coordinate all aspects of State Department activity on Iran.

Some experts assert that the threat posed by Iran stems from the nature and ideology of Iran's regime, and that the underlying, if unstated, goal of Trump Administration policy is to bring about regime collapse. A regime change strategy presumably would take advantage of divisions and fissures within Iran, as well as evident popular unrest. Hassan Rouhani, a moderate who seeks to improve Iran's relations with the West, including the United States, won successive presidential elections in 2013 and 2017, and reformist and moderate candidates won overwhelmingly in concurrent municipal council elections in all the major cities. But hardliners continue to control the state institutions that maintain internal security in large part through suppression. In part as a response to repression as well as economic conditions, unrest erupts periodically, most recently during December 2017-January 2018, and more sporadically since then.

President Trump has indicated a willingness to meet with Iranian leaders, but his key foreign policy subordinates have set strict conditions for any broader improvement in relations—conditions the regime is highly unlikely to meet. As of mid-2018, Administration officials have been increasingly highlighting Iran's human rights abuses and systemic corruption in an apparent attempt to weaken support for the regime within Iran.

POLITICAL HISTORY

Iran is a country of nearly 80 million people, located in the heart of the Persian Gulf region. The United States was an ally of the late Shah of Iran, Mohammad Reza Pahlavi ("the Shah"), who ruled from 1941 until his ouster in February 1979. The Shah assumed the throne when Britain and Russia forced his father, Reza Shah Pahlavi (Reza Shah), from power because of his perceived alignment with Germany in World War II. Reza Shah had assumed power in 1921 when, as an officer in Iran's only military force, the Cossack Brigade (reflecting Russian influence in Iran in the early 20th century), he launched a coup against the government of the Qajar royal family, which had ruled since 1794. Reza Shah was proclaimed Shah in 1925, founding the Pahlavi dynasty. The Qajar dynasty had been in decline for many years before Reza Shah's takeover. That dynasty's perceived manipulation by Britain and Russia had been one of the causes of the 1906 constitutionalist movement, which forced the Qajar dynasty to form Iran's first Majles (parliament) in August 1906 and promulgate a constitution in December 1906. Prior to the Qajars, what is now Iran was the center of several Persian empires and dynasties whose reach had shrunk steadily over time. After the 16th century, Iranian empires lost control of Bahrain (1521), Baghdad (1638), the Caucasus (1828), western Afghanistan (1857), Baluchistan (1872), and what is now Turkmenistan (1894). Iran adopted Shiite Islam under the Safavid Dynasty (1500-1722), which ended a series of Turkic and Mongol conquests.

The Shah was anti-Communist, and the United States viewed his government as a bulwark against the expansion of Soviet influence in the Persian Gulf and a counterweight to pro-Soviet Arab regimes and movements. Israel maintained a representative office in Iran during the Shah's time and the Shah supported a peaceful resolution of the Arab-Israeli dispute. In 1951, under pressure from nationalists in the *Majles* (parliament) who gained strength in the 1949 Majles elections, he appointed a popular nationalist parliamentarian, Dr. Mohammad Mossadeq, as prime minister. Mossadeq was widely considered left-leaning, and the United States was wary of his drive for nationalization of the oil industry, which had been controlled since 1913 by the AngloPersian Oil Company. His followers began an uprising in August 1953 when the Shah tried to dismiss him, and the Shah fled. The Shah was restored to power in a CIA-supported uprising that toppled Mossadeq ("Operation Ajax") on August 19, 1953.

The Shah tried to modernize Iran and orient it toward the West, but in so doing he alienated the Shiite clergy and religious Iranians. He incurred broader resentment by using his SAVAK intelligence service to repress dissent. The Shah exiled Ayatollah Ruhollah Khomeini in 1964 because of Khomeini's active opposition to what he asserted were the Shah's anticlerical policies and forfeiture of Iran's sovereignty to the United States. Khomeini fled to and taught in Najaf, Iraq, a major Shiite theological center. In 1978, three years after the March 6, 1975, Algiers Accords between the Shah and Iraq's Baathist leaders that temporarily ended mutual hostile actions, Iraq expelled Khomeini to France, where he continued to agitate for revolution that would establish Islamic government in Iran. Mass demonstrations and guerrilla activity by pro-Khomeini forces caused the Shah's government to collapse. Khomeini returned from France on February 1, 1979, and, on February 11, 1979, he declared an Islamic Republic of Iran. Khomeini's concept of *velayat-e-faqih* (rule by a supreme Islamic jurisprudent, or "Supreme Leader") was enshrined in the constitution that was adopted in a public referendum in December 1979 (and amended in 1989). The constitution provided for the post of Supreme Leader of the Revolution. The regime based itself on strong opposition to Western influence, and relations between the United States and the Islamic Republic turned openly hostile after the November 4, 1979, seizure of the U.S. Embassy and its U.S. diplomats by pro-Khomeini radicals, which began the so-called hostage crisis that ended in January 1981 with the release of the hostages.[1] Ayatollah Khomeini died on June 3, 1989, and was succeeded by Ayatollah Ali Khamene'i.

The regime faced serious unrest in its first few years, including a June 1981 bombing at the headquarters of the Islamic Republican Party (IRP) and the prime minister's office that killed several senior elected and clerical leaders, including then-Prime Minister Javad

[1] The U.S. Embassy hostages are to be compensated for their detention in Iran from proceeds received from various banks to settle allegations of concealing financial transactions on behalf of Iranian clients, under a provision of the FY2016 Consolidated Appropriation.

Bahonar, elected President Ali Raja'i, and IRP head and top Khomeini disciple Ayatollah Mohammad Hussein Beheshti. The regime used these events, along with the hostage crisis with the United States, to justify purging many of the secular, liberal, and left-wing personalities that had been prominent in the years just after the revolution. Examples included the regime's first Prime Minister Mehdi Bazargan; the pro-Moscow Tudeh Party (Communist); the People's Mojahedin Organization of Iran (PMOI, see below); and the first elected president, Abolhassan Bani Sadr. The regime was under economic and military threat during the 1980-1988 Iran-Iraq War, which at times nearly halted Iran's oil exports. Since that war, Iran has not faced severe external military threats but domestic political rifts have continued.

REGIME STRUCTURE, STABILITY, AND OPPOSITION

Some experts attribute the acrimony that has characterized U.S.-Iran relations since the Islamic revolution to the structure of Iran's regime. Although there are some elected leadership posts and diversity of opinion, Iran's constitution—adopted in public referenda in 1980 and again in 1989—reserves paramount decisionmaking authority for a "Supreme Leader" (known formally in Iran as "Leader of the Revolution"). The President and the *Majles* (unicameral parliament) are directly elected, and since 2013, there have been elections for municipal councils that set local development priorities and select mayors. Even within the unelected institutions, factional disputes between those who insist on ideological purity and those considered more pragmatic are evident. In part because of the preponderant political power of the clerics and the security services, the regime has faced repeated periods of unrest from minorities, intellectuals, students, labor groups, the poor, women, and members of Iran's minority groups. (Iran's demographics are depicted in a text box below).

U.S. officials in successive Administrations have accused Iran's regime of widespread corruption, both within the government and among its pillars of support. In a speech on Iran on July 22, 2018, Secretary of State Michael Pompeo characterized Iran's government as "something that resembles the mafia more than a government." He detailed allegations of the abuse of privileges enjoyed by Iran's leaders and supporting elites to enrich themselves and their supporters at the expense of the public good.[2]

[2] Secretary of State Michael Pompeo. "Supporting Iranian Voices." Reagan Library, July 22, 2018.

Supreme Leader: Grand Ayatollah Ali Khamene'i.

Born in July 1939 to an Azeri (Turkic) family from the northern city of Mashhad. Was jailed by the Shah of Iran for supporting Ayatollah Khomeini's revolution. After the regime took power in 1979, helped organize Revolutionary Guard and other security organs. Lost some use of right arm in purported assassination attempt in June 1981. Was elected president in 1981 and served until 1989. Was selected Khomeini's successor in June 1989. Upon that selection, Khamene'i's religious ranking was advanced in official organs to "Grand Ayatollah" from the lower ranking "Hojjat ol-Islam." Still lacks the undisputed authority to end factional disputes and the public adoration Khomeini had. Has taken more of a day-to-day role since the 2009 uprising, including establishing strict parameters for Iran's nuclear negotiating team during the JCPOA talks. As to Khamene'i's health situation, the government acknowledged that he underwent prostate surgery in September 2014 but Khamene'i has since appeared in public regularly, including occasionally performing light physical tasks. Has not traveled outside Iran since becoming Supreme Leader. Lives in the Pasteur district of Tehran, named after French biologist Louis Pasteur.

Policies

Throughout career, has consistently taken hardline stances on regional issues, particularly toward Israel, repeatedly calling it a "cancerous tumor" that needs to be excised from the region. In March 2014, publicly questioned whether the Holocaust occurred—an issue highlighted by former president Ahmadinejad. He is widely believed to fear direct military confrontation with United States on Iranian soil. He meets with few Western officials and is avowedly suspicious of relations with the West, particularly the United States, as potentially making Iran vulnerable to Western cultural influence, spying, and possible regime destabilization efforts. Largely bowing to public opinion, Khamene'i acquiesced to the election in 2013 of the relatively moderate President Hassan Rouhani, who favors opening to the West. Khamene'i did not oppose the JCPOA, paving the way for its adoption by the *Majles* and the Council of Guardians. In 2016, he accused the United States of not implementing JCPOA-related sanctions relief fully and thereby deterring foreign firms from returning to Iran. Earlier, he reputedly issued religious proclamation (2003) against Iran acquiring a nuclear weapon, and has publicly (2012) called doing so a "sin." He fully backs efforts by Revolutionary Guard and other Iranian organs to support regional pro-Iranian movements and governments.

Earlier in his career, Khamene'i tended to support the business community (bazaaris), and opposed state control of the economy, but as Supreme Leader he has asserted that officials, including Rouhani, need to promote a self-sufficient economy that can withstand the effects of international sanctions ("resistance economy"). Attributed late 2017-early 2018 unrest to meddling by the United States, Saudi Arabia, and Israel, but also acknowledged that protesters had legitimate grievances.

Khamene'i's office is run by Mohammad Mohammadi Golpayegani, with significant input from Khamene'i's second and increasingly influential son, Mojtaba. Also advised by *Keyhan* editor Hossein Shariatmadari and former Foreign Minister Ali Akbar Velayati.

Photograph from http://www.leader.ir.

Unelected or Indirectly Elected Institutions: The Supreme Leader, Council of Guardians, and Expediency Council

Iran's power structure consists of unelected or indirectly elected persons and institutions.

The Supreme Leader

At the apex of the Islamic Republic's power structure is the "Supreme Leader." He is required to be a senior cleric and is chosen by an elected body—the Assembly of Experts—which also has the constitutional power to remove him, as well as to rewrite Iran's constitution (subject to approval in a national referendum). Upon Ayatollah Khomeini's death, the Assembly selected one of his disciples, Ayatollah Ali Khamene'i, as Supreme Leader.[3] Although he has never had Khomeini's undisputed political or religious authority, the powers of the office ensure that Khamene'i is Iran's paramount leader. Under the constitution, the Supreme Leader is commander-in-chief of the armed forces, giving him the power to appoint commanders.

Khamene'i makes five out of the nine appointments to the country's highest national security body, the *Supreme National Security Council (SNSC),* including its top official, the secretary of the body. Khamene's also has a representative of his office as one of the nine members, who typically are members of the regime's top military, foreign policy, and domestic security organizations. The Supreme Leader can remove an elected president, if the judiciary or the *Majles* (parliament) assert cause for removal. The

[3] At the time of his selection as Supreme Leader, Khamene'i was generally referred to at the rank of Hojjat ol-Islam, one rank below Ayatollah, suggesting his religious elevation was political rather than through traditional mechanisms.

Supreme Leader appoints half of the 12-member *Council of Guardians*, all members of the *Expediency Council*, and the judiciary head.

Succession to Khamene'i

There is no announced consensus choice to succeed Khamene'i. Khamene'i reportedly favors as his successor Ibrahim Raisi, who Khamene'i appointed in 2016 to head the powerful Shrine of Imam Reza (Astan-e Qods Razavi) in Mashhad, which controls vast property and many businesses in the province. Raisi is a hardliner who has served as state prosecutor and was allegedly involved in the 1988 massacre of prisoners and other acts of repression.[4] However, the Assembly would not necessarily take his preferences into account after his passing, and Raisi's chances of achieving that post might have been diminished by Raisi's election defeat in the May 19, 2017, presidential elections.

Other commonly mentioned possible successors include former judiciary chief Ayatollah Mahmoud Shahroudi, who was appointed in August 2017 to head the Expediency Council. Other contenders include judiciary head Ayatollah Sadeq Larijani and hardline Tehran Friday prayer leader Ayatollah Ahmad Khatemi. The succession chances of another potential candidate, hardline senior cleric Ayatollah Mohammad Taqi Mesbah-Yazdi, were likely reduced by his loss of an Assembly of Experts seat in the February 2016 elections.

The January 2017 death of regime stalwart Ayatollah Ali Akbar Hashemi-Rafsanjani removed from contention the one potential successor who was a constant presence at Ayatollah Khomeini's side in the 1979 revolution. Rafsanjani's protege, President Hassan Rouhani, is also a possible successor to Khamene'i. Rafsanjani was *Majles* speaker during 1981-1989 and president 1989 1997, and his family owns a large share of Iran's total pistachio production, which enabled him to atronize many key Iranian players. Rafsanjani's ouster as Assembly of Experts chairman in 2011 and the denial of his candidacy in the 2013 presidential elections were widely attributed to his tacit support of the 2009 protest movement and to the political activities of his children. The Assembly of Experts could conceivably use a constitutional provision to set up a three-person leadership council rather than select one person as a new Supreme Leader.

Council of Guardians and Expediency Council

Two appointed councils play a major role on legislation, election candidate vetting, and policy formulation.

---

4 https://www.washingtonpost.com/opinions/global-opinions/irans-likely-next-supreme-leader-is-no-friend-of-the-west/2016/09/26/eb3becc0-79fb-11e6-bd86-b7bbd53d2b5d_story.html?utm_term=.e6499d61d0be.

Table 1. Other Major Institutions, Factions and Individuals

Regime/Pro-Regime	
The regime derives support from a network of organizations and institutions such as those discussed below.	
Senior Shiite Clerics/Grand Ayatollahs	The most senior Shiite clerics, most of whom are in Qom, are generally "quietists"—they assert that the senior clergy should generally refrain from involvement in politics, although they do speak out on political issues. The ranks of the most senior clergy include Grand Ayatollah Nasser Makarem Shirazi and Grand Ayatollah Yusuf Sanei. Secretary of State Pompeo accused Shirazi in a July 22, 2018, speech of enriching himself through illicit trading of sugar. Another senior cleric is the hardline Ayatollah Mohammad Taqi Mesbah-Yazdi, who represents the "vocal" school of the senior clergy and is an assertive defender of the powers of the Supreme Leader. Helost his Assembly of Experts seat in February 2016 elections.
Religious Foundations ("Bonyads")	Iran has several major religious foundations, called "*bonyads.*" Examples include the Martyr's Foundation, the Foundation for the Oppressed and Disabled, the Astan Qods Razavi Foundation (linked to the Shrine of Imam Rezain Mashhad), and the Fifteen Khordad Foundation (which offers a bounty for the killing of author Salman Rushdie). The bonyads, controlled by clerics and their allies, control vast amounts of property and valuable businesses, some of which were built from assets left behind when the Shah and his allies fled Iran in1979. The bonyads are loosely regulated and largely exempt from taxation.
The Islamic Revolutionary Guard Corps (IRGC)	The IRGC is a military and internal security force, and an instrument of Iran's regional policy. The IRGC is sanctioned under several U.S. Executive orders, including most recently E.O. 13224 that sanctions entities determined to be supporting acts of international terrorism.
Society of Militant Clerics	Longtime organization of moderate-to-hardline clerics. Its Secretary-General is Ayatollah Mohammad Ali Movahedi-Kermani. President Rouhani is a member.

Sources: Various press accounts and author conversations with Iran experts in and outside Washington, DC. Secretary of State Michael Pompeo "Supporting Iranian Voices." Reagan Library, California, July 22, 2018.

Council of Guardians

The 12-member Council of Guardians (COG) consists of six Islamic jurists appointed by the Supreme Leader and six lawyers selected by the judiciary and confirmed by the *Majles*. Each councilor serves a six-year term, staggered such that half the body turns over every three years. Currently headed by Ayatollah Ahmad Jannati, the conservative-controlled body reviews legislation to ensure it conforms to Islamic law. It also vets election candidates by evaluating their backgrounds according to constitutional requirements that each candidate demonstrate knowledge of Islam, loyalty to the Islamic system of government, and other criteria that are largely subjective. The COG also certifies election results. Municipal council candidates are vetted not by the COG but by local committees established by the *Majles*.

Expediency Council

The Expediency Council was established in 1988 to resolve legislative disagreements between the *Majles* and the COG. It has since evolved into more of a policy advisory body for the Supreme Leader and an overseer of the performance of the president and his cabinet. Its members serve five-year terms. Longtime regime stalwart Ayatollah Ali

Akbar Hashemi-Rafsanjani was reappointed as its chairman in February 2007 and again in March 2012, but his January 2017 death left the top position vacant. In August 2017, the Supreme Leader named a new, expanded (from 42 to 45 members) Council, with former judiciary head Ayatollah Mahmoud Hashemi Shahroudi as the new chairman. The Expediency Council's executive officer is former Revolutionary Guard commander-in-chief Mohsen Reza'i. The council appointed in August 2017 includes former president Ahmadinejad. President Hassan Rouhani and Majles Speaker Ali Larijani were not reappointed as Council members but attend the body's sessions in their official capacities.

Domestic Security Organs

The leaders and senior officials of a variety of overlapping domestic security organizations form a parallel power structure that is largely under the direct control of the Supreme Leader in his capacity as Commander-in-Chief of the Armed Forces. The domestic security organs include

- The Islamic Revolutionary Guard Corps (IRGC). The military and security organ that is widely discussed in this chapter. Its domestic security role is usually implemented through the volunteer militia force called the *Basij* that monitors adherence to the regime's directives and compliance with the country's law and customs. It is the *Basij* that is widely accused of arresting women who violate the regime's public dress codes and raiding Western-style parties in which alcohol, which is illegal in Iran, might be served.
- Law Enforcement Forces. This body is an amalgam of regular police, gendarmerie, and riot police that serve throughout the country. It is the regime's first "line of defense" in suppressing antiregime demonstrations or other unrest.
- Ministry of Interior. The ministry, headed by Abdolreza Fazli, exercises civilian supervision of Iran's police and domestic security forces. However, the IRGC and Basij are generally outside Ministry control.
- Ministry of Intelligence and Security (MOIS). Headed by Mahmoud Alavi, the MOIS conducts domestic surveillance to identify regime opponents and try to penetrate antiregime cells. The Ministry works closely with the IRGC and *Basij*.

The leaders of most of these organizations, including the IRGC and the ministers of Interior and of Intelligence and Security, are represented on the Supreme National Security Council. Several of these organizations and their senior leaders or commanders are sanctioned by the United States for human rights abuses and other violations of U.S. Executive Orders such as E.O. 13553.

Elected Institutions/Recent Elections

Several major institutional positions are directly elected by the population, but international observers question the credibility of Iran's elections because of the role of the COG in vetting candidates and limiting the number and ideological diversity of the candidate field. Women can vote and run for most offices, and some women serve as mayors, but the COG interprets the Iranian constitution as prohibiting women from running for the office of president. Candidates for all offices must receive more than 50% of the vote, otherwise a runoff is held several weeks later.

Another criticism of the political process in Iran is the relative absence of political parties; establishing a party requires the permission of the Interior Ministry under Article 10 of Iran's constitution. The standards to obtain approval are high: to date, numerous parties have filed for permission since the regime was founded, but only those considered loyal to the regime have been granted license to operate. Some have been licensed and then banned after their leaders opposed regime policies, such as the Islamic Iran Participation Front and Organization of Mojahedin of the Islamic Revolution, discussed in the text box below.

The Presidency

The main directly elected institution is the presidency, which is formally and in practice subordinate to the Supreme Leader. Virtually every successive president has tried but failed to expand his authority relative to the Supreme Leader. Presidential authority, particularly on matters of national security, is also often circumscribed by key clerics and the generally hardline military and security organization called the Islamic Revolutionary Guard Corps (IRGC). But, the presidency is often the most influential economic policymaking position, as well as a source of patronage. The president appoints and supervises the cabinet, develops the budgets of cabinet departments, and imposes and collects taxes on corporations and other bodies. The presidency also runs oversight bodies such as the Anticorruption Headquarters and the General Inspection Organization, to which government officials are required to submit annual financial disclosures.

Prior to 1989, Iran had both an elected president and a prime minister selected by the elected Majles (parliament). However, the holders of the two positions were constantly in institutional conflict and a 1989 constitutional revision eliminated the prime ministership. Because Iran's presidents have sometimes asserted the powers of their institution against the office of the Supreme Leader itself, in October 2011, Khamene'i raised the possibility of eventually eliminating the post of president and restoring the post of prime minister.

The Majles

Iran's *Majles*, or parliament, is a 290-seat, all-elected, unicameral body. There are five "reserved seats" for "recognized" minority communities—Jews, Zoroastrians, and

Christians (three seats of the five). The *Majles* votes on each nominee to a cabinet post, and drafts and acts on legislation. Among its main duties is to consider and enact a proposed national budget (which runs from March 21 to March 20 each year, coinciding with Nowruz). It legislates on domestic economic and social issues, and tends to defer to executive and security institutions on defense and foreign policy issues. It is constitutionally required to ratify major international agreements, and it ratified the JCPOA in October 2015. The ratification was affirmed by the COG. Women regularly run and small numbers generally win election; there is no "quota" for the number of women to be elected. *Majles* elections occur one year prior to the presidential elections; the latest were held on February 26, 2016.

The Assembly of Experts

A major but little publicized elected institution is the 88-seat *Assembly of Experts.* Akin to a standing electoral college, it is empowered to choose a new Supreme Leader upon the death of the incumbent, and it formally "oversees" the work of the Supreme Leader. The Assembly can replace him if necessary, although invoking that power would, in practice, most likely occur in the event of a severe health crisis. The Assembly is also empowered to amend the constitution. It generally meets two times a year.

Elections to the Assembly are held every 8-10 years (some variation in the term), conducted on a provincial basis. Assembly candidates must be able to interpret Islamic law. After the fourth election for the Assembly in December 2006, Rafsanjani was named its deputy chairman. He became its chairman in September 2007, but his opposition to the crackdown on the 2009 uprising ran him afoul of the Supreme Leader and he was replaced as chair of the body in March 2011 by the aging compromise candidate Ayatollah Mohammad Reza Mahdavi-Kani. After Mahdavi-Kani died in 2014 and his successor, Mohammad Yazdi lost his seat in the Assembly of Experts election on February 26, 2016 (concurrent with the Majles elections), COG Chairman Ayatollah Ahmad Jannati was appointed concurrently as the Assembly chairman in May 2016.

Recent Elections

Following the post-Khomeini Rafsanjani presidency of 1989-1997, a reformist, Mohammad Khatemi, who won landslide victories in the elections of 1997 and 2001. However, hardliners marginalized him by the end of his term in 2005. Aided by widespread voiding of reformist candidacies by the CoG, conservatives won a slim majority of the 290 *Majles* seats in the February 20, 2004, elections. In June 2005, the CoG allowed eight candidates to compete (out of the 1,014 persons who filed), including Rafsanjani,[5] Ali Larijani, IRGC stalwart Mohammad Baqer Qalibaf, and Tehran mayor

---

[5] Rafsanjani was constitutionally permitted to run because a third term would not have been consecutive with his previous two terms. In the 2001 presidential election, the Council permitted 10 out of the 814 registered candidates.

Mahmoud Ahmadinejad. With reported tacit backing from Khamene'i, Ahmadinejad advanced to a runoff against Rafsanjani, and then won by a 62% to 36% vote. During Ahmadinejad's first term, splits widened between Ahmadinejad and other conservatives to the point where pro-Ahmadinejad and pro-Khamene'i conservatives competed against each other in the March 2008 *Majles* elections.

Disputed 2009 Election. Reformists sought to unseat Ahmadinejad in the June 12, 2009, presidential election by rallying to Mir Hossein Musavi, who served as prime minister during the 1980-1988 Iran-Iraq War and, to a lesser extent, former *Majles* speaker Mehdi Karrubi. Musavi's generally young, urban supporters used social media to organize large rallies in Tehran, but proAhmadinejad rallies were large as well. Turnout was about 85%. The Interior Ministry pronounced Ahmadinejad the winner (63% of the vote) only two hours after the polls closed. Supporters of Musavi, who received the second-highest total (about 35% of the vote) immediately protested the results as fraudulent because of the hasty announcement of the results—but some outside analysts said the results tracked preelection polls.[6] Large antigovernment demonstrations occurred June 13-19, 2009. Security forces killed over 100 protesters (opposition figure—Iran government figure was 27), including a 19-year-old woman, Neda Soltani, who became an icon of the uprising.

Reformist Leaders and Organizations

The figures discussed below are "reformists"—seeking dramatic change on issues such as freedom of expression, but not outright replacement of the regime. These reformist leaders were not widely used as symbols by protestors in the December 2017-January 2018 unrest in Iran.

Mir Hossein Musavi is the titular leader of the Green Movement, the coalition of youth and intellectuals that led the 2009-2010 uprising. A noncleric and former Khomeini aide, Musavi served as foreign minister in 1980 and as Iran's last prime minister from 1981 to 1989, at which time constitutional reforms abolished the post. An advocate of state-controlled economy, as prime minister, Musavi often feuded with Khamene'i, who was president at that time. He was arrested in 2011 for sedition and he and his wife, activist Zahra Rahnevard, remain under house arrest. Khamene'i has termed Musavi and Karrubi (below) as "seditionists" and has insisted that they remain confined.

Mehdi Karrubi is an Iranian cleric, former Majles Speaker (1989-1992, 2000-2004), and supporter of the Green Movement. Failed presidential campaigns in 2005 and 2009 led Karrubi to question the elections' validity and to support runner-up Mir Hossein Musavi's dispute over the election in 2009. Imprisoned in the 1970s for protesting the government of Mohammad Reza Shah, Karrubi became a leading politician of the Islamic left following the 1979 revolution. Karrubi shares Musavi's political views on the need for state-controlled economy

[6] A paper published by Chatham House and the University of St. Andrews strongly questions how Ahmadinejad's vote could have been as large as reported by official results, in light of past voting patterns throughout Iran. "Preliminary Analysis of the Voting Figures in Iran's 2009 Presidential Election." http://www.chathamhouse.org.uk.

and civil rights for women. In 2014, Karrubi was moved from a detention facility to house arrest. In August 2017, Karrubi challenged the regime by going on a hunger strike to demand a formal trial and a withdrawal of security forces from his home. Security forces left but remain outside his home to control visits. He reportedly is in poor health.

Mohammad Khatemi captured global attention for his overwhelming 1997 and 2001 presidential election victories, and his subsequent attempts to ease social and political restrictions in the country. However, supporters became disillusioned when Khatemi failed to buck hardliners on reform issues, leaving him largely marginalized by the end of his presidency in 2005. Khatemi endorsed Musavi in the 2009 election and, following the 2009 uprising, had his travel restricted and discussion or images of him banned in Iranian media. Khatemi reportedly helped organize reformists and other pro-Rouhani candidates in the 2016 Majles elections, and Rouhani has sought to end the media ban on discussions of Khatemi.

Pro-Reformist Organizations

The reformists are supported by several long-standing factions that supported the regime but fell out with hardliners and have become vocal regime critics.

National Trust (*Etemad-e-Melli*). Opposition grouping formed by Karrubi after his defeat in the 2005 election. Some of its leaders, such as Hengameh Shahidi, have been arrested and harassed by authorities.

Islamic Iran Participation Front (IIPF). The most prominent and best organized proreform grouping, but in 2009 lost political ground to Green Movement groups. IIPF leaders include Mohammed Khatemi's brother, Mohammad Reza Khatemi (deputy speaker in the 2000-2004 Majles) and Mohsen Mirdamadi. Backed Musavi in June 2009 election, and several IIPF leaders detained and prosecuted in postelection dispute. The party was outlawed in September 2010.

Mojahedin of the Islamic Revolution Organization (MIR) Composed mainly of left-leaning Iranian figures who support state control of the economy, but want greater political pluralism and relaxation of rules on social behavior. A major constituency of the reformist camp. Its leader is former Heavy Industries Minister Behzad Nabavi, who supported Musavi in 2009 election and has been incarcerated for most of the time since June 2009. The organization was outlawed by the regime simultaneously with the outlawing of the IIPF, above.

Combatant Clerics Association The group was formed in 1988 and its name is similar to the Society of Militant Clerics, but the group is run by reformists. Leading figures include Mohammad Khatemi, former Interior Minister Ali Akbar Mohtashemi-Pur, and former Prosecutor General Ali Asgar Musavi-Koiniha.

The opposition congealed into the "Green Movement of Hope and Change." Some protests in December 2009 overwhelmed regime security forces in some parts of Tehran, but the movement's activity declined after the regime successfully suppressed its demonstration on the February 11, 2010, anniversary of the founding of the Islamic Republic. As unrest ebbed, Ahmadinejad promoted his loyalists and a nationalist version of Islam that limits clerical authority, bringing him into conflict with Supreme Leader

Khamene'i. Amid that rift, in the March 2012 Majles elections, two blocs of candidates supported by Khamene'i won about 75% of the seats, weakening Ahmadinejad.

June 2013 Election of Rouhani

In the June 14, 2013, presidential elections, held concurrently with municipal elections, the major candidates included the following:

- Several hardliners that included Qalibaf (see above); Khamene'i foreign policy advisor Velayati; and then-chief nuclear negotiator Seyed Jalilli.
- Former chief nuclear negotiator Hassan Rouhani, a moderate and Rafsanjani ally.
- The CoG denial of Rafsanjani's candidacy, which shocked many Iranians because of Rafsanjani's prominent place in the regime, as well as the candidacy of an Ahmadinejad ally.

Green Movement supporters, who were first expected to boycott the vote, mobilized behind Rouhani after regime officials stressed that they were committed to a fair election. The vote produced a 70% turnout and a first-round victory for Rouhani, garnering about 50.7% of the 36 million votes cast. Hardliners generally garnered control of municipal councils in the major cities. Most prominent in Rouhani's first term cabinet were

- Foreign Minister: Mohammad Javad Zarif, a former Ambassador to the United Nations in New York, who was assigned to serve concurrently as chief nuclear negotiator, a post traditionally held by the chairman of the Supreme National Security Council. In September 2013, Rouhani appointed senior IRGC leader and former Defense Minister Ali Shamkhani as secretary (head) of that body; Shamkhani has espoused more moderate views than his IRGC peers.
- Oil Minister: Bijan Zanganeh, who served in the same post during the Khatemi presidency and attracted significant foreign investment to the sector. He replaced Rostam Qasemi, who was associated with the corporate arm of the IRGC.
- Defense Minister: Hosein Dehgan. An IRGC stalwart, he was an early organizer of the IRGC's Lebanon contingent that evolved into the IRGC-Qods Force. He also was IRGC Air Force commander and deputy Defense Minister.
- Justice Minister: Mostafa Pour-Mohammadi. As deputy Intelligence Minister in late 1980s, he was reportedly a decisionmaker in the 1988 mass executions of Iranian prisoners. He was Interior Minister under Ahmadinejad. Proposed legislation in the 115th Congress (H.Res. 188) would condemned Iran for the massacre and urged the United Nations to fully investigate it.

Dr. Hassan Rouhani.

Hassan Rouhani is a Hojjat ol-Islam in the Shiite clergy, one rank below Ayatollah. He was born in 1948. He holds a Ph.D. in law from Glasgow Caledonian University in Scotland. Rouhani is a long-time regime stalwart who was part of Ayatollah Khomeini's circle prior to the triumph of the Islamic revolution. He is also an associate and protégé of Rafsanjani, and Rouhani's pragmatic policy approach on issues such as the nuclear issue and relations with the United States has complicated Rouhani's relations with Khamene'i. Khamene'i criticized Rouhani's economic and foreign policies during the 2017 presidential election period, appearing to seek Rouhani's defeat.

Career Background

Often nicknamed the "diplomat sheikh," Rouhani was chief nuclear negotiator during 2003-2005, when Iran did agree to suspend uranium enrichment. Rouhani is a longtime member of the political establishment. Then-President Rafsanjani appointed him a member of the Supreme National Security Council in 1989, and he remains on that body. He has been a member of the Assembly of Experts since 1999 (and reelected to that body in the February 2016 election), and was a member of the Majles during 1980-2000, serving twice as deputy speaker. He has also been a member of the Expediency Council since 1991. He headed the Center for Strategic Studies, a foreign policy think tank that has advised the Expediency Council and the Supreme Leader, since 1992. Although he supported the crackdown against an earlier student uprising in July 1999, during the presidency of reformist figure Mohammad Khatemi, in 2013, Rouhani campaigned on a platform of easing the Islamic Republic's social restrictions and its suppression of free expression, helping him draw support from reformists.

Rouhani Presidency

Rouhani has focused mainly on negotiating and institutionalizing the JCPOA and on rebuilding Iran's international and regional economic ties, but not on seeking changes in Iran's regional policies. Hardliners who opposed Iranian concessions in the JCPOA were unable to persuade Khamene'i, the *Majles*, or the COG to block the accord. Sanctions relief caused the economy to grow since sanctions were lifted, but Khamene'i's speeches in 2016 and 2017 advocating building a "resistance economy," have been widely interpreted as contradicting Rouhani's emphasis on expanding trade relations with developed world.

Rouhani has sought to promote freedom of expression and political tolerance over the objections and contrary actions by hardliners in the judiciary and the security services. In September 2016, Rouhani achieved adoption of a new "charter for citizen's rights," and he has achieved the release of some prisoners incarcerated for involvement in the 2009 uprising, including prominent human rights lawyer Nasrin Sotoudeh. However, the judiciary and security institutions have continued to arrest and prosecute U.S.-Iran dual nationals and other dual nationals for alleged efforts to undermine the regime. And neither Mousavi or Karrubi (see above) has been released. The arrest of Rouhani's brother in July 2017 for unspecified financial misfeasance was widely viewed as a move by judicial hardliners to undermine Rouhani's authority. Appears to have successfully managed public unrest in late 2017-early 2018 by restraining hardline institutions from a major crackdown and by acknowledging protester economic grievances. Has also apparently prevailed on hardliners to ease enforcement of the public dress code for women. Has not succeeded, to date, in marginalizing IRGC role in Iranian economy, and he could face a serious hardliner political threat if the United States ceases implementing the JCPOA, which Rouhani negotiated.

Photograph from http://www.rouhani.ir.

Majles and Assembly of Experts Elections in 2016

On February 26, 2016, Iran held concurrent elections for the *Majles* and for the Assembly of Experts. A runoff round for 68 Majles seats was held on April 29. For the Majles, 6,200 candidates were approved, including 586 female candidates. Oversight bodies invalidated the candidacies of about 6,000, including all but 100 reformists. Still, pro-Rouhani candidates won about 140 seats, close to a majority, and the number of hardliners in the body was reduced significantly. Independents, whose alignments vary by issue, hold about 50 seats. Seventeen women were elected—the largest female contingent since the revolution. The *Majles*, which convened on May 27, 2016, reelected Ali Larijani as Speaker.

For the Assembly of Experts election, 161 candidates were approved out of 800 who applied to run. Reformists and their pro-Rouhani allies succeeded in defeating for an Assembly seat at least two prominent hardliners—current Assembly Chairman Mohammad Yazdi and Ayatollah Mohammad Taqi Mesbah-Yazdi. COG head Ayatollah Jannati retained his seat, but came in last for the 30 seats elected from Tehran Province. He was subsequently named chairman of the body.

Presidential Election on May 19, 2017

In the latest presidential election on May 19, 2017, Rouhani won a first-round victory with about 57% of the vote. He defeated a major figure, Hojjat ol-Eslam Ibrahim Raisi—a close ally of Khamene'i appointed by him in 2016 to head the large Astan-e-Qods

Razavi Foundation. Even though other major hardliners had dropped out of the race to improve Raisi's chances of winning, Raisi received only about 38% of the vote.[7]

Municipal elections were held concurrently. After vetting by local committees established by the *Majles*, about 260,000 candidates competed for about 127,000 seats nationwide. Over 6% of the candidates were women. The same alliance of reformists and moderate-conservatives that gave Rouhani a resounding victory also won control of the municipal councils of Iran's largest cities, including all 21 seats on the Tehran municipal council. The term of the existing councils expired in September 2017 and a reformist official, Mohammad Ali Najafi, replaced Qalibaf as Tehran mayor. However, Najafi resigned in March 2018 after criticism from hardliners for his viewing of a dance performance by young girls during a celebration of a national holiday. In April 2018, the deputy head of the department of the environment, Kaveh Madani, resigned after photos of him dancing in the United States five years prior surfaced on the internet.

Second Term Cabinet

Rouhani was sworn into a second term in early August 2017. His second term cabinet nominations retained most of the same officials in key posts, including Foreign Minister Zarif, Interior Minister Abdolreza Fazli, and Oil Minister Zanganeh. However, key changes included the following:

- Minister of Justice nominee Seyed Alireza Avayee replaced the controversial Pour-Mohammadi. Formerly a state prosecutor, he oversaw trials of protesters in the 2009 uprising and is subject to EU travel ban and asset freeze. His speech at a U.N. Human Rights Council meeting in Geneva in February 2018 prompted a walkout by several European diplomats.
- Defense Minister Amir Hatami, a regular military officer, replaced IRGC stalwart Hosein Dehgan and became the first non-IRGC Defense Minister in more than 20 years and the first regular military officer to serve in the position. The change was interpreted as an effort by Rouhani to reduce the power of the IRGC.
- Rouhani named two females as vice presidents, and one other as a member of the cabinet (but not heading any ministry).

---

[7] For more information on the 2017 presidential election, see CRS Insight IN10699, *Iran's Presidential Elections*, by Kenneth Katzman.

2017-2018 Unrest Challenges Regime[8]

Rouhani's presidency has been marked by the JCPOA, reintegration into the global community, efforts at domestic reform, and success in preserving the Asad regime in Syria. In December 2017, authorities announced that they would no longer arrest women who violated the public dress code but, shortly thereafter, significant unrest erupted. Demonstrations were smaller than the 2009-2010 protests, but were more widespread, occurring in more than 80 cities. Protests initially cited economic concerns—the high prices of staple foods—but quickly evolved to expressions of opposition to Iran's leadership and the expenditure of resources on interventions throughout the Middle East. Some protesters were motivated by Rouhani's 2018-2019 budget proposals to increase funds for clerical business enterprises ("bonyads") and the IRGC, while at the same time continuing to cut subsidies that Iranian economic experts argued were inflationary.

Rouhani sought to defuse the unrest by acknowledging the right to protest and the legitimacy of some demonstrator grievances. Khamene'i at first attributed the unrest to covert action by Iran's adversaries, particularly the United States, Saudi Arabia, and Israel, but he later acknowledged unspecified "problems" in the administration of justice.[9] Security officers used force against protester violence in some cities, but generally were cited by experts as exercising relative restraint. The government also temporarily shut down access to the social media site Instagram and a widely used messaging system called "Telegram" that is widely followed by younger Iranians. The IRGC announced on January 7 that the unrest had been "defeated," but some reports indicated that unrest continued in some cities and spawned groups that advocate forcefully defending protesters against regime security forces. Iran media reported that 25 were killed and nearly 4,000 were arrested during the unrest. Since February 2018, some women have continued protesting against the strict public dress code, and some have been detained. Small protests and other acts of defiance have continued since, including significant unrest in the Tehran bazaar in July 2018 in the context of shortages of some goods and shop closures due to the inability to price their goods for profit.

Primarily in the form of several Twitter messages, President Trump and other senior officials have strongly supported the protesters, in part by warning the regime against using force and vowing to hold officials responsible for harming protestors.

---

[8] The following information is derived from a wide range of press reporting in major newspapers and websites subsequent to December 28, 2017. Some activist sources report widely different numbers of protest sizes, cities involved, numbers killed or arrested, and other figures. CRS has no way to corroborate exact numbers cited.

[9] https://www.wsj.com/articles/irans-khamenei-recognizes-protesters-grievances-1515511134; National Council of Resistance. "Khamene'i's Belated Confession to Injustice and Inability to Revform, a Desperate Attempt to Escape Overthrow. February 19, 2018.

Demographics/Ethnic and Religious Minorities

General. Iran's population is about 83 million persons. In terms of ethnicity, about 60% is Persian; about 20%-25% is Azeri; about 7% are Kurds; about 4% are Arabs; and about 2% are Baluchis. Iran is about 99% Muslim, of which more than 90% are Shiites; about 8% are Sunnis; and 1% are Jewish, Christian, Zoroastrian, Baha'i', or other religions.

Azeris. Azeris, who have a Turkic ethnicity, are predominant in northern Iran, particularly in areas bordering Azerbaijan. Azeris in Iran are mostly well integrated into government and society (Khamene'i himself is of Azeri heritage), but many Azeris complain of ethnic and linguistic discrimination. Each year, there are arrests of Azeris who press for their right to celebrate their culture and history. The government accuses them of promoting separatism.

Christians. Christians, who number about 300,000, are a "protected minority" with three seats reserved in the Majles. The majority of Christians in Iran are ethnic Armenians, with Assyrian Christians contributing about 10,000-20,000 practitioners. The IRGC oversees churches in the country, suggesting official scrutiny of Christian religious practice, and numerous Christians remain incarcerated on charges related to their religious practices, such as using wine in certain services. At times, there have been unexplained assassinations of pastors in Iran, as well as prosecutions of Christians for converting from Islam—a practice illegal for any Iranian Muslim. Christians— along with the other two protected minorities, Zoroastrians and Jews—cannot publicly practice or advocate for their religion. One pastor, Yousef Nadarkhani, has been repeatedly arrested, released since 2006, including his May 2016 rearrest and release on bail in July 2016.

Kurds. There are about 5 million-11 million Kurds in Iran. The Kurdish language is not banned, but schools do not teach it and Kurdish political organizations, activists, and media outlets are routinely scrutinized, harassed, and closed down for supporting greater Kurdish autonomy. Abuses of Kurds are widely cited as providing political support for the Kurdish armed factions, with several Kurdish oppositionists having been executed since 2010. In May 2015, violent unrest broke out in the Kurdish city of Mahabad after a local woman was killed in unclear circumstances in a hotel room there, reportedly while with a member of Iran's intelligence services. Iranian Kurds recruited by the Islamic State terrorist organization conducted a major attack on Iran's parliament and the tomb of Ayatollah Khomeini in June 2017, killing 17 persons.

Arabs. Ethnic Arabs are prominent in southwestern Iran, particularly Khuzestan Province, where they are known as Ahwazi Arabs. The approximately 3 million Arabs in Iran encounter systematic oppression and discrimination, including torture and a prohibition on speaking or studying Arabic.

Baluchis. Iran has about 1.4 million Baluchis, living primarily in poorly developed and economically depressed southeastern Iran, in the area bordering Pakistan. Baluchis in Iran are mostly Sunni Muslims.

Jews. Also a "recognized minority" with one seat in the Majles, the approximately 10,000 member (according to the Tehran Jewish Committee) Jewish community enjoys somewhat more freedoms than Jews in several other Muslim states. On September 4, 2013, Rouhani's Twitter account issued greetings to Jews on the occasion of Jewish New Year ("Rosh Hashanah") and the Jewish Majles member accompanied Rouhani on his visit to the U.N.

General Assembly meetings in September 2013. However, the Iranian government ignores and sometimes promotes anti-Semitic rhetoric in state-sanctioned media, statements, books, and other publications. Former President Ahmadinejad, for example, often questioned the existence of the Holocaust, claiming it to be a Zionist propaganda tool. In June 1999, Iran arrested 13 Jews that it said were part of an "espionage ring" for Israel, and 10 were convicted. All were released by April 2003.

Baha'is. There are an estimated 20,000 Baha'is in Iran, where this religion started, based on a 19th century self-declared Iranian prophet named Baha'ullah. The regime has subjected the Baha'is to unrelenting repression as members of what it describes as a "heretical" religion. Baha'i leaders have been repeated imprisoned, land and property of Baha'i adherents has been seized, Baha'is are banned from serving in goverment, and Baha'is have been routinely discriminated against for job and university positions. Virtually yearly, resolutions in the U.S. Congress have condemned the repression of the Baha'is of Iran. The March 17, 2017, report of the U.N. Special Rapporteur on Iran human rights (A/HRC/34/65) contained an extensive appendix listing Baha'is in prison in Iran. Two of seven Baha'i leaders (the "Yaran") sentenced in 2008 to 20 years imprisonment for espionage were released in the fall of 2018; the other five remain in jail.

Sufis. In February 2018, Iran arrested 300 Sufis demanding the release of their fellow faith members. Hundreds of Sufis remain in prison for their religious beliefs.

The Administration also requested a U.N. Security Council meeting to consider Iran's crackdown on the unrest, although other countries used the meeting to criticize the U.S. position or urge that the United States not use the unrest as a justification to withdraw from the JCPOA. The Administration imposed U.S. sanctions on identified regime officials and institutions responsible for abuses against protestors, including judiciary chief Sadeq Larijani. The designation of Larijani for human rights sanctions represented the highest level Iranian official sanctioned by the United States to date. In Congress, several resolutions were introduced supporting the rights of protestors and condemning the use of force against them by the Iranian government: H.Res. 676 (passed House January 9), S.Res. 367, H.Res. 675, and S.Res. 368.

Human Rights Practices[10]

U.S. State Department reports and reports from a U.N. Special Rapporteur have long cited Iran for a wide range of abuses—aside from its suppression of political opposition—including escalating use of capital punishment, executions of minors, denial of fair public trial, harsh and life-threatening conditions in prison, and unlawful detention and torture. In a speech on Iran on July 22, 2018, Secretary of State Pompeo recited a

[10] Much of the information in this section comes from the State Department human rights report for 2017: https://www.state.gov/j/drl/rls/hrrpt/humanrightsreport/index.htm#wrapper.

litany of U.S. accusations of Iranian human rights abuses, and stated "America is unafraid to expose human rights violations and support those who are being silenced."

Table 2. Human Rights Practices: General Categories

Media Freedoms	The Ministry of Culture and Islamic Guidance monitors journalists reporting from Iran as well as media and communications operations. The government continues to block pro-reform websites, social media applications, and blogs—particularly during times of unrest—and to close newspapers critical of the government, but some editors say that the government has become more tolerant of critical media since Rouhani took office. In response to the November 2012 death in custody of blogger Sattar Beheshti, seven security officers were arrested and the Tehran "Cyber Police" commander was removed. Iran has set up a national network that has a monopoly on internet service for Iranians. The Committee to Protect Journalists reported on December 13, 2016, that Iran had only 8 journalists in Iranian prisons, compared with 19 the year earlier. Some individuals have been arrested in recent years for posting videos of themselves on social media dancing or performing Western music in clothing that violates Iran's dress code.
Labor Restrictions	Independent unions are legal but cannot operate in practice. Many trade unionists remain in jail for protesting unpaid wages, precarious working conditions, and poor living conditions, or for peaceful trade union activities. The sole authorized national labor organization is a state-controlled "Workers' House" umbrella. In 2014, Iran ratified an additional International Labour Organization convention.
Religious Freedom	Each year since 1999, the Secretary of State has designated Iran as a "Country of Particular Concern" under the International Religious Freedom Act (IRFA) for engaging in or tolerating particularly severe violations of religious freedom. No sanctions have been added on Iran under IRFA, on the grounds that Iran is already subject to extensive U.S. sanctions. The constitution specifies Ja'afari Shiite Islam as the official state religion and restrictions on religious freedom for some non-Shiite groups have been noted consistently in State Department and other reports. Iran's penal code provides the death penalty for attempts by non-Muslims to convert Muslims, as well as *moharebeh* (enmity against God) and *sabb al-nabi* (insulting the prophets)—crimes that critics say are selectively applied to regime opponents.
Executions Policy	Human rights observer groups say the government has increased executions since Rouhani took office, and continues to execute minors. Total executions numbered about 1,000 for 2015, about 500 for 2016, and over 400 in 2017. Iran is a party to the International Covenant on Civil and Political Rights and the Convention on the Rights of the Child, and is obligated to cease the executions of minors. Iran has not held accountable any officials involved in the summer 1988 executions of thousands of prisoners of conscience in Iran's prisons.
Human Trafficking	Since 2005, State Department "Trafficking in Persons" reports (including the report for 2018) have placed Iran in Tier 3 (worst level) for failing to take significant action to prevent trafficking in persons. Iranian women, boys, and girls are trafficked for sexual exploitation in Iran as well as to Pakistan, the Persian Gulf, and Europe. However, the State Department's 2017 report said the government had set up some centers to assist trafficking victims. The 2018 report credits Iran with taking steps to ratify the U.N. Convention against Transnational Organized Crime.
Corporal Punishments/ Stoning	Iran's judiciary continues to sanction corporal punishment, including flogging, blinding, stoning, and amputation. In 2002, the then head of Iran's judiciary, Ayatollah Shahroudi (mentioned above) issued a ban on stoning. However, Iranian officials later called that directive "advisory," thus putting stoning sentences at the discretion of individual judges, and the practice reportedly continues.

Sources: State Department reports on human rights practices, on international religious freedom, and trafficking in persons. Trafficking in persons report for 2018: https://www.state.gov/j/tip/rls/tiprpt/2018/index.htm. International Religious Freedom report for 2017: https://www.state.gov/documents/organization/269134.pdf.

State Department and Special Rapporteur reports have noted that the 2013 revisions to the Islamic Penal Code and the 2015 revisions to the Criminal Procedure Code made some reforms, including eliminating death sentences for children convicted of drug-related offenses and protecting the rights of the accused. A "Citizen's Rights Charter," issued December 19, 2016, at least nominally protects free expression and is intended to raise public awareness of citizen rights. It also purportedly commits the government to implement the Charter's 120 articles. In August 2017, Rouhani appointed a woman, former vice president Shahindokht Molaverdi, to oversee implementation of the Charter. The State Department's human rights report for 2017 says that key Charter protections for individual rights have not been implemented, to date.

Women's Rights

Women can vote and run for office but female candidates for president have always been barred from running by the Council of Guardians. They can and have served in cabinet and vice presidential positions, as well as in mayoral positions, but are not permitted to serve as judges. As noted above, in August 2017, Rouhani named three women to his second term cabinet, but he disappointed women's groups by not appointing any to ministerial posts.

Women have been subject to arrest if they do not cover their head in public, generally with a garment called a chador, but, in late December 2017, just before the latest round of significant unrest began, authorities announced they would no longer arrest dress code violators. Instead, violators are required to attend classes to correct their behavior. Still, small numbers of women in various cities have been protesting the code since February 2018 by taking off their hijab and holding them up in front of gathered crowds. In May 2018, one activist was sentenced to 20 years in prison for protesting the compulsory wearing of the hijab.

Women are permitted to drive and work outside the home without restriction, including owning their own businesses, although less than 20% of the workforce is female. Despite female majorities in higher education in past years, women are a third less likely to work after graduation than their male counterparts.

Women do not have inheritance or divorce rights equal to those of men, and their court testimony carries half the weight of a male's. A woman's husband has the power to restrict his wife's travel abroad, as well as limit her job prospects. Laws against rape are not enforced effectively. The law permits a man to have up to four wives as well as "temporary wives"—an arrangement reached after a religious ceremony and civil contract outlining the relationship's conditions. Women have also been banned from attending male sports matches, although that restriction has been relaxed somewhat since early 2017.[11]

A U.N. Special Rapporteur on Iran human rights was reestablished in March 2011 by the U.N. Human Rights Council (22 to 7 vote), resuming work done by a Special Rapporteur on Iran human rights during 1988-2002. Former Maldives Foreign Minister Ahmad Shaheed was appointed to this role in June 2011, and he was replaced by Asma Jahangir in September 2016. She issued two Iran human rights reports, the latest of which was dated August 14, 2017 (A/72/322), before passing away in February 2018. Her report

[11] https://www.huffingtonpost.com/entry/bowing-to-pressure-iran-grants-women-spectators-access_us_58a92da2e4b0fa149f9ac73d.

findings were largely consistent with those of the State Department and those of her predecessor. The special rapporteur mandate was extended on March 24, 2018. On July 6, 2018, the U.N. Human Rights Council appointed British-Pakistani lawyer Javaid Rehman as her replacement. The U.N. General Assembly has insisted that Iran cooperate with the efforts of the Special Rapporteur by allowing the official's visits to Iran. Iran has refused, agreeing instead to respond to Special Rapporteur inquiries through agreed "special procedures."

In November 2016, the U.N. General Assembly's Third Committee (which oversees human rights issues) adopted a resolution (85 in favor, 35 opposed, and 63 abstaining) expressing concern over Iran's "alarmingly" frequent use of the death penalty and again urging access to Iran by the Special Rapporteur. Despite the criticism of its human rights record, on April 29, 2010, Iran acceded to the U.N. Commission on the Status of Women. It also sits on the boards of the U.N. Development Program (UNDP) and UNICEF. Iran's U.N. dues are about $9 million per year.

Iran has an official body, the High Council for Human Rights, headed by former Foreign Minister Mohammad Javad Larijani (brother of the Majles speaker and the judiciary head). It generally defends the government's actions to outside bodies rather than encourages improvement of the government's human rights practices, although Larijani has, according to the Special Rapporteur, questioned the effectiveness of drug-related executions.

As part of its efforts to try to compel Iran to improve its human rights practices, the United States has imposed sanctions on Iranian officials alleged to have committed human rights abuses, and on firms that help Iranian authorities censor or monitor the internet. In April 2014, the European Parliament passed a resolution calling on European Union (EU) diplomats to raise Iran's human rights record at official engagements.

U.S.-Iran Relations, U.S. Policy, and Options

The February 11, 1979, fall of the Shah of Iran, who was a key U.S. ally, shattered U.S.-Iran relations. The Carter Administration's efforts to build a relationship with the new regime in Iran ended after the November 4, 1979, takeover of the U.S. Embassy in Tehran by radical pro-Khomeini "Students in the Line of the Imam." The 66 U.S. diplomats there were held hostage for 444 days, released minutes after President Reagan's inauguration on January 20, 1981. The United States broke relations with Iran on April 7, 1980, two weeks prior to a failed U.S. military attempt to rescue the hostages.

Iran has since then pursued policies that successive Administrations considered inimical to U.S. interests in the Near East region and beyond.[12] Iran's authoritarian political system and human rights abuses have contributed to, but have not necessarily been central to, the U.S.-Iran rift, although some observers assert that Iran's behavior flows directly from the nature of its regime.

Iran has an interest section in Washington, DC, under the auspices of the Embassy of Pakistan, and staffed by Iranian Americans. The former Iranian Embassy closed in April 1980 when the two countries broke diplomatic relations, and remains under the control of the State Department. Iran's Mission to the United Nations in New York runs most of Iran's diplomacy inside the United States. The U.S. interests section in Tehran, under the auspices of the Embassy of Switzerland, has no American personnel.

U.S.-Iran Relations since the Hostage Crisis

- ***Reagan Administration***. The Reagan Administration designated Iran a "state sponsor of terrorism" in January 1984, primarily because of Iran's support for Lebanese Hezbollah. The designation reinforced a U.S. "tilt" toward Iraq in the 1980-1988 Iran-Iraq War, which included diplomatic efforts to block conventional arms sales to Iran.[13] During 1987-1988, U.S. naval forces engaged in several skirmishes with Iranian naval elements in the course of U.S. efforts to protect oil shipments transiting the Persian Gulf from Iranian mines and other attacks. On April 18, 1988, Iran lost one-quarter of its larger naval ships in an engagement with the U.S. Navy, including a frigate sunk. However, the Administration contradicted its efforts to favor Iraq's war effort by providing arms to Iran ("TOW" antitank weapons and I-Hawk air defense batteries) in exchange for Iran's help in the releasing of U.S. hostages in held in Lebanon. On July 3, 1988, U.S. forces in the Gulf mistakenly shot down Iran Air Flight 655 over the Gulf, killing all 290 on board, contributing to Iran's decision to accept a ceasefire in the war with Iraq in August 1988.
- ***George H. W. Bush Administration***. In his January 1989 inaugural speech, President George H.W. Bush stated that "goodwill begets goodwill" with respect to Iran—implying that U.S.-Iran relations could improve if Iran helped obtain the release of U.S. hostages held by Hezbollah in Lebanon. Iran apparently did assist in obtaining their release and all remaining U.S. hostages there were freed by the end of December 1991. However, no U.S.-Iran thaw followed, possibly because

[12] Those policies, such as its national security policies and its development of an extensive nuclear program, are assessed in detail in CRS Report R44017, *Iran's Foreign and Defense Policies*, by Kenneth Katzman.

[13] Elaine Sciolino, *The Outlaw State: Saddam Hussein's Quest for Power and the Gulf Crisis* (New York: John Wiley and Sons, 1991), p. 168.

Iran continued to back terrorist groups in the Middle East and to oppose the U.S. push for Arab-Israeli peace that began after the 1991 U.S. liberation of Kuwait.

- ***Clinton Administration***. The Clinton Administration articulated a strategy of "dual containment" of Iran and Iraq—an attempt to keep both countries simultaneously weak rather than alternately tilting to one or the other. In 1995-1996, the Administration and Congress banned U.S. trade and investment with Iran and imposed penalties on foreign investment in Iran's energy sector, in response to Iran's support for terrorist groups seeking to undermine the Israeli-Palestinian peace process. The election of the moderate Mohammad Khatemi as president in May 1997 precipitated a U.S. offer of direct dialogue without preconditions, but Khatemi did not pursue the offer. In June 1998, then-Secretary of State Madeleine Albright called for mutual confidence building measures that could lead to a "road map" for normalization. In a March 17, 2000, speech, she admitted past U.S. interference in Iran.
- ***George W. Bush Administration***. In his January 2002 State of the Union message, President Bush named Iran as part of an "axis of evil" including Iraq and North Korea. However, the Administration enlisted Iran's diplomatic help in efforts to try to stabilize post-Taliban Afghanistan and post-Saddam Iraq.[14] The Administration rebuffed a reported May 2003 Iranian overture transmitted by the Swiss Ambassador to Iran for an agreement on all major issues of mutual concern ("grand bargain" proposal).[15] State Department officials disputed that the proposal was fully vetted within Iran's leadership. The Administration aided victims of the December 2003 earthquake in Bam, Iran, including through U.S. military aircraft deliveries into Iran. As Iran's nuclear program advanced, the Administration worked with several European countries to persuade Iran to agree to limit its nuclear program. President Bush's January 20, 2005, second inaugural address and his January 31, 2006, State of the Union message stated that the United States would be a close ally of a "free and democratic" Iran—appearing to support regime change.[16]

Obama Administration: Pressure, Engagement, and the JCPOA

President Obama asserted that there was an opportunity to persuade Iran to limit its nuclear program through diplomacy and to potentially rebuild a U.S.-Iran relationship after decades of mutual animosity. The approach emerged in President Obama's first

---

[14] Robin Wright, "U.S. In 'Useful' Talks With Iran," *Los Angeles Times*, May 13, 2003.

[15] http://www.armscontrol.org/pdf/2003_Spring_Iran_Proposal.pdf.

[16] Helene Cooper and David Sanger, "Strategy on Iran Stirs New Debate at White House," *New York Times*, June 16, 2007.

message to the Iranian people on the occasion of Nowruz (Persian New Year) on March 21, 2009, in which he stated that the United States "is now committed to diplomacy that addresses the full range of issues before us, and to pursuing constructive ties among the United States, Iran, and the international community." He referred to Iran as "The Islamic Republic of Iran," signaling opposition to a policy of regime change. The Administration reportedly also loosened restrictions on U.S. diplomats' meeting with their Iranian counterparts at international meetings. In addition

- President Obama exchanged several letters with Supreme Leader Khamene'i, reportedly expressing the Administration's support for engagement with Iran.
- In a major speech to the "Muslim World" in Cairo on June 4, 2009, President Obama acknowledged that the United States had played a role in the overthrow of Mossadeq and said that Iran had a right to peaceful nuclear power.

2009-2013: Emphasis on Economic Pressure

In 2009, Iran's crackdown on the Green Movement uprising and its refusal to accept compromises to limit its nuclear program caused the Obama Administration to shift to a "two track" strategy: stronger economic pressure coupled with offers of negotiations that could produce sanctions relief. The sanctions imposed during 2010-2013 received broad international cooperation and caused economic difficulty in Iran. The Administration also altered U.S. trade regulations to help Iranians circumvent their government's restrictions on internet usage, and funded exchanges with civil society activists in Iran. In 2013, before the election of Rouhani, the Administration began direct but unpublicized talks with Iranian officials in the Sultanate of Oman to probe Iran's willingness to reach a comprehensive nuclear accord.[17] The Administration also repeatedly stated that a military option is "on the table."

2013-2017: Rouhani Elected, JCPOA Implemented

The election of Rouhani in June 2013 contributed to a U.S. to emphasizing diplomacy, even though U.S.-Iran nuclear negotiations had begun in the Sultanate of Oman in early 2013, prior to Rouhani's election. On September 20, 2013, on the eve of U.N. General Assembly meetings, the *Washington Post* published an op-ed by Rouhani stating a commitment to engage in constructive interaction with the world. President Obama, in his September 24, 2013, U.N. speech, confirmed that he had exchanged letters with Rouhani stating the U.S. willingness to resolve the nuclear issue peacefully and that the United States "[is] not seeking regime change."[18] The two presidents spoke by phone

---

[17] http://www.al-monitor.com/pulse/originals/2015/08/iran-us-nuclear-khamenei-salehi-jcpoa-diplomacy.html#.

[18] Remarks by President Obama in Address to the United Nations General Assembly, September 24, 2013.

on September 27, 2013—the first direct U.S.-Iran presidential level contact since Iran's revolution.

President Obama expressed hope that the JCPOA would "usher[] in a new era in U.S.-Iranian relations,"[19] while at the same time asserting that the JCPOA would benefit U.S. national security even without such a broader rapprochement. After the JCPOA was finalized in July 2015, the United States and Iran held bilateral meetings at the margins of all nuclear talks and in other settings, covering regional as well as bilateral issues. President Obama met Foreign Minister Zarif at the September 2015 General Assembly session, but no U.S.-Iran meetings occurred during the September 2016 U.N. General Assembly session. However, some post-JCPOA actions by Iran, prevented a broad warming of U.S.-Iran relations. Subsequent to the JCPOA finalization:

- In December 2015, Iranian officials argued that new U.S. visa requirements in the FY2016 Consolidated Appropriations Act (P.L. 114-113) would cause European businessmen to hesitate to travel to Iran and thereby limit reengagement in Iran's economy. Then-Secretary of State Kerry wrote a letter to Foreign Minister Zarif on December 19, 2015, stating that the United States would implement the provision in a manner that avoids interfering with "legitimate business interests of Iran."
- In January 2016, Kerry worked with Foreign Minister Zarif to achieve the rapid release of 10 U.S. Navy personnel who the IRGC took into custody when their two riverine crafts strayed into what Iran considers its territorial waters.
- Coinciding with Implementation Day of the JCPOA (January 16, 2016), the dual citizens held by Iran at that time were released and a long-standing Iranian claim for funds paid for undelivered military equipment from the Shah's era was settled—resulting in $1.7 billion in payments to Iran ($400 million in foreign currency for the original DOD monies and $1.3 billion in foreign currency for an agreed amount of interest). Administration officials asserted that the nuclear diplomacy provided an opportunity to resolve these outstanding issues simultaneously, but some Members of Congress criticized the simultaneity of the financial settlement as appearing to pay "ransom" to Iran. Administration officials asserted that it had long been assumed that the United States would need to return monies to Iran for the undelivered military equipment and that the amount of interest agreed was likely less than what Iran might have been awarded by the U.S.-Iran Claims Tribunal.
- Iran conducted at least four ballistic missile tests from the time the JCPOA was finalized in 2015 until the end of the Obama Administration. The tests prompted

[19] Roger Cohen. "U.S. Embassy, Tehran." *New York Times*, April 8, 2015.

additional U.S. designations for sanctions of entities that support Iran's program and the Administration called the tests "defiant of" Resolution 2231.
- Obama Administration officials asserted that Iran's regional behavior did not changed significantly after the JCPOA. In October 2016, the Houthi rebels in Yemen fired anti-ship missiles possibly supplied by Iran at U.S. and UAE ships in the Red Sea. Iranian naval vessels also conducted occasional "high speed intercepts" of U.S. warships in the Persian Gulf throughout 2016, and Iran continued to threaten to close the Strait of Hormuz if Iran were attacked.
- After releasing all remaining jailed dual nationals in connection with Implementation Day, Iran subsequently jailed several other dual nationals. Some assert that Iran wants additional sanctions relief in exchange for their release.

According to Obama Administration officials, there was no discussion of any enhancements of mutual diplomatic representation, the posting of U.S. nationals to staff the U.S. interests section in Tehran, or a visit to Iran by then-Secretary of State Kerry. In 2014, Iran appointed one of those involved in the 1979 seizure of the U.S. embassy in Tehran—Hamid Aboutalebi—as ambassador to the United Nations. But, in April 2014, Congress passed S. 2195 (P.L. 113-100), which gave the Administration authority to deny him a visa to take up his duties. The United States subsequently announced he would not be admitted to the United States. Iran replaced him with Gholam Ali Khoshroo, who studied in the United States and served in Khatemi's reformist government. In May 2015, the two governments granted each other permission to move their respective interests sections in Washington, DC, and in Tehran to more spacious locations.

Trump Administration Policy and the JCPOA

Trump Administration policy to date has centered on the criticism that the JCPOA addressed only nuclear issues, and hindered the U.S. ability to pressure Iran on all other fronts, including its "malign" activities in the region and its development of ballistic missiles. According to Administration statements, the policy is to pressure Iran's economy to (1) compel it to renegotiate the JCPOA to address the JCPOA's deficiencies and (2) deny Iran the revenue to continue to intervene throughout the region. An unstated element of the policy is to create enough economic difficulties to stoke unrest in Iran, possibly to the point where the regime collapses. The policy has unfolded with specific statements and actions as follows:

- Citing Iran's arming of the Houthis in Yemen, on February 1, 2017, then-National Security Adviser Michael Flynn stated that Iran was "officially on notice" about its provocative behavior and that the United States would counter Iran on multiple fronts.

- In April 2017, the Administration announced a six-month Iran policy review, based on the premise that the JCPOA "only delays [Iran's] goal of becoming a nuclear state" and had failed to curb Iran's objectionable regional behavior.
- The Administration did not congratulate Rouhani or otherwise respond to his reelection in the May 19, 2017, vote in Iran.
- During his May 20-24, 2017, visit to the region, President Trump told an "Arab Islamic American Summit" in Saudi Arabia that "Until the Iranian regime is willing to be a partner for peace, all nations of conscience must work together to isolate Iran, deny it funding for terrorism, and pray for the day when the Iranian people have the just and righteous government they deserve." The following month, then-Secretary of State Tillerson testified before Congress that the Administration would work to support elements in Iran that would lead to a "peaceful transition" of Iran's government.[20]
- On October 13, 2017, President Trump announced the results of the six-month policy review. On the JCPOA, the President said that he would not make a certification of Iranian JCPOA compliance (under the INARA law Iran Nuclear Agreement Review Act, P.L. 114-17), and he demanded, as a condition of keeping the United States in the accord, that Congress and U.S. allies act to (1) address the expiration of JCPOA nuclear restrictions, (2) curb Iran's ballistic missile program, and (3) counter Iran's regional activities. The noncertification under INARA triggered a 60-day period for Congress to take legislative action under expedited procedures to reimpose those sanctions that were lifted. Congress did not take such action.
- On January 12, 2018, the President announced he would continue to waive sanctions at their mid-January expiration and again not certify Iranian compliance under INARA. However, President Trump said that he would not waive sanctions at the next waiver expiration deadline (May 12) unless his demands to address JCPOA weaknesses were addressed by Congress and U.S. allies in Europe. Visits by the leaders of France and Germany in April 2018 were intended to persuade President Trump to remain in the JCPOA.

Withdrawal from the JCPOA and Beyond

On May 8, 2018, President Trump announced that the United States would withdraw from the JCPOA and reimpose all U.S. secondary sanctions that were suspended (waived) or revoked to implement the accord. The reimposition goes into effect over a

[20] http://www.irannewsupdate.com/news/terrorism/3934-iran-u-s-policy-moving-toward-regime-change.html.

maximum 180-day period (by November 4, 2018),[21] with some of the sanctions (on rial trading, Iran's auto sector, and other sectors aside from energy and banking) being reimposed on August 6, 2018.

Statements by President Trump and Secretary of States Pompeo subsequent to the JCPOA withdrawal indicated that U.S. policy has shifted to apply maximum pressure on Iran's economy with the apparent intent to cause Iran's economy and political system to collapse; the stated intent of causing Iran to renegotiate the JCPOA to meet all U.S. demands; and the intent to deny Iran the revenue to continue to implement its defense programs and regional activities.

- On May 21, 2018, in his first speech as Secretary of State, Michael Pompeo announced a return to a U.S. strategy of pressuring Iran through sanctions and by working with allies against Iran's regional activities and proxies, as well as against its ballistic missile program, cyberattacks, and human rights abuses.[22] He also expressed U.S. "solidarity" with the Iranian people—indicating support for domestic opponents of Iran's regime.
- On July 22, 2018, in a speech to Iranian-Americans at the Reagan Library in California, Secretary Pompeo recited a litany of Iranian human rights abuses, official corruption, and efforts to destabilize the region. The Secretary stated that "I have a message for the people of Iran. The United States hears you; the United States supports you; the United States is with you."
- On July 23, 2018, following threats by Rouhani and other Iranian leaders to cut off the flow of oil through the Persian Gulf if Iran's oil exports are prevented by sanctions, President Trump issued a Twitter post from his personal account: "To Iranian President Rouhani: NEVER, EVER THREATEN THE UNITED STATES AGAIN OR YOU WILL SUFFER CONSEQUENCES THE LIKES OF WHICH FEW THROUGHOUT HISTORY HAVE EVER SUFFERED BEFORE. WE ARE NO LONGER A COUNTRY THAT WILL STAND FOR YOUR DEMENTED WORDS OF VIOLENCE & DEATH. BE CAUTIOUS!" The tweet suggested to some that the United States might be intent on military action against Iran, but no hostilities appeared imminent by either side.
- On August 16, 2018, Secretary Pompeo announced the creation of an "Iran Actions Group" at the State Department responsible for "directing, reviewing, and coordinating" all aspects of the department's Iran-related activities. He announced the group would be headed by the director of Policy Planning at the Department, Brian Hook, who would take on the additional title of "Special Representative for Iran."

---

[21] White House. Statement by the President on the JCPOA. May 8, 2018.

[22] Statement by Secretary of State Mike Pompeo at the Heritage Foundation. May 21, 2018.

Detentions of U.S. Nationals and Dual Nationals

Iran does not recognize any dual nationality and detained dual nationals are not given help from foreign diplomats.

Recent Past Detentions

2007: Iranian-American academic Haleh Esfandiari was imprisoned for several months in 2007 for allegations that her employer, the Woodrow Wilson Center, was involved in democracy promotion efforts in Iran.

2009: Iranian-American journalist Roxanna Saberi was imprisoned for five months for expired press credentials.

2009-2011: American hikers Sara Shourd, Shane Bauer, and Josh Fattal were arrested in August 2009 after crossing into Iran from a hike in northern Iraq. Their 2010-2011 releases were brokered by Oman.

On January 16, 2016, in concert with JCPOA "Implementation Day," several detainees were released, including former U.S. Marine Amir Hekmati, who was arrested in 2011 for spying for the United States; Reverend Saeed Abedini, a Christian convert of Iranian origin imprisoned since December 2012 for setting up Christian orphanages in Iran; *Washington Post* journalist Jason Rezaian, who was detained in July 2014; Nosratollah "Fred" Khosravi-Roodsari, who remained in Iran; and U.S. citizen Matthew Trevithick, a student arrested in 2015. In exchange, the United States released 7 Iranian-Americans/Iranians imprisoned in the United States for violating Iran sanctions, and dropped outstanding charges against 14 others not in U.S. custody. The releases were not addressed in the JCPOA.

Still in Custody or Missing

- Nizar Zakka (permanent resident, Lebanon national), information technology professional detained in September 2015 and sentenced to 10 years in prison in October 2016.
- Siamak and Baquer Namazi: In November 2015, Iran arrested U.S.-Iran national, Siamak Namazi, a business consultant, on unspecified charges. Iran detained his father, Baquer Namazi, in February 2016. In October 2016, the Namazis were sentenced to 10 years in prison. Baquer Namazi is held despite failing health.
- Reza "Robin" Shahini: In July 2016, Iran detained U.S.-Iran dual national Reza "Robin" Shahini, for crimes against the Islamic Republic and on October 25 he was sentenced to 18 years in prison. He was released on bail in late March 2017, pending appeal, but he is still apparently not permitted to leave Iran.
- Karan Vafadari: Vafadari, an Iranian American, was arrested in July 2016, along with his wife, U.S. permanent resident Afarin Niasari. The art gallery owners, who are Zoroastrians, were sentenced in January 2018 to 27 years in jail for "engaging in corruption and depravity" referring to allegedly serving alcohol at their home.
- On July 16, 2017, Iranian judiciary officials announced that Xiyue Want, a U.S. citizen and a graduate student at Princeton University, had been sentenced to 10 years in

prison for spying for the United States. Mr. Wang was arrested in the summer of 2016 while conducting research in Iran on that country's Qajar dynasty.

- Robert Levinson: Former FBI agent Robert Levinson remains missing after a visit to Kish Island in March 2007 to meet an Iranian contact. In March 2018, Iran again denied knowing his status or location. In January 2013, his family released recent photos of him provided by captors through uncertain channels.
- Mohrad Tahbaz a U.S.-British-Iranian national, was arrested in January 2018, along with seven members of the Persian Heritage Wildlife Foundation. His colleague, Canadian-Iranian national Kavous Seyed-Emami, died in custody a few weeks after his arrest under unexplained circumstances.

Non-U.S. Dual Nationals.

May 2011: British-Iranian dual national Kamal Foroughi was arrested and sentenced to eight years in prison in 2013 for unspecified charges. 2016: British-Iranian dual national Nazanin ZaghariRatcliffe and Canadian-Iranian dual national Homa Hoodfar were arrested. Hoodfar was released in September 2016, and Ratchliffe was given a three-day furlough from prison in late August 2018. April 2016: French-Iranian Nazak Afshar was arrested upon return to Iran, sentenced to six years in prison, and released on bail. She had been arrested in 2009 but was freed following French government intervention. British-Iranian dual national 2016: Abdolrasoul Dorri-Esfahani, a former member of Iran's nuclear negotiating team focused on financial issues, was jailed for alleged spying for British intelligence. March 2018: British-Iran national Shahabeddin Mansouri-Kermani, a banker, was sentenced on spying charges. May 2018: Iran-British national Mahan Abedin detained upon arrival from Britain, where he works for the British Council. Also arrested was Iranian national Aras Amiri, who was studying in Britain.

Bills in the 115th Congress, H.R. 4744 and S. 2365 would require U.S. sanctions to be imposed on Iranians responsible for detaining American citizens.

Source: State Department report mandated by Section 110 of the Countering America's Adversaries through Sanctions Act (CAATSA, P.L. 115-44); various press reports.

Policy Elements and Options

As have its predecessors, the Trump Administration has not publicly taken any policy option "off the table." Some options, such as sanctions, are being emphasized, while others are being considered or threatened to varying degrees.

Engagement and Improved Bilateral Relations

Successive Administrations have debated the degree to which to pursue engagement with Iran. Included in that debate has been whether to set conditions for engagement. As noted above, the Trump Administration has publicly welcomed engagement, but it has set strict conditions for any significant improvement in U.S.-Iran relations. For example, Secretary Pompeo, in his May 21, 2018, speech referenced above, stipulated an extensive list of demands for behavior changes by Iran that, if met, could potentially produce an improved U.S.-Iran relationship. Many of the demands enumerated by Secretary Pompeo—such as ending support for Lebanese Hezbollah and withdrawing entirely from Syria—go to the core of Iran's revolution and are unlikely to be met by Iran under any circumstances.

In his July speech in California, discussed above, Secretary of State Pompeo said "As President Trump has said, we're willing to talk with the regime in Iran, but relief from American pressure will only come when we see tangible, demonstrated, and sustained shifts in Tehran's policies."[23] Subsequently, at a July 30 press conference, President Trump stated he would be willing to meet President Rouhani without conditions. Press reports indicate that U.S. officials might have sought a Trump-Rouhani meeting at the September 2017 General Assembly meetings in New York, but Iranian officials refused to try to arrange a meeting. In a statement accompanying the August 6, 2018, reimposition of some sanctions on Iran, President Trump said "I am open to reaching a more comprehensive deal that addresses the full range of the regime's malign activities, including its ballistic missile program and its support for terrorism."[24] Iranian leaders have not indicated an inclination to arrange presidential-level U.S.-Iran talks, or to enter into new negotiations on a nuclear accord that would address all U.S. concerns.

Military Action

Successive U.S. Administrations have sought to back up other policy options with a capability to exercise military force against Iran. Prior to the JCPOA, supporters of military action against Iran's nuclear program argued that such action could set back Iran's nuclear program substantially.[25] A U.S. ground invasion to remove Iran's regime does not appear to have gained serious consideration at any time.

The Obama Administration repeatedly stated that "all options are on the table" to prevent Iran from acquiring a nuclear weapon, including military action against Iran's nuclear facilities.[26] However, the Obama Administration argued that military action

---

[23] Secretary of State Pompeo at the Reagan Library. Op. cit.

[24] Statement by the President on the Reimposition of United States Sanctions With Respect to Iran. August 6, 2018.

[25] Joby Warrick, "Iran: Underground Sites Vulnerable, Experts Say," *Washington Post*, March 1, 2012. For an extended discussion of U.S. air strike options on Iran, see Rogers, Paul. *Iran: Consequences of a War*. Oxford Research Group, February 2006.

[26] Jeffrey Goldberg, "Obama to Iran and Israel: 'As President of the United States, I Don't Bluff'," *The Atlantic*, March 2, 2012.

would set back Iran's nuclear advancement with far less certainty or duration than would a nuclear agreement. And Iranian retaliation could potentially escalate and expand throughout the region, reduce Iran's regional isolation, strengthen Iran's regime domestically, and raise oil prices.[27] After the JCPOA was finalized, President Obama reiterated the availability of this option should Iran violate the agreement.[28] Obama Administration officials articulated that U.S. military action against Iran might also be used if Iran (1) attacks or prepares to attack U.S. allies; or (2) attempts to interrupt the free flow of oil or shipping in the Gulf or elsewhere.

The Trump Administration has similarly stated that "all options are open," referring to military action. The Administration's pullout from the JCPOA was accompanied by threats to take unspecified action if Iran were to leave the accord and restart banned aspects of its nuclear program. The Administration's threats to counter Iran's threats to the freedom of navigation, cyberattacks, regional malign activities, and missile program could also suggest that the Administration is more willing to employ military options against Iran than was the Obama Administration. The apparent propensity to counter threatening Iranian actions with U.S. military action appeared to be reflected in President Trump's July 23, 2018, tweet that was cited above. In early August 2018, following Iranian threats to close the Strait of Hormuz in response to the reimposition of U.S. sanctions, CENTCOM Commander General Joseph Votel said that U.S. forces in the region were "watching for changes in the environment"—a veiled warning that U.S. forces would counter any Iranian military action that threatened U.S. interests.[29] The Votel warning also followed threatening comments by the commander of the IRGC-QF, Major General Qasem Soleimani.

With regard to presidential authorities, S.J.Res. 41, which passed the Senate on September 22, 2012, in the 112th Congress, rejects any U.S. policy that relies on "containment" of a potential nuclear Iran. No legislation has been enacted that would limit the President's authority to use military force against Iran, but neither has there been legislation authorizing the use of force against Iran, either on Iranian territory or against Iranian allied or proxy forces in the region.

Economic Sanctions

The U.S. withdrawal from the JCPOA and reimposition of all U.S. sanctions has major implications. The table below summarizes sanctions that have been used against Iran.

---

[27] http://2scottmontgomery.blogspot.com/2011/12/panetta-brookings-speech.html.

[28] Speech by President Obama at American University. August 7, 2015. President Obama Interview with CNN's Fareed Zakaria. Broadcast on August 9, 2015.

[29] Missy Ryan. U.S. Military Warns Iran over Activity in Shipping Passageway. Washington Post, August 9, 2018.

Table 3. Summary of U.S. Sanctions against Iran

Ban on U.S. Trade With and Investment in Iran. Executive Order 12959 (May 6, 1995) bans almost all U.S. trade with and investment in Iran. P.L. 111-195 (Comprehensive Iran Sanctions, Accountability, and Divestment Act, CISADA) codifies the trade ban, which generally does not apply to foreign subsidiaries of U.S. firms. Generally remains in force.
Energy Sector Sanctions. The Iran Sanctions Act (P.L. 104-172), as amended, authorizes the imposition of five out of a menu of 12 sanctions on firms that invest more than $20 million to develop Iran's petroleum (oil and gas) sector; sold Iran more than $1 million worth of gasoline or equipment to import gasoline or refine oil into gasoline; sold $1 million or more worth of energy equipment to Iran; provided shipping services to transport oil from Iran; engaged in an energy joint venture with Iran outside Iran; or bought Iran's sovereign debt. Another law—P.L. 112-239—sanctions most foreign dealings with Iran's energy, shipping, and shipbuilding sector, as well as the sale of certain items for Iranian industrial processes and the transfer to Iran of precious metals (often a form of payment for oil or gas). Waived in accordance with the JCPOA.
Sanctions On Iran's Central Bank. Section 1245 of the FY2012 National Defense Act (P.L. 112-81) prevents foreign banks that do business with Iran's Central Bank from opening U.S. accounts unless the parent countries of the banks earn an exemption by "significantly reducing" their purchases of Iranian oil. Another law, the Comprehensive Iran Sanctions, Accountability, and Divestment Act (P.L. 111-195, CISADA) bans U.S. accounts for banks that do business with sanctioned entities. The Department of the Treasury in November 2011 declared Iran's financial system an entity of primary money laundering concern. CISADA remains active but entities "delisted" for sanctions under the JCPOA are no longer subject to CISADA sanctions.
Terrorism Sanctions. Iran's designation by the Secretary of State as a "state sponsor of terrorism" triggers: (1) a ban on the provision of U.S. foreign assistance to Iran under Section 620A of the Foreign Assistance Act; (2) a ban on arms exports to Iran under Section 40 of the Arms Export Control Act (P.L. 95-92, as amended); (3) under Section 6(j) of the Export Administration Act (P.L. 96-72, as amended), a significant restriction—amended by other laws to a "presumption of denial"—on U.S. exports to Iran of items that could have military applications; (4) under Section 327 of the Anti-Terrorism and Effective Death Penalty Act (P.L. 104-132), a requirement that U.S. representatives to international financial institutions vote against international loans to terrorism list states. Executive Order 13224 (September 23, 2001) authorizes a ban on U.S. transactions with entities determined to be supporting international terrorism. The Order was not specific to Iran, but several Iranian entities have been designated. All remains in force.
Sanctions Against Foreign Firms that Aid Iranian Military or Weapons of Mass Destruction Capacity. The Iran-Syria-North Korea Nonproliferation Act (P.L. 106-178, March 14, 2000, as amended) authorizes the Administration to impose sanctions on foreign persons or firms determined to have provided assistance to Iran's weapons of mass destruction (WMD) programs. Sanctions include restrictions on U.S. trade with the sanctioned entity. Remains in force. The Iran-Iraq Arms Nonproliferation Act (P.L. 102-484, October 23, 1992, as amended) provides for U.S. sanctions against foreign firms that sell Iran "destabilizing numbers and types

of conventional weapons" or WMD technology. Executive Order 13382 (June 28, 2005) amended previous executive orders to provide for a ban on U.S. transactions with entities determined to be supporting international proliferation. Numerous Iranian entities, including the IRGC itself, have been designated.

Divestment. A Title in CISADA authorizes and protects from lawsuits various investment managers who divest from shares of firms that conduct specified business with Iran. Remains in force.

Sanctions Against Human Rights Abuses, Internet Monitoring, and Regional Activities. Various laws and Executive Orders (including CISADA, E.O 13553) impose sanctions on named Iranian human rights abusers, on firms that sell equipment Iran can use to monitor the internet usage of citizens or employ against demonstrators and on Iranian persons or entities that suppress human rights in Syria or contribute to destabilizing Iraq. Remains in force.

Source: CRS. For analysis and extended discussion of U.S. and international sanctions against Iran, see CRS Report RS20871, *Iran Sanctions*, by Kenneth Katzman.

Regime Change Option

One recurring U.S. policy question has been whether the United States should support efforts within Iran to overthrow Iran's leadership. The Obama Administration faced this question during the 2009 Green Movement uprising, deciding in that case that effusive U.S. support for the uprising would undermine the opposition's position in Iran. President Obama did, however, give some public support to the demonstrators, and his 2011 Nowruz (Persian New Year) address mentioned specific dissidents and said "young people of Iran ... I want you to know that I am with you."[30] In a September 24, 2013, General Assembly speech, amid preliminary discussions with Iran on a possible nuclear agreement, President Obama explicitly stated that the United States does not seek to change Iran's regime.

The Trump Administration—in cited statements by Secretary Pompeo and other U.S. officials— asserts that its policy is not to change Iran's regime but instead to change Iran's behavior and cause it to "make a strategic decision about how to ensure its well-being and the well-being of its people."[31] However, the content of these and other statements by Administration officials, in particular Secretary Pompeo's speech to Iranian-Americans at the Reagan Library on July 22, 2018, suggest support for a regime change outcome. In his speech on May 21, 2017, in Saudi Arabia, President Trump stated that his Administration is hoping that Iran's government will change to one that the Administration considers "just and righteous." In testimony before two congressional committees in June 2017, then-Secretary of State Rex Tillerson said the Administration supports a "philosophy of regime change" for Iran (Senate Appropriations Committee)

[30] White House, "Remarks of President Obama Marking Nowruz," March 20, 2011.
[31] Pompeo speech at the Reagan Library, July 22, 2018, op.cit.

and that the Administration would "work toward support of those elements inside of Iran that would lead to a peaceful transition of that government" (House Foreign Affairs Committee). In his October 13, 2017, policy announcement on Iran, President Trump stated that

> we stand in total solidarity with the Iranian regime's longest-suffering victims: its own people. The citizens of Iran have paid a heavy price for the violence and extremism of their leaders. The Iranian people long to—and they just are longing, to reclaim their country's proud history, its culture, its civilization, its cooperation with its neighbors.

Subsequently, President Trump issued statements of support for the December 2017-January 2018 protests in Iran on Twitter and in other formats. In his May 8, 2018, announcement of a U.S. withdrawal from the JCPOA, President Trump stated

The Shah's Son, Student Activists, and Other Prominent Dissidents

Some Iranians abroad, including in the United States, want to replace the regime with a constitutional monarchy led by Reza Pahlavi, the U.S.-based son of the late former Shah and a U.S.-trained combat pilot. The Shah's son, born in 1960, has condemned the regime for the 2009 crackdown and called for the international community to withdraw representation in Tehran. He appears periodically in broadcasts in Iran through Iranian exile-run stations in California, as well as in other Iran-oriented media.

Pahlavi has always retained some support from the older generations in Iran, but he has tried to broaden his following by denying he seeks to restore the monarchy. Since March 2011, he has increasingly cooperated with— and possibly attempted to co-opt—younger leaders in a "National Council of Iran" (NCI), which was established with over 30 groups in April 2013. The Council drafted democratic principles for a post-Islamic republic Iran but it suffered defections and its activity level diminished to the point where it largely disbanded. In April 2018, a discovery in Tehran of a mumified body was possibly that of his grandfather, Reza Shah, who ruled from 1925- 1941 and is remembered fondly by some Iranians for instituting law and order.

Student dissident groups composed of well-educated, Westernized urban youth have been the backbone of the Iranian opposition. The Office of Consolidation of Unity is the student group that led the 1999 riots but which later became controlled by regime loyalists. An offshoot, the Confederation of Iranian Students (CIS), led by U.S.- based Amir Abbas Fakhravar, believes in regime replacement and in 2013 formed a "National Iran Congress" to advocate that outcome. The group has drafted a constitution for a future republic of Iran and, in concert with 2017-2018 protests in Iran, supports the formation of a "revolutionary council" that could take power if the regime were to collapse. Cofounder Arzhang Davoodi has been in prison since 2002 and in July 2014 was sentenced to death. The sentence has not been implemented to date.

Other dissidents, some in Iran, others in exile (including in the United States), have criticized the regime for decades.

Journalist Akbar Ganji left Iran in 2006 after serving 6 years in prison for alleging high-level involvement in the 100 murders of Iranian dissident intellectuals.

Religion scholar Abdolkarim Soroush left Iran in 2001 after challenging the doctrine of clerical rule.

Former Revolutionary Guard organizer Mohsen Sazegara broadcasts online to Iran from his base in the United States.

Nobel Peace Prize laureate (2003) and Iran human rights activist lawyer Shirin Abadi, who for many years represented clients persecuted or prosecuted by the regime, left Iran after the 2009 uprising.

Other significant dissidents in exile include former Culture Minister Ataollah Mohajerani, Mohsen Kadivar, and U.S.-based Fatemah Haghighatjoo.

Some well-known dissidents have been incarcerated periodically or continuously since 2010, including filmmaker Jafar Panahi and famed blogger Hossein Derakshan, and journalist Abdolreza Tajik. The elderly leader of the Iran Freedom Movement, Ibrahim Yazdi, was released from prison in April 2011 after resigning as the movement's leader. Human rights lawyer Nasrin Sotoudeh was released from prison in September 2013. In May 2015, the regime arrested Narges Mohammadi, a well-known activist against regime executions.

> Finally, I want to deliver a message to the long-suffering people of Iran. The people of America stand with you.... But the future of Iran belongs to its people. They are the rightful heirs to a rich culture and an ancient land, and they deserve a nation that does justice to their dreams, honor to their history and glory to God.

In his speech to the Heritage Foundation on May 21, Secretary of State Pompeo added that the United States expresses total solidarity with the Iranian people. In his Reagan Library speech on July 22, 2018, Pompeo recited a litany of Iranian regime human rights abuses and governmental corruption that called into question its legitimacy and, in several passages and answers to questions, clearly expressed the hope that the Iranian people will oust the current regime. The apparent support for a regime change policy was furthered by Secretary Pompeo's announcement during that speech that the Broadcasting Board of Governors is launching a new full-time Persian-language service for television, radio, digital, and social media to help "ordinary Iranians inside of Iran and around the globe can know that America stands with them."

At times, some in Congress have advocated that the United States adopt a formal policy of overthrow of the regime. In the 111th Congress, one bill said that it should be U.S. policy to promote the overthrow of the regime (the Iran Democratic Transition Act, S. 3008).

Many of Iran's leaders, particularly Supreme Leader Khamene'i, continue to articulate a perception that the United States has never accepted the 1979 Islamic revolution. Khamene'i and other Iranian figures note that the United States provided funding to antiregime groups, mainly promonarchists, during the 1980s.[32] Comments by various U.S. Administrations on the issue of Iran regime change have been noted above.

Democracy Promotion and Internet Freedom Efforts

Successive Administrations and Congresses have sought to at least lay the groundwork for eventual regime change through "democracy promotion" programs and sanctions on Iranian human rights abuses. Legislation authorizing democracy promotion in Iran was enacted in the 109th Congress. The Iran Freedom Support Act (P.L. 109-293, signed September 30, 2006) authorized funds (no specific dollar amount) for Iran democracy promotion.[33] Several laws and Executive Orders issued since 2010 are intended to promote internet freedom, and the Administration has amended U.S.-Iran trade regulations to allow for the sale to Iranians of consumer electronics and software that help them communicate. Then-Under Secretary of State Wendy Sherman testified on October 14, 2011, that some of the democracy promotion funding for Iran was used to train Iranians to use technologies that circumvent regime internet censorship.

Many have argued that U.S. funding for such programs is counterproductive. Even before the post-2009 election crackdown, Iran was arresting civil society activists by alleging they are accepting the U.S. democracy promotion funds, while others have refused to participate in U.S. funded programs, fearing arrest.[34] Perhaps to address these criticisms, the Obama Administration altered Iran democracy promotion programs somewhat toward working directly with Iranians inside Iran who are organized around apolitical issues such as health, education, science, and the environment.[35] The State Department, which often uses appropriated funds to support prodemocracy programs run by organizations based in the United States and in Europe, refuses to name grantees for security reasons. The funds shown below have been obligated through DRL and the Bureau of Near Eastern Affairs in partnership with USAID. Some of the funds have also been used for cultural exchanges, public diplomacy, and broadcasting to Iran. A further indication of the sensitivity of specifying the use of the funds is that, since FY2010, funds

---

[32] CRS conversations with U.S. officials responsible for Iran policy. 1980-1990. After a period of suspension of such assistance, in 1995, the Clinton Administration accepted a House-Senate conference agreement to include $18-$20 million in funding authority for covert operations against Iran in the FY1996 Intelligence Authorization Act (H.R. 1655), according to a *Washington Post* report of December 22, 1995. The Clinton Administration reportedly focused the covert aid on changing the regime's behavior, rather than its overthrow.

[33] This legislation was a modification of H.R. 282, which passed the House on April 26, 2006, by a vote of 397-21, and S. 333, which was introduced in the Senate.

[34] Three other Iranian Americans were arrested and accused by the Intelligence Ministry of actions contrary to national security in May 2007: U.S. funded broadcast (Radio Farda) journalist Parnaz Azima (who was not in jail but was not allowed to leave Iran); Kian Tajbacksh of the Open Society Institute funded by George Soros; and businessman and peace activist Ali Shakeri. Several congressional resolutions called on Iran to release Esfandiari (S.Res. 214 agreed to by the Senate on May 24; H.Res. 430, passed by the House on June 5; and S.Res. 199). All were released by October 2007. Tajbacksh was rearrested in September 2009 and remains incarcerated.

[35] CRS conversation with U.S. officials of the "Iran Office" of the U.S. Consulate in Dubai, October 2009.

have been provided for Iran civil society/democracy promotion as part of a broader "Near East regional democracy programs."

Iran asserts that funding democracy promotion represents a violation of the 1981 "Algiers Accords" that settled the Iran hostage crisis and provide for noninterference in each other's internal affairs. The George W. Bush Administration asserted that open funding of Iranian prodemocracy activists (see below) was a stated effort to change regime behavior, not to overthrow the regime, although some saw the Bush Administration's efforts as a cover to achieve a regime change objective.

Broadcasting/Public Diplomacy Issues

Another part of the democracy promotion effort has been the development of Iran-specific U.S. broadcasting services to Iran. Radio *Farda* ("tomorrow," in Farsi) began under Radio Free Europe/Radio Liberty (RFE/RL), in partnership with the Voice of America (VOA), in 2002. The service was established as a successor to a smaller Iran broadcasting effort begun with an initial $4 million from the FY1998 Commerce/State/Justice appropriation (P.L. 105-119). It was to be called Radio Free Iran but was never formally given that name by RFE/RL. Based in Prague, Radio *Farda* broadcasts 24 hours/day and has 59 full-time employees. Its budget is approximately $11 million per year. No U.S. assistance has been provided to Iranian exile-run stations.[36] As noted above, Secretary Pompeo has announced a new Persian-language channel for Iranians through various media; it is not clear whether this new service will be located in existing programs or as part of an entirely new program.

Table 4. Iran Democracy Promotion Funding

FY2004	Foreign operations appropriation (P.L. 108-199) earmarked $1.5 million for "educational, humanitarian and non-governmental organizations and individuals inside Iran to support the advancement of democracy and human rights in Iran." The State Department Bureau of Democracy and Labor (DRL) gave $1 million to a unit of Yale University, and $500,000 to National Endowment for Democracy.
FY2005	$3 million from FY2005 foreign aid appropriation (P.L. 108-447) for democracy promotion. Priority areas: political party development, media, labor rights, civil society promotion, and human rights.
FY2006	$11.15 million for democracy promotion from regular FY2006 foreign aid appropriation (P.L. 109102). $4.15 million administered by DRL and $7 million for the Bureau of Near Eastern Affairs.
FY2006 supp.	Total of $66.1 million (of $75 million requested) from FY2006 supplemental (P.L. 109-234): $20 million for democracy promotion; $5 million for public diplomacy directed at the Iranian population; $5 million for cultural exchanges; and $36.1 million for Voice of America-TV and "Radio *Farda*" broadcasting. Broadcasting funds are provided through the Broadcasting Board of Governors.
FY2007	FY2007 continuing resolution provided $6.55 million for Iran (and Syria) to be administered through DRL. $3.04 million was used for Iran. No funds were requested.
FY2008	$60 million (of $75 million requested) is contained in Consolidated Appropriation (H.R. 2764, P.L. 110-161), of which, according to the conference report, $21.6 million is ESF for prodemocracy programs, including nonviolent efforts to oppose Iran's meddling in other countries. $7.9 million is from a

[36] The conference report on the FY2006 regular foreign aid appropriations stated the sense of Congress that such support should be considered.

	"Democracy Fund" for use by DRL. The appropriation also fully funded additional $33.6 million requested for Iran broadcasting: $20 million for VOA Persian service; $8.1 million for Radio Farda; and $5.5 million for exchanges with Iran.
FY2009	Request was for $65 million in ESF "to support the aspirations of the Iranian people for a democratic and open society by promoting civil society, civic participation, media freedom, and freedom of information." H.R. 1105 (P.L. 111-8) provides $25 million for democracy promotion programs in the region, including in Iran.
FY2010	$40 million requested and used for Near East Regional Democracy programming. Programs to promote human rights, civil society, and public diplomacy in Iran constitute a significant use of these region-wide funds.
FY2011	$40 million requested and will be used for Near East Regional Democracy programs. Programming for Iran with these funds to be similar to FY2010.
FY2012	$35 million for Near East Regional Democracy (NERD), and Iran-related use similar to FY2010 and FY2011.
FY2013	$30 million for NERD, with Iran use similar to prior two fiscal years. About $583,000 was obligated for Iran democracy promotion.
FY2014	$30 million for NERD. About $1 million was obligated for Iran democracy promotion.
FY2004	Foreign operations appropriation (P.L. 108-199) earmarked $1.5 million for "educational, humanitarian and non-governmental organizations and individuals inside Iran to support the advancement of democracy and human rights in Iran." The State Department Bureau of Democracy and Labor (DRL) gave $1 million to a unit of Yale University, and $500,000 to National Endowment for Democracy.
FY2015	$30 million for NERD. About $675,000 was obligated for Iran democracy promotion
FY2016	$32 million for NERD, About $900,000 was obligated for Iran democracy promotion.
FY2017	$30 million for NERD, with Iran use likely similar to prior years.
FY2018	$15 million requested, with Iran use likely similar to prior years.

Sources: Information provided by State Department and reviewed by Department's Iran Office, February 1, 2010; State Department Congressional Budget Justifications; USAID Explorer database.

Ethnicity- and Sect-Based Armed Groups

Sunni Armed Opposition: Jundullah

Jundullah is composed of Sunni Muslims primarily from the Baluchistan region bordering Pakistan. The region is inhabited by members of the Baluch minority and is far less developed than other parts of Iran. On the grounds that *Jundullah* has attacked civilians in the course of violent attacks in Iran, the State Department formally named it an FTO on November 4, 2010. *Jundullah* has conducted several attacks on Iranian security and civilian officials, including a May 2009 bombing of a mosque in Zahedan and the October 2009 killing of five IRGC commanders in Sistan va Baluchistan Province. The regime claimed a victory against the group in February 2010 with the capture of its top leader, Abdolmalek Rigi. The regime executed him in June 2010, but the group retaliated in July 2010 with a Zahedan bombing that killed 28 persons, including some IRGC personnel. The group was responsible for a December 15, 2010, bombing at a mosque in Chahbahar that killed 38.

Kurdish Armed Groups

One armed Kurdish group operating out of Iraq is the Free Life Party, known by its acronym PJAK. Its leader is believed to be Abdul Rahman Hajji Ahmadi, born in 1941, who is a citizen of Germany and lives in that country. Many PJAK fighters reportedly are women.

PJAK was designated by the Department of the Treasury in early February 2009 as a terrorism supporting entity under Executive Order 13224, although the designation statement indicated the decision was based mainly on PJAK's association with the Turkish Kurdish opposition group Kongra Gel, also known as the PKK. Five Kurds executed by Iran's regime in May 2010 were alleged members of PJAK. In July 2016, the Kurdistan Democratic Party of Iran (KDP-I) announced a resumption of "armed struggle" against the regime, which had been suspended for 25 years, following clashes with the IRGC that left several dead on both sides. KDP-I fighters involved in the clashes reportedly had entered Iran from Kurdish-controlled territory in Iraq. The Kurds who were recruited by the Islamic State for the June 2017 attacks in Tehran, discussed above, did not have clear affiliations with the established Kurdish armed groups discussed above.

Arab Oppositionists/Ahwazi Arabs

Another militant group, the *Ahwazi Arabs*, operates in the largely Arab-inhabited areas of southwest Iran. Relatively inactive over the past few years, and the regime continues to execute captured members of the organization.

VOA Persian Service

The VOA established a Persian-language service to Iran in July 2003. It consists of radio broadcasting (one hour a day of original programming); television (six hours a day of primetime programming, rebroadcast throughout a 24-hour period); and internet. The service has come been criticized by observers for losing much of its audience among young, educated, antiregime Iranians who are looking for signs of U.S. official support. The costs for the service are about $20 million per year.

State Department Public Diplomacy Efforts

The State Department has sought outreach to the Iranian population.

- In May 2003, the State Department added a Persian-language website to its list of foreign-language websites, under the authority of the Bureau of International Information Programs. The website was announced as a source of information about the United States and its policy toward Iran.
- In February 14, 2011, the State Department began Persian-language Twitter feeds in an effort to connect better with internet users in Iran.
- In part to augment U.S. public diplomacy, the State Department announced in April 2011 that a Persian-speaking U.S. diplomat based at the U.S. Consulate in Dubai would make regular appearances on Iranian media.

People's Mojahedin Organization of Iran (MEK, PMOI)/National Council of Resistance of Iran (NCRI)

The best-known exiled opposition group is the Mojahedin-e-Khalq Organization (MEK), also known as the People's Mojahedin Organization of Iran (PMOI). It is the main organization within the National Council of Resistance of Iran (NCRI), which acts as a parliament-in-exile. Secular and left-leaning, the PMOI was formed in 1965 by university students opposed to the Shah of Iran. It has been widely characterized by experts as blending several left-leaning ideologies with Islam, but it publicly advocates universal suffrage, a non-nuclear Iran, and abolition of use Sharia law in Iran. The group allied with pro-Khomeini forces during the Islamic revolution and, according to State Department reports, supported the November 1979 takeover of the U.S. Embassy in Tehran. The group's members were killed or exiled after unsuccessfully rising up against the Khomeini regime in mid-1981, and thousands of its members have since been executed, including those massacred in prison in 1988. The PMOI was led until 1989 by spouses Maryam and Massoud Rajavi, the former of which has been NCRI President-elect since 1992. Mrs. Rajavi is based in France and the whereabouts of Massoud Rajavi are unknown. The PMOI elects a Secretary General every two years and the Rajavis are no longer involved in its day-to-day operations.

The State Department designated the PMOI as an FTO in October 1997, during the presidency of the relatively moderate Mohammad Khatemi, with whom the Clinton Administration was trying to forge dialogue. In August 2003, the Department of the Treasury ordered the NCRI's offices in the United States closed. The FTO designation was based on State Department reports asserting that the members of the PMOI were responsible for the killing of seven American military personnel and contract advisers to the former Shah during 1973-1976; and bombings at U.S. government and U.S. corporate offices in Tehran to protest the 1972 visits to Iran of President Nixon and Secretary of State Kissinger. The reports also listed as terrorism several attacks by the group against regime targets (including 1981 bombings that killed high-ranking officials), attacks on Iranian government facilities, and attacks on Iranian security officials. The group has denied involvement in the attacks. The group's alliance with Saddam Hussein's regime apparently contributed to the designation, even though Saddam was a U.S. ally when the group moved there in 1987.

The PMOI challenged the FTO listing in the U.S. court system and, in June 2012, the Appeals Court gave the State Department until October 1, 2012, to decide on the FTO designation, without prescribing an outcome. On September 28, 2012, maintaining there had not been confirmed acts of PMOI terrorism for more than a decade and that it had cooperated on the Camp Ashraf issue (below), the group was removed from the FTO list and was "de-listed" from its designation as a terrorist group under Executive Order 13224. State Department officials, in a background briefing that day, said, "We do not see the [PMOI] as a viable or democratic opposition movement." However, regime officials often blame the PMOI for stoking unrest in Iran, suggesting regime nervousness about the group's support level within Iran and degree of organization. The group has also been credited for exposing Iranian nuclear sites and other proliferation-related locations and actions. The State Department has been meeting with the MEK since its removal from the FTO list, including in Iraq. The NCR-I reopened its offices in Washington, DC, in April 2013.

Camp Ashraf Issue

The situation of PMOI members in Iraq has been resolved. U.S. forces attacked PMOI military installations in Iraq during Operation Iraqi Freedom (March 2003) and negotiated a ceasefire with PMOI elements in Iraq, under which the 3,400 PMOI members consolidated at Camp Ashraf, near the border with Iran. Its weaponry was placed in storage, guarded by U.S. and Iraqi personnel. In July 2004, the United States granted the Ashraf detainees "protected persons" status under the 4th Geneva Convention, although that designation lapsed when Iraq resumed full sovereignty in June 2004. The Iraqi government's pledges to adhere to all international obligations with respect to the PMOI in Iraq have come into question on several occasions: on July 28, 2009, Iraq used force to overcome resident resistance to setting up a police post in the camp, killing 13 residents of the camp. On April 8, 2011, Iraq Security Forces killed 36 Ashraf residents. In December 2011, the Iraqi government and the United Nations agreed to relocate Ashraf residents to the former U.S. military base Camp Liberty, near Baghdad's main airport. The relocation was completed by September 17, 2012, leaving a residual group of 101 PMOI persons at Ashraf. Despite the move, the government failed to prevent Iraqi Shiite militias from attacking Camp Liberty residents with rockets and other weaponry. And, on September 1, 2013, 52 of the residual Ashraf residents were killed by gunmen that appeared to have assistance from Iraqi forces. Seven went missing. The FY2016 National Defense Authorization Act (P.L. 114-92) called for "prompt and appropriate steps" to promote the protection of camp residents. In September 2016, the 280 remaining residents of Camp Liberty were resettled in Albania and there are no more PMOI members there.

Sources: Various press reports and CRS conversations with NCR-I representatives and experts.

Since 2006, the State Department has been increasing the presence of Persian-speaking U.S. diplomats in U.S. diplomatic missions around Iran, in part to help identify and facilitate Iranian participation in U.S. democracy-promotion programs. The Iran unit at the U.S. consulate in Dubai has been enlarged significantly into a "regional presence" office, and "Iran-watcher" positions have been added to U.S. diplomatic facilities in Baku, Azerbaijan; Istanbul, Turkey; Frankfurt, Germany; London; and Ashkabad, Turkmenistan, all of which have large expatriate Iranian populations and/or proximity to Iran.[37] An "Office of Iran Affairs" has been formed at the State Department, and it is reportedly engaged in contacts with U.S.-based exile groups such as those discussed earlier.

[37] Farah Stockman, "'Long Struggle' With Iran Seen Ahead," *Boston Globe*, March 9, 2006.

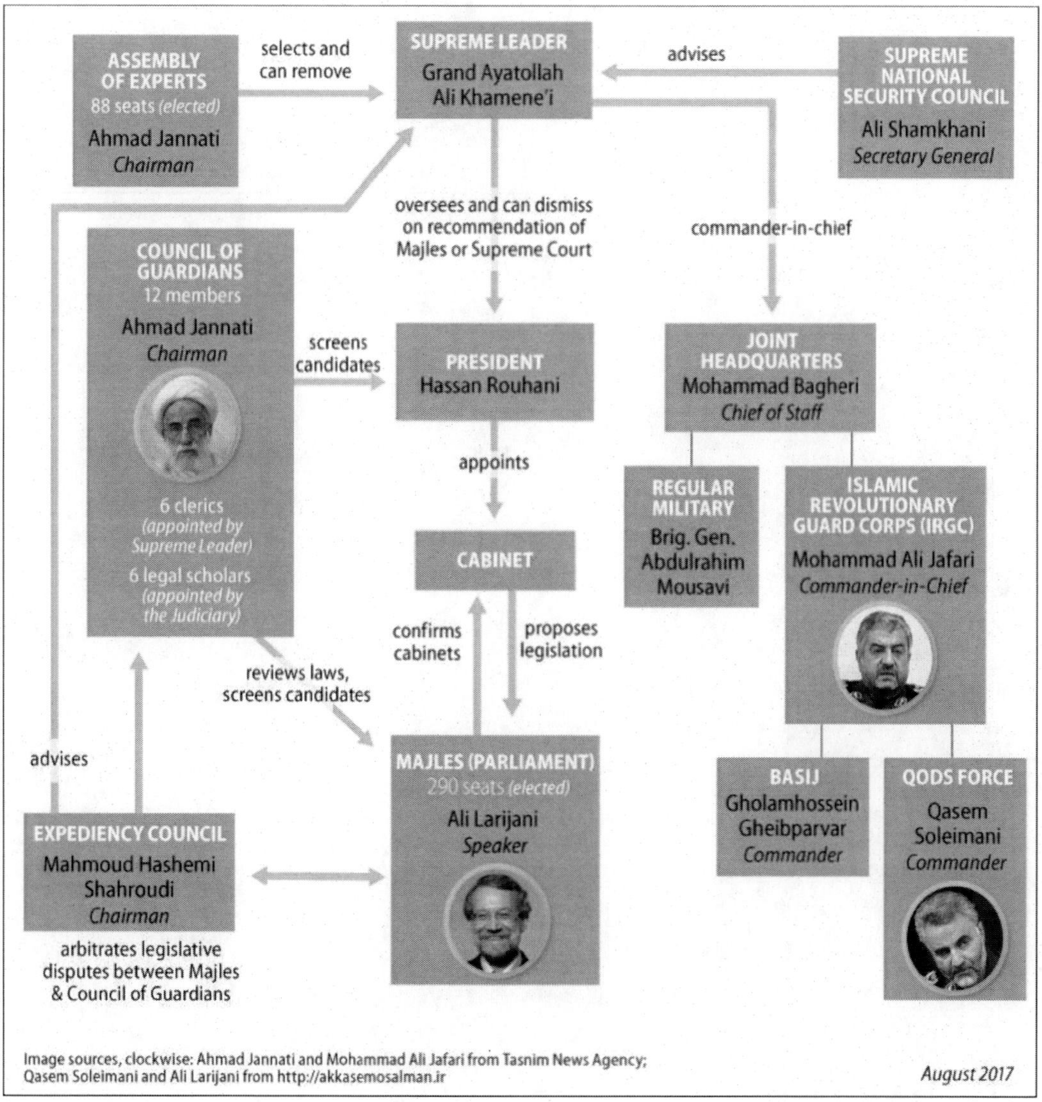

Source: CRS.

Figure 1. Structure of the Iranian Government.

Source: Map boundaries from Map Resources, 2005. Graphic: CRS.

Figure 2. Map of Iran.

ACKNOWLEDGMENTS

The author wishes to acknowledge the research contribution of Sarah Manning, Research Associate, CRS Foreign Affairs, Defense and Trade Division, in the preparation of this chapter.

In: Iran: Economic, Political and Nuclear Policies
Editor: Everett Fowler
ISBN: 978-1-53614-827-5

Chapter 5

IRAN'S FOREIGN AND DEFENSE POLICIES*

Kenneth Katzman

ABSTRACT

Iran's national security policy is the product of many overlapping and sometimes competing factors such as the ideology of Iran's Islamic revolution; perception of threats to the regime and to the country; long-standing Iranian national interests; and the interaction of the Iranian regime's factions and constituencies. Iran's leadership

- seeks to deter or thwart U.S. or other efforts to invade or intimidate Iran or to bring about a change of regime.
- has sought to take advantage of opportunities of regional conflicts to overturn a power structure in the Middle East that it asserts favors the United States, Israel, Saudi Arabia, and other Sunni Muslim Arab regimes.
- seeks to enhance its international prestige and restore a sense of "greatness" reminiscent of ancient Persian empires.
- provides material support to allied governments and armed factions such as the Asad regime in Syria, Lebanese Hezbollah, Houthi rebels in Yemen, Iraqi Shiite militias, and Bahraini militant groups. Iranian officials characterize this support as helping the region's "oppressed" and assert that Saudi Arabia, in particular, is instigating sectarian tensions and trying to exclude Iran from regional affairs.
- has sought to use sanctions relief provided by the July 2015 multilateral nuclear agreement (Joint Comprehensive Plan of Action, JCPOA) to emerge as a regional energy and trade hub and to negotiate future weapons buys.
- sometimes disagrees on tactics and strategies. Supreme Leader Ali Khamene'i and key hardline institutions, such as the Islamic Revolutionary Guard Corps (IRGC), oppose any compromises of Iran's national security core goals, but support the reintegration into regional and international diplomacy that is advocated by Iran's elected president, Hassan Rouhani.

---

* This is an edited, reformatted and augmented version of Congressional Research Service, Publication No. R44017, dated October 9, 2018.

- supports acts of international terrorism, as the "leading" or "most active" state sponsor of terrorism, according to each annual State Department report on international terrorism since the early 1990s.

The Trump Administration has articulated a strategy to counter Iran's "malign activities" and its behavior more broadly, based primarily on reducing Iran's financial resources. The Administration argued that the JCPOA failed to address Iran's regional activities and, partly on these grounds, President Trump withdrew the United States from the JCPOA on May 8, 2018, and announced that all U.S. sanctions would be reimposed. Additional aspects of Administration strategy for countering Iran's malign activities—which include working with partner governments and factions in the region—are enumerated in a report submitted to Congress in late August 2018, a report mandated by the Countering America's Adversaries through Sanctions Act (P.L. 115-44). President Trump and other senior U.S. officials also have indirectly threatened military action against Iranian actions that pose an immediate threat to U.S. regional interests or allies. In late September 2018, the Administration issued a report ("Outlaw Regime: A Chronicle of Iran's Destructive Activities") broadly indicting Iran's malign activities as well as a litany of other activities the Administration termed "Iranian regime's destructive behavior at home and abroad."

INTRODUCTION

Successive Administrations have identified Iran as a key national security challenge, citing Iran's nuclear and missile programs as well as its long-standing attempts to counter many U.S. objectives in the region. Director of National Intelligence Dan Coats, in his February 13, 2018, annual worldwide threat assessment testimony before Congress, assessed that "Iran will seek to expand its influence in Iraq, Syria, and Yemen, where it sees conflicts generally trending in Tehran's favor ..." and "Iran will develop military capabilities that threaten U.S. forces and allies in the region...." Successive National Defense Authorization Acts (NDAAs) have required an annual report on Iran's military power, which has in recent years contained assessments of Iran similar to those presented publicly by the intelligence community.[1]

IRAN'S POLICY MOTIVATORS

Iran's foreign and defense policies are products of overlapping, and sometimes contradictory, motivations. One expert has characterized these contradictions as indecision over whether Iran is a "nation or a cause."[2]

---

1 "Fiscal Year 2016 Report on the Military Power of Iran." Defense Department, Unclassified Executive Summary. January 2017. The FY2016 and FY2017 NDAAs (P.L. 114-92 and P.L. 114-328) extended the annual DOD reporting requirement until the end of 2025 and required that the report include information on Iran's offensive and defensive cyber capabilities, and its cooperation with other state or nonstate actors to conduct or mask its cyber operations.

2 Foreign Policy Association. "A Candid Discussion with Karim Sadjadpour." May 6, 2013. http://foreignpolicyblogs.com/2013/05/06/a-candid-discussion-with-karim-sadjadpour/.

Threat Perception

Iran's leaders are apparently motivated, at least to some extent, by the perception of threat to their regime and their national interests Ayatollah posed by the United States and its allies.

- Iran's paramount decisionmaker since 1989, Supreme Leader Grand Ayatollah Ali Khamene'i, has repeatedly stated that the United States seeks to overturn Iran's regime through support for its domestic opponents, imposition of economic sanctions, and support for Iran's regional adversaries.[3] He frequently warns against Western "cultural influence"—social behavior that he asserts does not comport with Iran's societal and Islamic values. U.S. officials and reports have said that "Supreme Leader Ali Khamene'i maintains a deep distrust of U.S. intentions toward Iran...."[4]
- Iran's leaders assert that the U.S. maintenance of a large military presence in the Persian Gulf region and in other countries around Iran reflects intent to intimidate Iran or attack it if Iran pursues policies the United States finds inimical.[5]
- Iran's leaders assert that the United States' support for Sunni Arab regimes that oppose Iran has led to the empowerment of radical Sunni Islamist groups and spawned Sunni-dominated terrorist groups such as the Islamic State.[6]

Ideology

The ideology of Iran's 1979 Islamic revolution continues to infuse Iran's foreign policy. The revolution overthrew a secular, authoritarian leader, the Shah, who the leaders of the revolution asserted had suppressed Islam and its clergy. A clerical regime was established in which ultimate power is invested in a "Supreme Leader" who melds political and religious authority.

- In the early years after the revolution, Iran attempted to "export" its revolution to nearby Muslim states. In the late 1990s, Iran appeared to abandon that goal

---

[3] Khamene'i: "U.S. Would Overthrow Iranian Government If It Could—Media." *Reuters*, February 8, 2014.

[4] https://fas.org/man/eprint/dod_iran_2016.pdf.

[5] Erik Slavin. "Iran Emphasizes Nuclear Reconciliation, Criticizes U.S. Military Posture in Persian Gulf." *Stars and Stripes*, March 5, 2014. http://www.stripes.com/news/iran-emphasizes-nuclear-reconciliation-criticizes-us-militaryposture-in-persian-gulf-1.271204.

[6] Ramin Mostaghim. "Iranians Rally to Support Iraq; Some Blame U.S. for Sunni Insurgency." *Los Angeles Times*, June 24, 2014. http://www.latimes.com/world/middleeast/la-fg-iran-volunteers-militants-iraq-20140624-story.html.

because its promotion produced resistance to Iran in the region.[7] However, the various conflicts in the region that arose from the 2011 "Arab Spring" uprisings have appeared to give Iran opportunities to revive that goal to some extent.

- Iran's leaders assert that the political and economic structures of the Middle East are heavily weighted against "oppressed" peoples and in favor of the United States and its regional allies. Iranian leaders generally describe as "oppressed" peoples the Palestinians, who do not have a state of their own, and Shiite Muslims, who are underrepresented and economically disadvantaged minorities in many countries of the region.
- Iran claims that the region's politics and economics have been distorted by Western intervention and economic domination. Iranian officials claim that the creation of Israel is a manifestation of Western intervention that deprived the Palestinians of legitimate rights.
- Iran claims its ideology is pan-Islamic and nonsectarian. It cites its support for Sunni groups such as Hamas and for secular Palestinian groups as evidence that it works with non-Islamist, non-Shiite groups to promote the rights of the Palestinians.

National Interests

Iran's national interests usually dovetail with, but sometimes conflict with, Iran's ideology.

- Iran's leaders, stressing Iran's well-developed civilization and historic independence, claim a right to be recognized as a major power in the region. They contrast Iran's history with that of the six Persian Gulf monarchy states (Saudi Arabia, Kuwait, United Arab Emirates, Qatar, Bahrain, and Oman of the Gulf Cooperation Council, GCC), most of which gained independence only in the 1960s and 1970s. To this extent, many of Iran's foreign policy actions are similar to those undertaken by the Shah of Iran and prior Iranian dynasties.
- Iran has sometimes tempered its commitment to aid other Shiites to promote its geopolitical interests. For example, it has supported mostly Christian-inhabited Armenia, rather than Shiite-inhabited Azerbaijan, in part to thwart cross-border Azeri nationalism among Iran's large Azeri minority. It has refrained from backing Islamist movements in the Central Asian countries, which are mainly Sunni inhabited and whose Islamist movements are largely hostile toward Iran.

---

[7] Soner Cagaptay, James F. Jeffrey, and Mehdi Khalaji. "Iran Won't Give Up on Its Revolution." *New York Times*, op-ed, April 26, 2015.

- Even though Iranian leaders accuse U.S. allies of contributing to U.S. efforts to structure the Middle East to the advantage of the United States and Israel, Iranian officials have sought to engage with and benefit from transactions with historic U.S. allies, such as Turkey, to try to thwart international sanctions.

Factional Interests, Competition, and Public Opinion

Iran's foreign policy often appears to reflect differing approaches and outlooks among key players and interest groups.

- According to Iran's constitution and in practice, Iran's Supreme Leader has final say over major foreign policy decisions. Grand Ayatollah Ali Khamene'i, Supreme Leader since 1989, consistently expresses mistrust of U.S. intentions toward Iran. His consistent refrain, and the title of his book widely available in Iran, is "I am a revolutionary, not a diplomat."[8] Leaders of Iran's Islamic Revolutionary Guard Corps (IRGC), the military and internal security force created after the Islamic revolution, consistently support regional interventions.
- More moderate Iranian leaders, including President Hassan Rouhani, argue that Iran should not have any "permanent enemies." They maintain that a pragmatic foreign policy resulted in easing of international sanctions under the JCPOA, increased worldwide attention to Iran's views, and the positioning of Iran as a trade and transportation hub. Rouhani tends to draw support from Iran's youth and intellectuals, who say they want greater integration with the international community and who helped Rouhani achieve a first-round reelection victory on May 19, 2017, with 57% of the vote against a hardline candidate.
- Public opinion might be a growing factor in Iranian foreign policy. Significant protests occurred in Iran over economic and other issues in December 2017-January 2018. Many protesters expressed opposition to the use of Iran's financial resources for regional interventions rather than to improve the living standards of the population.

INSTRUMENTS OF IRAN'S NATIONAL SECURITY STRATEGY

Iran employs a number of different methods and mechanisms to implement its foreign policy, including supporting armed factions.

---

[8] http://www.nytimes.com/2014/11/21/world/middleeast/iran-us-nuclear-talks.html?_r=0.

Financial and Military Support to Allied Regimes and Groups

- Iran provides arms, training, and military advisers in support of allied governments and movements, such as the regime of President Bashar Al Asad of Syria, Lebanese Hezbollah, Hamas, Houthi rebels in Yemen, and Shiite militias in Iraq. Iran supports some Sunni Muslim groups: most Palestinians are Sunni Muslims and several Palestinian FTOs receive Iranian support because they are antagonists of Israel.
- The State Department report on international terrorism for 2016 stated that Iran remained the foremost state sponsor of terrorism in 2016, and continued to play a "destabilizing role" in military conflicts in Iraq, Syria, and Yemen. Iran also has been implicated in supporting violent Shiite opposition group attacks in Bahrain. Iran was joined in these efforts by Hezbollah.[9]
- DNI Dan Coats, in a worldwide threat assessment testimony to Congress on February 13, 2018, repeated the decades-long U.S. assertion that Iran "continues to be the foremost state sponsor of terrorism."[10] Many of the groups Iran supports are named as Foreign Terrorist Organizations (FTOs) by the United States, and because of that support, Iran was placed on the U.S. list of state sponsors of terrorism ("terrorism list") in January 1984.[11]
- Some armed factions that Iran supports have not been named as FTOs and have no record of committing acts of international terrorism. Such groups include the Houthi ("Ansar Allah") movement in Yemen (composed of Zaidi Shiite Muslims) and some underground Shiite opposition factions in Bahrain.
- Iran generally opposes Sunni terrorist groups that work against Iran's core interests, such as Al Qaeda and the Islamic State organizations.[12] Iran actively worked against the Islamic State organization in Syria and Iraq. Iran has expelled some Al Qaeda activists who it allowed to take refuge there after the September 11, 2001, attacks, but some reportedly remain—perhaps in an effort by Iran to exert leverage against the United States or Saudi Arabia.
- Iran's operations in support of its allies—which generally include arms shipments, provision of advisers, training, and funding—are carried out by the Qods (Jerusalem) Force of the IRGC (IRGC-QF). That force is headed by IRGC Major General Qasem Soleimani, who is said to report directly to Khamene'i.[13] IRGC and IRGC-QF leaders have on numerous occasions publicly acknowledged

---

[9] The text of the section on Iran can be found at https://www.state.gov/j/ct/rls/crt/2016/index.htm.

[10] Director of National Intelligence Dan Coats. Statement for the Record. Worldwide Threat Assessment of the US Intelligence Community. Senate Select Committee on Intelligence. May 11, 2017, and February 13, 2018.

[11] The other two countries still on the terrorism list are Syria and Sudan.

[12] http://nationalinterest.org/blog/the-buzz/iranians-are-terrified-irans-isis-nightmare-10856.

[13] http://www.newyorker.com/reporting/2013/09/30/130930fa_fact_filkins?printable=true&currentPage=all.

these activities,[14] although often characterizing Iran's support as humanitarian in nature or in order to protect Shiite religious shrines or sacred sites. Much of the weaponry Iran supplies to its allies includes specialized anti-tank systems ("explosively-forced projectiles" EFPs), artillery rockets, mortars, short-range missiles, and anti-ship cruise missiles.[15]

Table 1. Selected Iran or Iran-Related Terrorism Attacks or Plots

Date	Incident/Event	Claimed/Likely Perpetrator
November 4, 1979	U.S. Embassy in Tehran seized and 66 U.S. diplomats held for 444 days (until January 21, 1981).	Hardline Iranian regime elements
April 18, 1983	Truck bombing of U.S. Embassy in Beirut, Lebanon. 63 dead, including 17 U.S. citizens.	Factions that formed Lebanese Hezbollah claimed responsibility.
October 23, 1983	Truck bombing of U.S. Marine barracks in Beirut. 241 Marines killed.	Same as above
December 12, 1983	Bombings of U.S. and French embassies in Kuwait City. 5 fatalities.	Da'wa Party of Iraq. 17 Da'wa activists imprisoned in Kuwait
March 16, 1984	U.S. Embassy Beirut Political Officer William Buckley taken hostage in Beirut, others later. Last hostage released December 1991.	Factions that eventually formed Lebanese Hezbollah.
September 20, 1984	Truck bombing of U.S. embassy annex in Beirut. 23killed.	Factions that eventually formed Hezbollah
July 31, 1984	Air France aircraft hijacked to Iran	Factions that formed Hezbollah
May 25, 1985	Bombing of Amir of Kuwait's motorcade	Da'wa Party of Iraq
June 14, 1985	Hijacking of TWA Flight 847. One fatality, Navy diver Robert Stetham	Hezbollah
1985-86	Soft targets in Paris bombed, killing 12	Hezbollah/Iran intelligence
February 17, 1988	Col. William Higgins, serving with U.N. peacekeeping operation, was kidnapped in southern Lebanon; video of his corpse was released 18 months later.	Hezbollah
April 5, 1988	Hijacking of Kuwait Air passenger plane. Two killed.	Hezbollah
July 13, 1989	Assassination of Iranian Kurdish leader Qassemlu	Hezbollah/Iran
August 5, 1991	Assassination of former Prime Minister Bakhtiar	Iran intelligence
March 17, 1992	Bombing of Israeli Embassy in Buenos Aires. 29 killed.	Hezbollah, assisted by Iranian intelligence/diplomats.
July 18, 1994	Bombing of Argentine-Jewish Mutual Association (AMIA) building in Buenos Aires.	Same as above
June 25, 1996	Bombing of Khobar Towers housing complex near Dhahran, Saudi Arabia. 19 U.S. Air Force killed.	Saudi Hezbollah, but some assessments point to Al Qaeda.
October 11, 2011	U.S. Justice Dept. unveiled discovery of alleged plot involving at least one IRGC-QF officer, to assassinate Saudi Ambassador in Washington, DC.	IRGC-QF reportedly working with U.S.-based person and Mexican drug cartel.
February 13, 2012	Wife of Israeli diplomat wounded in Delhi, India	Lebanese Hezbollah
July 19, 2012	Bombing in Sofia, Bulgaria, killed five Israeli tourists, followed arrest of IRGC-QF operative surveilling synagogue in Sofia.	Lebanese Hezbollah, IRGC-QF
March 22, 2018	Two Iranian operatives charged with terrorism in Tirana, Albania	IRGC-QF or Iran intelligence

Sources: Recent State Department Country Reports on Terrorism; State Department "Select Iran-Sponsored Operational Activity in Europe, 1979-2018 (July 5, 2018); various press.

[14] *Al Jazeera*, August 20, 2016.

[15] Farzin Nadimi. "How Iran's Revived Weapons Exports Could Boost its Proxies." Washington Institute for Near East Policy, August 17, 2015.

Direct Military Action

- Whereas Iran seemingly prefers indirect action through proxies and armed factions it supports, Iran does sometimes undertake direct military action.
- Iran has, although less so in the past year, conducted "high speed intercepts" of U.S. ships in the Persian Gulf, as an apparent show of strength. Iran has, on some occasions, diverted or detained international shipping transiting the Gulf.
- Iran appears to be making increasingly frequent use of missile strikes on regional opponents. In September, Iran fired missiles at a Kurdish opposition group based in northern Iraq. In early October, Iran fired, from Iranian territory, several missiles at Islamic State positions in Syria.

Other Political Action/Cyber Attacks

Iran's national security is not limited to militarily supporting allies and armed factions.

- A wide range of observers report that Iran has provided funding to political candidates in neighboring Iraq and Afghanistan to cultivate allies there.[16]
- Iran has reportedly provided direct payments to leaders of neighboring states in an effort to gain and maintain their support. In 2010, then-President of Afghanistan Hamid Karzai publicly acknowledged that his office had received cash payments from Iran.[17]
- Iran has established some training and education programs that bring young Muslims to study in Iran. One such program runs in Latin America, despite the small percentage of Muslims there.[18]
- Since 2012, Iran has dedicated significant resources toward cyber-espionage and has conducted cyber attacks against the United States and U.S. allies in the Persian Gulf. Iranian hackers, supported by the Iranian government, have conducted a series of cyber attacks against oil and gas companies in the Persian Gulf.[19]

---

[16] See, for example. http://www.newsweek.com/what-are-iranians-doing-iraq-303107. Also reported in author conversations with U.S. and Iraq and Afghan officials, 2009-2015.

[17] http://www.theguardian.com/commentisfree/2010/oct/26/iran-cash-payments-to-afghanistan.

[18] http://www.crethiplethi.com/subversion-and-exporting-the-islamic-revolution-in-latin-america/islamic-countries/iran-islamic-countries/2012/.

[19] Letter to SFRC Chairman Bob Corker, including report to Congress pursuant to the Countering America's Adversaries through Sanctions Act. Letter dated August 29, 2018.

Diplomacy

Iran also uses traditional diplomatic tools.

- Iran has an active Foreign Ministry and maintains embassies or representation in all countries with which it has diplomatic relations. Khamene'i has rarely traveled outside Iran as Supreme Leader—and not at all in recent years—but Iranian presidents travel outside Iran regularly, including to Europe and U.N. meetings in New York. Khamene'i frequently hosts foreign leaders in Tehran, including hosting Russia's president Vladimir Putin on several occasions, most recently in early September 2018.
- From August 2012 until August 2015, Iran held the presidency of the Non-Aligned Movement (NAM), which has about 120 member states and 17 observer countries and generally shares Iran's criticisms of big power influence over global affairs. In August 2012, Iran hosted the NAM annual summit.
- Iran is a party to all major nonproliferation conventions, including the Nuclear Non-Proliferation Treaty (NPT) and the Chemical Weapons Convention (CWC). Iran insists that it has adhered to all its commitments under these conventions, but the international community asserted that it did not meet all its NPT obligations and that Iran needed to prove that its nuclear program is for purely peaceful purposes. Nuclear negotiations between Iran and international powers began in 2003 and culminated with the July 2015 JCPOA.
- Iran is actively seeking to expand its participation in multilateral organizations. It has sought to join the World Trade Organization (WTO) since the mid-1990s. Iran also seeks full membership regional organizations including the South Asian Association of Regional Cooperation (SAARC) and the Shanghai Cooperation Organization (SCO). Officials from some SCO countries have said that the JCPOA removed obstacles to Iran's obtaining full membership, but opposition from some members have blocked Iran's accession to date.[20]
- Iran has participated in multilateral negotiations to try to resolve the civil conflict in Syria, even though Iran's main goal is to ensure Asad's continuation in power.

---

[20] http://www.globalresearch.ca/geopolitical-shift-iran-to-become-full-member-of-the-shanghai-cooperation-organization-sco/5465355.

IRAN'S NUCLEAR AND DEFENSE PROGRAMS

Iran has pursued a wide range of defense programs, as well as a nuclear program that the international community perceived could be intended to eventually produce a nuclear weapon. These programs are discussed in the following sections.

Nuclear Program[21]

Iran's nuclear program has been a paramount U.S. concern for successive Administrations, in part because Iran's acquisition of an operational nuclear weapon could cause Iran to perceive that it is immune from outside military pressure and could produce a nuclear arms race in one of the world's most volatile regions. Experts also have expressed concerns that Iran might transfer nuclear technology to extremist groups, and Israeli leaders characterize an Iranian nuclear weapon as a threat to Israel's existence. Some Iranian leaders argue that a nuclear weapon could end Iran's historic vulnerability to great power invasion, domination, or regime change attempts.

Iran's nuclear program has been a significant U.S. national security issue in 2002, when U.S. officials confirmed that Iran was building a uranium enrichment facility at Natanz and a heavy water production plant at Arak.[22] The perceived threat escalated significantly in 2010, when Iran began enriching uranium to 20% purity, which requires most of the work needed to enrich further to weapons-grade uranium (90%+). Another requirement for a nuclear weapon is a detonation mechanism that the International Atomic Energy Agency (IAEA) concluded that Iran researched as late as 2009. The United States and its partners also have insisted that Iran must not possess a nuclear-capable missile.[23]

Iran's Nuclear Intentions and Activities

The U.S. intelligence community has stated in recent years that it "does not know whether Iran will eventually decide to build nuclear weapons." Iranian leaders cite Supreme Leader Khamene'i's 2003 formal pronouncement (*fatwa*) that nuclear weapons are un-Islamic as evidence that a nuclear weapon is inconsistent with Iran's ideology. Iranian leaders assert that Iran's nuclear program was always intended for civilian uses, including medicine and electricity generation. Iran argued that uranium enrichment is its "right" as a party to the 1968 Nuclear Non-Proliferation Treaty and that it wants to make

---

[21] More extensive information on Iran's nuclear program can be found in CRS Report R43333, *Iran Nuclear Agreement and U.S. Exit*, by Paul K. Kerr and Kenneth Katzman.

[22] In November 2006, the IAEA, at U.S. urging, declined to provide technical assistance to the Arak facility on the grounds that it was likely for proliferation purposes.

[23] White House Office of the Press Secretary. Statement by the President on the Iran Nuclear Deal. January 12, 2018.

its own nuclear fuel to avoid potential supply disruptions. U.S. officials have said that Iran's use of nuclear energy is acceptable. IAEA findings that Iran researched a nuclear explosive device—detailed in a December 2, 2015, International Atomic Energy Agency (IAEA) report—cast doubt on Iran's assertions of purely peaceful nuclear intent. There have been no assertions that Iran diverted nuclear material to a weapons program.[24]

Nuclear Weapons Time Frame Estimates

In April 2015, then-Vice President Biden told a Washington, DC, research institute that Iran could likely have enough fissile material for a nuclear weapon within two to three months of a decision to manufacture that material. U.S. officials said that the JCPOA increased the "breakout time"— an all-out effort by Iran to develop a nuclear weapon using declared facilities or undeclared covert facilities—to at least 12 months. When the JCPOA was agreed, Iran had about 19,000 total installed centrifuges to enrich uranium, of which about 10,000 were operating. Prior to the interim nuclear agreement (Joint Plan of Action, JPA), Iran had a stockpile of 400 lbs of 20% enriched uranium (short of the 550 lbs. that would be needed to produce one nuclear weapon). Weapons grade uranium is uranium that is enriched to 90%.

Under the JCPOA, Iran is allowed to operate only about 5,000 centrifuges and was required to reduce its stockpile of 3.67% enriched uranium to 300 kilograms (660 lbs.). These restrictions start to come off beginning in October 2025—10 years from Adoption Day (October 2015). Another means of acquiring fissile material for a nuclear weapon is to reprocess plutonium, a material that could be produced by Iran's heavy water plant at Arak. In accordance with the JCPOA, Iran rendered inactive the core of the reactor and limits its stockpile of heavy water.

The JCPOA does not prohibit civilian nuclear plants such as the one Russia built at Bushehr. Under a 1995 bilateral agreement, Russia supplies nuclear fuel for that plant and takes back the spent nuclear material for reprocessing. It became operational in 2012.

International Diplomatic Efforts to Address Iran's Nuclear Program

The JCPOA was the product of a long international effort to persuade Iran to negotiate limits on its nuclear program. That effort began when it was revealed by the United States that Iran was building facilities to enrich uranium. In 2003, France, Britain, and Germany (the "EU-3") opened a diplomatic track to negotiate curbs on Iran's program. On October 21, 2003, Iran pledged, in return for peaceful nuclear technology, to suspend uranium enrichment activities and sign and ratify the "Additional Protocol" to the NPT (allowing for enhanced inspections). Iran signed the Additional Protocol on December 18, 2003, although the *Majles* did not ratify it.

---

[24] The February 25, 2011, IAEA report listed Iran's declared nuclear sites as well as a summary of all the NPT obligations Iran is not meeting. IAEA report of February 25, 2011. http://lewis.armscontrolwonk.com/files/2011/02/ gov2011-7.pdf.

Iran ended the suspension after several months, but the EU-3 and Iran subsequently reached a November 14, 2004, "Paris Agreement," under which Iran suspended uranium enrichment in exchange for trade talks and other non-U.S. aid. The Bush Administration supported the agreement with a March 11, 2005, announcement by dropping the U.S. objection to Iran's applying to join the World Trade Organization (WTO). That agreement broke down in 2005 when Iran rejected an EU-3 proposal for a permanent nuclear accord as offering insufficient benefits. In August 2005, Iran began uranium "conversion" (one step before enrichment) at its Esfahan facility and, on February 4, 2006, the IAEA board voted 27-3[25] to refer the case to the Security Council. The Council set an April 29, 2006, deadline to cease enrichment.

"P5+1" Formed. In May 2006, the Bush Administration join the talks, triggering an expanded negotiating group called the "Permanent Five Plus 1" (P5+1: United States, Russia, China, France, Britain, and Germany). A month after it formed, the P5+1 offered Iran guaranteed Iran nuclear fuel for its civilian reactor (Annex I to Resolution 1747) and threatened sanctions if Iran did not agree (sanctions were imposed in subsequent years).[26]

U.N. Security Council Resolutions Adopted

The U.N. Security Council subsequently imposed sanctions on Iran in an effort to shift Iran's calculations toward compromise. (The resolutions below, as well as Resolution 1929, were formally superseded on January 16, 2016, by Resolution 2231.)

- *Resolution 1696* (July 31, 2006). The Security Council voted 14-1 for U.N. Security Council Resolution 1696, giving Iran until August 31, 2006, to suspend enrichment suspension, suspend construction of the Arak heavy-water reactor, and ratify the Additional Protocol to Iran's IAEA Safeguards Agreement. It was passed under Article 40 of the U.N. Charter, which makes compliance mandatory, but not under Article 41, which refers to economic sanctions, or Article 42, which authorizes military action.
- *Resolution 1737* (December 23, 2006). After Iran refused a proposal to temporarily suspend enrichment, the Security Council adopted U.N. Security Council Resolution 1737 unanimously, under Chapter 7, Article 41 of the U.N. Charter. It demanded enrichment suspension by February 21, 2007, prohibited sale to Iran of nuclear technology, and required U.N. member states to freeze the financial assets of named Iranian nuclear and missile firms and related persons.
- *Resolution 1747* (March 24, 2007) Resolution 1747, adopted unanimously, demanded Iran suspend enrichment by May 24, 2007. It banned arms transfers by Iran (a provision directed at stopping Iran's arms supplies to its regional allies

[25] Voting no: Cuba, Syria, Venezuela. Abstaining: Algeria, Belarus, Indonesia, Libya, South Africa.

[26] One source purports to have obtained the contents of the package from ABC News: http://www.basicint.org/pubs/Notes/BN060609.htm.

and proxies) and called for countries to cease selling Iran arms or dual use items and for countries and international financial institutions to avoid giving Iran any new loans or grants (except loans for humanitarian purposes).

- *Resolution 1803* (March 3, 2008) Adopted 14-0, Resolution 1803 banned travel by named sanctioned persons; banned virtually all sales of dual use items to Iran; and authorized inspections of Iran Air Cargo and Islamic Republic of Iran Shipping Line shipments, if there is cause to believe that the shipments contain banned goods. In May 2008, the P5+1 added political and enhanced energy cooperation with Iran to previous incentives, and the enhanced offer was attached as an Annex to Resolution 1929 (see below).
- *Resolution 1835* (September 27, 2008). In July 2008, Iran it indicated it might be ready to accept a temporary "freeze for freeze": the P5+1 would impose no new sanctions and Iran would stop expanding uranium enrichment. No agreement on that concept was reached, even though the Bush Administration sent an Under Secretary of State for Political Affairs to a P5+1-Iran meeting in Geneva in July 2008. Resolution 1835 demanded compliance but did not add any sanctions.

Developments during the Obama Administration

The P5+1 met in February 2009 to incorporate the Obama Administration's stated commitment to direct U.S. engagement with Iran and,[27] in April 2009, U.S. officials announced that a U.S. diplomat would attend P5+1 meetings with Iran. In July 2009, the United States and its allies demanded that Iran offer constructive proposals by late September 2009 or face "crippling sanctions." A September 9, 2009, Iranian proposal led to an October 1, 2009, P5+1-Iran meeting in Geneva that produced a tentative agreement for Iran to allow Russia and France to reprocess 75% of Iran's low-enriched uranium stockpile for medical use. A draft agreement was approved by the P5+1 countries following technical talks in Vienna on October 19-21, 2009, but the Supreme Leader decided that Iran's concessions were excessive and no accord was finalized.

In April 2010, Brazil and Turkey negotiated with Iran to revive the October arrangement. On May 17, 2010, the three countries signed a "Tehran Declaration" for Iran to send 2,600 pounds of low enriched uranium to Turkey in exchange for medically useful uranium.[28] Iran submitted to the IAEA an acceptance letter, but the Administration rejected the plan as failing to address enrichment to the 20% level.

U.N. Security Council Resolution 1929

Immediately after the Brazil-Turkey mediation failed, then-Secretary of State Clinton announced that the P5+1 had reached agreement on a new U.N. Security Council Resolution that would give U.S. allies authority to take substantial new economic

---

[27] Dempsey, Judy. "U.S. Urged to Talk With Iran." *International Herald Tribune*, February 5, 2009.

[28] Text of the pact is at http://www.cfr.org/publication/22140/.

measures against Iran. Adopted on June 9, 2010,[29] Resolution 1929, was pivotal by linking Iran's economy to its nuclear capabilities and thereby authorizing U.N. member states to sanction key Iranian economic sectors. An annex to the Resolution presented a modified offer of incentives to Iran.[30] Negotiations subsequent to the adoption of Resolution 1929,—in December 2010, in Geneva and January 2011, in Istanbul — floundered over Iran's demand for immediate lifting of international sanctions. Additional rounds of P5+1-Iran talks in 2012 and 2013 (2012: April in Istanbul; May in Baghdad; and June in Moscow; 2013: Almaty, Kazakhstan, in February and in April) did not reach agreement on a P5+1 proposals that Iran halt enrichment to the 20% level; close the Fordow facility; and remove its stockpile of 20% enriched uranium.

Joint Plan of Action (JPA)

The June 2013 election of Rouhani as Iran's president improved the prospects for a nuclear settlement and, in advance of his visit to the U.N. General Assembly in New York during September 23-27, 2013, Rouhani stated that the Supreme Leader had given him authority to negotiate a nuclear deal. The Supreme Leader affirmed that authority in a speech on September 17, 2013, stating that he believes in the concept of "heroic flexibility"—adopting "proper and logical diplomatic moves...."[31] An interim nuclear agreement, the Joint Plan of Action (JPA), was announced on November 24, 2013, providing modest sanctions relief in exchange for Iran to (1) eliminating its stockpile of 20% enriched uranium, (2) ceasing to enrich to that level, and (3) not increasing its stockpile of 3.5% enriched uranium.

The Joint Comprehensive Plan of Action (JCPOA)[32]

P5+1-Iran negotiations on a comprehensive settlement began in February 2014 but missed several self-imposed deadlines. On April 2, 2015, the parties reached a framework for a JCPOA, and the JCPOA was finalized on July 14, 2015. U.N. Security Council Resolution 2231 of July 20, 2015, endorsed the JCPOA and contains restrictions (less stringent than in Resolution 1929) on Iran's importation or exportation of conventional arms (for up to five years), and on development and testing of ballistic missiles capable of delivering a nuclear weapon (for up to eight years). On January 16, 2016, the IAEA certified that Iran completed the work required for sanctions relief and "Implementation Day" was declared.

---

[29] It was adopted by a vote of 12-2 (Turkey and Brazil voting no) with one abstention (Lebanon).

[30] Text of the resolution is at http://www.isis-online.org/uploads/isis-reports/documents/Draft_resolution_on_Iran_annexes.pdf.

[31] Open Source Center, "Iran: Leader Outlines Guard Corps Role, Talks of 'Heroic Flexibility,'" published September 18, 2013.

[32] For detail on the JCPOA, see CRS Report R43333, *Iran Nuclear Agreement and U.S. Exit*, by Paul K. Kerr and Kenneth Katzman.

The Trump Administration, the JCPOA, and Iran Policy

The Trump Administration criticized the JCPOA for not addressing key U.S. concerns about Iran's continuing "malign activities" in the region or its ballistic missile program, and the expiration of key nuclear restrictions.[33] In October 2017, the Administration withheld certification of Iranian compliance under the Iran Nuclear Agreement Review Act (INARA, P.L. 114-17) on the grounds that sanctions relief is not proportional to the limitations on Iran's nuclear program. The noncertification enabled Congress to act under expedited rules to reimpose U.S. sanctions, but Congress did not take such action. Until May 2018, President Trump continued to renew all waivers of U.S. sanctions required to continue implementing U.S. JCPOA commitments.

In speeches and statements on October 13, 2017, and January 12, 2018, the President threatened to reimpose sanctions (and withdraw the United States from the JCPOA) unless Congress and the European countries acted to (1) extend the JCPOA's nuclear restrictions beyond current deadlines to ensure that Iran never comes close to developing a nuclear weapon; (2) impose strict sanctions on Iran's development of ballistic missiles; and (3) ensure that Iran allows "immediate" access to any site that the IAEA wants to visit. Separately, President Trump and other U.S. officials insisted that U.S. allies address Iran's "malign activities" in the region. The European countries negotiated with the United States to try to meet President Trump's requirements but they did not meet all of his stipulated conditions. On May 8, 2018, President Trump withdrew the United States from the JCPOA and announced that all U.S. sanctions would be reimposed by November 4, 2018.

On August 29, 2018, the Administration provided Congress with a report mandated by the Countering America's Adversaries through Sanctions Act (P.L. 115-44) on its strategy to counter "Iran's conventional and assymetric threats." The elements of the strategy are discussed throughout this chapter.

Missile Programs and Chemical and Biological Weapons Capability

Iran has an active missile development program, as well as other WMD programs at varying stages of activity and capability, as discussed further below.

Chemical and Biological Weapons[34]

U.S. reports indicate that Iran has the capability to produce chemical warfare (CW) agents and "probably" has the capability to produce some biological warfare agents for

---

[33] Department of State. Press Briefing by Secretary of State Rex Tillerson. August 1, 2017.

[34] Information in this section is derived from the August 2018 Administration report to Congress under the Countering America's Adversaries through Sanctions Act.

offensive purposes, if it made the decision to do so.[35] Iran signed the Chemical Weapons Convention on January 13, 1993, and ratified on June 8, 1997. The U.S. A 2017 "Annual Report on Compliance with the Chemical Weapons Convention" states that the United States cannot certify that Iran has met its obligations under the Convention to declare chemical weapons production facilities; to report any retransfer of chemical weapons; and to declare retention of any undeclared chemical weapons stockpile. Iran also has ratified the Biological and Toxin Weapons Convention (BTWC), but it engages in dual-use activities with possible biological weapons applications that could potentially be inconsistent with the Convention. Iran is widely believed to be unlikely to use chemical or biological weapons or to transfer them to its regional proxies or allies because of the potential for international powers to discover their origin and retaliate against Iran for any use.

Missiles[36]

According to the September 2018 Administration report "Outlaw Regime: A Chronicle of Iran's Destructive Activities," Iran has "the largest ballistic missile force in the Middle East, with more than ten ballistic missile systems either in its inventory or in development, and a stockpile of hundreds of missiles that threaten its neighbors in the region."[37] The intelligence community has said publicly that Iran "can strike targets up to 2,000 kilometers from Iran's borders."

Iran is not known to possess an Intercontinental Ballistic Missile (ICBM) capability (missiles of ranges over 2,900 miles), but the DNI threat assessment testimony of February 13, 2018, stated that "Tehran's desire to deter the United States might drive it to field an ICBM."[38] However, IRGC Commander-in-Chief Ali Jafari said in October 2017 that the existing ranges of Iran's missiles are "sufficient for now," suggesting that Iran has no plans to develop an ICBM.[39] If there is a decision to do so, progress on Iran's space program could shorten the pathway to an ICBM because space launch vehicles use similar technology. Iran's missile programs are run by the IRGC Air Force, particularly the IRGC Air Force Al Ghadir Missile Command—an entity sanctioned under Executive Order 13382. There are persistent reports that Iran-North Korea missile cooperation is extensive, but it is not known from published material whether North Korea and Iran have recently exchanged missile hardware.

---

35 Deputy Director of National Intelligence for Analysis, "Unclassified Report to Congress on the Acquisition of Technology Relating to Weapons of Mass Destruction and Advanced Conventional Munitions, Covering 1 January to 31 December 2010," March 2011.

36 For more information on Iran's missile arsenal, see CRS Report R42849, *Iran's Ballistic Missile and Space Launch Programs*, by Steven A. Hildreth.

37 The report can be downloaded at https://www.state.gov/secretary/remarks/2018/09/286216.htm.

38 Worldwide Threat Assessment of the US Intelligence Community. Testimony before the Senate Select Committee on Intelligence. February 13, 2018.

39 "Iran: No Need to Extend 2,000 km Ballistic Missile Range." Al Jazeera, October 31, 2017.

At the more tactical level, Iran is acquiring, developing, and exporting short range ballistic and cruise missiles that Iran's forces can use and/or transfer to regional allies and proxies to protect them and to enhance Iran's ability to project power. The DNI's February 13, 2018, threat assessment testimony stated that Iran "continues to develop and improve a range of new military capabilities to target US and allied military assets in the region, including armed UAVs, ballistic missiles, advanced naval mines, unmanned explosive boats, submarines and advanced torpedoes, and anti-ship and land-attack cruise missiles."[40]

Resolution 2231 (the operative Security Council resolution on Iran) "calls on" Iran not to develop or test ballistic missiles "designed to be capable of" delivering a nuclear weapon, for up to eight years from Adoption Day of the JCPOA (October 18, 2015). The wording is far less restrictive than that of Resolution 1929, which clearly prohibited Iran's development of ballistic missiles. The JCPOA itself does not specifically contain ballistic missile restraints.

Iran has continued developing and testing missiles, despite Resolution 2231, which took effect on January 16, 2016, "Implementation Day."

- On October 11, 2015, and reportedly again on November 21, 2015, Iran tested a 1,200-mile-range ballistic missile, which U.S. intelligence officials called "more accurate" than previous Iranian missiles of similar range.
- Iran conducted ballistic missile tests on March 8-9, 2016—the first such tests after Implementation Day.
- Iran reportedly conducted a missile test in May 2016, although Iranian media had varying accounts of the range of the missile tested.
- A July 11-21, 2016, test of a missile of a range of 2,500 miles, akin to North Korea's Musudan missile, reportedly failed. It is not clear whether North Korea provided any technology or had any involvement in the test.[41]
- On January 29, 2017, Iran tested what Trump Administration officials called a version of the Shahab missile, although press reports say the test failed when the missile exploded after traveling about 600 miles.
- On July 27, 2017, Iran's *Simorgh* rocket launched a satellite into space.
- Iran continues to periodically test short-range ballistic missiles.

U.S. and U.N. Responses to Iran's Missile Tests

The Obama and Trump Administrations have termed Iran's post-Implementation Day ballistic missile tests as "provocative and destabilizing," "inconsistent with" Resolution 2231—stopping short of accusing Iran of "violation" of 2231.

---

[40] Worldwide Threat Assessment of the US Intelligence Community. op. cit.

[41] Lucas Tomlinson. "Iran Conducts 4th Missile Test Since Signing Nuke Deal." *Fox News*, July 15, 2016.

The Trump Administration termed Iran's July 27, 2017, space launch a "violation" of the Resolution because of that technology's inherent capability to carry a nuclear warhead.

Table 2. Iran's Missile Arsenal

Shahab-3 ("Meteor")	The 600-mile range missile is operational, and Defense Department (DOD) reports indicate Tehran is improving its lethality and effectiveness.
Shahab-3 "Variants"	Iran appears to be developing several extended-range variants of the Shahab, under a variety of names including: Sijil, Ashoura, Emad, Ghadr, and Khorramshahr. These missiles have ranges of about 1,000-1,200 miles, putting the entire Middle East region within reach from Iran. Some use sold fuel and others use liquid fuel. Some Shahab variants inscribed with the phrase "Israel must be wiped off the face of the earth"—were launched on March8-9, 2016.
BM-25/Musudan Variant	This missile, with a reported rangeof up to 2,500 miles, is of North Korean design, and in turn based on the Soviet-era "SS-N-6" missile. Reports in 2006 that North Korea supplied the missile or components of it to Iran have not been corroborated, but Iran reportedly tried to test its own version of this missile in July 2016.
Short Range Ballistic Missiles and Cruise Missiles	Iran fields a wide variety of increasingly capable short-range ballistic and anti-ship cruise missiles. One short-range ballistic missile (the Qiam, with 400 mile range) was first tested in August 2010. Iran has also developed150-200 mile-range Fateh 110 and 313 and Hormuz solid fuel missilesand arelatedKhaliji Fars (Persian Gulf) anti-ship ballistic missile. Iran has armedits patrol boats (and supplied allies and proxies) with Chinese-made C-802 anti-ship cruise missilesand Iranian variants of that weapon. Iran also has C-802s and other missiles emplaced along Iran's coast, including the Chinese-made CSSC-2 (Silkworm) and the CSSC-3 (Seersucker). Iran also possesses a few hundred short-range ballistic missiles, including the *Shahab-1*(Scud-b), the *Shahab-2*(Scud-C), and the *Tondar-69*(CSS-8). Iran also reportedly has transferred some of these missiles to allies in Lebanon, Syria, Yemen, and Iraq.
ICBMs	An ICBM is a ballistic missile with a range of 5,500 kilometers (about 2,900 miles). After long estimating that Iran might have an ICBM capability by 2010, the U.S. intelligence community has not stated that Iran has produced an ICBM, to date.
Space Vehicles	In February 2009, Iran successfully launched a small, low-earth satellite on a Safir-2 rocket (range about 155 miles). Iran claimed additional satellite launches subsequently, including the launch and return of a vehicle carrying a small primate in December 2013. Since March2016, Iran has been reported to readying the *Simorgh*vehicle for a space launch, and the launch occurred on July 27, 2017.
Warheads	*Wall Street Journal*report of September 14, 2005, said that U.S. intelligence believes Iran is working to adapt the Shahab-3 to deliver a nuclear warhead. Subsequent press reports said that U.S. intelligence captured an Iranian computer in mid-2004 showing plans to construct a nuclear warhead for the Shahab.[42] No further information has been reported since.

Sources: Testimony of U.S. intelligence community officials, 2005-2018; various press.

The U.N. Security Council referred the 2016 and 2017 tests to its sanctions committee but has not imposed any additional sanctions on Iran to date.Several successive Administrations have designated Iranian missile-related entities for sanctions under Executive Order 13382 and the Iran, North Korea, and Syria Nonproliferation Act. In his January 12, 2018, statement, President Trump demanded, as a condition of remaining in the JCPOA, enactment of legislation that explicitly states that Iran's "long-

[42] William Broad and David Sanger, "Relying On Computer, U.S. Seeks to Prove Iran's Nuclear Aims," *New York Times*, November 13, 2005.

range missile and nuclear weapons programs are inseparable" and that Iran's development and testing of missiles should be subject to "severe sanctions."

Section 1226 of the FY2017 National Defense Authorization Act (S. 2943, P.L. 114-328) requires the DNI, as well as the Secretary of State and the Secretary of the Treasury, to each submit quarterly reports to Congress on Iranian missile launches in the one preceding year, and on efforts, if any, to impose sanctions on entities assisting those launches. The provision sunsets on December 31, 2019.

Iran asserts that conventionally armed missiles are an integral part of its defense strategy and the tests will continue. Iran argues that it is not developing a nuclear weapon and therefore is not designing its missile to carry a nuclear weapon. Iranian officials say they will not negotiate any new curbs on Iran's missile program.

U.S. and Other Missile Defenses

Successive U.S. Administrations have sought to build up regional missile defense systems. The United States and Israel have a broad program of cooperation on missile defense as well as on defenses against shorter range rockets and missiles such as those Iran supplies to Lebanese Hezbollah. Through sales of the Patriot system (PAC-3) and more advanced "THAAD" (Theater High Altitude Area Defense) to the Gulf states, the United States has sought to construct a coordinated GCC missile defense system.

The United States has sought a defense against an eventual long-range Iranian missile system by emplacing missile defense systems in various Eastern European countries and on ship-based systems. The United States has helped Israel develop the Arrow missile defense system that is intended to intercept Iranian (or other) ballistic missiles launched at Israel. Other Israeli systems developed with U.S. help, including Iron Dome and David's Sling, are intended to intercept rockets launched by Iranian allies Hezbollah and Hamas. The FY2013 national defense authorization act (P.L. 112-239) contained provisions urging the Administration to undertake more extensive efforts, in cooperation with U.S. partners and others, to defend against the missile programs of Iran (and North Korea).

Conventional and "Asymmetric Warfare" Capability[43]

Iran appears to be able to defend against any conceivable aggression from Iran's neighbors, while lacking the ability to project conventional military power outside the region or across waterways. Iran's forces are widely assessed as incapable of defeating the United States in a classic military confrontation, but they could potentially inflict

[43] For detailed analysis of Iran's military strategy, doctrine, procurement policy, and related issues, see International Institute for Strategic Studies. "Gulf Security after 2020." December 2017.

significant damage or casualties on the U.S. military. CENTCOM Commander General Joseph Votel testified on February 27, 2018, that Iran's ground forces are "improving their ability to quickly mobilize and deploy in response to internal and external threats."

Organizationally, Iran's armed forces are divided to perform functions appropriate to their roles. The Islamic Revolutionary Guard Corps (IRGC, known in Persian as the *Sepah-e-Pasdaran Enghelab Islami*)[44] controls the *Basij* (Mobilization of the Oppressed) volunteer militia that has been the main instrument to repress domestic dissent. The IRGC also has a national defense role and it and the regular military (*Artesh*)—the national army that existed under the former Shah— report to a joint headquarters. In June 2016, Supreme Leader Khamene'i replaced the longtime Chief of Staff (head) of the Joint Headquarters with IRGC Major General Mohammad Hossein Bagheri, an early IRGC recruit who fought against Kurdish insurgents and in the Iran-Iraq War. The appointment of an IRGC officer to head the joint headquarters again demonstrates the IRGC's dominance within Iran's military and security structure. On the other hand, Rouhani's August 2017 appointment of a senior *Artesh* figure, Brigadier General Amir Hatami, as Defense Minister suggests that the *Artesh* remains a respected institution in the defense establishment. The *Artesh* is deployed mainly at bases outside cities and has no internal security role.

The IRGC Navy and regular Navy (Islamic Republic of Iran Navy, IRIN) are distinct forces; the IRIN has responsibility for the Gulf of Oman, whereas the IRGC Navy has responsibility for the closer-in Persian Gulf and Strait of Hormuz. The regular Air Force controls most of Iran's combat aircraft, whereas the IRGC Air Force runs Iran's ballistic missile programs. Iran has a small number of warships on its Caspian Sea coast. Since 2014, Iran sent warships into the Atlantic Ocean on a few occasions as a demonstration of growing naval strength. In August 2018, the hardline IRGC General Alireza Tangsiri was appointed commander of the IRGC Navy.

Asymmetric Warfare Capacity

Iran compensates for its conventional military deficiencies by expanding its capacity for "asymmetric warfare." Administration reports and testimony continue to assess that Iran is developing forces and tactics to control the approaches to Iran, including the Strait of Hormuz. Iran's naval strategy appears to be center on developing an ability to "swarm" U.S. naval assets with its fleet of small boats and large numbers of anti-ship cruise missiles and its inventory of coastal defense cruise missiles. It is also developing increasingly lethal systems such as more advanced naval mines and "small but capable submarines," according to DOD reports and the August 2018 report required by the Countering America's Adversaries through Sanctions Act. Iran has added naval bases along its coast in recent years, enhancing its ability to threaten shipping in the strait. As

[44] For a more extensive discussion of the IRGC, see Katzman, Kenneth, "The Warriors of Islam: Iran's Revolutionary Guard," *Westview Press*, 1993.

discussed further later in this report, IRGC Navy vessels have conducted "high-speed intercepts"—close-approaches of U.S. naval vessels in the Persian Gulf—sometimes causing U.S. evasive action or warning shots.

Iran's arming of regional allies and proxies represents another aspect of Iran's development of asymmetric warfare capabilities. Iran's allies and proxies control territory within which Iran can emplace missiles, rockets, and factories to build military equipment. These allies help Iran expand its influence and project power with little direct risk, giving Tehran a measure of deniability. For example, Iran's provision of anti-ship and coastal defense missiles to the Houthi rebels in Yemen, discussed further below, could represent an effort by Tehran to project military power into the key Bab el-Mandeb Strait chokepoint.

In the event of confrontation with the United States, Iran could also try to retaliate against through terrorist attacks inside the United States or against U.S. embassies and facilities in Europe or the Persian Gulf. Iran could also try to direct Iran-supported forces in Afghanistan or Iraq to attack U.S. personnel there. Iran's support for regional terrorist groups and other armed factions was a key justification for Iran's addition to the U.S. list of state sponsors of terrorism ("terrorism list") in January 1984.

Military-to-Military Relationships

Iran's armed forces have few formal relationships with foreign militaries outside the region. Iran's military-to-military relationships with Russia, China, Ukraine, Belarus, and North Korea generally have focused on Iranian arms purchases or upgrades, but Iran and Russia are cooperating militarily in Syria to assist the Asad regime. According to the August 2018 report to Congress mandated by the Countering America's Adversaries through Sanctions Act, Iran "has obtained missile and aircraft technology from foreign suppliers, including China and North Korea. In August 2016, Iran allowed Russia's bomber aircraft, for a brief time, to use Iran's western airbase at Hamadan to launch strikes in Syria—the first time the Islamic Republic gave a foreign military use of Iran's military facilities.[45] Iran and India have a "strategic dialogue" and some Iranian naval officers reportedly underwent some training in India in the 1990s. Iran's military also conducted joint exercises with the Pakistani armed forces in the early 1990s. In September 2014, two Chinese warships docked at Iran's port of Bandar Abbas, for the first time in history, to conduct four days of naval exercises,[46] and in October 2015, the leader of Iran's regular (not IRGC) Navy made the first visit ever to China by an Iranian Navy commander. In August 2017, the chief of Iran's joint military headquarters made the first top-level military visit to Turkey since Iran's 1979 revolution.

---

[45] A provision of the House version of the FY2017 NDAA (Section 1259M of H.R. 4909) required an Administration report on Iran-Russia military cooperation worldwide, but the provision was removed in conference action.

[46] Thomas Erdbrink and Chris Buckley. "China's Navy Sends Ships for Exercises with Iran." *New York Times*, September 22, 2014.

Iranian Arms Transfers and U.N. Restrictions

Sales to Iran of most conventional arms (arms on a U.N. Register of Conventional Arms) were banned by U.N. Resolution 1929. Resolution 2231, which supersedes Resolution 1929, requires (for a maximum of five years from Adoption Day—until October 17, 2020)

Table 3. Iran's Conventional Military Arsenal

Military and Security Personnel: 700,000 total. Regular army ground force is about 350,000, Revolutionary Guard Corps (IRGC) ground force is about 125,000. IRGC navy is about 20,000 and regular navy is about 18,000. Regular Air Force has about 30,000 personnel and IRGC Air Force (which runs Iran's missile programs) is of unknown size. Security forces number about 40,000-60,000 law enforcement forces, with another 100,000 Basij (volunteer militia under IRGC control) permanently deployed. Hundreds of thousands of additional Basij could be mobilized in the event or an all-out war.
Tanks: 1,650+ Includes 480 Russian-made T-72. Iran reportedly discussing purchase of Russian-made T-90s.
Surface Ships and Submarines: 100+ (IRGC and regular Navy) Includes 4 Corvette; 18 IRGC-controlled Chinese-made patrol boats, several hundred small boats.) Also has 3 Kilo subs (reg. Navy controlled). Iran has been long said to possess several small subs, possibly purchased assembled or in kit form from North Korea. Iran claimed on November 29, 2007, to have produced a new small sub equipped with sonar-evading technology, and it deployed four Iranian-made "Ghadir class" subs to the Red Sea in June 2011. Iran reportedly seeks to buy from Russia additional frigates and submarines. Iran has stockpiled a wide array of naval mines.
Combat Aircraft/Helicopters: 330+ Includes 25 MiG-29 and 30 Su-24. Still dependent on U.S. F-4s, F-5s and F14 bought during Shah's era. Iran reportedly negotiating with Russia to purchase Su-30s (Flanker) equipped with advanced air to air and air to ground missiles (Yakhont ant-ship missile). Iran reportedly seeks to purchase Russia-made Mi-17 attack helicopters.
Artillery Rockets. Iran has developed "Explosively Formed Projectiles" (EFPs) anti-tank rockets used to significant effect against U.S. forces in Iraq (2003-11). Iran provides the weapon to its regional allies and proxies.
Anti-aircraft Missile Systems: Iran has 150+ U.S.-made I-Hawk (from Iran-Contra Affair) plus possibly some Stingers acquired in Afghanistan. Russia delivered to Iran (January 2007) 30 anti-aircraft missile systems (Tor M1), worth over $1 billion. In December 2007, Russia agreed to sell five batteries of the highly capable S-300 air defense system at an estimated cost of $800 million. Sale of the system did not technically violate U.N. Resolution 1929, because the system is not covered in the U.N. Registry on Conventional Arms, but Russia refused to deliver the system as long as that sanction remained in place. After the April 2, 2015, framework nuclear accord, Russian officials indicated they would proceed with the S-300 delivery, and the weapon is operational as of 2018. Iran reportedly also seeks to buy the S-400 anti-aircraft system from Russia.

Sources: IISS Military Balance (2017)—Section on Middle East and North Africa, and various press reports; testimony of CENTCOM Commander Gen. Joseph Votel before the House Armed Services Committee on February 27, 2018.

Table 4. The Islamic Revolutionary Guard Corps (IRGC)

The IRGC is generally loyal to Iran's political hardliners and is clearly more politically influential than is Iran's regular military, which is numerically larger, but was held over from the Shah's era. The IRGC's political influence has grown sharply as the regime has relied on it to suppress dissent. A Rand Corporation study stated: "Founded by a decree from Ayatollah Khomeini shortly after the victory of the 1978-1979 Islamic Revolution, Iran's Islamic Revolutionary Guards Corps (IRGC) has evolved well beyond its original foundations as an ideological guard for the nascent revolutionary regime.... The IRGC's presence is particularly powerful in Iran's highly factionalized political system, in which [many senior figures] hail from the ranks of the IRGC...." Its overall commander, IRGC Major General Mohammad Ali Jafari, who has been in the position since September 2007, is considered a hardliner against political dissent and a close ally of the Supreme Leader. He criticized Rouhani for accepting a phone call from President Obama on September 27, 2013, and opposed major concessions in the JCPOA negotiations.
Militarily, the IRGC fields a ground force of about 100,000 for national defense. The IRGC Navy has responsibility to patrol the Strait of Hormuz and the regular Navy has responsibility for the broader Arabian Sea and Gulf of Oman (deeper waters further off the coast). The IRGC Air Force runs Iran's ballistic missile programs, but combat and support military aviation is operated exclusively by the regular Air Force, which has the required pilots and sustainment infrastructure for air force operations.
The IRGC is the key organization for maintaining internal security. The *Basij* militia, which reports to the IRGC commander in chief, operates from thousands of positions in Iran's institutions and, as of 2008, has been integrated at the provincial level with the IRGC's provincial units. As of December 2016, the Basij is led by hardliner Gholam Hosein Gheibparvar. In November 2009, the regime gave the IRGC's intelligence units greater authority, surpassing that of the Ministry of Intelligence.
Through its Qods (Jerusalem) Force (QF), the IRGC has a foreign policy role in exerting influence throughout the region by supporting pro-Iranian movements and leaders. The IRGC-QF commander, Brigadier General Qassem Soleimani, reportedly has an independent channel to Khamene'i. The IRGC-QF numbers approximately 10,000- 15,000 personnel who provide advice, support, and arrange weapons deliveries to pro-Iranian factions or leaders in Lebanon, Iraq, Syria, Persian Gulf states, Gaza/West Bank, Afghanistan, and Central Asia. IRGC leaders have confirmed the QF is in Syria to assist the regime of Bashar al-Assad against an armed uprising, and it is advising the Iraqi government against the Islamic State (also known as ISIS or ISIL)—tacitly aligning it there with U.S. forces. Section 1223 of the FY2016 National Defense Authorization Act (P.L. 114-92) required a DOD report any U.S. military interaction with the IRGC-QF, presumably in Iraq. The IRGC-QF commander during 1988-1995 was Brigadier General Ahmad Vahidi, who served as defense minister during 2009-2013. He led the QF when it allegedly assisted Lebanese Hezbollah carry out two bombings of Israeli and Jewish targets in Buenos Aires (1992 and 1994) and is wanted by Interpol. He allegedly recruited

Saudi Hezbollah activists later accused of the June 1996 Khobar Towers bombing.
As noted, the IRGC is also increasingly involved in Iran's economy, acting through a network of contracting businesses it has set up, most notably *Ghorb* (also called *Khatem ol-Anbiya*, Persian for "Seal of the Prophet"). Active duty IRGC senior commanders reportedly serve on Ghorb's board of directors and its chief executive, Rostam Ghasemi, served as Oil Minister during 2011-2013. In 2009, the IRGC bought a 50% stake in Iran Telecommunication Company at a cost of $7.8 billion, although that firm was later privatized. Then CIA Director Mike Pompeo estimated in 2017 that the IRGC affiliates might control about 20% of Iran's overall economy, but estimates vary widely and the actual figure is widely considered uncertain.
Numerous IRGC and affiliated entities, including the IRGC itself and the QF, have been designated for U.S. sanctions as proliferation, terrorism supporting, and human rights abusing entities. The United States did not remove any IRGC-related designations under the JCPOA, but the EU will be doing so in 2023.

Sources: Frederic Wehrey et al.,"The Rise of the Pasdaran," Rand Corporation, 2009; Katzman, Kenneth, "The Warriors of Islam: Iran's Revolutionary Guard," Westview Press, 1993; Department of the Treasury; http://www.newyorker.com/reporting/2013/09/30/130930fa_fact_filkins?printable=true&currentPage=all; https://www.defenddemocracy.org/content/uploads/documents/Transcript_FINAL_Pompeo.pdf.

Security Council approval for any transfer of weapons or military technology, or related training or financial assistance, to Iran. The Resolution names the weapons systems subject to the restriction as

> Battle tanks; armored combat vehicles; large caliber artillery systems; combat aircraft; attack helicopters; warships; missiles or missile systems, as defined by the U.N. Register of Conventional Arms, or related material, including spare parts...and the provision to Iran.. of technical training, financial resources or services, advice, other services or assistance related to the supply, sale, transfer, manufacture, maintenance, or use of arms and related materiel....

Defense Minister Hossein Dehgan visited Moscow in February 2016, reportedly to discuss possible purchases of $8 billion worth of new conventional arms, including T-90 tanks, Su-30 aircraft, attack helicopters, anti-ship missiles, frigates, and submarines. Such purchases would require Security Council approval under Resolution 2231, and U.S. officials have said the United States would use its veto power to deny approval for the sale.

Resolution 2231 also requires Security Council approval for Iranian transfers of any weaponry outside Iran until October 17, 2020. Separate U.N. Security Council resolutions ban arms shipments to such conflict areas as Yemen (Resolution 2216) and Lebanon (Resolution 1701). There is no U.N. ban on arms exports to Syria. As noted in sections on Iran's regional activities below, Iran appears to have violated this restriction on numerous occasions, but the U.N. Security Council has not, to date, agreed on any punishments for these apparent violations.

Defense Budget

Iran's defense budget generally runs about 4% of GDP. Of the defense budget, about two-thirds funds the IRGC and its subordinate units, and about one-third funds the regular military (*Artesh*) and its units. Iran's national budget is about $300 billion. President Trump stated in his May 8, 2018, announcement of the U.S. withdrawal from the JCPOA that Iran's defense budget has increased 40% since the JCPOA has been implemented. Other sources say the increase has been a more modest 30% since 2015.[47] Incorporating the increase, Iran's 2018-2019 defense budget is about $20-$25 billion.[48] The increase since the JCPOA was forged is likely due to improved revenues from sales of crude oil and other goods resulting from JCPOA-related sanctions relief. By contrast, GCC combined defense spending is expected by defense industry experts to reach $100 billion in 2019.[49]

COUNTERING IRAN'S MALIGN ACTIVITIES

The Trump Administration has articulated a multi-layered strategy to try to counter Iran's malign activities and "roll back" Iranian influence in the region. The centerpiece of the strategy is to impose economic sanctions on Iran in order to deny it the resources it needs to conduct operations outside its borders. The Administration justified its exit from the JCPOA as an effort to deny Iran the financial resources to exert influence in the region. The State Department report "Outlaw Regime: A Chronicle of Iran's Destructive Activities" asserts that Iran has spent over $16 billion since 2012 "propping up the Assad regime and supporting [Iran's] other partners and proxies in Syria, Iraq, and Yemen."

In addition, the Administration has threatened military retaliation for Iranian direct action, and, on September 21, 2018, Secretary of State Pompeo threatened action against Iran for activities undertaken by Iran's proxies. According to the Secretary, "We have told the Islamic Republic of Iran that using a proxy force to attack an American interest will not prevent us from responding against the prime actor." The United States also works with local leaders and factions that seek to counter Iranian influence. The applications of Administration strategy are discussed in the sections below.

The Administration has also articulated 12 specific demands for Iran to change its behavior in exchange for a new JCPOA. The demands pertaining to Iran's regional activities, as stipulated in the May 21, 2018, speech by Secretary of State Pompeo at the Heritage Foundation are that Iran:

---

47 https://www.cnn.com/2018/05/12/politics/trump-tweet-iran-military-nuclear-deal/index.html.
48 https://en.radiofarda.com/a/iran-military-budget-irgc/28980550.html.
49 "Gulf States' Defence Budgets to Hit $100bn in 2019: report." Al Jazeera, September 6, 2018.

- End support to Middle East terrorist groups, including Lebanese Hizballah, Hamas, and the Palestinian Islamic Jihad.
- Respect the sovereignty of the Iraqi government and permit the disarming, demobilization, and reintegration of Shiite militias
- End military support to the Houthi militia and work towards a peaceful political settlement in Yemen.
- Withdraw all forces under Iranian command throughout the entirety of Syria.
- End support for the Taliban and other terrorists in Afghanistan and the region, and cease harboring senior al-Qaeda leaders.
- End the IRGC-QF's support for terrorists and militant partners around the world.
- End its threatening behavior against its neighbors, including: threats to destroy Israel, firing of missiles into Saudi Arabia and the UAE, threats to international shipping, and destructive cyberattacks.

The basis of and context for these demands are discussed in the sections below.

Near East Region

The focus of Iranian security policy is the Near East, where Iran employs all instruments of its national power. Successive Administrations have described many of Iran's regional operations as "malign activities." Director of National Intelligence Dan Coats, in February 13, 2018, delivery of the annual worldwide threat assessment testimony before Congress, assessed that "Iran will seek to expand its influence in Iraq, Syria, and Yemen, where it sees conflicts generally trending in Tehran's favor." Secretary of State Pompeo described a litany of Iranian malign activities in his speech to the Heritage Foundation on May 21, 2018—a speech in which he stipulated as one among many demands for normalization of relations with Iran that the regime cease its malign regional activities.

Dollar Value of Iranian Funding to Allies and Proxies. A question that often proves difficult is that of the dollar value of material support that the IRGC-QF provides to Iran's allies and proxies. Published estimates vary widely and are difficult to corroborate. Information from official U.S. government sources sometimes provides broad dollar figures without breakdowns or clear information on how those figures were derived. Section 1230E of the House version of the FY2019 NDAA (H.R. 5515, P.L. 115-232) would require an annual administration report on the amounts spent by the IRGC-QF in the preceding year to support: Hezbollah, Hamas, the Houthis in Yemen, and "proxy forces in Iraq and Syria."

The Persian Gulf

Iran has a 1,100-mile coastline on the Persian Gulf and Gulf of Oman, and intimidating and influencing the Persian Gulf monarchy states have always been a key focus of Iran's foreign policy—even during the reign of the Shah of Iran. In 1981, perceiving a threat from revolutionary Iran and spillover from the Iran-Iraq War that began in September 1980, the six Gulf states formed the Gulf Cooperation Council alliance (GCC: Saudi Arabia, Kuwait, Bahrain, Qatar, Oman, and the United Arab Emirates). U.S.-GCC security cooperation, developed during the 1980-1988 Iran-Iraq War, expanded significantly after the 1990 Iraqi invasion of Kuwait. Prior to 2003 the extensive U.S. presence in the Gulf was also intended to contain Saddam Hussein's Iraq, but, with Iraq militarily weak since the fall of Saddam Hussein, the U.S. military presence in the Gulf focuses on containing Iran and conducting operations against regional terrorist groups. The GCC states host significant numbers of U.S. forces at their military facilities and procure sophisticated U.S. military equipment.

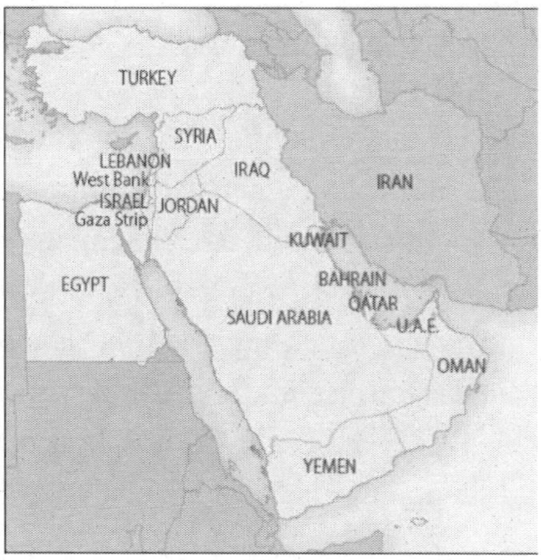

Source: Created by CRS.

Figure 1. Map of Near East.

Several of the GCC leaders have accused Iran of fomenting unrest among Shiite communities in the GCC states, particularly those in the Eastern Provinces of Saudi Arabia and in Bahrain, which has a majority Shiite population. At the same time, all the GCC states maintain relatively normal trading relations with Iran, and some have undertaken joint energy and infrastructure projects with it. In 2017, Iran sought to ease tensions with the GCC countries in an exchange of letters and a February 2017 visit by President Hassan Rouhani to Kuwait and Oman, but the same regional issues that divide Iran and the GCC countries thwarted the initiative.

The willingness of Qatar, Kuwait, and Oman to engage Iran contributed to a rift within the GCC in which Saudi Arabia, UAE, and Bahrain—joined by a few other

Muslim countries—announced on June 5, 2017, an air, land, and sea boycott of Qatar.[50] The rift has given Iran an opportunity to accomplish a long-standing goal of weakening the GCC alliance. The GCC rift came two weeks after President Donald Trump visited Saudi Arabia and expressed strong support for its policies.

Saudi Arabia[51]

Iranian and Saudi leaders accuse each other of seeking hegemony and to exclude the other from regional influence. Saudi leaders also accuse Iran of supporting Shiite dissidents in the kingdom's largely Shiite Eastern Province. The mutual animosity has aggravated sectarian tensions and contributed to an Iran-Saudi regional war by proxy.[52] Most notably, in 2015, Saudi Arabia led a coalition that intervened in Yemen's internal conflict in an effort to roll back Iranian influence by reducing the territory under the control of Houthi rebels there. Iran's arming of the Houthi rebels in Yemen has increased Iran's potential to threaten the Kingdom militarily, and Saudi Arabia has blamed Iran directly for supplying the Houthis with ballistic missiles that have been fired on the Kingdom on several occasions. The Saudi claims have been backed up by reports from the U.N. panels of experts on the Yemen conflict. In 2017, Saudi leaders unsuccessfully sought to undermine Lebanese Hezbollah's by pressuring Saudi ally and Lebanon Prime Minister, Sa'd Hariri, to expose Hezbollah's pervasive influence over the government of Lebanon. Saudi leaders have sought since mid-2017 to engage Baghdad and various Iraqi factions to draw the country closer to the Arab world and away from Iran. Iran blamed Saudi Arabia, among other adversaries that included the Islamic State organization, for the September 22, 2018, attack on a military parade in Ahwaz, in mostly Arab southwestern Iran, which killed 25 persons. However, Iran did not direct its retaliation against Saudi Arabia, instead launching missiles against Islamic State positions in Syria on October 1.

The Saudi-Iran rift expanded in January 2016 when Saudi Arabia severed diplomatic relations with Iran in the wake of violent attacks and vandalism against its embassy in Tehran and consulate in Mashhad, Iran. The attacks were a reaction to Saudi Arabia's January 2, 2016, execution of an outspoken Shia cleric, Nimr Baqr al Nimr, alongside dozens of Al Qaeda members; all had been convicted of treason and/or terrorism charges. Subsequently, Saudi Arabia and Bahrain broke diplomatic relations with Iran, and Qatar, Kuwait, and UAE recalled their ambassadors from Iran. In December 2016, Saudi Arabia executed 15 Saudi Shiites sentenced to death for "spying" for Iran.

---

[50] The intra-GCC rift with Qatar has many antecedents beyond differences over Iran policy, as discussed in CRS Insight IN10712, *Qatar and its Neighbors: Disputes and Possible Implications*, by Kenneth Katzman and Christopher M. Blanchard, and CRS Report R44533, *Qatar: Governance, Security, and U.S. Policy*, by Kenneth Katzman.

[51] For detailed information on Saudi Arabia's policy toward Iran, see CRS Report RL33533, *Saudi Arabia: Background and U.S. Relations*, by Christopher M. Blanchard.

[52] Statement for the Record. U.S. Director for National Intelligence James Clapper. Senate Armed Services Committee, February 2015, p. 14.

Saudi leaders have criticized the JCPOA's shortfalls in terms similar to those used by the Trump Administration, but Saudi officials publicly support the accord's continuation. Still, Saudi Arabia publicly applauded the Trump Administration's May 2018 exit from the JCPOA. Saudi Crown Prince Mohammad bin Salman Al Saudi, on the eve of a March 20, 2018, meeting with President Trump, stated that Saudi Arabia would acquire a nuclear weapon if Iran does. Saudi Arabia is seeking to forge a civilian nuclear cooperation agreement with the United States, perhaps in part to signal to Iran that it will not have a monopoly in the Gulf on nuclear technology.

Saudi officials repeatedly cite past Iran-inspired actions as a reason for distrusting Iran. These actions include Iran's encouragement of violent demonstrations at some Hajj pilgrimages in Mecca in the 1980s and 1990s, which caused a break in relations from 1987 to 1991. The two countries increased mutual criticism of each other's actions in the context of the 2016 Hajj. Saudi Arabia asserts that Iran instigated the June 1996 Khobar Towers bombing and accuses it of sheltering the alleged mastermind of the bombing, Ahmad Mughassil, a leader of Saudi Hezbollah. Mughassil was arrested in Beirut in August 2015.

United Arab Emirates (UAE)[53]

The UAE is aligned with Saudi Arabia against Iran, opposing extensive diplomatic engagement and as a core member of the Saudi-led coalition combatting the Houthi rebels in Yemen. As noted above, the UAE withdrew its ambassador from Iran in solidarity with Saudi Arabia in connection with the Nimr execution in January 2016. The UAE criticized the deficiencies of the JCPOA, later supported its continuation as a stabilizing force in the region, but then applauded the U.S. pullout from the JCPOA. UAE leaders blamed Iran for arming the Houthis with anti-ship missiles that damaged a UAE naval vessel in the Bab el-Mandeb Strait in late 2016.

The UAE is alone in the GCC in having a long-standing territorial dispute with Iran, concerning the Persian Gulf islands of Abu Musa and the Greater and Lesser Tunb islands. The Tunbs were seized by the Shah of Iran in 1971, and the Islamic Republic took full control of Abu Musa in 1992, violating a 1971 agreement to share control of that island. The UAE has sought to refer the dispute to the International Court of Justice (ICJ), but Iran insists on resolving the issue bilaterally. (ICJ referral requires concurrence from both parties to a dispute.) In 2013-2014, the two countries held direct apparently productive discussions on the issue and Iran reportedly removed some military equipment from the islands.[54] However, no resolution has been announced. The GCC has consistently backed the UAE position.

---

[53] For detailed information on Iran-UAE relations, see CRS Report RS21852, *The United Arab Emirates (UAE): Issues for U.S. Policy*, by Kenneth Katzman.

[54] http://archive.defensenews.com/article/20140115/DEFREG04/301150034/Source-UAE-Iran-Reach-Accord-Disputed-Hormuz-Islands.

Despite their political and territorial differences, the UAE and Iran maintain extensive trade and commercial ties. Iranian-origin residents of Dubai emirate number about 300,000, and many Iranian-owned businesses are located there, including branch offices of large trading companies based in Tehran and elsewhere in Iran.

Qatar[55]

Since 1995, Qatar has occupied a "middle ground" between anti-Iran animosity and sustained engagement with Iran. Qatar maintains periodic high-level contact with Iran; the speaker of Iran's *Majles* (parliament) visited Qatar in March 2015 and the Qatari government allowed him to meet with Hamas leaders in exile there. Qatar also pursues policies that are opposed to Iran's interests, for example by providing arms and funds to factions in Syria opposed to Syrian President Bashar Al Asad and by joining Saudi-led military intervention in Yemen (which ceased after Qatar pulled out of Yemen as a consequence of the intra-GCC rift). Qatar has sometimes used its engagement with Iran to obtain the release of prisoners held by Iran or its allies, and strongly refutes Saudi-led assertions that it is aligned with or politically close to Iran. Qatar did withdraw its Ambassador from Iran in connection with the Nimr execution discussed above, but restored relations in August 2017 in large part to reciprocate Iran's support for Qatar in the intra-GCC rift. Iran has increased its food exports to Qatar as Qatar finds alternative sources to imports from Saudi Arabia.

Qatar does not have territorial disputes with Iran, but Qatari officials reportedly remain wary that Iran could try to encroach on the large natural gas field Qatar shares with Iran (called North Field by Qatar and South Pars by Iran). In April 2004, the Iran's then-deputy oil minister said that Qatar is probably producing more gas than "her right share" from the field.

Bahrain[56]

Bahrain, ruled by the Sunni Al Khalifa family and still unsettled by unrest among its majority Shiite population, is a strident critic of Iran. Bahrain's leaders consistently allege that Iran is agitating Bahrain's Shiite community, some of which is of Persian origin, to try to overturn Bahrain's power structure. In 1981 and again in 1996, Bahrain publicly claimed to have thwarted Iran-backed efforts by Bahraini Shiite dissidents to violently overthrow the ruling family. Bahrain has consistently accused Iran of supporting radical Shiite factions within an opposition dominated by peaceful political societies.[57] On several occasions, Bahrain has temporarily withdrawn its Ambassador from Iran

---

[55] For detailed information on Iran-Qatar relations, see CRS Report R44533, *Qatar: Governance, Security, and U.S. Policy*, by Kenneth Katzman.

[56] For detailed information on Iran-Bahrain relations, see CRS Report 95-1013, *Bahrain: Reform, Security, and U.S. Policy*, by Kenneth Katzman.

[57] http://www.aljazeera.com/news/middleeast/2014/01/bahrain-accuses-iran-training-rebels201413144049814960.html.

following Iranian criticism of Bahrain's treatment of its Shiite population or alleged Iranian anti-government plots. Bahrain broke ties with Iran in concert with Saudi Arabia in January 2016 over the Nimr execution dispute.

Some reports in indicate that Iran's efforts to support violent factions in Bahrain includes providing weapons, explosives, and weapons-making equipment. In late 2016, Bahraini authorities uncovered a large warehouse containing equipment, apparently supplied by Iran, that is tailored for constructing "explosively-forced projectiles" (EFPs) such as those Iran-backed Shiite militias used against U.S. armor in Iraq during 2004-2011. No EFPs have actually been used in Bahrain, to date.[58] On January 1, 2017, 10 detainees who had been convicted of militant activities such as those discussed above broke out of Bahrain's Jaw prison with the help of attackers outside the jail. In March 2017, security forces arrested a group of persons that authorities claimed were plotting to assassinate senior government officials, asserting that the cell received military training by IRGC-QF. Six Bahraini Shiites were sentenced to death for this alleged plot on December 25, 2017. In late October 2017, 29 Bahrainis were convicted for having links to Iran and conducting espionage in Bahrain.

On March 17, 2017, the State Department named two members of a Bahrain militant group, the Al Ashtar Brigades, as Specially Designated Global Terrorists (SDGTs), asserting the group is funded and supported by Iran.[59] In July 2018, the State Department named the Al Ashtar Brigades as a Foreign Terrorist Organization (FTO). The State Department report on international terrorism for 2016, released in July 2017, stated that

> Iran has provided weapons, funding, and training to Bahraini militant Shia groups that have conducted attacks on the Bahraini security forces. On January 6, 2016, Bahraini security officials dismantled a terrorist cell, linked to IRGC-QF, planning to carry out a series of bombings throughout the country.

Tensions also have flared occasionally over Iranian attempts to question the legitimacy of a 1970 U.N.-run referendum in which Bahrainis chose independence rather than affiliation with Iran. In March 2016, a former IRGC senior commander and adviser to Supreme Leader Khamene'i reignited the issue by saying that Bahrain is an Iranian province and should be annexed.[60]

As did Saudi Arabia and the UAE, Bahrain criticized the JCPOA, later supported its continuation as a stabilizing force, but then supported the Trump Administration's withdrawal from the accord.

---

[58] Souad Mekhennet and Joby Warrick. "In Bahrain's Militant Cells, U.S. Sees Iran." *Washington Post*, April 2, 2017.

[59] State Department Terrorist Designations of Ahmad Hasan Yusuf and Alsayed Murtadha Majeed Ramadhan Alawi. March 17, 2017.

[60] Gam News, Iran, as reported by Middle East Media Research Institute (MEMRI), March 17, 2016.

Kuwait[61]

Kuwait cooperates with U.S.-led efforts to contain Iranian power and is participating in Saudi-led military action against Iran-backed Houthi rebels in Yemen, but it also has tried to mediate a settlement of the Yemen conflict and broker a GCC-Iran rapprochement. Kuwait also exchanges leadership-level visits with Iran; Kuwait's Amir Sabah al-Ahmad Al Sabah visited Iran in June 2014, meeting with Rouhani and Supreme Leader Khamene'i. Kuwait's Foreign Minister visited Iran in late January 2017 to advance Iran-GCC reconciliation, and Rouhani visited Kuwait (and Oman) in February 2017 as part of that abortive effort. Kuwaiti leaders appear to view Iran as helpful in stabilizing Iraq, a country that occupies a central place in Kuwait's foreign policy because of Iraq's 1990 invasion. Kuwait has extensively engaged Iraq's Shiite leaders despite criticism of their marginalization of Sunni Iraqis.

Kuwait is differentiated from some of the other GCC states by its integration of Shiites into the political process and the economy. About 25% of Kuwaitis are Shiite Muslims, but Shiites have not been restive there and Iran was not able to mobilize Kuwaiti Shiites to end Kuwait's support for the Iraqi war effort in the Iran-Iraq War (1980-1988). However, on numerous occasions, Kuwaiti courts have convicted Kuwaitis with spying for the IRGC-QF or Iran's intelligence service. Kuwait recalled its Ambassador from Iran in connection with the Saudi-Iran dispute over the Saudi execution of Al Nimr.

Oman[62]

Omani officials assert that engagement with Iran is a more effective means to moderate Iran's foreign policy than to isolate or threaten Iran, and Oman has the most consistent engagement with Iran's leadership of any of the Gulf states. Omani leaders express gratitude for the Shah's sending of troops to help the Sultan suppress rebellion in the Dhofar region in the 1970s, even though Iran's regime changed since then.[63] Iranian President Hassan Rouhani has visited Oman in 2014 and in 2017. Sultan Qaboos visited Iran in August 2013, reportedly to explore with the newly elected Rouhani concepts for improved U.S.-Iran relations and nuclear negotiations that ultimately led to the JCPOA. Since sanctions on Iran were lifted, Iran and Oman have accelerated their joint development of the Omani port of Duqm, which Iran envisions as a trading and transportation outlet for Iran. Since late 2016, Oman also has been a repository of Iranian heavy water to help Iran comply with the JCPOA.

Oman has not supported any factions fighting the Asad regime in Syria and has not joined the Saudi-led Arab intervention in Yemen, enabling Oman to undertake the role of

---

[61] For detailed information on Iran-Kuwait relations, see CRS Report RS21513, *Kuwait: Governance, Security, and U.S. Policy*, by Kenneth Katzman.

[62] For detailed information on Iran-Oman relations, see CRS Report RS21534, *Oman: Reform, Security, and U.S. Policy*, by Kenneth Katzman.

[63] As reported in author conversations in Oman and with Omani officials, 1988-2015.

mediator in both of those conflicts. Oman has denied that Iran has used its territory to smuggle weaponry to the Houthi rebels in Yemen that Iran is supporting, but U.N. experts have identified land routes through Oman that could be possible channels for Iranian weapons exports to the Houthis.[64] Oman was the only GCC country to not downgrade its relations with Iran in connection with the January 2016 Nimr dispute. And, Oman drew closer to Iran in 2017 because of Iran's support for Qatar in the intra-GCC rift, which Omani leaders assert was the result of misguided action by Saudi Arabia and the UAE.

Iranian Threat to the Gulf and U.S.-GCC Efforts to Counter Iran

The Gulf countries have been considered lynchpins in U.S. strategy over successive U.S. Administrations to contain Iranian power. One key threat that the United States and GCC cooperate to address is the potential threat Iran represents to the long-asserted core U.S. interest in preserving both the free flow of oil and freedom of navigation in the Persian Gulf, which is only about 20 miles wide at its narrowest point. The Strait of Hormuz is identified by the Energy Information Administration as an important possible "chokepoint" for the world economy. Each day, about 17 million barrels of oil flow through the strait, which is 35% of all seaborne traded oil and 20% of all worldwide traded oil.[65] U.S. and GCC officials view Iran as posing a possible threat to both the free flow of oil and freedom of navigation; CENTCOM Commander General Joseph Votel testified before the House Armed Services Committee on February 27, 2018, that: "With little warning, Iran could quickly close the Strait of Hormuz using stockpiles of naval mines and disrupt key maritime chokepoints throughout the region." In mid-2015, Iran stopped several commercial ships transiting the strait as part of an effort to resolve commercial disputes with the shipping companies involved—stoppages possibly intended to demonstrate Iran's potential ability to control the strait.

In early July 2018, Iran's President Rouhani indirectly threatened the free flow of oil in the Gulf should the Trump Administration succeed in compelling Iran's oil customers to cease buying Iranian oil entirely. In late August 2018, the newly appointed IRGC Navy commander Alireza Tangsiri inflamed fears of Iranian action in the Gulf by saying that Iran had "full control" of the Gulf and the Strait of Hormuz.[66] In early August 2018, General Votel stated that the U.S. military is "paying attention" to Iranian military movements in the Gulf. Subsequently, in late August 2018, the newly appointed IRGC Navy commander Tangsiri stated that Ian "has full control" of the gulf and Strait of Hormuz. However, no significant changes in the Iranian naval posture has been reported.

Iran has sometimes challenged U.S. forces in the Gulf, perhaps in part to demonstrate that it is not intimidated by U.S. power. During 2016-2017, according to DNI Coats,

---

[64] See, for example, S/2018/68, Final report of the Panel of Experts on Yemen, January 26, 2018.

[65] http://www.eia.gov/todayinenergy/detail.cfm?id=18991.

[66] Fox News, August 27, 2018.

about 10% of U.S. Navy interactions with the IRGC-Navy were "unsafe, abnormal, or unprofessional." IRGC-Navy elements conducted numerous "high speed intercepts" of U.S. naval vessels in the Gulf and, in some cases, fired rockets near U.S. warships. During some of these incidents, U.S. vessels have fired warning shots at approaching Iranian naval craft. However, U.S. Navy and other military commanders say that, since August 2017, Iran has largely ceased the naval challenges. The shift in Iranian behavior might have been prompted by concerns that that the Trump Administration might authorize the use of deadly force in future such incidents.

President Trump has stated an intent to counter Iranian actions in the Gulf or more broadly, including potentially with military action. On July 22, President Trump issued the tweet below:

> To Iranian President Rouhani: NEVER, EVER THREATEN THE UNITED STATES AGAIN OR YOU WILL SUFFER CONSEQUENCES THE LIKES OF WHICH FEW THROUGHOUT HISTORY HAVE EVER SUFFERED BEFORE. WE ARE NO LONGER A COUNTRY THAT WILL STAND FOR YOUR DEMENTED WORDS OF VIOLENCE & DEATH. BE CAUTIOUS!

11:24 PM - Jul 22, 2018

U.S.-GCC Cooperation Structures

The Obama Administration sought to add structure to the U.S.-GCC strategic partnership by instituting a "U.S.-GCC Strategic Dialogue" in March 2012. Earlier, in February 2010, then-Secretary Clinton also raised the issue of a possible U.S. extension of a "security umbrella" or guarantee to regional states against Iran.[67] However, no such formal U.S. security pledge was issued.

The JCPOA prompted GCC concerns that the United States might reduce its commitment to Gulf security and President Obama and the GCC leaders held two summit meetings—in May 2015 and April 2016—to reassure the GCC of U.S. support against Iran. The statement following the 2015 summit at Camp David said:

> In the event of [ ] aggression or the threat of [ ] aggression [against the GCC states], the United States stands ready to work with our GCC partners to determine urgently what action may be appropriate, using the means at our collective disposal, including the potential use of military force, for the defense of our GCC partners.[68]

---

[67] Paul Richter and Alexandra Davis. "U.S. Promises to Beef up Defense Aid to Persian Gulf Allies." *Los Angeles Times*, April 7, 2015.

[68] https://www.whitehouse.gov/the-press-office/2015/05/14/us-gulf-cooperation-council-camp-david-joint-statement.

The summit meetings produced announcements of a U.S.-GCC strategic partnership and specific commitments to (1) facilitate U.S. arms transfers to the GCC states; (2) increase U.S.-GCC cooperation on maritime security, cybersecurity, and counterterrorism; (3) organize additional large-scale joint military exercises and U.S. training; and (4) implement a Gulf-wide coordinated ballistic missile defense capability, which the United States has sought to promote in recent years.[69] Perhaps indicating reassurance, the GCC states expressed support for the JCPOA.[70]

The Trump Administration's characterization of Iran as a major regional threat eased GCC state concerns about U.S. policy toward Iran. The GCC states all expressed support for the Trump Administration's relaxation of restrictions on arms sales to the GCC states and de-emphasizing concerns over GCC human rights practices or other issues. Saudi Arabia, the UAE, and Bahrain all publicly supported the Trump Administration exit from the JCPOA, whereas—reflecting divisions within the GCC—Qatar, Kuwait, and Oman expressed "understanding" for the exit. U.S. officials have stated that the intra-GCC rift centered on Qatar is harming the U.S.-led effort to forge a united strategy against Iran, and, since April 2018, President Trump reportedly has been insisting that Gulf leaders resolve the rift.[71]

Building on the exit from the JCPOA, the Trump Administration reportedly is attempting to build a new coalition to counter Iran, composed of the GCC states plus Egypt, Jordan, and possibly also Morocco. The Administration reportedly sought to unveil this "Middle East Strategic Alliance" (MESA) in advance of a planned U.S.-GCC summit on October 12-13, 2018. However, because of the ongoing intra-GCC dispute and other factors, the meeting has been postponed until an unspecified time in 2019.[72]

U.S. Forces in the Gulf and Defense Agreements

The GCC states are pivotal to U.S. efforts to counter Iran militarily. There are about 35,000 U.S. forces in the Gulf region currently, most of which are stationed at military facilities in the GCC states that the United States accesses under formal defense cooperation agreements (DCAs) with Kuwait, Bahrain, Qatar, and the UAE; a facilities access agreement with Oman; and memoranda of understanding with Saudi Arabia. U.S. defense agreements with the GCC states also reportedly provide for the United States to preposition substantial military equipment, to train the GCC countries' forces; to sell arms to those states; and, in some cases, for consultations in the event of a major threat to

---

[69] https://www.whitehouse.gov/the-press-office/2015/05/14/annex-us-gulf-cooperation-council-camp-david-joint-statement.

[70] State Department, Joint Statement of the U.S.-GCC Foreign Ministers Meeting. August 3, 2015; https://www.whitehouse.gov/the-press-office/2015/09/04/joint-statement-meeting-between-president-barack-obamaand-king-salman.

[71] https://www.reuters.com/article/us-usa-gulf/in-call-with-saudi-king-trump-demanded-quick-end-to-gulf-rift-u-s-officials-idUSKBN1HI332.

[72] Jack Detsch. "Trump Shelves Gulf Talks Until Next Year." Al Monitor, September 6, 2018.

the state in question.[73] Some U.S. forces in the Gulf are aboard a U.S. aircraft carrier task force that is in the Gulf region nearly constantly. The Defense Department also uses authority in Section 2282 of U.S.C. Title 10 to program Counterterrorism Partnerships Funds CTPF) for U.S. special operations forces training to enhance GCC counterterrorism capabilities.

Arms Sales. U.S. arms sales to the GCC countries have improved GCC air and naval capabilities and their interoperability with U.S. forces. With the exception of post-2011 uprising Bahrain, the United States has tended to approve virtually all arms purchase requests by the GCC states, including such equipment as combat aircraft, precision-guided munitions, combat ships, radar systems, and communications gear. Congress has generally not sought to block such sales, although a Senate vote in June 2017 nearly blocked a sale of precision-guided munitions to Saudi Arabia over its tactics in its war effort in Yemen. And, the intra-GCC rift has slowed the process of concluding new arms sales to the GCC states: Senate Foreign Relations Committee Chairman Bob Corker has said he would withhold informal concurrence on major new arms sales to the GCC states until the rift is resolved.

The following sections discuss specific U.S.-Gulf defense relationships.[74]

- *Saudi Arabia.* The United States and Saudi Arabia have utilized memoranda of understanding, limited in scope, to enable a few hundred U.S. military personnel to train the military, National Guard (SANG), and Ministry of Interior forces in Saudi Arabia. The Saudi force has about 225,000 active duty personnel, with about 600 tanks, of which 200 are U.S.-made M1A2 "Abrams" tanks. The Saudi Air Force flies the F-15. Saudi Arabia reportedly is contemplating buying the sophisticated missile defense system Theater High Altitude Air Defense system (THAAD).
- *Kuwait.* The United States has had a DCA with Kuwait since 1991, and over 13,000 mostly U.S. Army personnel are stationed there, including ground combat troops. Kuwait has hosted the U.S.-led headquarters for Operation Inherent Resolve (OIR), the military component of the campaign against the Islamic State.
- U.S. forces operate from such facilities as Camp Arifjan, south of Kuwait City, where the United States prepositions ground armor including Mine Resistant Ambush Protected (MRAP) vehicles, as well as from several Kuwaiti air bases.

[73] The texts of the DCAs and related agreements are classified, but general information on the provisions of the agreements has been provided in some open sources, including http://www.strategicstudiesinstitute.army.mil/pdffiles/pub185.pdf. Section 1234 of the FY2016 NDAA (P.L. 114-92) required a report within 120 days of enactment (by March 30, 2016) on any U.S. security commitments to Middle Eastern countries, including the GCC, and the U.S. force posture required for those commitments.

[74] The U.S. deployments in the Gulf are discussed in greater detail in CRS reports on the individual GCC states. Information in this section is derived from author visits to the GCC states since 1993 and conversations with U.S. and Gulf state diplomats. See also International Institute for Strategic Studies, "The Military Balance, 2015."

U.S. forces train at Camp Buehring, about 50 miles west of the capital. Kuwait has a small force (about 15,000 active military personnel) that relies on U.S. arms, including Abrams tanks and F/A-18 combat aircraft. The Trump Administration stated during the September 2017 visit to Washington, DC, of Kuwait's Amir that it would proceed with selling Kuwait 32 additional F/A-18s.

- *Qatar*. The United States has had a DCA with Qatar since 1992, which was revised in December 2013. Nearly 10,000 U.S. military personnel, mostly Air Force, are in Qatar, manning the forward headquarters of U.S. Central Command (CENTCOM), which has responsibility for the Middle East and Central Asia; a Combined Air Operations Center (CAOC) that oversees U.S. combat aircraft missions in the region; the large Al Udeid Air Base; and the *As Saliyah* army prepositioning site where U.S. tanks are prepositioned. Qatar's armed force is small with about 12,000 active military personnel. Qatar has historically relied on French military equipment, including Mirage combat aircraft, but in late 2016, the Obama Administration approved selling up to 72 F-15s to Qatar. The F-15 deal, with an estimated value of $21 billion, was formally signed between Qatar and the Trump Administration on June 14, 2017. Qatari officials say they will expand Al Udeid air base and are allowing fixed housing and other facilities to be built on the base to better accommodate U.S. personnel deployed there.
- *UAE*. The United States has had a DCA with UAE nearly continuously since 1994. About 5,000 U.S. forces, mostly Air Force and Navy, are stationed in UAE, operating surveillance and refueling aircraft from Al Dhafra Air Base, and servicing U.S. Navy and contract ships which dock at the large commercial port of Jebel Ali. The UAE armed forces include about 63,000 active duty personnel. Its ground forces use primarily French-made tanks purchased in the 1990s, but its air forces are equipped with F-16s the country has bought from the United States in recent years. The UAE has stated that it wants to buy the F-35 Joint Strike Fighter, but U.S. officials have indicated that the potential sale would be evaluated in accordance with U.S. policy to maintain Israel's Qualitative Military Edge (QME). The Trump Administration said in early 2018 that it is considering providing the UAE with advanced briefings on the aircraft. The UAE is the only GCC state to date that has taken delivery of the THAAD anti-missile system.
- *Bahrain*. The United States has had a DCA with Bahrain since 1991. More than 8,000 U.S. personnel, mostly Navy, operate out of the large Naval Support Activity facility that houses the U.S. command structure for U.S. naval operations in the Gulf. U.S. Air Force personnel also access Shaykh Isa Air Base. Bahrain has only about 6,000 active military personnel, and another 11,000 internal security forces under the Ministry of Interior. The United States has given Bahrain older model U.S. M60A3 tanks and a frigate ship as grant "excess defense articles," and the country has bought U.S.-made F-16s with national

funds. The Obama Administration told Congress in late 2016 that it would not finalize approval of a Bahrain request to purchase additional F-16s unless the government demonstrates progress on human rights issues, but in March 2017, the Trump Administration dropped that condition and is proceeding with the sale, while maintaining a ban on arms sales to Bahrain's internal security forces.

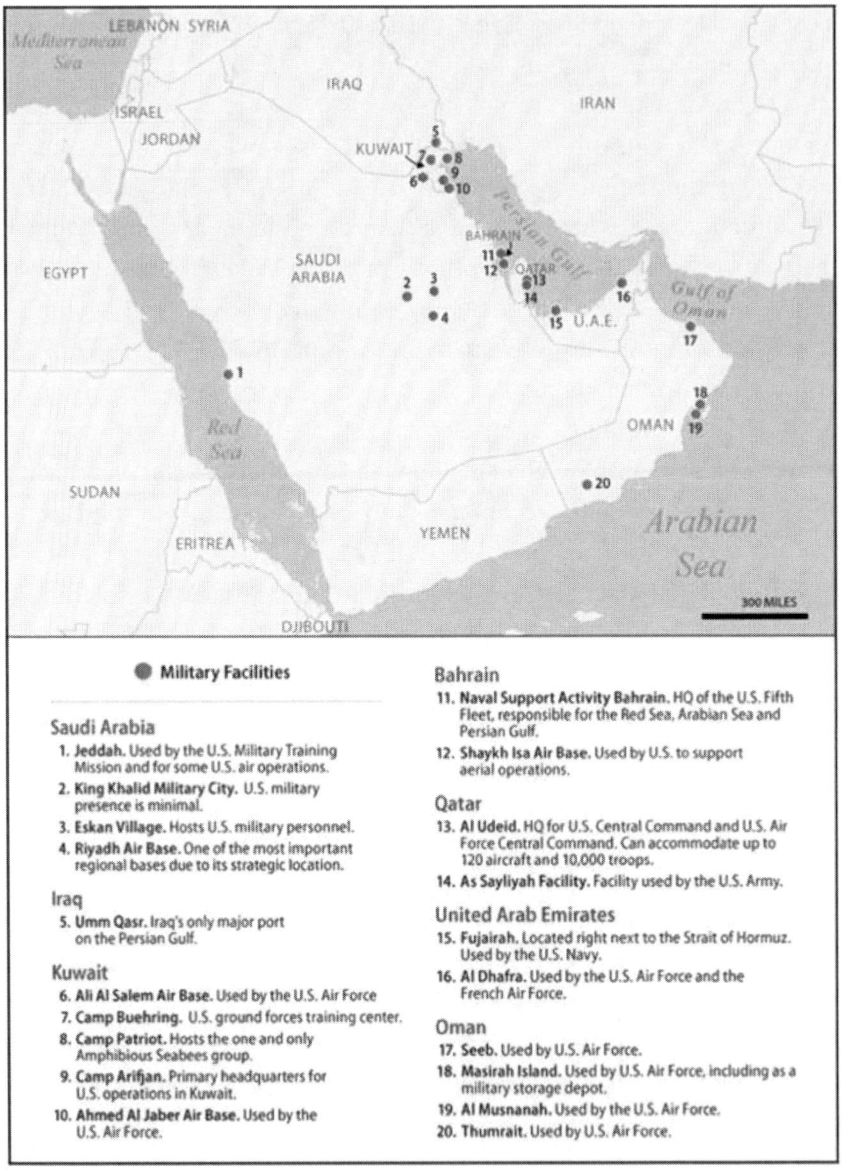

Source: http://www.darkgovernment.com/news/wp-content/uploads/2012/01/persian-gulf.jpg.

Figure 2. Major Persian Gulf Military Facilities.

- *Oman*. The United States has had a "facilities access agreement" with Oman since April 1980, under which a few hundred U.S. forces (mostly Air Force) are deployed at and have access to Omani air bases such as those at Seeb, Masirah Island, Thumrait, and Musnanah. Oman has a 25,000-person force that has historically relied on British-made military equipment. The United States has provided some M60A3 tanks as excess defense articles, and Oman has bought F-16s using national funds.
- *Assistance Issues*. The GCC states are considered wealthy states and most receive little or virtually no U.S. assistance. The least wealthy Gulf states Bahrain and Oman receive a few million dollars per year in Foreign Military Financing (FMF) and International Military Education and Training Funds (IMET). Small amounts of State Department funds are provided to all the Gulf states for counterterrorism/border security programs (nonproliferation, anti-terrorism, de-mining and related, NADR, funds)

Iranian Policy on Iraq, Syria, and the Islamic State[75]

Iran's policy has been to support the Shiite-led governments in Iraq and Syria against armed insurgencies or other domestic strife that might threaten those governments. That policy faced a significant challenge from the Islamic State organization, a Sunni radical Islamist movement that used internal dissension to capture significant territory in both of those countries in 2014, but which has been beaten back substantially by a U.S.-led coalition as well as Iran-supported government and militia forces in both countries. Iran has taken advantage of the Islamic State's defeats to improve Iran's regional strategic position.

Iraq

In Iraq, the U.S. military ousting of Saddam Hussein in 2003 removed a long-time antagonist and produced a government led by Shiite Islamists with long-standing ties to Iran.[76] The June 2014 offensive led by the Islamic State organization at one point brought Islamic State forces to within 50 miles of the Iranian border. Iran responded by supplying the Baghdad government as well as the *peshmerga* forces of the autonomous Kurdistan Regional Government (KRG) with IRGC-QF advisers, intelligence drone surveillance, weapons shipments, and other direct military assistance.[77] And, Iranian leaders reportedly

[75] For information, see CRS Report R43612, *The Islamic State and U.S. Policy*, by Christopher M. Blanchard and Carla E. Humud.

[76] Michael Gordon, "Iran Supplying Syrian Military Via Iraqi Airspace," *New York Times*, September 5, 2012.

[77] "Iran News Agency Reports Death of Iranian Pilot in Iraq." Radio Free Europe/Radio Liberty. July 5, 2014.

acquiesced to U.S. insistence that Iran's longtime ally Maliki be replaced by a different Shiite Islamist, Haider al-Abadi, who pledged to be more inclusive of Sunni leaders.[78]

Table 5. Military Assets of the Gulf Cooperation Council Member States

	Bahrain	Kuwait	Oman	Qatar	Saudi Arabia	UAE
Total Manpower	8,200+	15,500 +	42,600+	11,800	225,000+	63,000
Army and National Guard						
Personnel	6,000	11,000	25,000	8,500	175,000	44,400
Main Battle Tanks	180	293	154	39	600	467
AIFV/APC	225	789	206	230	3,011	1,957
Artillery	151	218	233	91+	771	579+
Attack Helicopters	—	—	—	—	15	—
SAMs	91	136+	48	75	1,805	N/A
Navy						
Personnel	700	2,000	4,200	1,800	13,500	2,500
Destroyers /Frigates	1	—	3	—	7	—
Submarines	—	—	2	—	—	10
Patrol/Coastal Combatants	64	52	46	23	83	141
Amphibious Landing Craft	1	4	—	—	8	—
Air Force						
Personnel (Air Defense)	1,500	2,500	5,000	1,500	20,000 (16,000)	4,500
Fighter Aircraft	33	39	15	12	261	138
Attack Helicopters	28	16	—	8	—	37
Missile Defense						
Patriot PAC-2	Yes	Yes	—	Yes	Yes	Yes
Patriot PAC-3	Yes	Yes	—	Yes	Yes	Yes
THAAD	—	—	Considering	Considering	Sale approved by Dept. of State (10/17)	Delivered

Sources: *The Military Balance*, 2017, published by the International Institute for Strategic Studies, and various press; https://www.reuters.com/article/us-usa-saudi-missiles/u-s-approves-possible-15-billion-sale-of-thaadmissiles-to-saudi-arabia-idUSKBN1CB2IN.

Notes: AIFV = Armored Infantry Fighting Vehicle, APC = Armored Personnel Carrier, SAM = Surface-to-Air Missile, THAAD = Terminal High Altitude Area Defense.

With Iraq now largely in a post-ISIS period, Iran's influence in Iraq was cast into some doubt with the strong May 12, 2018, election showing of Iraqi nationalist Moqtada al-Sadr's faction, although the strongly pro-Iranian Shiite militia commander Hadi al-Ameri's faction unexpectedly won the second most number of seats in the Iraqi parliament. Abadi's "Victory" faction finished an unexpectedly weak third. In October 2018, coalition negotiations named relatively pro-American figures as president and presumptive prime minister.

Iraq's new political leadership notwithstanding, Iran will continue to wield substantial influence on Iraq because the IRGC-QF arms, trains, and advises several

[78] Babak Dehghanpisheh. "Iran Dramatically Shifts Iraq Policy to Confront Islamic State." *Reuters*, September 2, 2014.

Shiite militias that earlier fought the United States during 2003-2011. Iran's supplies of these groups with rocket-propelled munitions, such as Improvised Rocket Assisted Munitions (IRAMs) contributed to the deaths of about 500 U.S. military personnel during those years.[79] Iran has typically appointed members of or associates of the IRGC-QF as its Ambassador to Iraq. In late August 2018, there were unconfirmed reports that Iran had transferred short-range ballistic missiles to some of its Shiite militia allies in Iraq, possibly for the purpose or projecting force further into the region.[80] Secretary of State Michael Pompeo reacted to the reports by stating in a tweet that he is:

> "Deeply concerned about reports of #Iran transferring ballistic missiles into Iraq. If true, this would be a gross violation of Iraqi sovereignty and of UNSCR 2231. Baghdad should determine what happens in Iraq, not Tehran.

Current estimates of the total Shiite militiamen in Iraq number about 110,000-120,000, of which about two-thirds are members of Iran-backed militias.[81] Collectively, all of the Shiite militias are known as Popular Mobilization Forces or Units (PMFs or PMUs).

The commanders of the most powerful Iran-backed militias, including Asa'ib Ahl Al Haq (AAH) leader Qais Khazali, the Badr Organization's Hadi al-Amiri (see above), and Kata'ib Hezbollah's Abu Mahdi al-Muhandis, are said to wield significant political influence. They have close ties to Iran dating from their underground struggle against Saddam Hussein in the 1980s and 1990s, and the commanders have publicly pressured the government to reduce reliance on the United States and ally more closely with Iran. Some of these commanders advocate a U.S. withdrawal from Iraq now that the Islamic State has been mostly defeated in Iraq. Khazali is a member of Iraq's parliament. These figures have largely resisted incorporated their forces into the formal security structure.

Despite good relations with the Iraqi Kurdish political leadership, Iran, as does the United States, supports the territorial integrity of Iraq and opposed the September 25, 2017, KRG referendum on independence. At the same time, Iran is wary of the ability of some anti-Iran government Kurdish movements to operate in northern Iraq. In September 2018, Iran fired seven Fateh-110 short-range ballistic missiles at a base in northern Iraq operated by the Kurdistan Democratic Party of Iran—an Iranian Kurdish opposition group. The KDP-I's Secretary General and other figures of the group were reportedly among those wounded.[82]

---

[79] http://www.militarytimes.com/story/military/capitol-hill/2015/07/14/iran-linked-to-deaths-of-500-us-troops-in-iraqafghanistan/30131097/.

[80] "Exclusive: Iran Moves Missile to Iraq in Warning to Enemies." Reuters, August 31, 2018.

[81] http://www.foxnews.com/politics/2016/08/16/us-officials-up-to-100000-iran-backed-fighters-now-in-iraq.html.

[82] https://www.apnews.com/39a6e79233574b0fb8ef2a794625ed33.

Iranian Funding to Iraqi Militias

In 2014, a senior Iranian cleric estimated the dollar value of Iran's assistance to Iraq at about $1 billion—a large increase over an estimated baseline level of about $150 million per year.[83]

Sadrist Militias and Their Offshoots

Several of the Iran-backed militias are offshoots of the "Mahdi Army" militia that the junior Shiite cleric Moqtada Al Sadr formed in 2004 to combat the U.S. military presence in Iraq. As the U.S. intervention in Iraq ended in 2011, the Mahdi Army evolved into a social services network but, in response to the Islamic State offensive in 2014, it reorganized as the "Salaam (Peace) Brigade," with about 15,000 fighters.

One Mahdi Army offshoot, Kata'ib Hezbollah (KAH) was designated by the State Department as a Foreign Terrorist Organization (FTO) in June 2009. KAH has an estimated 20,000 fighters.[84] In July 2009, the Department of the Treasury designated it and its commander, Muhandis, as threats to Iraqi stability under Executive Order 13438. Muhandis was a Da'wa party operative during Saddam's rule, and was convicted in absentia by Kuwaiti courts for the Da'wa assassination attempt on the ruler of Kuwait in May 1985 and the 1983 Da'wa bombings of the U.S. and French embassies there. After these attacks, he served as leader of the Badr Corps of the IRGCbacked Supreme Council for the Islamic Revolution in Iraq (SCIRI), but he broke with the group in 2003 because of its support for the U.S. invasion of Iraq. He joined the Mahdi Army during 2003-2006 but then broke to form KAH.

AAH leader Qais al-Khazali headed the Mahdi Army "Special Groups" breakaway faction during 2006-2007, until his capture and incarceration by U.S. forces for his alleged role in a 2005 raid that killed five American soldiers. During his imprisonment, his followers formed AAH. After his release in 2010, Khazali took refuge in Iran, returning in 2011 to take resume command of AAH while also converting it into a political movement and social service network. AAH resumed military activities after the 2014 Islamic State offensive, and has about 15,000 fighters.

The Badr Organization

The Badr Organization, the armed wing of the Islamic Supreme Council of Iraq (ISCI, formerly SCIRI), the mainstream Shiite party headed now by Ammar al-Hakim. did not oppose the 2003 11 U.S. intervention in Iraq. The Badr forces (then known as the Badr Brigades or Badr Corps) received training and support from the IRGC-QF in its failed efforts to overthrow Saddam during the 1980s and 1990s. The Badr Organization largely disarmed after Saddam's fall and integrated into the political process, supporting the United States as a facilitator of Iraq's transition to Shiite rule. Its leader is Hadi al-

---

[83] "Iran Dramatically Shifts Iraq Policy to Confront Islamic State." Reuters, September 2, 2014.

[84] http://www.aljazeera.com/indepth/opinion/2016/02/iraq-popular-demobilisation-160224050939178.html.

Amiri, an elected member of the National Assembly who advocates for government reliance on the Shiite militias. The Amiri-led faction, called "Conquest," won the second-highest number of seats in the May 12, 2018, Iraqi election, positioning Amiri to wield significant influence. Badr has an estimated 20,000 militia fighters.[85]

Iran-Backed Militias Formed after the 2011 U.S. Withdrawal

Some reputedly Iran-backed Shiite militias formed after the U.S. withdrawal. One such militia formed in 2013 to assist the Asad regime—the Harakat Hezbollah al-Nujaba or "Nujaba Movement," led by Shaykh Akram al-Ka'bi. In Syria, the group increased its presence on the Aleppo front in 2016 to help the Asad regime recapture the whole city. Ka'bi was designated as a threat to Iraq's stability under E.O. 13438 in 2008, when he was then a leader of a Mahdi Army offshoot termed the "Special Groups." Another Shiite militia, the "Mukhtar Army," formed in 2013 to help the government suppress Sunni protests. It was led by Wathiq al-Battat, who reportedly was killed in late 2014.[86] The Mukhtar Army claimed responsibility for a late October 2015 attack on Iranian dissidents inhabiting the "Camp Liberty" facility, discussed below. These militias might total 10,000 personnel.

U.S. Policy to Curb Iranian Influence in Iraq

U.S. policy has been to try to counterbalance Iranian influence in Iraq by working with Iraqi leaders who are well-disposed to the United States and relatively nonsectarian. The United States supported Abadi's reelection bid in Iraq as contributing to efforts to counter Iran's influence there, but the newly named president and prime minister, Barham Salih and Adel Abdul Mahdi, respectively, are well known to U.S. officials and favor continued U.S. involvement in Iraq. In 2014, U.S. officials initially refused to support Iraqi Shiite militias in the anti-Islamic State effort, but U.S. policy after 2015 supported those PMFs identified by U.S. officials as not backed by Iran. October 2017, then-Secretary of State Rex Tillerson called on Iran-backed militias to disarm and for their Iranian advisors to "go home."[87] Although Abadi's office publicly rebuked that U.S. call, the Trump Administration reportedly has worked with Abadi, with mixed success, to integrate the militias into the official security forces or demobilize and merge into the political process.

Still, there is potential for the activities of Iran-backed militias to become issues in broader Trump Administration Iran policy. On September 11, 2018, following rocket attacks near U.S. diplomatic facilities in Iraq, the Administration blamed Iran for not "act[ing] to stop these attacks."[88] Subsequently, as noted above, Secretary of State

---

[85] http://www.aljazeera.com/indepth/opinion/2016/02/iraq-popular-demobilisation-160224050939178.html.

[86] http://www.longwarjournal.org/archives/2014/12/leader_of_iran-suppo.php.

[87] https://www.reuters.com/article/us-usa-gulf-tillerson-iraq/go-home-tillerson-tells-iranian-backed-militias-in-iraq-idUSKBN1CR0JR.

[88] White House. Statement by the Press Secretary, September 11, 2018.

Pompeo threatened potential U.S. military action against Iran if its proxies, including the Iran-backed militias in Iraq, attacked U.S. interests. And U.S. officials reportedly are strongly resisting the appointment of high-ranking Iran-backed militia members to a new Iraqi cabinet.

With respect to sanctions, Executive Order 12438 blocks property and prevents U.S. visas for persons determined to threaten stabilization efforts in Iraq. In the 115th Congress, H.R. 4591 would essentially codify that executive order. Other legislations, such as S.3431 and H.R. 4238, would require sanctions on two of the Iran-backed militias, specifically naming Asa'ib Ahl al-Haq and Harakat Hezbollah al-Nujaba. On the other hand, these organizations are believed to have virtually no U.S.-based assets or financial interests that would be susceptible to U.S. sanctions.

Syria[89]

Iranian leaders characterize Syrian President Bashar al Asad as a key ally, despite Asad's secular ideology, and Iran has sustained a major effort to keep him in power. The reasons for Iran's consistent and extensive support for Asad include: (1) Syria's cooperation is key to Iran's arming and protection of Hezbollah; (2) the Asad regime has been Iran's closest Arab ally in a region where most governments oppose Iran; (3) a Sunni opposition government hostile to Iran might come to power if Asad fell; and (4) the Asad regime can help block Sunni extremist groups from attacking Hezbollah in Lebanon from across the Syria border. Most observers conclude that Iran's strategic interest in the Asad regime's survival is sufficiently compelling that Iran will resist any Russian or other attempts to persuade it to completely withdraw Iranian forces from Syria. In late August 2018. Iran and Syria signed a military cooperation agreement, perhaps suggesting Iranian intent to remain militarily in Syria for the indefinite future.

Iranian support to Asad against the rebellion is extensive, including the provision of substantial funds, weapons, and IRGC-QF advisors to the Syrian regime. After 2012, Iran gradually escalated its intervention to the point where regional security sources estimated that, by late 2015, it was deploying nearly 2,000 military personnel in Syria, including IRGC-QF, IRGC ground force, and even some regular army special forces personnel.[90] The deployment of Iranian regular army forces in Syria was significant because Iran's regular military has historically not deployed beyond Iran's borders since the 1980-88 Iran-Iraq War. The IRGC-QF recruited a reported 50,000-80,000 Shiite fighters to operating under Iranian command in Syria,[91] including about 7,000 Hezbollah militiamen, Iraqi militias such as Harakat Hezbollah al-Nujaba, and brigades composed

---

[89] For more information on the conflicts in Syria, see CRS Report RL33487, *Armed Conflict in Syria: Overview and U.S. Response*, coordinated by Carla E. Humud.

[90] Dan Williams. "Israel Says 55 Iranians Killed in Syria's War." *Reuters*, November 19, 2015; American Enterprise News Round Up. April 4, 2016; FY2016 DOD report on the military power of Iran, released January 2017 (unclassified summary).

[91] Department of State, Country Reports on Terrorism 2016. See also: Institute for the Study of War. "Iranian Strategy in Syria," by Will Fulton, Joseph Holliday, and Sam Wyer. May 2013.

of Afghan and Pakistani Shiites. These militias advanced east to the point where they can potentially help Iran form a secure supply corridor from Iran to the Lebanon. On several occasions, Iran-backed forces approached U.S. training locations for Syrian forces in southeast Syria combatting the Islamic State and were subjected to U.S.-led fire to halt their advances. On October 1, 2018, Iran fired six ballistic missiles from western Iran on suspected Islamic State positions near Hanjin. Syria. Iran claimed the strikes were retaliation for the September 2018 attack on Iran's military parade in Ahwaz (see above), but the attack, which were near areas in which U.S. and U.S.-backed forces in Syria operate, could be interpreted as signaling Iran's ability to project power in Syria from Iran's homeland itself.

Iran's extensive involvement in Syria has alarmed Israeli leaders who now apparently perceive Iran as using Syrian territory to exert greater leverage against Israel—adding to the threat posed by Hezbollah on Israel's northern border. Israel accuses Iran of constructing bases in Syria, including rocket and missile factories that can safely supply Hezbollah. Among the bases Iran reportedly is present in Syria include Tiyas and al Shayrat airfields near Homs, Damascus airport, Nayrab airfield near Aleppo, and a base at al-Qiswah. Iran tested Israel's capabilities in February 2018 by launching a drone over Israeli territory, which Israel shot down but which precipitated an Israel-Syria clash that resulted in the downing of one Israeli combat aircraft. Further clashes in April and May, culminating in a large Israeli strike on Iranian facilities in Syria, including those locations mentioned above, during May 9-10, 2018, have sparked widespread concerns that a broader Israel-Iran war could erupt. The clashes also indicate that Israel has not succeeded in influencing Russia to compel Iran-backed forces to withdraw to areas far from Israeli-controlled territory.[92] Persuading Russia to do so has been a focus of Prime Minister Benjamin Netanyahu's several meetings with Russia's President Vladimir Putin in 2017 and 2018, and most recently on July 11, 2018.

Iran has not hidden its involvement or its losses in Syria. Deaths of high-ranking IRGC commanders in battles in Syria have been widely publicized in state-run media. Their deaths have been portrayed by the regime as heroic sacrifices on behalf of the Iranian revolution and Iran's national interests. At least 2,100 Iranian military personnel have died in Syria, including several high-level IRGC-QF commanders.[93] Iranian and Iran-controlled forces are likely to play a role in any Syrian government offensive to recapture Idlib province, the last major bastion of opposition forces. A September 7, 2018, Tehran summit attended by President Rouhani, President Putin, and Turkey's President Recep Tayyip Erdrogan reportedly did not agree to Turkish requests for a ceasefire in Idlib, which would spare civilians there a battle for the province.

Prior to the Russian intervention, Iran participated in multilateral diplomacy on a political solution in Syria and put forward proposals for a peaceful transition in Syria. In

---

[92] Amos Yadlin. "How to Understand Israel's Strike on Syria." *New York Times*, September 9, 2017.

[93] Pasdar Toll in Syria Heavier than all U.S. Deaths in Mideast. Iran Times, March 16, 2018.

2015, Iran attended meetings of and did not publicly dissent from joint statements issued by, an international contact group on Syria, which included the United States. Iran was invited to participate in this "Vienna process" after the United States dropped its objections on the grounds that, in the wake of the July 2015 Iran nuclear agreement, Iran could potentially contribute to a Syria solution. However, Russia's intervention in Syria created the potential for Iran to achieve its maximum goals in Syria, and in 2016-2018, Iran has apparently continued to pursue those goals in negotiations brokered by Russia and Turkey ("Astana Process"). However, the August 2018 Administration report on Iran mandated by the Countering America's Adversaries through Sanctions Act said that Iran "is not playing a constructive role in Syria...despite Iran's status as a 'guarantor' of the Astana ceasefire zones ostensibly in place..." In the event that there is a political transition, Iran will presumably seek to establish a government that would allow it to continue to use Syria to supply Hezbollah.

Iranian Financial Support to Asad

Estimates of Iran's spending to support Asad's effort against the rebellion vary widely. In June 2015, the office of the U.N. Special Envoy to Syria Staffan de Mistura, estimated Iran's aid to Syria, including military and economic aid, to total about $6 billion per year.[94] Iranian aid to Syria is difficult to gauge with precision, in part because it includes a combination of economic aid (for which some figures, such as lines of credit, are publicly available in official statements), subsidized oil and commodity transfers, as well as military aid (for which numbers are difficult to obtain). The State Department's "Outlaw Regime" report (graphic, page 11), referenced above, indicates that Iran has extended "at least $4.6 billion in credit to the Assad regime" since 2012.

U.S. Policy to Limit Iranian Influence in Syria

A stated U.S. goal in Syria is to limit Iranian influence there, in part to help protect Israel and in part as a component of a larger U.S. strategy of rolling back Iran's regional influence. Then-Secretary of State Rex Tillerson devoted much of a January 17, 2018, speech on U.S. policy toward Syria to explaining that the United States would maintain, for an unspecified time, 2,000 U.S. troops in Syria in part for the purpose of diminishing Iranian influence in Syria and denying Iran's "dreams of a northern arch" (from Iran to the Mediterranean).[95] He explained that, a U.S. Russia de-escalation agreement for southwest Syria "... addresses Israel's security by requiring Iranian-backed militias, most notably Hezbollah, to move away from Israel's border."

In September 2018, U.S. officials appeared to link policy in Syria more closely to overall Iran policy by indicating that U.S. forces in Syria would stay for the foreseeable

[94] Eli Lake. "Iran Spends Billions to Prop Up Asad," *Bloomberg View*, June 9, 2015.

[95] Department of State. Secretary of State Rex Tillerson. Remarks on the Way Forward for the United States Regarding Syria. January 17, 2018.

future, in part to exercise leverage to reduce Iran's presence in Syria. National Security Adviser John Bolton made that linkage explicit in a speech on September 10, 2018.[96] Still, the U.S. forces have not been ordered—to preemptively attack Iranian or pro-Iranian forces in Syria, raising questions about how the United States will a demands, stated by Secretary of State Pompeo in his May 21, 2018, speech at Heritage Foundation, that "Iran must withdraw all forces under Iranian command throughout the entirety of Syria."[97] The Administration has supported Israeli strikes on Iranian positions in Syria that is part of Israel's effort to deny Iran the opportunity to conduct an extensive military infrastructure there.

Executive Order 13572 blocks U.S.-based property and prevents U.S. visas for persons determined to be responsible for human rights abuses and repression of the Syrian people. Several IRGC-QF commanders have been designated for sanctions under the order. In the 115th Congress, H.R. 4012 would direct the Director of National Intelligence to produce a National Intelligence Estimate on Iranian support to proxy forces in Syria (and Lebanon).

Hamas, Hezbollah, and other Anti-Israel Groups[98]

A significant component of Iran's policy in the region is to pressure Israel strategically, as discussed below.

Israel

Iran's leaders assert that Israel is an illegitimate creation of the West and an oppressor of the Palestinians—a position that differs from that of the Shah of Iran, whose government maintained relatively normal relations with Israel. Supreme Leader Khamene'i has repeatedly described Israel as a "cancerous tumor" that should be removed from the region. In a September 2015 speech, Khamene'i stated that Israel will likely not exist in 25 years—the time frame for the last of the JCPOA nuclear restriction to expire.[99] These statements underpin Israeli assertions that a nuclear-armed Iran would be an "existential threat" to Israel.

Iran's leaders routinely state that Israel presents a serious strategic threat to Iran and that the international community applies a "double standard" to Iran in that Israel has faced no sanctions even though it is the only Middle Eastern country to possess nuclear

---

96 https://www.defensenews.com/global/the-americas/2018/09/24/bolton-us-troops-staying-in-syria-until-iran-leaves/.

97 State Dept. "After the Deal: A New Iran Strategy." Secretary of State Mike Pompeo before the Heritage Foundation. May 21, 2018.

98 For more information, see CRS Report R41514, *Hamas: Background and Issues for Congress*, by Jim Zanotti; and CRS Report RL33476, *Israel: Background and U.S. Relations*, by Jim Zanotti.

99 http://www.cnn.com/2015/09/10/middleeast/iran-khamenei-israel-will-not-exist-25-years/.

weapons and not to become a party to the Nuclear Non-Proliferation Treaty (NPT). Iran's leaders regularly cite Israeli statements that Israel retains the option to unilaterally strike Iran's nuclear facilities, and assert that Israel's purported nuclear arsenal is a main obstacle to establishing a weapons-of-massdestruction (WMD) free zone in the Middle East.

Iran materially supports nonstate actors such as Hamas and Hezbollah that have undertaken armed action against Israel, possibly as an attempt to apply pressure to Israel to compel it to make concessions. Alternately, Iran might be attempting to disrupt prosperity, morale, and perceptions of security among Israel's population. Iran's material support for militant anti-Israel groups has long concerned not only Israel but successive U.S. Administrations. For more than two decades, the annual State Department report on international terrorism has asserted that Iran provides funding, weapons (including advanced rockets), and training to a variety of U.S.-designated FTOs, including Hezbollah, Hamas, Palestinian Islamic Jihad—Shiqaqi Faction (PIJ), the Al Aqsa Martyrs Brigades (a militant offshoot of the dominant Palestinian faction Fatah), and the Popular Front for the Liberation of Palestine-General Command (PFLP-GC).

Israel and the Obama Administration disagreed over the JCPOA—Prime Minister Benjamin Netanyahu called it a "historic mistake," and, in September 2017 and in March 2018, he reportedly urged President Trump to seek to renegotiate it or to terminate U.S. participation in it. Netanyahu's policy preference was adopted when the Trump Administration exited the JCPOA on May 8, 2018. Israel retains the option of a military strike on Iran's nuclear facilities should Iran responds to the U.S. exit by abrogating the JCPOA and resuming the nuclear activities prohibited or limited by the agreement. Israel also counters Iran forces and allies and proxies directly, using its own forces and U.S.-supplied military and intelligence technology, as demonstrated in its repeated strikes on Iranian and Iran-supported militia forces in Syria.

Hamas[100]

U.S. officials assert that Iran gives Hamas funds, weapons, and training. Hamas seized control of the Gaza Strip in 2007 and has since administered that territory, but it ceded formal authority over Gaza in June 2014 to a consensus Palestinian Authority (PA) government and turned over further authority to the PA as part of an October 2017 reconciliation agreement. Hamas terrorist attacks within Israel have decreased since 2005, but Hamas has used Iran-supplied rockets and other weaponry during three conflicts with Israel since 2008, the latest of which was in 2014. Smaller scale trading of rocket attacks and air strikes have taken place in the summer of 2018.

The Iran-Hamas relationship was forged in the 1990s as part of an apparent attempt to disrupt the Israeli-Palestinian peace process through Hamas attacks on buses,

[100] For more information, see CRS Report RL34074, *The Palestinians: Background and U.S. Relations*, by Jim Zanotti.

restaurants, and other civilian targets inside Israel. However, in 2012, their differing positions on the ongoing Syria conflict caused a rift. Largely out of sectarian sympathy with Sunni rebels in Syria, Hamas opposed the efforts by Asad to defeat the rebellion militarily. Iran reduced its support to Hamas in its brief 2014 conflict with Israel as compared to previous Hamas-Israel conflicts in which Iran backed Hamas extensively. Since then, Iran has apparently sought to rebuild the relationship by providing missile technology that Hamas used to construct its own rockets and by helping it rebuild tunnels destroyed in the conflict with Israel.[101] Hamas leaders restored the group's relations with Iran during a Hamas delegation visit to Tehran in October 2017.

Iranian Financial Support

Iran's support to Hamas has been estimated to be as high as $300 million per year (funds and in-kind support, including weapons) during periods of substantial Iran-Hamas collaboration,[102] but is widely assessed at a baseline amount in the tens of millions per year. The State Department's September 2018 "Outlaw Regime" report states that Iran "provides up to $100 million annually in combined support to Palestinian terrorist groups," including Hamas, PIJ, and the PFLP-GC.

Hezbollah

Lebanese Hezbollah, which Iranian leaders portray as successful "exportation" of Iran's Islamic revolution, is Iran's most significant nonstate ally. Hezbollah's actions to support its own as well as Iranian interests take many forms, including acts of terrorism and training and combat in countries in the region.[103] Recent State Department reports on international terrorism state that "the group generally follows the religious guidance of the Iranian Supreme Leader, which [is] [Grand Ayatollah] Ali Khamenei."[104]

Iran's close relationship to the group began when Lebanese Shia clerics of the pro-Iranian Lebanese Da'wa (Islamic Call) Party—many of whom had studied under the leader of Iran's revolution, Grand Ayatollah Ruhollah Khomeini—began to organize in 1982 into what later was unveiled in 1985 as Hezbollah. IRGC forces were sent to Lebanon to help develop a military wing, and these IRGC forces subsequently evolved into the IRGC-QF. The IRGC-QF and its commander, IRGC Major General Qasem Soleimani, have been designated for U.S. sanctions under Executive Order 13224.

Illustrating the degree to which Iranian assistance has helped Hezbollah become a potential global terrorism threat, the State Department report on international terrorism for 2016 repeated assertions that Hezbollah continues to be "capable of operating around

---

[101] Stuart Winer. "Iran Boasts of Rocket Aid to Palestinians, Hezbollah." *The Times of Israel*, February 3, 2015; and, http://www.wsj.com/articles/iran-rekindles-relations-with-hamas-1429658562.

[102] Robert Tait, "Iran Cuts Hamas Funding Over Syria." *Telegraph*, May 31, 2013.

[103] See Ben Hubbard. "Hezbollah Wields Rising Power as Iran's Enforcer." *New York Times*, August 28, 2017.

[104] Department of State. Bureau of Counterterrorism and Countering Violent Extremism. Country Reports on Terrorism: 2016.

the world." According to the State Department and many other assessments, Iran assisted Hezbollah to several terrorist attacks that are depicted in the table above.

Iranian leaders have long worked with Hezbollah as an instrument to pressure Israel. Hezbollah's attacks on Israeli forces in Israel's self-declared "security zone" in southern Lebanon contributed to an Israeli withdrawal from that territory in May 2000. Hezbollah fired Iranian-supplied rockets on Israel's northern towns and cities during the July-August 2006 war with Israel, and in July 2006 Hezbollah damaged an Israeli warship with a Chinese-made C-802 anti-ship missile of the type that Iran reportedly bought in significant quantity from China in the 1990s. Hezbollah's leadership asserted that it was victorious in that war for holding out against Israel.[105]

Hezbollah has become a major force in Lebanon's politics, in part due to the arms and funding it gets from Iran. Hezbollah now plays a major role in decisionmaking and leadership selections in Lebanon. Hezbollah's militia rivals the Lebanese Armed Forces (LAF). However, there has been vocal criticism of Hezbollah in and outside Lebanon for its support for Asad, which has diluted Hezbollah's image as a steadfast opponent of Israel and has embroiled it in war against other Muslims. In November 2017, the resignation of Prime Minister Sa'd Hariri appeared intended to expose and undermine Hezbollah's influence in Lebanon—a move he undertook immediately after close consultations with Riyadh. The resignation was rescinded by popular pressure in Lebanon and did not diminish Hezbollah's position. Hezbollah's allies increased their number of seats as a result of April 2018 parliamentary elections in Lebanon, although the number of seats held by Hezbollah itself stayed at the 13 it held previously.

Iranian Financial Support

Iranian financial support for the group probably fluctuates: Iran likely has provided high levels of aid to the group since its combat intervention in Syria and at times such as the 2006 Hezbollah war with Israel, whereas financial support likely wanes when the group is not involved in significant operations.[106] The State Department report for 2016 asserted that Iran provides "the majority of financial support for Hezbollah in Lebanon," and "has trained thousands of [Hezbollah] fighters at camps in Iran." The State Department report for 2015 contained a specific figure, stating that Iran has provided Hezbollah with "hundreds of millions of dollars."[107] However, on June 5, 2018, Under Secretary of the Treasury for Terrorism and Financial Intelligence Sigal Mandelker cited a figure of $700 million in Iranian support to Hezbollah per year[108]—far higher than specific figures previously cited in any U.S. official reports. The higher figure could

---

105 "Nasrallah Wins the War." *The Economist*, August 17, 2006.

106 Author conversations with various experts and U.S. officials in Washington, DC, 1985-2017.

107 Department of State. Bureau of Counterterrorism and Countering Violent Extremism. Country Reports on Terrorism; 2015.

108 Treasury Under Secretary for Terrorism and Financial Intelligence Sigal Mandelker Delivers Remarks at the Foundation for Defense of Democracies. CQ Newsmaker Transcripts. June 5, 2018.

represent a U.S. reassessment of its previous estimates, or perhaps reflect a large increase due to Hezbollah's extensive combat on various battlefronts in Syria. The State Department's September 2018 "Outlaw Regime" report repeats the $700 million figure.

Similarly, the number of IRGC-QF advisers working with Hezbollah has apparently fluctuated according to the operational level of activity of the group. In the early 1980s, Iran was widely reported to have a few thousand IRGC personnel helping to establish what became Hezbollah. More recently, Hezbollah has become more self-sufficient[109] and able to assist IRGC-QF operations elsewhere, such as in Syria, Iraq, and Yemen.[110] In Syria, the IRGC-QF has facilitated Hezbollah's extensive involvement on behalf of the Asad regime, whose continuation in power is in the interests of both Iran and Hezbollah. Syria is the key conduit through which the IRGC-QF has historically armed and assisted Hezbollah.

Regarding weapons transfers, the State Department report on international terrorism for 2016 says that, according to the Israeli government, since that conflict, Hezbollah has stockpiled more than 130,000 rockets and missiles,[111] presumably supplied mostly by Iran. Some are said to be capable of reaching Tel Aviv and other population centers in central Israel from south Lebanon. The State Department report adds that Israeli experts assert that Iran also has transferred to Hezbollah anti-ship and anti-aircraft capabilities.[112]

U.S. Policy to Reduce Iran's Support for Hezbollah

The Trump Administration has followed its predecessors in trying to disrupt the Iran-Hezbollah relationship, although without evident success. The United States has not acted against Hezbollah militarily, but it has publicly supported Israeli air strikes in Syria that are intended, at least in part, to disrupt Iranian weapons supplies to Hezbollah. In January 2015, apparently in response to one of these air strikes, Hezbollah attacked an Israeli military convoy near the Lebanon-Israel-Syria tri-border area, killing two Israeli soldiers, but the incident did not result in an escalation. The United States has imposed sanctions on Iranian entities involved in supplying Hezbollah as well as on Hezbollah and its related entities, although without apparent effect in light of the fact that such entities do not generally operate in the international financial or commercial system. Congress is considering additional legislation, including H.R. 3329 and S. 1595, what would seek to sever Hezbollah's access to the global financial system, although the effect of such sanctions might be minimal insofar as major international banks already shun Hezbollah.

---

[109] Ibid.
[110] Ben Hubbard. *New York Times*, op. cit.
[111] State Department terrorism report for 2016, op. cit.
[112] Ibid.

Yemen[113]

Iranian leaders have not generally identified Yemen as a core Iranian security interest, but Iranian leaders appear to perceive Yemen's instability as an opportunity to acquire additional leverage against Saudi Arabia and U.S. interests. A 2011 "Arab Spring"-related uprising in Yemen forced longtime President Ali Abdullah Saleh to resign in January 2012. Iran reportedly assisted the Zaydi Shiite revivalist movement known as the "Houthis" (Ansar Allah) in its seizure of the capital, Sana'a that forced Saleh's successor, Abd Rabu Mansur Al Hadi, to flee. In March 2015, Saudi Arabia assembled an Arab coalition that, with logistical help from U.S. forces, has recaptured some territory lost to the Houthis but not yet achieved a political solution to the conflict there.[114]

The increasingly sophisticated nature of Iran's support for the Houthis could suggest that Iran perceives the Houthis as a potential proxy to project power on the southwestern coast of the Arabian Peninsula. Iranian weapons shipments to the Houthis are banned by Resolution 2231 on Iran and also by Resolution 2216 on Yemen, discussed above. The State Department's "Outlaw Regime" report cites press reports that Iran might have sent some militia forces from Syria to fight alongside the Houthis in Yemen.

A July 2016 report on Iran by the U.N. Secretary-General reiterated the assertion[115] made previously by U.N. experts, that Iran has shipped arms to the Houthis. Among the systems Iran is providing are anti-ship cruise missiles that are of increasing concern to U.S. commanders. The Houthis fired anti-ship missiles at UAE and U.S. ships in the Red Sea in October 2016, and which prompted U.S. strikes on Houthi-controlled radar installations. Iran subsequently deployed several warships to the Yemen seacoast as an apparent sign of support for the Houthis. In January 2017, the Houthis damaged a Saudi ship in the Red Sea—an action that contributed to the February 1, 2017, Trump Administration statement putting Iran "on notice" for its regional malign activities. The degree of U.S. concern about Iran's supplies of missiles to the Houthis was reflected in U.S. CENTCOM commander General Joseph Votel's March 29, 2017, testimony before the House Armed Services Committee, referring to the Bab el-Mandeb Strait:

> It is a choke point, it is a major transit area for commerce, not only ours but for international ships. About 60 to 70 ships go through there a day. What we have seen, I believe, that the— with the support of Iran, we have seen the migration of capabilities that we previously observed in the Straits of Hormuz, a layered defense, consists of coastal defense missiles and radar systems, mines, explosive boats that have been migrated from

---

[113] For more information, see CRS Report R43960, *Yemen: Civil War and Regional Intervention*, by Jeremy M. Sharp.

[114] Ali al-Mujahed and Hugh Naylor. "Yemen Rebels Defy Saudi-led Attacks." *Washington Post*, March 28, 2015.

[115] Report of the Secretary-General on the Implementation of Security Council Resolution 2231 (2015). U.N. Document Number S/2016/589, July 12, 2016.

the Straits of Hormuz to this particular area right here, threatening commerce and ships and our security operations in that particular area.

Saudi Arabia, with U.S. and some U.N. backing, accuses Iran of providing the ballistic missiles that the Houthis have fired on Riyadh on several occasions. A December 8, 2017, report by the U.N. Secretary-General on implementation of Resolution 2231 generally supports those allegations as well as allegations that Iran had shipped other weapons to the Houthis.[116] U.S. Ambassador to the U.N. Nikki Haley cited that report in a December 14, 2017, presentation to the Security Council that asserted definitively that Iran had given the Houthis the missiles fired on Riyadh.[117] A report by a U.N. panel of experts in January 2018 reportedly found that two missiles fired on Saudi Arabia by the Houthis, on July 22 and November 4, 2017, were consistent with the design of Iranian missiles,[118] but the panel did not state definitively who supplied the missiles or how they were transported to Yemen. In late February 2018, Russia blocked a U.N. Security Council resolution from identifying Iran directly as a violator of the U.N. ban on weapons shipments to Yemen (Resolution 2216). Iran has denied providing the Houthis with missiles and assert that they are from a government arsenal assembled before the 2011 civil strife.

Financial Support

Many observers assess that Iran's support for the Houthis has been modest. However, the State Department's "Outlaw Regime" report states that since 2012, Iran "has spent hundreds of millions of dollars" aiding the Houthis.

U.S. Policy to Counter Iranian Influence in Yemen

In his May 21, 2018, speech, Secretary Pompeo stipulated as one U.S. demand on Iran that the country "must also end its military support for the Houthi militia and work towards a peaceful political settlement in Yemen." The United States has sought to prevent Iran from delivering weapons to the Houthis by conducting joint naval patrols with members of the Saudi-led coalition. Some weapons shipments have been intercepted. Some reports indicate that, to evade the naval scrutiny, Iran has been transferring its weapons deliveries to a variety of small boats in the northern Persian Gulf, from where they sail to Yemen.[119] The United States also is increasing its assistance to Oman to train its personnel to prevent smuggling through its territory, presumably including the smuggling of Iranian weaponry to the Houthis. U.S. forces have not

---

[116] Fourth Report of the Secretary-General on the Implementation of Security Council Resolution 2231 (2015). S/2017/1030. December 8, 2017.

[117] http://foreignpolicy.com/2017/12/14/nikki-haley-yemen-houthi-rebels-iran-missiles-press-conference-pentagon-skepticism-united-nations-trump-nuclear-deal-diplomacy/.

[118] https://www.washingtonpost.com/world/un-probe-details-fallout-of-proxy-war-in-yemen-between-saudi-coalitionand-iran-/2018/01/11/3e3f9302-f644-11e7-9af7-a50bc3300042_story.html.

[119] https://www.reuters.com/article/us-gulf-kuwait-iran-exclusive-idUSKBN1AH4I4.

engaged in any bombing of the Houthis or Iranian advisers in Yemen, although U.S. forces continue to operate on the ground in Yemen against the Al Qaeda in the Arabian Peninsula (AQAP) terrorist group that operates in southeastern Yemen.

Turkey[120]

Iran and Turkey, which share a short border, have extensive economic relations but sometimes tense political relations. Turkey is a member of NATO, and Iran has sought to limit Turkey's cooperation with any NATO plan to emplace military technology near Iran's borders. Iran and Turkey's disputes on some regional issues might be caused, at least in part, by the sectarian differences between Sunni-inhabited Turkey and Shiite Iran. Turkey has advocated Asad's ouster as part of a solution for conflict-torn Syria whereas Iran is a key supporter of Asad. However, following a failed Turkish military coup in July 2016, and mutual concerns over the empowerment of Syrian Kurdish forces, Turkey-Iran differences narrowed. Turkey's President Recep Tayip Erdogan has come to publicly accept that Asad might remain in power in Syria and both countries are integral part of Russia-led talks on an overall political solution for Syria. Iran and Turkey cooperate to try to halt cross border attacks by Kurdish groups that oppose the governments of Turkey (Kurdistan Workers' Party, PKK) and of Iran (Free Life Party, PJAK), and which enjoy safe have in northern Iraq. In August 2017, the first high-level Iranian military visit to Turkey since the Iranian revolution took place when the chief of staff of Iran's joint military headquarters, Hamid Baqeri, who rose through IRGC ranks, visited Ankara.

Turkey supported the JCPOA, and sanctions relief on Iran has enabled Iran-Turkey trade to expand. Iran supplies as much as 50% of Turkey's oil and over 5% of its natural gas, the latter flowing through a joint pipeline that began operations in the late 1990s and has since been supplemented by an additional line. President Erdogan has indicated that Turkey will not cooperate with the reimposition of sanctions on Iran related to the U.S. exit from the JCPOA.

In the 1990s and early 2000s, Iran and Turkey were at odds over the strategic engagement of Turkey's then leaders with Israel. The Iran-Turkey dissonance on the issue faded after Erdogan's Islamist-rooted Justice and Development Party (AKP) came to power in Turkey. Turkey has since been a significant supporter of Hamas and other Islamist movements.

---

[120] For analysis on Turkey's foreign policy and U.S. relations, see CRS Report R44000, *Turkey: Background and U.S. Relations In Brief*, by Jim Zanotti.

North Africa

Two countries in North Africa, Egypt and Morocco, have been mentioned as potential members of the planned "Middle East Strategic Alliance" (MESA) to counter Iran.

Egypt[121]

Iran's relations with Egypt have been strained for decades, spanning various Egyptian regimes. Egypt is a Sunni-dominated state that is aligned politically and strategically with other Sunni governments that are critical of Iran. Iran broke relations with Egypt shortly after the 1979 peace treaty Egypt signed with Israel. The two countries reportedly have been close to reestablishing full relations numerous times, including after the election of a Muslim Brotherhood leader, Mohammad Morsi, as Egypt's president. Morsi visited Iran in August 2012. However, relations worsened again after the military's overthrow of the Morsi government. Egypt, particularly under the government of President Abd al Fattah Sisi, views Hamas as an Islamist threat and has sought to choke off Iranian and other weapons supplies to that movement. On the other hand, Egypt and Iran have found some common ground on Syria insofar as Sisi has not sought Asad's ouster.

Morocco[122]

In May 2018, Morocco announced that it would sever diplomatic ties with Iran because of alleged Iranian support (via its ally Lebanese Hezbollah) for the Polisario Front, which seeks independence for the Western Sahara.[123] Morocco's foreign minister claimed that Hezbollah had provided surface-to-air missiles to the Polisario; that evidence was reportedly presented to Iran but has not been made public. No other publicly available evidence appears to support of those specific allegations, and both Iran and Hezbollah denied the accusations. Morocco previously cut ties with Iran in March 2009 due to alleged Iranian efforts to spread Shiism in largely Sunni Morocco; diplomatic relations were reestablished in January 2017. Morocco has close relations with Saudi Arabia, which supported Morocco's severing ties with Iran.

An intent to be part of the MESA coalition could give Morocco incentive to be as hardline on Iran as possible, and potential to accuse Iran of activities for which there might not be a lot of independently corroborated evidence. There has been little, if any, evidence that influencing politics or political outcomes in Morocco has been a significant feature of Iran's regional policies or its intent. Iranian leaders rarely, if ever, mention

---

[121] For comprehensive analysis on Egypt, see: CRS Report RL33003, *Egypt: Background and U.S. Relations*, by Jeremy M. Sharp.

[122] For comprehensive analysis on Morocco, see: CRS Report RS21579, *Morocco: Current Issues*, by Alexis Arieff.

[123] Al Jazeera, may 1, 2018. https://www.aljazeera.com/news/2018/05/morocco-cuts-diplomatic-ties-iran-western-sahara-feud-180501173229190.html.

Morocco when they outline Iranian policy in the Middle East region. In part this might be because there are few easily identifiable factions in Morocco that are pro-Iranian or with which the IRGC-QF can work.

SOUTH AND CENTRAL ASIA

Iran's relations with countries in the Caucasus, Central Asia, and South Asia vary significantly, but most countries in these regions conduct relatively normal trade and diplomacy with Iran. Some of them face significant domestic threats from radical Sunni Islamist extremist movements similar to those that Iran characterizes as a threat.

Most of the Central Asia states that were part of the Soviet Union are governed by authoritarian leaders. Afghanistan remains politically weak, and Iran is able to exert influence there. Some countries in the region, particularly India, seek greater integration with the United States and other world powers and tend to downplay cooperation with Iran. The following sections address countries that have significant economic and political relationships with Iran.

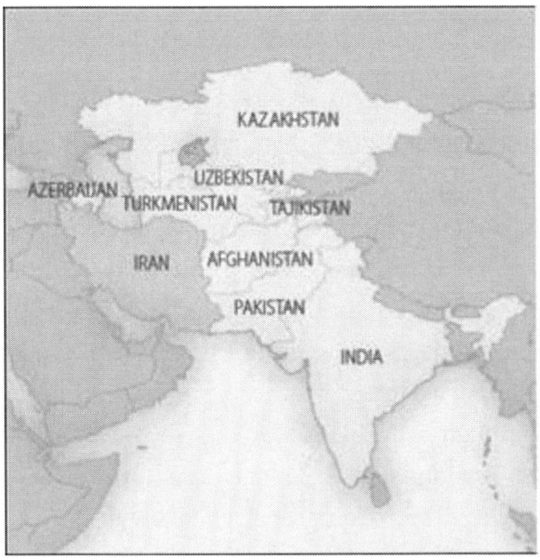

Source: Created by CRS.

Figure 3. South and Central Asia Region.

The South Caucasus: Azerbaijan and Armenia

Azerbaijan is, like Iran, mostly Shiite Muslim-inhabited. However, Azerbaijan is ethnically Turkic and its leadership is secular. Iran and Azerbaijan also have territorial differences over boundaries in the Caspian Sea. Iran asserts that Azeri nationalism might stoke separatism among Iran's large Azeri Turkic population, which has sometimes been restive. Iran has generally tilted toward Armenia, which is Christian, in Armenia's conflict with Azerbaijan over the Nagorno-Karabakh enclave. The relationship is expanding among Iran, Armenia, and Georgia now that Iran is not under international economic sanctions. On December 21, 2016, President Rouhani visited Armenia to discuss a Persian Gulf-Black Sea transit and transport corridor.[124]

For more than two decades, Azerbaijan has engaged in strategic cooperation with the United States against Iran (and Russia), including Azerbaijan's deployments of troops to and facilitation of supply routes to Afghanistan,[125] and counterterrorism cooperation. In the 1990s, the United States successfully backed construction of the Baku-Tblisi-Ceyhan oil pipeline, intended in part to provide non-Iranian and non-Russian export routes. On the other hand, the United States has accepted Azerbaijan's need to deal with Iran on some major regional energy projects. Several U.S. sanctions laws exempted from sanctions long-standing joint natural gas projects that involve some Iranian firms—particularly the Shah Deniz natural gas field and pipeline in the Caspian Sea. The project is run by a consortium in which Iran's Naftiran Intertrade Company (NICO) holds a passive 10% share. (Other major partners are BP, Azerbaijan's national energy firm SOCAR, and Russia's Lukoil.)[126]

The lifting of sanctions on Iran has caused Azerbaijan to alter its policy toward Iran somewhat. In August 2016, Azerbaijan's President Ilham Aliyev hosted Rouhani and Russia's President Vladimir Putin to a "Baku Summit," in which a major topic was a long-discussed "North-South Transport Corridor" involving rail, road, and shipping infrastructure from Russia to Iran, through Azerbaijan. The project is estimated to cost $400 million. And, some press reports indicate that Iranian investors previously or still linked to Iranian governing institutions have engaged in real estate and other projects in Azerbaijan.

Central Asia

Iran has generally sought positive relations with the leaderships of the Central Asian states, even though most of these leaderships are secular and all of the Central Asian states are mostly Sunni inhabited. Almost all of the Central Asian states share a common language and culture with Turkey; Tajikistan is alone among them in sharing a language with Iran. Several have active Sunni Islamist opposition movements, such as the Islamic

---

[124] http://www.tehrantimes.com/news/409363/Iran-Armenia-discuss-Persian-Gulf-Black-Sea-corridor.
[125] http://foreignpolicynews.org/2014/04/10/azerbaijans-strategic-relations-united-states/.
[126] For more information, see CRS Report RS20871, *Iran Sanctions*, by Kenneth Katzman.

Movement of Uzbekistan (IMU),[127] giving the Central Asian countries common cause with Iran to prevent Sunni jihadist terrorist actions. The IMU, which is active in Afghanistan, in mid-2015, declared its loyalty to the Islamic State organization.[128]

Iran and the Central Asian states are expanding economic relations, perhaps in part to fit into China's "One Belt, One Road" initiative to build up infrastructure in countries west of China— akin to reviving the old "Silk Road. In December 2014, a new railway was inaugurated through Iran, Kazakhstan, and Turkmenistan, providing a link from the Persian Gulf to Central Asia.[129] And, the lifting of sanctions could position Iran as central to energy and transportation routes linking East Asia with Europe, a vision that was discussed with Iranian leaders during the January 2016 visit to Iran of China's President Xi Jinping.

Along with India and Pakistan, Iran has been given observer status in a Central Asian security grouping called the Shanghai Cooperation Organization (SCO—Russia, China, Kazakhstan, Kyrgyzstan, Uzbekistan, and Tajikistan). In April 2008, Iran applied for full membership in the organization. Apparently in an effort to cooperate with international efforts to pressure Iran, in June 2010, the SCO barred admission to Iran on the grounds that it is under U.N. Security Council sanctions.[130] Some officials from SCO member countries have stated that the the JCPOA removes that formal obstacles to Iran's obtaining full membership, but opposition to Iran's full membership among some SCO countries has denied Iran from full membership, to date. Rouhani attended the late May 2018 SCO meeting in China which, among other issues, reportedly discussed how to react to the May 8, 2018, U.S. exit from the JCPOA.[131]

Turkmenistan

Turkmenistan and Iran have a land border in Iran's northeast. Supreme Leader Khamene'i is of Turkic origin; his family has close ties to the Iranian city of Mashhad, capital of Khorasan Province, which borders Turkmenistan. The two countries are also both rich in natural gas reserves. A natural gas pipeline from Iran to Turkey, fed with Turkmenistan's gas, began operations in 1997, and a second pipeline was completed in 2010. Turkmenistan still exports some natural gas through the Iran-Turkey gas pipeline, but China has since become Turkmenistan's largest natural gas customer.

---

[127] Sebastien Peyrouse. "Iran's Growing Role in Central Asia? Geopolitical, Economic, and Political Profit and Loss Account. Al Jazeera Center for Studies. April 6, 2014. http://studies.aljazeera.net/en/dossiers/2014/04/2014416940377354.html.

[128] Stratfor. "Re-Examining the Threat of Central Asian Militancy" January 21, 2015. http://www.stratfor.com/analysis/ re-examining-threat-central-asian-militancy#axzz3PTRMU0el.

[129] http://www.railwaygazette.com/news/news/asia/single-view/view/iran-turkmenistan-kazakhstan-rail-link-inaugurated.html.

[130] Substantially more detail on Iran's activities in Afghanistan is contained in CRS Report RL30588, *Afghanistan: Post-Taliban Governance, Security, and U.S. Policy*, by Kenneth Katzman.

[131] https://www.financialexpress.com/defence/sco-summit-2018-china-to-host-hassan-rouhani-amid-iran-nuclear-dealupheaval/1183681/.

Another potential project favored by Turkmenistan and the United States would likely reduce interest in pipelines that transit Iran. President Berdymukhamedov has revived his predecessor's 1996 proposal to build a gas pipeline through Afghanistan to Pakistan and India (termed the Turkmenistan-Afghanistan-Pakistan-India, or "TAPI" pipeline). In August 2015, Turkmenistan's state-owned gas company was named head of the pipeline consortium and Turkmenistan officials said the project was formally inaugurated in December 2015,[132] with completion expected in 2019. U.S. officials have expressed strong support for the project as "a very positive step forward and sort of a key example of what we're seeking with our New Silk Road Initiative, which aims at regional integration to lift all boats and create prosperity across the region."[133]

Tajikistan

Iran and Tajikistan share a common Persian language, as well as literary and cultural ties. Despite the similar ethnicity, the two do not share a border and the population of Tajikistan is mostly Sunni. President Imamali Rakhmonov has asserted that Iran and Tajikistan face common threats from arms races, international terrorism, political extremism, fundamentalism, separatism, drug trafficking, transnational organized crime, [and] the proliferation of weapons of mass destruction" and that close ties with neighboring states such as Iran would be based on noninterference in each other's internal affairs and the peaceful settlement of disputes, such as over border, water, and energy issues.[134] He indicated intent to expand relations with Iran, but few if any joint projects have materialized.

Some Sunni Islamist extremist groups that pose a threat to Tajikistan are allied with Al Qaeda or the Islamic State. Tajikistan's leaders appear particularly concerned about Islamist movements in part because the Islamist-led United Tajik Opposition posed a serious threat to the newly independent government in the early 1990s, and a settlement of the insurgency in the late 1990s did not fully resolve government-Islamist opposition tensions. The Tajikistan government has detained members of Jundallah (Warriors of Allah)—a Pakistan-based Islamic extremist group that has conducted bombings and attacks against Iranian security personnel and mosques in Sunni areas of eastern Iran. In part because the group attacked some civilian targets in Iran, in November 2010, the State Department named the group an FTO.

Kazakhstan

Kazakhstan, one of the seemingly more stable Central Asian states, is a significant power by virtue of its geographic location, large territory, and ample natural resources. It hosted a round of P5+1-Iran nuclear negotiations in 2013. In September 2014,

---

[132] http://www.reuters.com/article/2015/09/15/turkmenistan-pipeline-idUSL5N11L0RE20150915.
[133] State Department, Daily Press Briefing, May 23, 2012.
[134] Center for Effective Dispute Resolution (CEDR), March 16, 2013, Doc. No. CEL-54015758.

Kazakhstan's President Nursultan Nazarbayev held talks with President Rouhani and expressed the hope that a JCPOA would be achieved in order to better integrate economically into the Central Asian region.[135] Kazakhstan played a role in the commercial arrangements that produced the late December 2015 shipment out to Russia of almost all of Iran's stockpile of low-enriched uranium, an action that fulfilled a key JCPOA requirement. Kazakhstan's National Atomic Company Kazatomprom supplied Iran with 60 metric tons of natural uranium on commercial terms as compensation for the removal of the material, which Norway paid for.

With sanctions eased, Iran is open to additional opportunities to cooperate with Kazakhstan on energy and infrastructure projects. Kazakhstan possesses 30 billion barrels of proven oil reserves (about 2% of world reserves) and 45.7 trillion cubic feet of proven gas reserves (less than 1% of world reserves). Two major offshore oil fields in Kazakhstan's sector of the Caspian Sea— Kashagan and Kurmangazy—are estimated to contain at least 14 billion barrels of recoverable reserves. Iran and Kazakhstan do not have any joint energy ventures in the Caspian or elsewhere, but after the finalization of the JCPOA in July 2015, the two countries resumed Caspian oil swap arrangements that were discontinued in 2011.[136] The two countries are not at odds over specific sections of the Caspian Sea, but the territorial arrangements of the Caspian are not settled.[137]

Uzbekistan

During the 1990s, Uzbekistan, which has the largest military of the Central Asian states, identified Iran as a potential regional rival and as a supporter of Islamist movements in the region. However, since 1999, Uzbekistan and Iran—which do not share a common border or significant language or cultural links—have moved somewhat closer over shared stated concerns about Sunni Islamist extremist movements, particularly the Islamic Movement of Uzbekistan (IMU) extremist group. In February 1999, six bomb blasts in Tashkent's governmental area nearly killed then President Islam Karimov, who was expected to attend a high-level meeting there. The government alleged that the plot was orchestrated by the IMU with assistance from Afghanistan's Taliban, which was in power in Afghanistan and hosting Osama bin Laden. In September 2000, the State Department designated the IMU as an FTO.[138] The IMU itself has not claimed responsibility for any terrorist attacks in Iran and appears focused primarily on activities against the governments of Afghanistan and Uzbekistan.

Iran-Uzbekistan relations have not changed significantly since the August 2016 death of Uzbekistan's longtime President Islam Karimov and his replacement by Shavkat Mirziyoyev, who was at the time the Prime Minister. Uzbekistan has substantial natural

---

[135] http://english.farsnews.com/newstext.aspx?nn=13930618000811.
[136] http://en.mehrnews.com/news/109439/Kazakhstan-to-resume-oil-swap-with-Iran.
[137] http://www.eurasianet.org/node/79761.
[138] http://www.state.gov/j/ct/rls/crt/2001/html/10252.htm#imu.

gas resources but it and Iran do not have joint energy-related ventures. Most of Uzbekistan's natural gas production is for domestic consumption.

South Asia

The countries in South Asia face perhaps a greater degree of threat from Sunni Islamic extremist groups than do the countries of Central Asia. They also share significant common interests with Iran, which Iran used to foster cooperation against U.S. sanctions. This section focuses on several countries in South Asia that have substantial interaction with Iran.

Afghanistan

In Afghanistan, Iran is pursuing a multi-track strategy by helping develop Afghanistan economically, engaging the central government, supporting pro-Iranian groups and, at times, arming Taliban fighters. An Iranian goal appears to be to restore some of its traditional sway in eastern, central, and northern Afghanistan, where "Dari"-speaking (Dari is akin to Persian) supporters of the "Northern Alliance" grouping of non-Pashtun Afghan minorities predominate. Iran shares with the Afghan government concern about the growth of Islamic State affiliates in Afghanistan, such as Islamic State—Khorasan Province, ISKP, an affiliate of the Islamic State organization that Iran is trying to thwart on numerous fronts in the region. The two countries are said to be cooperating effectively in their shared struggle against narcotics trafficking. President Ghani and Iranian leaders meet periodically.[139]

Iran has sought influence in Afghanistan in part by supporting the Afghan government, which is dominated by Sunni Muslims and ethnic Pashtuns. In October 2010, then-President Hamid Karzai admitted that Iran was providing cash payments (about $2 million per year) to his government.[140] It is not known whether such payments continue. Iran's ally, Dr. Abdullah Abdullah, who is halfTajik and speaks Dari, is "Chief Executive Officer" of the Afghan government under a power-sharing arrangement with President Ashraf Ghani that followed the 2014 presidential election.

Even though it engages the Afghan government, Tehran has in the recent past sought leverage against U.S. forces in Afghanistan and in any Taliban-Afghan government peace settlement. Past State Department reports on international terrorism have accused Iran of providing materiel support, including 107mm rockets, to select Taliban and other militants in Afghanistan, and of training Taliban fighters in small unit tactics, small arms

---

[139] "Afghanistan, Iran to Work together Against "Macabre" IS Threat." RFE/RL, April 22, 2015.

[140] Dexter Filkins. "Iran Is Said to Give Top Karzai Aide Cash by the Bagful." *New York Times*, October 23, 2010.

use, explosives, and indirect weapons fire.[141] In July 2012, Iran allowed the Taliban to open an office in Zahedan (eastern Iran).[142] In December 2016, Iran invited several Taliban figures to an "Islamic Unity" conference in Tehran. Reflecting apparent concern about the U.S. military presence in Afghanistan, Iran reportedly tried to derail the U.S.-Afghanistan Bilateral Security Agreement (BSA), signed in September 2014, that allowed the United States to maintain troops in Afghanistan after 2014. It prohibits the United States from launching military action against other countries from Afghanistan. In his May 21, 2018, speech, Secretary Pompeo demanded that "Iran, too, must end support for the Taliban and other terrorists in Afghanistan and the region, and cease harboring senior Al Qaeda leaders."

Purported Iranian support to Taliban factions comes despite the fact that Iran saw the Taliban regime in Afghanistan of 1996-2001 as an adversary. The Taliban allegedly committed atrocities against Shiite Afghans (Hazara tribes) while seizing control of Persian-speaking areas of western and northern Afghanistan. Taliban fighters killed nine Iranian diplomats at Iran's consulate in Mazar-e-Sharif in August 1998, prompting Iran to mobilize ground forces to the Afghan border.

Pakistan[143]

Relations between Iran and Pakistan have been uneven. Pakistan supported Iran in the 1980-1988 Iran-Iraq War, and Iran and Pakistan engaged in substantial military cooperation in the early 1990s, and the two still conduct some military cooperation, such as joint naval exercises in April 2014. The founder of Pakistan's nuclear weapons program, A.Q. Khan, sold nuclear technology and designs to Iran.[144] However, a rift emerge between the two countries in the 1990s because Pakistan's support for the Afghan Taliban ran counter to Iran's support for the Persian-speaking and Shiite Muslim minorities who opposed Taliban rule. Iran reportedly is concerned that Pakistan might harbor ambitions of returning the Taliban movement to power in Afghanistan.[145] In addition, two Iranian Sunni Muslim militant groups that attack Iranian regime targets—*Jundullah* (named by the United States as an FTO, as discussed above) and Jaysh al-Adl— operate from western Pakistan.

A significant factor dividing them is Pakistan's relationship with Saudi Arabia. Pakistan declined a Saudi request that Pakistan participation in the Saudi-led coalition against the Houthis in Yemen, but Pakistan joined Saudi Arabia's 34-nation "anti-terrorism coalition" in December 2015. The coalition was announced as a response to the

---

141 State Department, Country Reports on International Terrorism: 2011. http://www.state.gov/j/ct/rls/crt/2011/195547.htm.

142 Maria Abi-Habib, "Tehran Builds On Outreach to Taliban," *Wall Street Journal*, August 1, 2012.

143 For detail on Pakistan's foreign policy and relations with the United States, see CRS Report R41832, *Pakistan-U.S. Relations*, by K. Alan Kronstadt.

144 John Lancaster and Kamran Khan, "Pakistanis Say Nuclear Scientists Aided Iran," *Washington Post*, January 24, 2004.

145 Author conversations with experts in Washington, DC, who consult with Iranian government officials. 2013-15.

Islamic State, but Iran asserts it is directed at reducing Iran's regional influence. In January 2017, the former Chief of Army Staff of Pakistan, Raheel Sharif, was appointed military commander of that coalition—an appointment that clearly signaled further Pakistani tilt toward Saudi Arabia. Experts have speculated that if Saudi Arabia sought to counter Iran's nuclear program with one of its own, the prime source of technology for the Saudi program would be Pakistan.

The two nations' bilateral agenda has increasingly focused on a joint major gas pipeline project that would ease Pakistan's energy shortages while providing Iran an additional customer for its large natural gas reserves. As originally conceived, the line would continue on to India, but India withdrew from the project at its early stages. Then-President of Iran Ahmadinejad and Pakistan's then-President Asif Ali Zardari formally inaugurated the project in March 2013. Iran has completed the line on its side of the border, but Pakistan was unable to finance the project on its side of the border until China agreed in April 2015 to build the pipeline at a cost of about $2 billion.[146] U.S. officials stated that the project could be subject to U.S. sanctions under the Iran Sanctions Act,[147] which will take effect again by November 4, 2018. There is little evident movement on the pipeline as of March 2018.

India[148]

India and Iran have overlapping histories and civilizations, and they are aligned on several strategic issues. Tens of millions of India's citizens are Shiite Muslims. Both countries have historically supported minority factions in Afghanistan that are generally at odds with Afghanistan's dominant Pashtun community.

As international sanctions on Iran increased in 2010-2013, India sought to preserve its longstanding ties with Iran while cooperating with the sanctions regime. In 2010, India's central bank ceased using a Tehran-based regional body, the Asian Clearing Union, to handle transactions with Iran. In January 2012, Iran agreed to accept India's local currency, the rupee, to settle nearly half of its sales to India. During 2011-2015, India reduced its purchases of Iranian oil—at some cost to its own development—in order to receive from the U.S. Administration exemptions from sanctions. India has increased oil purchases from Iran to nearly pre-2012 levels after sanctions were lifted, and in May 2016 India agreed to transfer to Iran about $6.5 billion that it owed for Iranian oil shipments but which was held up for payment due to sanctions. India's position has generally been that it will only enforce sanctions authorized by U.N. Security Council resolutions, rendering it likely that India will resist U.S. efforts to

---

[146] http://economictimes.indiatimes.com/news/international/world-news/china-to-build-pakistan-iran-gas-pipeline-pakistan-government/articleshow/46867932.cms.

[147] http://www.thenational.ae/business/energy/big-powers-block-iran-pakistan-gas-pipeline-plans.

[148] For detail on India's foreign policy and relations with the United States, see CRS Report R42823, *India-U.S. Security Relations: Current Engagement*, by K. Alan Kronstadt and Sonia Pinto.

compel it to comply with reimposed U.S. sanctions such as those that mandate cuts in oil purchases from Iran.

Some projects India has pursued in Iran involve not only economic issues but national strategy. India has long sought to develop Iran's Chabahar port, which would give India direct access to Afghanistan and Central Asia without relying on transit routes through Pakistan. India had hesitated to move forward on that project because of U.S. opposition to projects that benefit Iran. India has said that the implementation of JCPOA sanctions relief in January 2016 paved the way for work to begin in earnest on the Chabahar project. India, Iran, and Afghanistan held a ceremony in May 2016 to herald the start of work on the port based on an Indian pledge of a $500 million investment in it, with Iran to provide the remaining $500 million. Work was slowed by the difficulty equipment suppliers had in obtaining financing for the project, a consequence of hesitancy among banks about whether the United States might still try to sanction the project.[149] However, on December 3, 2017, Iran inaugurated the $1 billion expansion of Chabahar. During a visit to India in June 2018, U.S. Ambassador to the United Nations Nikki Haley said the Administration might consider providing exemptions to U.S. sanctions to enable the Chabahar work to continue because the project is vital to Afghanistan's development and reducing its dependence on Pakistan.[150] India has begun shipping wheat to Afghanistan through this new port. During Rouhani's visit to India in February 2018, in which he and India's Prime Minister Narendra Modi signed memoranda outlining future expanded energy cooperation.

In large part because of distrust between India and Pakistan, in 2009, India withdrew from the Iran-Pakistan gas pipeline project asserting it had concerns about the security of the pipeline, the location at which the gas would be transferred to India, pricing of the gas, and transit tariffs. During economic talks in July 2010, Iranian and Indian officials reportedly raised the issue of constructing a subsea natural gas pipeline, which would bypass Pakistani territory.[151]

During the late 1990s, U.S. officials expressed concern about India-Iran military-to-military ties. The relationship included visits to India by Iranian naval personnel, although India said these exchanges involved junior personnel and focused mainly on promoting interpersonal relations and not on India's provision to Iran of military expertise. The military relationship between the countries has withered in recent years.

---

[149] http://economictimes.indiatimes.com/industry/transportation/shipping-/-transport/india-slow-to-develop-chabaharport-as-china-races-ahead-at-rival-hub/articleshow/54693856.cms; https://www.reuters.com/article/us-india-iran-portsidUSKBN19024M.

[150] U.S. Envoy Haley Tells Modi Important to Cut Imports of Iranian Oil. Reuters, June 27, 2018.

[151] http://www.thehindu.com/news/international/world/iran-backs-deepsea-gas-pipeline-to-india/article5466999.ece.

RUSSIA

Iran attaches significant weight to its relations with Russia—a permanent member of the U.N. Security Council, a supplier of arms to Iran, a party to the JCPOA, and a key ally supporting the Asad regime. Russia appears to view Iran as a de facto ally in combating Sunni Islamist extremist movements, which have conducted attacks in Russia. Russian President Vladimir Putin visited Iran on November 23, 2015, to attend a conference of major international natural gas producers, and also held talks with Supreme Leader Khamene'i and President Rouhani, resulting in an announcement of a $5 billion line of credit to Iran for possible joint projects, including additional natural gas pipelines, railroads, and power plants.[152] Rouhani visited Moscow on March 28, 2017, to discuss with President Putin the issues discussed below. During Putin's visit to Tehran on November 1, 2017, the two countries agreed to collaborate on "strategic energy deals" valued at about $30 billion.[153] Russia opposed the U.S. exit from the JCPOA and has said it would not cooperate with reimposed U.S. secondary sanctions on Iran.

U.S. officials express concern primarily with Iran-Russia military cooperation, particularly in Syria. Russia-Iran cooperation has been pivotal to the Asad regime's recapture of much of rebel-held territory since 2015. Yet, the two countries' interests do not align precisely in Syria because Iranian leaders express far greater concern about protecting Hezbollah in any post-Asad regime than do leaders of Russia, whose interests appear to center on preserving the Asad regime and on Russia's overall presence in the Middle East. In August 2016, Iran briefly allowed Russia to stage bombing runs in Syria from a base in western Iran, near the city of Hamadan. The Russian use of the base ran counter to Iran's constitution, which bans foreign use of Iran's military facilities, and Iran subsequently ended the arrangement after Russia publicized it.

Russia has been Iran's main supplier of conventional weaponry and a significant supplier of missile-related technology. In February 2016, Iran's Defense Minister Hosein Dehgan visited Moscow reportedly to discuss purchasing Su-30 combat aircraft, T-90 tanks, helicopters, and other defense equipment. Under Resolution 2231, selling such gear would require Security Council approval, and U.S. officials have said publicly they would not support such a sale. Russia previously has abided by all U.N. sanctions to the point of initially cancelling a contract to sell Iran the advanced S-300 air defense system—even though Resolution 1929, which banned most arms sales to Iran, did not specifically ban the sale of the S-300. After the April 2, 2015, framework nuclear accord was announced, Russia lifted its ban on the S-300 sale. Russia has shipped the system,

---

152 "Russian President Putin, Iran's Ayatollah Khamenei Meet to Discuss Syria." *Wall Street Journal*, November 23, 2015.

153 "Russia and Iran Sign $30 bn Energy Agreements." *Financial Times*, November 1, 2017.

and Iran has begun deploying and testing it. In January 2015, Iran and Russia signed a memorandum of understanding on defense cooperation, including military drills.[154]

Russia built and still supplies fuel for Iran's only operating civilian nuclear power reactor at Bushehr, a project from which Russia earns significant revenues. In December 2015, Russia was the end destination of the shipment out of Iran of almost all of Iran's stockpile of low-enriched uranium—helping Iran meet a key requirement of the JCPOA.

EUROPE

U.S. and European approaches on Iran converged during 2006-2017 because of shared concerns about Iran's nuclear program. Prior to that time, European countries expressed only modest concern about Iran's policies and were reluctant to sanction it. After the passage of Resolution 1929 in June 2010, European Union (EU) sanctions on Iran became nearly as extensive as those of the United States.[155] In 2012, the EU banned imports of Iranian crude oil and natural gas. In concert with the JCPOA, the EU lifted nearly all of its sanctions on Iran and numerous European businesses resumed their relationships with Iran.[156] The EU opposed the U.S. exit from the JCPOA and are discussing ways in which to continue providing Iran with the economic benefits from the JCPOA and thereby hopefully persuade it to remain in the accord.[157]

Iran has always maintained full diplomatic relations with the EU countries, although relations have sometimes been disrupted as part of EU country reactions to Iranian assassinations of dissidents in Europe or attacks by Iranian militants on EU country diplomatic property in Iran. There are several daily flights from several European countries to Iran, and many Iranian students attend European universities. After the JCPOA was finalized in July 2015, then-British Foreign Secretary Phillip Hammond visited Iran and reopened Britain's embassy there, closed since a 2011 attack on it by pro-government protesters.

During the 1990s, U.S. and European policies toward Iran were in sharp contrast. The United States had no dialogue with Iran at all whereas the EU countries maintained a policy of "critical dialogue" and refused to join the 1995 U.S. trade and investment ban on Iran. The EU-Iran dialogue was suspended in April 1997 in response to the German terrorism trial ("Mykonos trial") that found high-level Iranian involvement in killing

---

[154] Ibid.

[155] For information on EU sanctions in place on Iran, see http://eeas.europa.eu/delegations/iran/eu_iran/restrictive_measures/index_en.htm. See also: CRS Insight IN10656, *Iran Policy and the European Union*, by Derek E. Mix and Kenneth Katzman and CRS Insight IN10809, *Doing Business with Iran: EU-Iran Trade and Investment Relations*, by Cathleen D. Cimino-Isaacs and Kenneth Katzman.

[156] For more information on the post-sanctions business relationships between Iran and the EU countries, see CRS Report RS20871, *Iran Sanctions*, by Kenneth Katzman.

[157] See: CRS In Focus IF10916, *Efforts to Preserve Economic Benefits of the Iran Nuclear Deal*, by Cathleen D. Cimino-Isaacs, Kenneth Katzman, and Derek E. Mix.

Iranian dissidents in Germany, but it resumed in May 1998 during Mohammad Khatemi's presidency of Iran. In the 1990s, European and Japanese creditors bucked U.S. objections and rescheduled about $16 billion in Iranian debt bilaterally, in spite of Paris Club rules that call for multilateral rescheduling. During 2002-2005, there were active negotiations between the European Union and Iran on a "Trade and Cooperation Agreement" (TCA) that would have lowered the tariffs or increased quotas for Iranian exports to the EU countries.[158] Negotiations were discontinued in late 2005 after Iran abrogated an agreement with several EU countries to suspend uranium enrichment.

EAST ASIA

East Asia includes three of Iran's five largest buyers of crude oil and one country, North Korea, that is widely accused of supplying Iran with missile and other military-related technology. The countries in Asia have not extensively intervened militarily or politically in the Middle East, and Iran rarely criticizes countries in Asia.

China[159]

China, a permanent member of the U.N. Security Council and a P5+1 party to the JCPOA, is Iran's largest oil customer. During U.N. Security Council deliberations on Iran during 2006-2013, China tended to argue for less stringent sanctions than did the United States, but China's compliance with U.S. sanctions was pivotal to U.S. efforts to reduce Iran's revenue from oil sales.

China opposed the U.S. withdrawal from the JCPOA and the government has said it would not abide by reimposed U.S. secondary sanctions by cutting its purchases of Iranian oil.

China faces a potential threat from Sunni Muslim extremists in western China and appears to see Shiite Iran as a potential ally against Sunni radicals. China also appears to agree with Iran's view that the Asad regime is preferable to the Islamic State and other Islamist rebel organizations.

Shortly after Implementation Day of the JCPOA, China's President Xi Jinping included Tehran on a visit to the Middle East region. His trip to Iran generally focused on China's vision of an energy and transportation corridor extending throughout Eurasia

[158] During the active period of talks, which began in December 2002, there were working groups focused not only on the TCA terms and proliferation issues but also on Iran's human rights record, Iran's efforts to derail the Middle East peace process, Iranian-sponsored terrorism, counternarcotics, refugees, migration issues, and the Iranian opposition PMOI.

[159] CRS In Focus IF10029, *China, U.S. Leadership, and Geopolitical Challenges in Asia*, by Susan V. Lawrence.

("One Belt, One Road," OBOR), and including Iran, and the two countries agreed to expand trade to $600 billion over the next decade. Iran's burgeoning economic and diplomatic relationships with the Central Asian states appear intended, at least in part, to enable Iran to take advantage of the substantial Chinese investment in the region that is required to implement its OBOR vision. As an example, in February 2016, the first rail cargo from China arrived in Iran via the Kazakhstan-TurkmenistanIran link discussed above.

China in the past supplied Iran with advanced conventional arms, including cruise missile-armed fast patrol boats that the IRGC Navy operates in the Persian Gulf; anti-ship missiles; ballistic missile guidance systems; and other WMD-related technology. A number of China-based entities have been sanctioned by the United States, including in 2017, for allegedly aiding Iran's missile, nuclear, and conventional weapons programs.

Japan and South Korea

Iran's primary interest in Japan and South Korea has been to expand commercial relations after sanctions were eased. Neither Japan nor South Korea has been heavily involved in security and strategic issues in the Middle East, but both countries are close allies of the United States. Both countries are wary of Iran's reported military and technology relations with North Korea.

During the period when the United States was implementing the JCPOA, South Korea's then-President Geun-hye Park visited Tehran in May 2016 for the first tour of Iran by a South Korean president to Iran since 1962, accompanied by representatives of 236 South Korean companies and organizations. The two sides signed a number of agreements in the fields of oil and gas, railroads, tourism, and technology, and agreed to reestablish direct flights between Tehran and Seoul.

Japan's Prime Minister Shinzo Abe reportedly had planned to visit Iran in late August 2016, but postponed the visit. During the U.N. General Assembly meetings in New York (September 18-21, 2017), Abe accepted an invitation from President Rouhani to visit Iran, according to Abe's spokesperson, but no date for the visit was announced. The visit, which would have been the first by a leader of Japan to the Islamic Republic, is unlikely now that the United States has exited the JCPOA.

Japanese and South Korean firms are consistently unwilling to risk their positions in the U.S. market by violating any U.S. sanctions on Iran, and these companies are starting to leave the Iran market now that U.S. secondary sanctions are being reimposed.

North Korea

Iran and North Korea have been aligned as "rogue states" subjected to wide-ranging international sanctions. North Korea is one of the few countries with which Iran has formal military-to-military relations, and the two countries have cooperated on a wide range of military and WMD-related ventures, particularly the development of ballistic missile technology. In the past, Iran reportedly funded and assisted in the retransfer of missile and possibly nuclear technology from North Korea to Syria.[160] North Korea also reportedly supplied Iran with small submarines. It is widely suspected that the two continue to cooperate on missile development, and possibly nuclear issues as well, but the extent of the cooperation, if any, is not known from published sources.

North Korea has not at any time pledged to abide by international sanctions against Iran, but its economy is too small to significantly help Iran. According to some observers, a portion of China's purchases of oil from Iran and other suppliers is re-exported to North Korea. After international sanctions on Iran's crude oil exports were removed, additional quantities of Iranian oil likely began reaching North Korea, most likely via China. However, the expansion of such retransfers are likely limited by the adoption in September 2017 of additional U.N. sanctions limiting the supply of oil to North Korea.

LATIN AMERICA[161]

Some U.S. officials and some in Congress have expressed concerns about Iran's relations with leaders in Latin America that share Iran's distrust of the United States. Some experts and U.S. officials have asserted that Iran has sought to position IRGC-QF operatives and Hezbollah members in Latin America to potentially carry out terrorist attacks against Israeli targets in the region or even in the United States itself.[162] Some U.S. officials have asserted that Iran and Hezbollah's activities in Latin America include money laundering and trafficking in drugs and counterfeit goods.[163] These concerns were heightened during the presidency of Mahmoud Ahmadinejad (2005 2013), who made repeated, high-profile visits to the region in an effort to circumvent U.S. sanctions and gain support for his criticisms of U.S. policies. However, few of the economic agreements that Ahmadinejad announced with Latin American countries were implemented, by all accounts.

---

[160] http://www.wsj.com/articles/SB10001424052702303763804579183231117914364.

[161] For more information on the issues discussed in this section, see CRS Report RS21049, *Latin America: Terrorism Issues*, by Mark P. Sullivan and June S. Beittel.

[162] Ilan Berman. "Iran Courts Latin America." Middle East Quarterly, Summer 2012. http://www.meforum.org/3297/iran-latin-america.

[163] Posture Statement of General John F. Kelly, Commander, U.S. Southern Command, before the 114th Congress, Senate Armed Services Committee, March 12, 2015.

Source: Created by CRS.

Figure 4. Latin America.

President Rouhani has generally expressed only modest interest in further expanding ties in Latin America, perhaps in part because Latin America is not pivotal to Iran's economy.[164] He made his first visit to the region in September 2016 (three years into his presidency) in the course of traveling to the annual U.N. General Assembly meetings in New York. He went to several of the countries that Foreign Minister Zarif did when Zarif met with leaders in Cuba, Chile, Bolivia, Ecuador, Nicaragua, and Venezuela in August 2016—the countries in that region that Ahmadinejad visited during his presidency as well. Iran's officials have stated that the purpose of the visits were to expand economic relations with Latin American countries now that international sanctions on Iran have been lifted.

In the 112th Congress, the Countering Iran in the Western Hemisphere Act, requiring the Administration to develop a strategy to counter Iran's influence in Latin America, was enacted (H.R. 3783, P.L. 112-220). The required report was provided to Congress in June 2013, asserting that "Iranian influence in Latin America and the Caribbean is waning" in part because of U.S. efforts to cause Latin American countries to assess the costs and benefits of closer relations with Iran.[165] Observers have directed particular attention to Iran's relationship with Venezuela (an OPEC member, as is Iran) because of its avowed anti-U.S. posture, and Argentina, because of the Iran-backed attacks on Israeli and Jewish targets there. Iran's relations with Cuba have been analyzed by experts in the

[164] http://www.thedialogue.org/resources/are-iran-trade-ties-important-for-latin-america/.

[165] State Department, "Annex A: Unclassified Summary of Policy Recommendations," June 2013.

past, but the U.S. opening to Cuba that began in late 2014 have eased concerns about Cuba-Iran relations. U.S. counterterrorism officials also have stated that the triborder area of Argentina, Brazil, and Paraguay is a "nexus" of arms, narcotics and human trafficking, counterfeiting, and other potential funding sources for terrorist organizations, including Hezbollah. Assertions in 2009 by some U.S. officials that Iran was significantly expanding its presence in Nicaragua were disputed by subsequent accounts.[166]

Venezuela[167]

During Ahmadinejad's presidency, Iran had particularly close relations with Venezuela and its president, Hugo Chavez, who died in office in March 2013. Neither Rouhani nor Chavez's successor, Nicolas Maduro, have expressed the enthusiasm for the relationship that Chavez and Ahmadinejad did. Even during the presidencies of Chavez and Ahmadinejad, the United States did not necessarily perceive a threat from the Iran-Venezuela relationship. In July 2012, President Obama stated that Iran-Venezuela ties have not had "a serious national security impact on the United States."[168] Very few of the economic agreements announced were implemented. A direct air link was reportedly restarted by President Maduro in January 2015 in order to try to promote tourism between the two countries.[169] Petroleos de Venezuela (PDVSA)—which operates the Citgo gasoline stations in the United States—has been supplying Iran with gasoline since 2009, in contravention of U.S. sanctions, and PDVSA was sanctioned under the Iran Sanctions Act in May 2011.[170] The United States "de-listed" PDVSA as stipulated in the JCPOA, but it will be "re-listed" in concert with the reimposition of U.S. sanctions on Iran in 2018.

Argentina[171]

In Argentina, Iran and Hezbollah carried out acts of terrorism against Israeli and Jewish targets in Buenos Aires that continue to affect Iran-Argentina relations. The major attacks were the 1992 bombing of the Israeli embassy and the 1994 bombing of a Jewish community center (Argentine-Israeli Mutual Association, AMIA). Based on indictments and the investigative information that has been revealed, there is a broad consensus that these attacks were carried out by Hezbollah operatives, assisted by Iranian diplomats and their diplomatic privileges.

---

[166] "Iran's Rumored 'Mega-Embassy' Set Off Alarms in U.S." *Washington Post*, June 13, 2009. http://www.washingtonpost.com/wp-dyn/content/article/2009/07/12/AR2009071202337.html.

[167] For more information, see CRS Report R43239, *Venezuela: Issues for Congress, 2013-2016*, by Mark P. Sullivan.

[168] Comments by President Barack Obama on "CNN: The Situation Room," July 11, 2012.

[169] http://panampost.com/sabrina-martin/2015/04/06/iran-takes-venezuelan-money-passes-on-deliveries/.

[170] http://www.reuters.com/article/2011/05/24/us-iran-usa-sanctions-idUSTRE74N47R20110524.

[171] For more information, see CRS Report R43816, *Argentina: Background and U.S. Relations*, by Mark P. Sullivan and Rebecca M. Nelson.

The Buenos Aires attacks took place more than 20 years ago and there have not been any recent public indications that Iran and/or Hezbollah are planning attacks in Argentina or elsewhere in Latin America. However, in February 2015, Uruguay stated that an Iranian diplomat posted there had left the country before Uruguay issued a formal complaint that the diplomat had tested the security measures of Israel's embassy in the capital, Montevideo.[172]

Many in Argentina's Jewish community opposed a January 2013 agreement between Iran and the government of then-President Cristina Fernandez de Kirchner to form a "truth commission" rather than to aggressively prosecute the Iranians involved. In May 2013, the Argentine prosecutor in the AMIA bombing case, Alberto Nisman, issued a 500-page report alleging that Iran has been working for decades in Latin America, setting up intelligence stations in the region by utilizing embassies, cultural organizations, and even mosques as a source of recruitment. In January 2015, Nisman was found dead of a gunshot wound, amid reports that he was to request indictment of Argentina's president for allegedly conspiring with Iran to downplay the AMIA bombing issue. President Kirchner was succeeded in December 2015 by Mauricio Macri, who has not sought to broaden relations with Iran,[173] possibly explaining why Argentina apparently was not on the itinerary for Rouhani's regional visit in 2016.

AFRICA

Sub-Saharan Africa has not generally been a focus of Iranian foreign policy, perhaps because of the relatively small size of most African economies and the limited ability of African countries to influence the actions of Iran's main regional rivals. Former President Ahmadinejad sought to deepen diplomatic and commercial ties to some African countries, focusing on those that have had historically tense relations with Western powers (such as Sudan, Zimbabwe, and South Africa). Many African countries, however, apparently did not want to risk their relationships with the United States or blowback from domestic Sunni constituencies by broadening relations with Iran.

The overwhelming majority of Muslims in Africa are Sunni, and Muslim-majority African countries have tended to be responsive to financial and diplomatic overtures from Iran's rival, Saudi Arabia. Amid the Saudi-Iran dispute in January 2016 over the Nimr execution, several African countries that Iran had cultivated as potential allies broke relations with Iran outright, including Djibouti, Comoros, and Somalia, as well as Sudan. Senegal, at one time seen as a primary focus of Ahmadinejad's Africa outreach, and Sudan have supported the Saudi-led military effort against the Iran-backed Houthis in

---

[172] "Questions Swirl over Incident Involving Iranian Diplomat in Uruguay." *LatinNews* Daily, February 9, 2015.

[173] http://www.thedialogue.org/resources/are-iran-trade-ties-important-for-latin-america/.

Yemen—in Sudan's case with some forces.[174] The UAE, in particular, has actively sought allies in the Horn of Africa to reduce Iranian influence, including by facilitating UAE operations against the Iran-backed Houthi rebels in Yemen. West Africa's large Lebanese diaspora communities may also be a target of Iranian influence operations and a conduit for Hezbollah financial and criminal activities.

Rouhani has made few statements on relations with countries in Africa and has apparently not made the continent a priority. Tehran appears, however, to retain an interest in cultivating African countries as trading partners—an interest that might increase now that the Trump Administration has decided to exit the JCPOA and reimpose all U.S. sanctions. Iran's leaders also apparently see Africa as a market for its arms exports and as sources of diplomatic support in U.N. forums.[175] African populations may also be seen as potential targets for Iranian "soft power" and religious influence. Iran's Al Mustafa University, which promotes Iran's message and Shiite religious orientation with branches worldwide, has numerous branches in various African countries.[176]

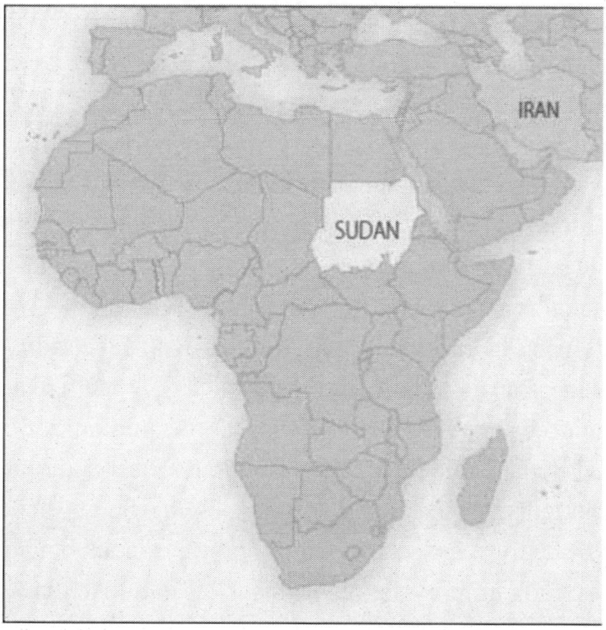

Source: Created by CRS.

Figure 5. Sudan.

---

[174] Senegal pledged in 2015 to deploy 2,100 troops in support of the Saudi-led coalition in Yemen, but it has yet to do so.

[175] On arms sales, see C.J. Chivers."A Trail of Bullet Casings Leads from Africa's Wars back to Iran." *New York Times*, January 11, 2013. https://www.nytimes.com/2013/01/12/world/africa/a-trail-of-bullet-casings-leads-fromafricas-wars-to-iran.html?mtrref=www.google.com&gwh=404CEDBD8247A8A74FBA1C19E2589305&gwt=pay.

[176] Iranain American Forum, "Al Mustafa University, Iran's Global Network of Islamic Schools." April 12, 2016. http://iranian-americans.com/irans-export-of-islamic-fundamentalism-al-mustafa-global-training-centers-2/.

The IRGC-QF has reportedly operated in some countries in Africa, in part to secure arms-supply routes for pro-Iranian movements in the Middle East but also to be positioned to act against U.S. or allied interests, to support friendly governments or factions, and act against Sunni extremist movements. Several African countries have claimed to disrupt purportedly IRGC-QF-backed arms trafficking or terrorism plots. In May 2013, a court in Kenya found two Iranian men guilty of planning to carry out bombings in Kenya, apparently against Israeli targets. In December 2016, two Iranians and a Kenyan who worked for Iran's embassy in Nairobi were charged with collecting information for a terrorist act after filming the Israeli embassy in that city. Senegal cut diplomatic ties with Iran between 2011 and 2013 after claiming that Iran had trafficked weapons to its domestic separatist insurgency.

Sudan

Iran's relations with the government of Sudan, which were extensive since the early 1990s, have diminished substantially since 2014 as Sudan has moved closer to Iran's rivals, Saudi Arabia and the UAE. Sudan, like Iran, is still named by the United States as a state sponsor of terrorism, although U.S. officials have praised the country's counterterrorism cooperation in recent years, possibly to the point where the Administration might decide to remove Sudan from the terrorism list.[177] Iran's relations with Sudan provided Iran with a channel to supply weapons to Hamas and other pro-Iranian groups in the Gaza Strip.[178] The relationship began in the 1990s when Islamist leaders in Sudan, who came to power in 1989, welcomed international Islamist movements to train and organize there. Iran began supplying Sudan with weapons it used on its various fronts, such as in its internal conflicts with rebels in what is now South Sudan as well as in the Darfur region, and the IRGC-QF reportedly armed and trained Sudanese forces, including the Popular Defense Force militia.[179] Some observers say Iranian pilots assisted Sudan's air force, and Iran's naval forces periodically visited Port Sudan. Iran also reportedly played a key role in helping Sudan build its own military industry.[180] Israel repeatedly accused Iran of shipping weapons bound for Gaza through Sudan[181] and, at times, took military action against sites in Sudan that Israel asserted were being used by Iran to arm Hamas.[182]

---

[177] State Department, Country Reports n Terrorism: 2016; Jina Moore. "U.S. is Open to Removing Sudan from Terrorism List, Diplomat Says." *New York Times*, November 16, 2017.

[178] Michael Lipin. "Sudan's Iran Alliance under Scrutiny." VOANews, October 31, 2012. http://www.voanews.com/content/article/1536472.html.

[179] "Did Israel Just Bow Up an Iranian Weapons Factory in Sudan?" *Christian Science Monitor*, October 25, 2012.

[180] See, e.g., Small Arms Survey. "Sudan's Military Industry Corporation Display at the 2015 IDEX Convention." March 9, 2015.

[181] "Were the Israelis Behind the 'Mystery' Air Strike in Sudan?" *Time*, April 6, 2011; "Car Blast in E. Sudan, Khartoum Points to Israel," *Reuters*, May 22, 2012; "Rockets and Meetings," Africa Confidential, May 25, 2012.Weapons Documented in South Kordofan," *Small Arms Survey*, April 2012.

[182] "Israel Navy Intercepts Gaza-Bound Iranian Rocket Ship Near Port Sudan." *Jerusalem Post*, March 5, 2014.

However, because Sudan is inhabited by Sunni Arabs, it has always been considered susceptible to overtures from Saudi Arabia and other GCC countries to distance itself from Iran. Since 2014, Saudi and UAE economic assistance to and investment in Sudan have caused Sudan to realign. In September 2014, the Sudan government closed all Iranian cultural centers in Sudan and expelled the cultural attaché and other Iranian diplomats on the grounds that Iran was using its facilities and personnel in Sudan to promote Shiite Islam.[183] In March 2015, Sudan joined the Saudi-led Arab coalition against the Houthis in Yemen, appearing to confirm that Sudan has significantly downgraded its strategic relations with Iran. In December 2015, Sudan joined the Saudi-led anti-terrorism coalition discussed earlier. In January 2016, Sudan severed ties with Iran in connection with the Saudi execution of Nimr.

ALTERNATIVE SCENARIOS

A key question is how U.S. actions might alter Iran's national security policies in ways more favorable to U.S. interests. To date, no U.S. strategy has reduced Iran's regional influence. Trump Administration officials assert that Iran has increased its regional malign activities since the JCPOA began Implementation Day, and cite that observation as one justification for exiting the accord. However, many experts argue that Iran's expanded regional influence is due more to opportunities provided by the region's conflicts than to an increase in Iran's financial resources.

As noted throughout, Administration efforts against Iran included imposition of sanctions on various Iranian activities; cooperation with regional leaders and groups who seek to limit Iranian influence; and deployment of U.S. forces to intercept Iranian weapons shipments and deter Iranian ground action. As General Votel testified on February 27, 2018, "Countering the Iranian regime's malign influence in the region is a key component of [U.S.] efforts to defend allies from military aggression, bolster [U.S.] partners against coercion, and share responsibilities for the common defense." However, additional U.S. pressure on Iran—particularly if such pressure involves military action—would likely embroil the United States more deeply in regional conflicts. In concert with exiting the JCPOA in May 2018, neither President Trump nor Secretary of State Pompeo cited specific new U.S. steps that would counter Iran's foreign and defense policies, other than attempting to reduce its financial resources through sanctions.

Whether the JCPOA continues to operate despite the U.S. withdrawal from it, those who argue that Iran is an increasingly challenging regional actor maintain that

---

[183] "Sudan Expels Iranian Diplomats and Closes Cultural Centers." *The Guardian*, September 2, 2014.

- Iran is likely to continue to supply its regional allies and proxies with larger quantities of and more accurate weaponry, including rockets and short-range missiles.
- Iran might, through its allies and proxies in Syria and Iraq, succeed in establishing a secure land corridor extending from Iran to Lebanon and in pressuring Israel from the Syrian border as well as the Lebanon border. The potential for major Iran-Israel conflict in Syria, and the possibility that clashes could escalate into a broader regional war, is significant.
- A further prolongation of the intra-GCC rift could complicate U.S. efforts to contain Iran militarily and hinder U.S. military operations in the region.
- The lifting of the U.N. ban on arms sales to Iran in October 2020 will enable Iran to modernize its armed forces. Acquiring additional systems could strengthen its capabilities to the point where it can move ground forces across waterways such as the Strait of Hormuz.
- Iran could further increase its assistance to hardline opposition factions in Bahrain, which has apparently been limited to date to only small, militant underground groups.[184]
- Iran might succeed in emerging as a major regional energy and trading hub, both within and outside its participation in China's OBOR initiative, potentially expanding Iran's political influence to an even greater extent.
- Various regional powers might establish or expand military cooperation with Iran, a development that could strengthen Iran's conventional capabilities.

On the other hand, in order to preserve the JCPOA, advance its reintegration into the international community, and avoid clashes with either the United States or Israel, Iran might be induced to shift its policies in ways that benefit U.S. and allied interests. Those who take this view argue that

- Iran might be induced to cooperate in identifying an alternative to Asad in Syria that resolves, or greatly attenuates, the civil conflict there and paves the way for Iran to draw down its forces there.
- Iran might be persuaded to curtail its delivery of additional long-range rockets or other military equipment to Hezbollah and Hamas, although Iran is unlikely under any circumstances to reduce its political support for Hezbollah.
- Iran might support a political solution in Yemen that gives the Houthis less influence in a new government than they are demanding.
- Iran and the UAE might resolve their territorial dispute over Abu Musa and the two Tunbs islands in the Persian Gulf.

[184] Ibid.

- Iran might increase the transparency of its financial system, including addressing all the concerns of the multilateral Financial Action Task Force (FATF) about the use of its banking system for money laundering and terrorism financing.
- Iran might gain admission to the Shanghai Cooperation Organization, which could lead to broader cooperation between Iran and Central Asian states against the Islamic State or other terrorist organizations.
- Iran might seek to finalize major regional economic projects that benefit the whole region, including development of oil and gas fields in the Caspian Sea; gas pipeline linkages between Iran and Kuwait, Bahrain, and Oman; the Iran-Pakistan natural gas pipeline; the development of the Chabahar port; and transportation routes linking Central Asia to China.

Domestic Iranian factors could cause Iran's foreign policy to shift. For example

- As noted, protesters in over 80 Iranian cities in December 2017-January 2018 complained, in part, about the regime's use of resources for foreign intervention rather than to improve living standards. Fear of future unrest could cause the regime to reduce the scope of its interventions, to cut its defense budget, or limit its missile development program.
- The departure from the scene of the Supreme Leader could change Iran's foreign policy sharply, depending on the views of his successor.

In: Iran: Economic, Political and Nuclear Policies
Editor: Everett Fowler ISBN: 978-1-53614-827-5

Chapter 6

IRAN'S THREATS, THE STRAIT OF HORMUZ, AND OIL MARKETS: IN BRIEF*

Michael Ratner

INTRODUCTION

The exchanges of threats between members of the governments of Iran and the United States, including the presidents of both countries, have again raised the specter of an interruption of shipping through the Strait of Hormuz (the Strait), a key waterway for the transit of oil and natural gas to world markets. In the first half of 2018, approximately 18 million barrels per day (bpd) of crude oil and condensate, almost 4 million bpd of petroleum products, and over 300 million cubic meters per day in liquefied natural gas (LNG) exited the Strait. Iran accounted for about 10% of oil and 0% of the natural gas through the Strait. In a speech on July 22, Iranian President Rouhani stated, "We are the... guarantor of security of the waterway of the region throughout the history. Don't play with the lion's tail; you will regret it."[1] (Western reporting took the reference to the waterway to mean the Strait of Hormuz, which is the narrow waterway that forms the entrance to the Persian Gulf from the Gulf of Oman and ultimately the Arabian Sea. See Figure 1). To which President Trump tweeted, "Never, Ever, Threaten the United States Again or You Will Suffer Consequences the Likes of Which Few Throughout History Have Ever Suffered Before..."[2] Earlier, on July 3, President Rouhani stated, "The

* This is an edited, reformatted and augmented version of Congressional Research Service, Publication No. R45281, dated August 6, 2018.

[1] Office of the President of Iran, press release, July 22, 2018, http://www.president.ir/en/105359.

[2] Joshua Berlinger, "Trump Tweets Explosive Threat to Iran," *CNN*, July 23, 2018, https://www.cnn.com/2018/07/23/ politics/trump-iran-intl/index.html. Capitalization is not for emphasis.

Americans have claimed they want to completely stop Iran's oil exports. They don't understand the meaning of this statement, because it has no meaning for Iranian oil not to be exported, while the region's oil is exported."[3]

This is not the first time Iran's leaders have threatened to close or hinder shipping through the Strait of Hormuz. Prior to sanctions targeting Iran's oil exports in 2011/12, Iranian leaders threatened to close the Strait of Hormuz.[4] Press reports that Iran is about to begin a large naval exercise in and around the Strait in early August 2018 is likely to inflame tensions further.

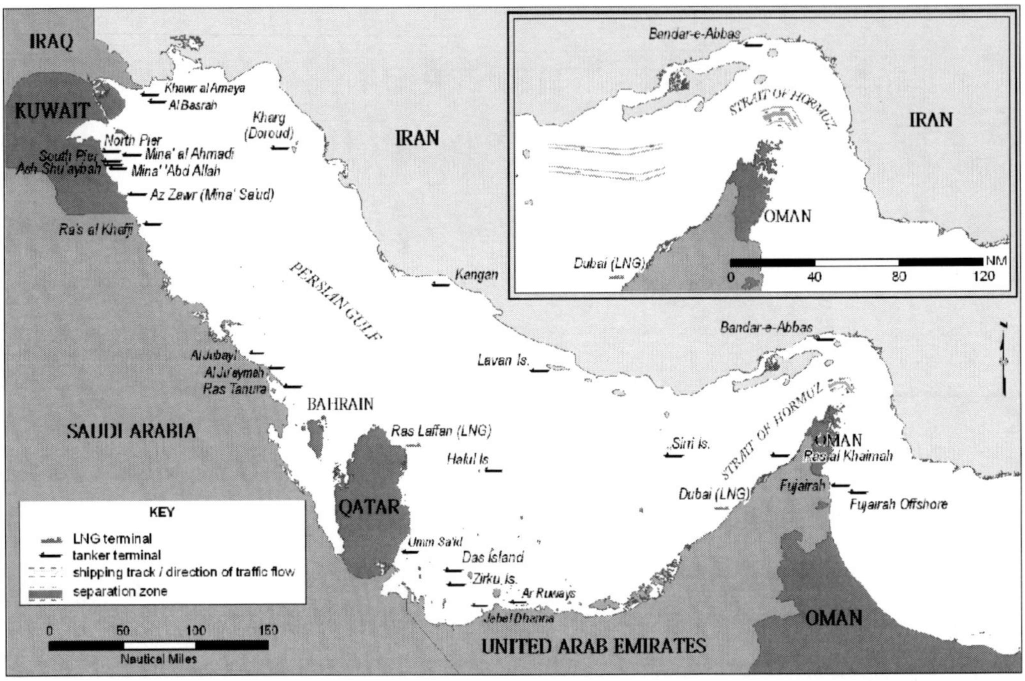

Source: Jacqueline Nolan, Library of Congress, with data from Petroleum Economist, National Oceanic and Atmospheric Administration, and Central Intelligence Agency.

Note: Location of terminal icons are indicative and not a precise location.

Figure 1. Persian Gulf and the Strait of Hormuz.

Congressional Interest

With the U.S. withdrawal from the Joint Comprehensive Plan of Action (JCPOA) on May 8, 2018, there may be increased potential for Congress to consider legislation regarding sanctions on Iran. A number of bills, mostly prior to the May 8 withdrawal,

---

[3] Silke Koltrowitz, "Iran's Rouhani Hints at Threat to Neighbors' Exports if Oil Sales Halted," *Reuters*, July 3, 2018, online edition.

[4] J. David Goodman. "Iran Warns U.S. Aircraft Carrier Not to Return to Gulf and a Strategic Strait." *New York Times*, January 4, 2012.

have been introduced in the 115th Congress targeting aspects of Iran's leadership, military, and economy.

The Strait of Hormuz

The Strait of Hormuz is the narrow waterway that forms the entrance to the Persian Gulf from the Gulf of Oman and ultimately the Arabian Sea. At its narrowest point it is 22 nautical miles wide and falls within Iranian and Omani territorial waters. There are two shipping lanes through the Strait, one in each direction. Each is two miles wide and they are separated by a two-mile buffer.

The United States and Sanctions[5]

On May 8, 2018, President Trump announced that the United States would no longer participate in the Joint Comprehensive Plan of Action (JCPOA) and that all U.S. secondary sanctions suspended to implement the JCPOA would be reinstated after a maximum "wind-down period" of 180 days (November 4, 2018). The U.S. sanctions that are going back into effect target all of Iran's core economic sectors. The Administration has indicated it will not look favorably on requests by foreign governments or companies for exemptions to allow them to avoid penalties for continuing to do business with Iran after that time.[6]

It remains uncertain whether reinstated U.S. sanctions based on the U.S. unilateral exit from the JCPOA will damage Iran's economy to the extent sanctions did during 2012-2015, when the global community was aligned in pressuring Iran. During that timeframe, Iran's economy shrank by 9% per year, crude oil exports fell from about 2.5 million bpd to about 1.1 million bpd, and Iran could not repatriate more than $120 billion in Iranian reserves held in banks abroad. JCPOA sanctions relief enabled Iran to increase its oil exports to nearly pre-sanctions levels, regain access to foreign exchange reserve funds and reintegrate into the international financial system, achieve about 7% yearly economic growth, attract foreign investments in key sectors, and buy new passenger aircraft. The sanctions relief reportedly contributed to Iranian President Hassan Rouhani's reelection in the May 19, 2017, vote. Yet, perceived economic grievances still sparked protests in Iran from December 2017 to January 2018.

---

[5] This section is drawn from the work of CRS analyst (name redacted). For additional information on Iran sanctions and the U.S. withdrawal, see CRS Report RS20871, *Iran Sanctions*, by (name redacted) , or CRS Report R43333, *Iran Nuclear Agreement and U.S. Exit*, by (name redacted)and (name redacted).

[6] See, for example, Brian Hook, "Briefing with an Iran Diplomacy Update," Department of State, July 2, 2018, https://www.state.gov/r/pa/prs/ps/2018/07/283669.htm.

The announced resumption of U.S. secondary sanctions has begun to harm Iran's economy because numerous major companies have announced decisions to exit the Iranian market rather than risk being penalized by the United States.[7] As an indicator of the effects, the value of Iran's currency sharply declined in June 2018, and some economic-based domestic unrest flared in concert. Smaller demonstrations and unrest have simmered since. If the European Union and other countries are unwilling or unable to keep at least the bulk of the economic benefits of the JCPOA flowing to Iran, there is substantial potential for Iranian leaders to decide to cease participating in the JCPOA.

IRAN'S PERSPECTIVE

Threats of U.S. sanctions that could reduce Iran's oil export earnings is a key impetus to Iran's threats to close the Strait of Hormuz. Historically, United Nations and multilateral sanctions had sought to reduce Iran's ability to develop its nuclear program by undermining its ability to develop its energy sector—targeting investment and financial linkages—but not directly targeting Iran's ability to export oil.[8] This changed in 2012.

Due to its own dependence on commerce through the Strait, Iran may be unlikely to attempt to close the waterway, but rather to shape the international debate on Iran policy. Oil exports are vital to the Iranian government's fiscal health and the Iranian economy as a whole. Iran relies on the Strait not only for its oil exports, averaging about 2.2 million bpd in the first half of 2018, but also for the imports of some needed food and medical products. Iran could attempt to re-route imports through ports outside the Strait, such as Jask, or via established overland trade routes through Pakistan or Iraq. In 2016, the International Monetary Fund (IMF) estimated Iran's oil exports account for between 50% and 60% of total exports and almost 15% of GDP.[9] The latter shows that Iran has a relatively diversified economy. However, many experts see Iran's warnings regarding the Strait of Hormuz as a reiteration of its long-held position to defend its oil exports. This implies that the likelihood that Iran might attempt to close the Strait increases if a broad embargo on purchases of Iran's oil emerges, either from countries complying with U.S. secondary sanctions or reinstating their own.

By threatening traffic through the Straits, Iran may risk alienating other nations, including its neighbors and customers, almost all of whom opposed the U.S. exit from the JCPOA and still want to engage economically with Iran. Most of the oil from the Persian

---

[7] For additional information, see CRS In Focus IF10916, *Efforts to Preserve Economic Benefits of the Iran Nuclear Deal*, by (name redacted), (name redacted), and (name redacted).

[8] Import of Iranian oil into the United States has been prohibited by U.S. law since 1995, but measures to end or reduce imports in Europe and other major markets are new.

[9] Selim Cakir, Magali Pinat, and Chady Ell-Khoury, et al., *Islamic Republic of Iran*, International Monetary Fund, IMF Country Report No. 18/94, March 29, 2018, p. 11.

Gulf, including from Iran, goes to Asian nations, with India and China being Iran's largest oil customers. Within weeks of the United States withdrawing from the JCPOA and stating its intention to reimpose sanctions, India's Foreign Minister Sushma Swaraj was quoted saying, "India follows only U.N. sanctions, and not unilateral sanctions by any country."[10] China has also indicated that it may not comply with the U.S. request to halt all imports from Iran.[11] Turkey, Iran's fourth largest oil importer, reportedly told U.S. officials it will not comply, as well.[12]

Iranian Options Regarding the Strait

Outright Closure

An outright closure of the Strait of Hormuz, a major artery of the global oil market, would be an unprecedented disruption of global oil supply and would likely contribute to higher global oil prices. However, at present, experts assess this to be a low probability event. Moreover, were this to occur, it is not likely to be prolonged. U.S. Secretary of Defense James Mattis asserted on July 27 that Iran's doing so would trigger a military response from the United States and others to preserve the freedom of navigation in that waterway.[13] The U.S. response could reach beyond simply reestablishing Strait transit.

Harassment and/or Infrastructure Damage

Iran could harass tanker traffic through the Strait through a range of measures without necessarily shutting down all traffic. This took place during the Iran-Iraq war in the 1980s. Also, critical energy production and export infrastructure could be damaged as a result of military action by Iran, the United States, or other actors. Harassment or infrastructure damage could contribute to lower exports of oil from the Persian Gulf, greater uncertainty around oil supply, higher shipping costs, and consequently higher oil prices. However, harassment also runs the risk of triggering a military response and alienating Iran's remaining oil customers.

---

[10] Nidhi Verma, "India Says It Only Follows U.N. Sanctions, Not U.S. Sanctions on Iran," *Reuters*, May 28, 2018, online edition, https://www.reuters.com/article/us-india-iran/india-says-it-only-follows-u-n-sanctions-not-u-s-sanctions-on-iran-idUSKCN1IT0WJ.

[11] Tetshushi Takahashi and Ryo Nakamura, "China to Ignore US Demand for Iran Oil Ban," *Nikkei Asian Review*, June 28, 2018, online edition, https://asia.nikkei.com/Economy/Trade-tensions/China-to-ignore-US-demand-for-Iran-oilban.

[12] David O'Byrne, "Turkey Informed US It Will Not Comply with Iran Sanctions," *S&P Global Platts*, July 24, 2018, online edition, https://www.spglobal.com/platts/en/market-insights/latest-news/natural-gas/072418-turkey-informed-usit-will-not-comply-with-iran-sanctions-report.

[13] Terri Moon Cronk, "'Communications Key in Solving International Disputes,' Mattis Says," *DoD News*, July 27, 2018, https://www.defense.gov/News/Article/Article/1586793/communications-key-in-solving-international-disputesmattis-says/.

Continued Threats

Iranian officials could continue to make threatening statements without taking action. Alternately, Iran could conduct naval exercises in the waterway that raise tensions, whether or not any offensive action is planned. Cable News Network reported that the Islamic Revolutionary Guard Corps (IRGC) Navy, which is responsible for Iran's defense of the Strait, plans a naval exercise in the Strait in early August, involving dozens of Iran's small boats.[14] The statements and maneuvers could still raise energy market tensions and contribute to higher oil prices, though only to the degree that oil market participants take such threats seriously.

OIL AND NATURAL GAS MARKET CONSIDERATIONS

The Strait of Hormuz is a key route of the global oil market. Persian Gulf oil exporters—Iraq, Kuwait, Saudi Arabia, the United Arab Emirates (UAE), and Qatar—shipped almost 22 million bpd of oil and products through the Strait in the first half of 2018, which is roughly 24% of the global oil market.[15] On average, 33 oil and LNGs tankers exited the Persian Gulf through the Strait each day with most of the crude oil and natural gas going to Asian countries, including China, Japan, India, and South Korea. According to the U.S. Energy Information Administration (EIA), the United States imported 1.7 million bpd of crude oil from Persian Gulf countries in 2017, less than 10% of U.S. consumption and no natural gas. Separately, about 28% of the world's liquefied natural gas (LNG) trade, equal to about 3% of global natural gas consumption, moves through the Strait each year.[16] This primarily entails exports from Qatar to Europe and Asia.

The Persian Gulf is also home to the world's spare oil production capacity. Some members of the Organization of the Petroleum Exporting Countries (OPEC), primarily Saudi Arabia, hold spare capacity as a result of their market management strategy. Kuwait and the United Arab Emirates hold small amounts of spare capacity as well. Spare capacity is viewed as a cushion to the oil market which can be used to offset supply disruptions. However, given its location, this spare capacity might not be available to offset a disruption to the Strait of Hormuz.

---

[14] Barbara Starr, Cable News Network, August 2, 2018, https://www.state.gov/r/pa/prs/ps/2018/07/283669.htm.

[15] Ranjith Raja and Giorgos Beleris, *Strait of Hormuz: The Aorta of Global Oil Flows*, Thomson Reuters, Dubai, July 2018, p. 3.

[16] Based on data from the BP Statistical Review of World Energy, http://www.bp.com/statisticalreview.

Table 1. Selected Iran-Related Events and Oil Price Changes

	Price Changes		
Event	Prior Month	Next Month	Commentary
Start of Iran/Iraq War, 9/23/1980[a]	0.1%	0.5%	The monthly oil price did not change much prior to this conflict beginning and even a month into it. However, six months into the conflict oil prices were up11%.
"Tanker War" begins, 3/27/1984	-0.2%	-0.9%	The "tanker war" included 44 attacks against tankers from other nations over the course of nine months. During this time, prices remained close to the March 27 price or lower, dropping 14% by the end of the period. The large drop is more reflective of the global oil market than the uncertainty created by the tanker war. Supply levels remained high during the time period, while demand was growing slowly.[b]
Re-flagged Bridgeton *hits a mine (Operation Earnest Will),* 7/24/1987	-1.6%	-1.1%	The *Bridgeton*, carrying the U.S. flag, hit a mine in the Persian Gulf. Under U.S. Operation Earnest Will, Kuwaiti tankers were re-flagged with the U.S. flag so that the U.S. Navy could protect them in the Persian Gulf. Prices stayed above the July 24thprice for almost three weeks before steadily declining. As minimal oil was interrupted overall, the risk to supply was decreased consequently putting downward pressure on prices.[c]
Operation Praying Mantis, 4/18/1988	10.7%	-4.6%	The U.S. operation destroyed almost 40% of Iran's navy. Prices after the event dropped immediately, with the biggest daily drop almost 5% two weeks later. Praying Mantis greatly diminished Iran's capabilities in the Persian Gulf, decreasing the likelihood of an oil cutoff. Leading up to U.S. Operation Praying Mantis, the overall oil market faced lower demand because of warm weather in Europe, and higher production as Saudi Arabia was producing at its OPEC quota and no longer below it and non-OPEC production was higher.[d]
Iran arms Strait of Hormuz, 3/28/1995	2.5%	4.9%	The Pentagon announced that it was monitoring Iranian installation of missiles in the Strait of Hormuz. Iran also took possession and fortified two nearby islands claimed by them and the United Arab Emirates. During the month after the announcement daily prices fluctuated up and down before jumping at the end of the period. However, about a week after the event began prices declined for eight consecutive days.
Iran threatens the Strait, 12/28/2011	1.0%	0.2%	Iran's first Vice President Mohammad Reza Rahimi was the first to threaten closure of the Strait. Prices initially rose almost daily from this event, peaking on January 4, 2012, almost 4% higher before declining.
United States withdraws from JCPOA, 5/8/2018	3.5%	-0.9%	The oil market appears to have accounted for the U.S. withdrawal from the JCPOA with a price rise prior to the event. The addition of other market events also put upward pressure on prices. However, since the announcement on May 8, prices have fallen, indicating the market has adjusted to the new circumstances.

Source: U.S. Energy Information Administration, Annual Oil Market Chronology, http://www.eia.gov/emeu/cabs/AOMC/8089.html.

Notes: Crude prices are NYMEX West Texas Intermediate crude prices (daily) except 1980, which is refiners acquisition cost of crude reported by EIA (monthly). A negative Prior Month price indicates that average 30-day price prior to the action data was greater than the price on the action date and therefore negative. A negative Next Month price means that the price on the action date was greater than the average 30-day price.

[a] Although there were events leading up to September 23, 1980, that contributed to hostilities, this date is used as a start date to the military conflict.

[b] U.S. Energy Information Administration (EIA), *Short-Term Energy Outlook*, DOE/EIA-0202(84/3Q), Washington, DC, August 1984, p. 12, http://www.eia.gov/forecasts/steo/archives/3Q84.pdf.

[c] EIA, *Short-Term Energy Outlook*, DOE/EIA-0202(87/4Q), Washington, DC, October 1987, p. 9, http://www.eia.gov/forecasts/steo/archives/4Q87.pdf.

[d] EIA, Short-Term Energy Outlook, DOE/EIA-0202(88/2Q), Washington, DC, April 1988, p. 7, http://www.eia.gov/forecasts/steo/archives/2Q88.pdf.

There are alternative oil pipeline routes to bypass the Strait, but not enough to account for all the oil that transits the Strait. According to EIA, there are three pipelines that transport oil from Saudi Arabia and the United Arab Emirates that go around the Strait—East-West Pipeline and Abqaiq-Yanbu Natural Gas Liquids Pipeline from Saudi Arabia, and the Abu Dhabi Crude Oil Pipeline from the UAE. As of 2016, when EIA last reported on these pipelines, the East-West Pipeline and the Abu Dhabi Crude Oil Pipeline could take additional volumes of oil, approximately 2.9 million bpd and 1.0 million bpd, respectively. This would leave approximately 18 million bpd stranded should the Strait of Hormuz be closed.

A disruption of oil through the Strait of Hormuz could significantly affect global oil prices. Though most of the oil that flows through the Strait goes to Asia, the oil market is globally integrated and a disruption anywhere can contribute to higher oil prices everywhere. For example, a disruption of oil exported from the Persian Gulf to Asia would leave Asian refineries bidding for oil from alternative sources. While actual disruptions and perceived disruption risks in the past have contributed to prices being higher than they might have otherwise been, actual Iran-related events since 1980 have not necessarily resulted in clear and significant price increases ex-post (see Table 1). Additionally, oil prices tend to quickly experience large price movements when supply deficits are in the 1.5 million bpd and 2 million bpd range. A supply deficit of 18 million bpd to 22 million bpd, an amount the market has never had to deal with, would likely result in significant upward pressure on prices. The numerous variables affecting the price of oil at any given time can make it difficult to estimate what specific change in price is due to a specific event. Nonetheless, reductions or threatened reductions to supply do tend to push oil prices up.

Key uncertainties for the impact of a disruption include how much global oil supply was reduced, risks of further reductions, and duration of the disruption. Risk of damage to oil production and export facilities in the Persian Gulf would also be of concern. Given limited bypass options, outright closure of the Strait would represent an unprecedented disruption to global oil supply and would likely cause a substantial increase in oil prices. However, as suggested above, outright closure may be unlikely, and even if it occurred, might not persist for very long.

In the event of a disruption, consumer countries would likely release strategic stocks to offset the impact on oil supply. As of May 2018, the United States held 660 million barrels of crude oil in the Strategic Petroleum Reserve (SPR),[17] a government held stockpile of crude oil to be used to offset supply disruptions.[18] The United States coordinates use of its SPR with other members of the International Energy Agency (IEA),

[17] Department of Energy, *SPR Quick Facts and FAQs*, https://www.energy.gov/fe/services/petroleum-reserves/strategic-petroleum-reserve/spr-quick-facts-and-faqs.

[18] For more background the SPR, see CRS Report R42460, *The Strategic Petroleum Reserve: Authorization, Operation, and Drawdown Policy*, by (name redacted).

which include Japan, Germany, South Korea, and other members of the Organization for Economic Cooperation and Development (OECD). Some non-IEA countries, such as China, also hold strategic stocks, and may or may not coordinate with an IEA member release. Oil importing members of the IEA have an obligation to hold oil stocks equal to at least 90 days-worth of net imports. As of April 2018, IEA member countries held about 4.4 billion barrels of crude oil and refined products in inventory, of which 1.6 billion are held by governments.[19] If drawn down at the maximum rate technically possible, these government-held stocks could be delivered to the market at an average rate of 10.4 million bpd of crude oil and 4 million bpd of products in the first month of an IEA collective action, diminishing thereafter.[20] (The rate diminishes as stocks are depleted.) By offsetting the loss of supply, a strategic stock release could blunt the impact a disruption can have on oil prices.

---

[19] International Energy Agency, *Oil Market Report*, July 12, 2018, p. Table 4, https://www.iea.org/media/omrreports/ tables/2018-07-12.pdf.

[20] International Energy Agency, *Fact Sheet: IEA Stocks and Drawdown Capacity*, February 25, 2011, http://www.iea.org/files/Potential_IEA_Stockdraw_Capacity.pdf.

In: Iran: Economic, Political and Nuclear Policies
Editor: Everett Fowler
ISBN: 978-1-53614-827-5

Chapter 7

IRAN'S PRESIDENTIAL ELECTIONS*

Kenneth Katzman

POLICY CONTEXT

Iranian voters go to the polls on May 19, 2017, to vote for president and municipal officials countrywide amid tensions between Iran and the United States. On April 19, the Trump Administration certified to Congress, pursuant to the Iran Nuclear Agreement Review Act (INARA, P.L. 114-17), that Iran is complying with the 2015 multilateral nuclear agreement (Joint Comprehensive Plan of Action, JCPOA).

Secretary of State Rex Tillerson stated, however, that the JCPOA "only delays [Iran's] goal of becoming a nuclear state" and has failed to curb Iran's objectionable regional behavior. He announced that the United States' Iran policy— including the JCPOA—is under review. In recent weeks, the Trump Administration has imposed sanctions on additional entities allegedly supporting Iran's missile program and has launched strikes on Iran's key regional ally, Syria, for its use of chemical weapons. The Administration reportedly is also contemplating increased support for an effort by a Saudi-led Arab coalition battling Iran-backed Houthi rebels in Yemen.

ELECTION FIELD FINALIZED

Iran holds presidential elections every four years. The post of president is subordinate to that of "Supreme Leader," but Iran's president has significant influence on economic

* This is an edited, reformatted and augmented version of Congressional Research Service, Publication No. IN10699, dated May 5, 2017.

policy and government operations. Iran's elections are characterized by the State Department as "falling short of international standards for free, fair elections," primarily because a 12-member appointed body called the Council of Guardians is empowered to vet all election candidates. Approximately 1,600 persons filed to run, including incumbent President Hassan Rouhani. On April 27, the Council of Guardians approved Rouhani and five other candidates to run—a winnowing of the field that was consistent with past elections. If no candidate receives more than 50% of the vote, a run-off is to be held about three weeks later.

The other five candidates are Ibrahim Raisi, a purported close ally of the Supreme Leader Grand Ayatollah Ali Khamene'i; Mohammad Baqr Qalibaf, Tehran mayor and a stalwart of the hardline Islamic Revolutionary Guard Corps (IRGC); Mostafa Mirsalim, the centrist former culture minister; and two moderate candidates, Rouhani's first Vice President Eshaq Jahangiri and Mostafa Hashemitaba. To improve Rouhani's chances of achieving a first-round victory, one main competitor for moderate votes, Jahangiri, is widely expected to drop out before the voting.

Rouhani emphasizes to his mainly urban, young, and intellectual supporters that he delivered sanctions relief under the JCPOA and ended Iran's international isolation. But, according to a substantial number of reports, many Iranians are not benefitting significantly from sanctions relief, perhaps adversely affecting Rouhani's election prospects. In 2013, Rouhani received 50.7% of the votes, narrowly avoiding a run-off in a divided field that included several hardline candidates. There are only two hardliners in the 2017 race. One is mid-ranking cleric Ibrahim Raisi, who is said to be Khamenei's favorite to succeed him as Supreme Leader. In mid-2016, Khamene'i appointed Raisi, a longtime state prosecutor and judicial official, as head of the large economic conglomerate (Astan-e-Qods Razavi Foundation) centered on the Shrine of Imam Reza in Mashhad. Raisi's fate in the election might determine his chances to eventually succeed Khamene'i.

Raisi is basing his campaign on an appeal to rural and working class voters, many of whom benefit from regime largesse such as that provided by state-linked foundations such as Astan-e-Qods Razavi and support the Supreme Leader. Khamene'i's recent speeches have criticized Rouhani for failing to advance the "resistance economy"—the hardline concept of building up Iran's domestic industries and reducing reliance on imports. On April 30, 2017, Khamene'i, referring to the JCPOA, stated that "it is not correct" when Rouhani says that since he took office, "the shadow of war has been faded away." Despite Khamene'i's apparent backing, Raisi's long prior service in the judiciary could harm his prospects—candidates who come from the judiciary and the security apparatus, including the IRGC, have tended to fare poorly in elections. Raisi was part of the judiciary apparatus that allegedly approved the 1988 execution of a significant number of Iranian prisoners. The other hardliner in the race, Qalibaf, has previously run twice and lost, although he generally receives praise for his performance as Tehran's mayor.

PROSPECTS AND IMPLICATIONS

The probable outcome of the election, including whether Rouhani can again garner enough votes to avoid a run-off, is unclear. Also unclear is the degree to which three televised candidate debates will affect voter preferences. One Iranian poll in early May indicated that if the election proceeds to a runoff, Rouhani would likely defeat either Raisi or Qalibaf. However, polling in Iran is widely considered to be unreliable. There is also the potential for the Supreme Leader and his allies to put the state apparatus to work on behalf of Rouhani's challenger, including tasking the IRGC and its Basij militia to distribute pro-Raisi leaflets and transport his likely supporters to the polls, and intimidate voters in cities where Rouhani voters are prevalent. Some of these steps were widely reported to have been taken by the regime in the 2005 and 2009 elections.

Any outcome will have significant implications for U.S. policy. Even though all the candidates have described the JCPOA as an established fixture and would be likely to continue implementing it, a more hardline president might discontinue Rouhani's efforts to promote diplomatic engagement with the West. A hardline president might also try to remove even those few restraints Rouhani has managed to impose on actions that U.S. officials characterize as provocative. Further provocative actions, which include missile tests and support for regional allies that act against U.S. interests or allies, could put Iran on a collision course with the Trump Administration, which has already taken several steps against Iran, as discussed above. The Trump Administration and Congress are considering imposing new sanctions on Iran's missile program and on the IRGC, but have refrained from announcing decisions on any possible actions, reportedly to avoid harming Rouhani's reelection prospects.

In: Iran: Economic, Political and Nuclear Policies
Editor: Everett Fowler
ISBN: 978-1-53614-827-5

Chapter 8

IRAN'S NUCLEAR PROGRAM: STATUS*

Paul K. Kerr

ABSTRACT

Iran's nuclear program began during the 1950s. The United States has expressed concern since the mid-1970s that Tehran might develop nuclear weapons. Iran's construction of gas centrifuge uranium enrichment facilities is currently the main source of proliferation concern. Gas centrifuges can produce both low-enriched uranium (LEU), which can be used in nuclear power reactors, and weapons-grade highly enriched uranium (HEU), which is one of the two types of fissile material used in nuclear weapons.

The United States has assessed that Tehran possesses the technological and industrial capacity to produce nuclear weapons, but has not yet mastered all of the necessary technologies for building such weapons. Whether Iran has a viable design for a nuclear weapon is unclear. A National Intelligence Estimate made public in 2007 assessed that Tehran "halted its nuclear weapons program" in 2003. The estimate, however, also assessed that Tehran is "keeping open the option to develop nuclear weapons" and that any decision to end a nuclear weapons program is "inherently reversible." U.S. intelligence officials have reaffirmed this judgment on several occasions.

Obtaining fissile material is widely regarded as the most difficult task in building nuclear weapons. As of January 2014, Iran had produced an amount of LEU containing up to 5% uranium-235 which, if further enriched, could theoretically have produced enough HEU for as many as eight nuclear weapons. Iran had also produced LEU containing nearly 20% uranium-235; the total amount of this LEU would, if it had been in the form of uranium hexafluoride and further enriched, have been sufficient for a nuclear weapon. After the Joint Plan of Action, which Tehran concluded with China, France, Germany, Russia, the United Kingdom, and the United States (collectively known as the "P5+1"), went into effect in January 2014, Iran either converted much of its LEU containing nearly 20% uranium-235 for use as fuel in a research reactor located in

* This is an edited, reformatted and augmented version of Congressional Research Service, Publication No. RL34544, dated September 19, 2018.

Tehran, or prepared it for that purpose. Iran has diluted the rest of that stockpile so that it contained no more than 5% uranium-235.

Although Iran claims that its nuclear program is exclusively for peaceful purposes, the program has generated considerable concern that Tehran is pursuing a nuclear weapons program. The U.N. Security Council responded to Iran's refusal to suspend work on its uranium enrichment program by adopting several resolutions that imposed sanctions on Tehran. Despite evidence that sanctions and other forms of pressure have slowed the program, Iran continued to enrich uranium, install additional centrifuges, and conduct research on new types of centrifuges. Tehran has also worked on a heavy-water reactor, which was a proliferation concern because its spent fuel would have contained plutonium—the other type of fissile material used in nuclear weapons. However, plutonium must be separated from spent fuel—a procedure called "reprocessing." Iran has said that it will not engage in reprocessing.

The International Atomic Energy Agency (IAEA) monitors Iran's nuclear facilities and has verified that Tehran's declared nuclear facilities and materials have not been diverted for military purposes. The agency has also verified that Iran has implemented various restrictions on, and provided the IAEA with additional information about, its uranium enrichment program and heavy-water reactor program pursuant to the July 2015 Joint Cooperative Plan of Action (JCPOA), which Tehran concluded with the P5+1. On the JCPOA's Implementation Day, which took place on January 16, 2016, all of the previous Security Council resolutions' requirements were terminated. The nuclear Nonproliferation Treaty (NPT) and U.N. Security Council Resolution 2231, which the Council adopted on July 20, 2015, comprise the current legal framework governing Iran's nuclear program. Iran has continued to comply with the JCPOA and resolution.

Iran and the IAEA agreed in 2007 on a work plan to clarify outstanding questions regarding Tehran's nuclear program, most of which concerned possible Iranian procurement activities and research directly applicable to nuclear weapons development. A December 2015, report to the IAEA Board of Governors from agency Director-General Yukiya Amano contains the IAEA's "final assessment on the resolution" of these outstanding issues.

Then-Under Secretary of State for Political Affairs Wendy Sherman explained during an October 2013 hearing of the Senate Committee on Foreign Relations that Iran would need as much as one year to produce a nuclear weapon if the government made the decision to do so. At the time, Tehran would have needed two to three months of this time to produce enough weapons-grade HEU for a nuclear weapon. Iran's compliance with the JCPOA has lengthened this time to one year, according to U.S. officials. These estimates apparently assume that Iran would use its declared nuclear facilities to produce fissile material for a weapon. However, Tehran would probably use covert facilities for this purpose; Iranian efforts to produce fissile material for nuclear weapons by using its known nuclear facilities would almost certainly be detected by the IAEA.

BACKGROUND

Iran's nuclear program began during the 1950s. Construction of a U.S.-supplied research reactor, called the Tehran Research Reactor (TRR), located in Tehran began in 1960; the reactor went critical in 1967.[1] During the 1970s, Tehran pursued an ambitious

[1] The United States and Iran signed a nuclear cooperation agreement in 1957; it entered into force in 1959. The two countries negotiated another such agreement during the 1970s, but it was never concluded. For a summary of

nuclear power program; according to contemporaneous U.S. documents, Iran wanted to construct 10-20 nuclear power reactors and produce more than 20,000 megawatts of nuclear power by 1994.[2] Iran also began constructing a light-water nuclear power reactor near the city of Bushehr and also considered obtaining uranium enrichment and reprocessing technology.

Iran took steps to demonstrate that it was not pursuing nuclear weapons. For example, Tehran signed the nuclear Nonproliferation Treaty (NPT) in 1968 and ratified it in 1970. Iran also submitted a draft resolution to the U.N. General Assembly in 1974 that called for establishing a nuclear-weapons-free zone in the Middle East. Nevertheless, mid-1970s U.S. intelligence reports expressed concern that Iran might pursue a nuclear weapons program.[3] Although Iran cancelled its nuclear program after its 1979 revolution, a 1981 Department of State draft paper argued that Iran might develop a nuclear weapons program in response to a then-suspected Iraqi nuclear weapons program, although Iran was not one of several countries of "near to medium term proliferation concern" to which the paper referred.[4]

Tehran "reinstituted" the nuclear program in 1982.[5] According to International Atomic Energy Agency (IAEA) reports, Iran conducted experiments during the 1980s and early 1990s related to uranium conversion, heavy water production, and nuclear reactor fuel fabrication. A 1985 National Intelligence Council report, which cited Iran as a potential "proliferation threat," stated that Tehran was "interested in developing facilities that ... could eventually produce fissile material that could be used in a [nuclear] weapon." The report, however, added that it "would take at least a decade" for Iran to do

---

these negotiations, see William Burr, "A Brief History of U.S.-Iranian Nuclear Negotiations," *Bulletin of the Atomic Scientists*, January/February 2009.

[2] The United States was willing to supply Iran with reprocessing technology, according to 1975 and 1976 National Security Council documents. Tehran also had a 1976 contract for a pilot uranium-enrichment facility using lasers (see *Implementation of the NPT Safeguards Agreement and Relevant Provisions of Security Council Resolutions 1737 (2006) and 1747 (2007) in the Islamic Republic of Iran*, Report by the Director General, GOV 2007/58, November 15, 2007. Additionally, according to a 1976 State Department cable, Iran engaged in uranium exploration in Iran and other countries, planned to reprocess spent reactor fuel in the future, and had contemplated building its own enrichment facility, (U.S. Embassy Tehran Airgram A-76 to State Department, "The Atomic Energy Organization of Iran," April 15, 1976).

[3] *Prospects for Further Proliferation of Nuclear Weapons*, Special National Intelligence Estimate, August 23, 1974. A 1975 Department of State memorandum referred to the "uncertainty over" Iran's "long-term objectives despite its NPT status" ("Memorandum for the Assistant to the President for National Security Affairs: Department of State Response to NSSM 219 (Nuclear Cooperation with Iran)," April 18, 1975). A 1975 CIA report identified Iran as one state with the "potential... to cross the explosives threshold within the next ten years." (*Managing Nuclear Proliferation: The Politics of Limited Choice*, Research Study, CIA, December 1975.) A 1988 CIA report (*Middle East-South Asia: Nuclear Handbook*) indicated that Iran had conducted nuclear weapons "design work" before the 1979 revolution.

[4] "Request for Review of Draft Paper on the Security Dimension of Non-Proliferation," Special Assistant for Nuclear Proliferation Intelligence, National Foreign Assessment Center, Central Intelligence Agency, to Resource Management Staff, Office of Program Assessment et al., April 9, 1981. Iraq pursued nuclear, chemical, and biological weapons during the 1980s. The paper argued that Iraq's nuclear program was "intended to provide the option of developing nuclear explosives in the future."

[5] *Middle East-South Asia: Nuclear Handbook*, CIA, May 1988.

so.[6] A 1986 CIA report went further, citing "the advantage of long-range missiles to deliver warheads quickly, virtually without warning, and-unlike aircraft-without facing any defense" as a "factor" that would incentivize Iranian development of nuclear weapons "in the late 1990s."[7] A U.S. intelligence report published 10 years later stated that Iran was "aggressively pursuing a nuclear weapons capability and, if significant foreign assistance were provided, could produce a weapon by the end of the decade."[8]

The Iranian government says that it plans to expand its reliance on nuclear power in order to generate electricity. This program will, Tehran says, substitute for some of Iran's oil and gas consumption and allow the country to export additional fossil fuels; the previous Iranian regime also made this argument.[9] Iran has begun to operate the Bushehr reactor, and Tehran says it intends to build additional reactors to generate 20,000 megawatts of power within the next 20 years.[10] The 2015 Joint Comprehensive Plan of Action (JCPOA) requires Iran to refrain from building heavy water-moderated reactors for 15 years, and Iran pledges to refrain from constructing any such reactors indefinitely. Iranian officials say that Tehran has begun design work on its first indigenously produced light-water reactor, which is to be constructed at Darkhovin. According to official U.S. and Iranian sources, France agreed to construct the reactor during the 1970s, but ended the project after the 1979 revolution in Iran.[11] President of the Atomic Energy Organization of Iran (AEOI) Ali Akbar Salehi stated in September 2016 that "we are almost about to sign a contract for designing" the reactor, "but it will take a rather long time."[12]

---

[6] *The Dynamics of Nuclear Proliferation: Balance of Power and Constraints*, National Intelligence Council, September 1985. A 1985 CIA report articulated a more sanguine view, observing that "there is no evidence that Iran is resuming nuclear research to develop nuclear weapons." ("Overview of Iran's Renewed Efforts for Nuclear Development," Central Intelligence Agency Directorate of Intelligence, August 5, 1985).

[7] *Iran-Iraq: Ballistic Missile Warfare and Its Regional Implications*, An Intelligence Assessment, Central Intelligence Agency Directorate of Intelligence, March 1986.

[8] *The Weapons Proliferation Threat*, Nonproliferation Center, March 1995.

[9] For example, according to a 1976 State Department cable, the President of the Atomic Energy Organization of Iran cited these arguments as reasons for starting an ambitious nuclear program (U.S. Embassy Tehran Airgram A-76 to State Department, 1976). Ambassador Ali Asghar Soltanieh, then Iran's Permanent Representative to the International Atomic Energy Agency, has explained that nuclear power would only meet "perhaps a small portion" of the projected national electricity demand. "Interview with Iran's Ambassador to IAEA," Campaign Against Sanctions and Military Intervention in Iran, June 29, 2008 (published July 2, 2008).

[10] "Iran to Follow Nuclear Timetable Regardless of IAEA Reports—Official," *Islamic Republic of Iran News Network*, February 25, 2009. A spokesperson for the Atomic Energy Organization of Iran stated on January 11, 2016, that the country "needs to generate 20,000 megawatts of nuclear electricity" and should produce 12,000 megawatts of nuclear electricity by 2025 (Sara Ma'sumi, Interview with Behruz Kamalvandi, "Less Than Seven Day to the Implementation of the JCPOA [Joint Comprehensive Plan of Action]," *E'temad*, January 11, 2016).

[11] "Iran Asks France to Remain Committed to N. Power Plant Construction Deal," *FARS News Agency*, October 28, 2014. Director of Central Intelligence, Joint Atomic Energy Intelligence Committee, *Iran's Nuclear Program: Building a Weapons Capability*, February 1993. France completed five percent of the project, according to former President of Iran's Atomic Energy Organization Reza Amrollahi ("If We Want Nuclear Energy, We Should Not Make a Fuss," *Sharq*, September 7, 2013).

[12] "Iran to Build More Power Plants—Nuclear Chief," *IRTV2*, September 10, 2016.

Iranian officials have repeatedly asserted that the country's nuclear program is exclusively for peaceful purposes (see Appendix A). Nevertheless, the United States and other governments have argued that Iran may be pursuing, at a minimum, the capability to produce nuclear weapons. Discerning a peaceful nuclear program from a nuclear weapons program can be difficult because much nuclear technology is dual-use. In addition, military nuclear programs may coexist with civilian programs, even without an explicit governmental decision to produce nuclear weapons.

Jose Goldemberg, Brazil's former secretary of state for science and technology, observed that a country developing the capability to produce nuclear fuel

> does not have to make an explicit early [political] decision to acquire nuclear weapons. In some countries, such a path is supported equally by those who genuinely want to explore an energy alternative and by government officials who either want nuclear weapons or just want to keep the option open.[13]

Some analysts argue that several past nuclear programs, such as those of France, Sweden, and Switzerland, illustrate this approach.[14] A Swedish official involved in that country's nuclear weapons program "argued that the main aim should be the generation of nuclear energy, with plutonium production, which would make possible the manufacture of nuclear weapons as a sideeffect."[15] Moreover, a 1975 U.S. intelligence assessment argued that countries might develop an "unweaponized" nuclear explosive device "to further their political, and even military, objectives."[16]

The main source of proliferation concern generated by Iran's nuclear program has been Tehran's construction of gas centrifuge uranium-enrichment facilities. Gas centrifuges enrich uranium by spinning uranium hexafluoride gas at high speeds to increase the concentration of the uranium-235 isotope. Such centrifuges can produce both low-enriched uranium (LEU), which can be used in nuclear power reactors, and highly enriched uranium (HEU), which is one of the two types of fissile material used in nuclear weapons. HEU can also be used as fuel in certain types of nuclear reactors.[17] Iran also has a uranium-conversion facility, which converts uranium ore concentrate into several

---

[13] Jose Goldemberg, "Looking Back: Lessons from the Denuclearization of Brazil and Argentina," *Arms Control Today*, April 2006.

[14] See James Acton, "The Problem with Nuclear Mind Reading," *Survival*, February-March 2009, pp. 119-142; Paul M. Cole, "Atomic Bombast: Nuclear Weapon Decision-making in Sweden 1945–1972," The Henry L. Stimson Center, 1996; "Neutral States: Sweden and Switzerland," in T.V. Paul, *Power Vs. Prudence: Why Nations Forgo Nuclear* Weapons (Montreal: McGill University Press), 2000, pp. 84-98; and Bruno Tertrais, "Has Iran Decided to Build the Bomb? Lessons from the French Experience," January 30, 2007.

[15] Thomas Jonter, "The Swedish Plans to Acquire Nuclear Weapons, 1945–1968: An Analysis of the Technical Preparations," *Science & Global Security*, 18:61–86, 2010.

[16] Memorandum to Holders, Special National Intelligence Estimate, *Prospects for Further Proliferation of Nuclear Weapons*, SNIE 4-1-74, December 18, 1975. The assessment did not discuss whether Iran was pursuing such an option.

[17] Highly enriched uranium used in nuclear weapons typically contains about 90% uranium-235, whereas low-enriched uranium used in nuclear reactors typically contains less than 5% uranium-235.

compounds, including uranium hexafluoride.[18] This program is currently constrained by the JCPOA. However, following the May 8, 2018, U.S. announcement that the United States would no longer participate in the JCPOA and would reimpose sanctions that had been suspended pursuant to the agreement, Iranian President Hassan Rouhani ordered the AEOI to "go ahead with adequate preparations to resume enrichment at the industrial level without any limit."[19] Iranian officials have asserted that the country can rapidly reconstitute its fissile material production capability.[20]

Iran claims that it wants to produce LEU fuel for its planned light-water nuclear power reactors, as well as the TRR and other planned future research reactors. The latter reactors will be used to produce isotopes for medical purposes, according to Tehran. Although Iran has expressed interest in purchasing nuclear fuel from other countries, Tehran asserts that the country should have an indigenous enrichment capability as a hedge against possible fuel supply disruptions.[21] President Rouhani ordered AEOI President Salehi on December 13, 2016, to provide a plan "for designing and manufacturing nuclear-propulsion system to be used in maritime transportation," as well as producing fuel for such a system.[22] However, Iranian officials have indicated that Tehran would not produce enriched uranium exceeding JCPOA-established enrichment limits.[23] In a January 2018 letter, Iran informed the IAEA of the government's "decision ... to construct naval nuclear propulsion in future."[24] Tehran explained in an April 2018 letter to the agency that "[f]or the first five years, no [nuclear] facility will be involved" and the "[n]uclear fuelled engines/reactors will be used for civilian purpose."[25]

A reactor moderated by heavy water, which Iran was constructing at Arak, was also been a source of concern. Although Tehran says that the reactor is intended for the production of radioisotopes for medical purposes, it had been a proliferation concern because its spent fuel would have contained plutonium well-suited for use in nuclear

---

[18] For a detailed description of the nuclear fuel cycle, see CRS Report RL34234, *Managing the Nuclear Fuel Cycle: Policy Implications of Expanding Global Access to Nuclear Power*, coordinated by Mary Beth D. Nikitin.

[19] "Iran Accepts Remaining in JCPOA Under Condition," *Islamic Republic News Agency*, May 9, 2018.

[20] See, for example, "Iran Can Resume 20 Per Cent Uranium Enrichment Only in 5 Days: Salehi," *Iranian Students News Agency (ISNA)*, August 22, 2017; "AEOI Chief: Iran Able to Resume 20% Enrichment in Maximum 5 Days," *FARS News Agency*, August 22, 2017.

[21] *What Are Iran's "Practical Needs" and Why Does Iran Want to Fuel Reactors on Its Own?*, nuclearenergy.ir, July 2014. "Soltaniyeh: Iran Has No Alternative but to Enrich Uranium," *Islamic Republic News Agency*, October 2, 2008; "Interview with Iran's Ambassador to IAEA," 2008.

[22] "Following U.S Delay, Negligence and Violation of JCPOA; President Orders FM, AEOI Head to Implement Legal Procedures, Produce Nuclear Fuel, Propulsion System," December 13, 2016. Available at http://president.ir/en/96776.

[23] "Iran Nuclear Propulsion Bids to 'Heed' 2015 Deal," *Tasnim News Agency Website*, December 26, 2016; "Salehi Discusses Nuclear Propulsion Systems, Content of Rouhani's Order with Amano," *Islamic Republic News Agency*, December 21, 2016; "AEOI Official: Russia, China Willing to Build Small N. Reactors in Iran," *FARS News Agency*, January 23, 2018.

[24] *Verification and Monitoring in the Islamic Republic of Iran in Light of United Nations Security Council Resolution 2231 (2015)*, Report by the Director General, International Atomic Energy Agency, GOV/2018/7, February 22, 2018.

[25] *Verification and Monitoring in the Islamic Republic of Iran in Light of United Nations Security Council Resolution 2231 (2015)*, Report by the Director General, International Atomic Energy Agency, GOV/2018/24, May 24, 2018.

weapons. Spent nuclear fuel from nuclear reactors contains plutonium, the other type of fissile material used in nuclear weapons. In order to be used in nuclear weapons, however, plutonium must be separated from the spent fuel—a procedure called "reprocessing." Iran has said that it will not engage in reprocessing. This reactor is designed to use natural uranium fuel, which does not require enrichment.

In addition to the dual-use nature of the nuclear programs described above, Iran's inconsistent cooperation with the IAEA contributed to suspicions that Tehran had a nuclear weapons program.[26] In the past, Iran has taken actions that interfered with the agency's investigation of its nuclear program, including concealing nuclear activities and providing misleading statements. Then-IAEA Director-General Mohamed ElBaradei explained in a 2008 interview that Iran's cooperation lagged behind IAEA demands:

> they [the Iranians] have concealed things from us in the past, but that doesn't prove that they are building a bomb today. They continue to insist that they are interested solely in using nuclear power for civilian purposes. We have yet to find a smoking gun that would prove them wrong. But there are suspicious circumstances and unsettling questions. The Iranians' willingness to cooperate leaves a lot to be desired. Iran must do more to provide us with access to certain individuals and documents. It must make a stronger contribution to clarifying the last unanswered set of questions—those relating to a possible military dimension of the Iranian nuclear program.[27]

Consistent with ElBaradei's statement, IAEA Director-General Amano explained in a 2012 interview that the IAEA did not claim that "Iran [has] made a decision to obtain nuclear weapons."[28] Notably, Tehran has implemented various restrictions on, and provided the IAEA with additional information about, its uranium enrichment program and heavy-water reactor program pursuant to the July 2015 Joint Cooperative Plan of Action (JCPOA), which Tehran concluded with China, France, Germany, Russia, the United Kingdom, and the United States.

Iran and the IAEA agreed in August 2007 on a work plan to clarify the outstanding questions regarding Tehran's nuclear program, most of which concerned possible Iranian procurement activities and research directly applicable to nuclear weapons development. A December 2015, report to the IAEA Board of Governors from agency Director-General Yukiya Amano contains the IAEA's "final assessment on the resolution" of these outstanding issues.[29] Iran also has extensive programs to develop ballistic missiles and cruise missiles.

---

[26] For a detailed description of Iran's compliance with its international obligations, see CRS Report R40094, *Iran's Nuclear Program: Tehran's Compliance with International Obligations*, by Paul K. Kerr.

[27] "Interview with IAEA Boss Mohamed ElBaradei," *Der Spiegel*, June 11, 2008.

[28] Jay Solomon and David Crawford, "An Interview with IAEA's Yukiya Amano," *Wall Street Journal*, June 9, 2012.

[29] *Final Assessment on Past and Present Outstanding Issues Regarding Iran's Nuclear Programme*, GOV/2015/68, December 2, 2015.

Current Nuclear Controversy

The current public controversy over Iran's nuclear program began in August 2002, when the National Council of Resistance on Iran (NCRI), an Iranian exile group, revealed information during a press conference (some of which later proved to be accurate) that Iran had built nuclear-related facilities at Natanz and Arak that it had not revealed to the IAEA. The United States had been aware of at least some of these activities, according to knowledgeable former officials.[30] During the mid-1990s, Israel's intelligence services detected Iranian "efforts to develop a military nuclear industry," according to a 2004 Israeli Knesset committee report.[31]

Iran ratified the NPT in 1970. States-parties to the treaty are obligated to conclude a comprehensive safeguards agreement with the IAEA; Tehran concluded such an agreement in 1974. In the case of nonnuclear-weapon states-parties to the treaty (of which Iran is one), such agreements are designed to enable the IAEA to detect the diversion of nuclear material from peaceful purposes to nuclear weapons uses, as well as to detect undeclared nuclear activities and material. As a practical matter, however, the IAEA's ability to inspect and monitor nuclear facilities, as well as obtain relevant information, pursuant to a comprehensive safeguards agreements is limited to facilities that have been declared by the government.[32] Additional Protocols to IAEA safeguards agreements augment the agency's ability to investigate clandestine nuclear facilities and activities by increasing the agency's authority to inspect certain facilities and demand additional information from states-parties.[33] The IAEA's statute requires the agency's Board of Governors to refer cases of noncompliance with safeguards agreements to the U.N. Security Council. Prior to the NCRI's revelations, the IAEA had expressed concerns that Iran had not been providing the agency with all relevant information about its nuclear programs, but had never found Iran in violation of its safeguards agreement.

In fall 2002, the IAEA began to investigate Iran's nuclear activities at Natanz and Arak; inspectors visited the sites the following February. During a June 2003 meeting, the IAEA board first expressed "concern" about Iran's past undeclared nuclear activities and urged Tehran to cooperate with the agency's investigation. The IAEA board's first resolution, which was adopted during a September 2003 meeting, called on Tehran to

---

[30] Gary Samore, Former Senior Director for Nonproliferation and Export Controls on the National Security Council, personal communication June 5, 2008; Former Director of Central Intelligence George J. Tenet, "DCI Remarks on Iraq's WMD Programs," February 5, 2004.

[31] *Report—Volume 1 (Unrestricted section)*, The Committee of Enquiry into the Intelligence System in Light of the War in Iraq, The Knesset Foreign Affairs and Defence Committee, March 2004.

[32] The IAEA does have other investigative tools, such as monitoring scientific publications from member-states. For more information, see CRS Report R40094, *Iran's Nuclear Program: Tehran's Compliance with International Obligations*, by Paul K. Kerr.

[33] NPT states are not required to conclude Additional Protocols. However, applicable U.N. Security Council resolutions require Iran to conclude such a protocol.

increase its cooperation with the agency's investigation and to suspend its uranium enrichment activities. For more detail about Iran's nuclear organization, see Appendix B.

President Rouhani identified the Atomic Energy Organization of Iran (AEOI) as "the authority that was," prior to the June 2003 IAEA board meeting, "basically handling all political and technical issues concerning" the agency's investigation of Iran's nuclear program.[34] Following that meeting, Iran's Supreme National Security Council created the Supreme Nuclear Committee, which was composed of officials from various agencies, including the AEOI and the ministries of defense, foreign affairs, and intelligence.[35] After the IAEA board adopted its September 2003 resolution, the government placed Rouhani, who was the head of the Supreme National Security Council at the time, in charge of the negotiations concerning Iran's nuclear program. Rouhani explained the resulting nuclear decisionmaking process in 2011:

> Even though some people thought the nuclear team was operating with complete prerogatives, the facts were otherwise. The work procedure for every issue was that we first had to discuss the matter in the Supreme Nuclear Committee, then we took that result to the Meeting of Leaders, and finally we acted in accordance with the decision of the leaders.[36]

In October 2003, Iran concluded an agreement with France, Germany, and the United Kingdom, collectively known as the "E3," to suspend its enrichment activities, sign and implement an Additional Protocol to its IAEA safeguards agreement, and comply fully with the IAEA's investigation.[37] As a result, the IAEA board decided to refrain from referring the matter to the U.N. Security Council, despite U.S. advocacy for such a referral.[38] Statements from current and former Iranian officials indicate that, during fall 2003, Tehran feared that the United States might use Security Council referral as a means to undertake military action or other coercive measures against Iran.[39] Rouhani argued in

---

34 "Beyond the Challenges Facing Iran and the IAEA Concerning the Nuclear Dossier," *Rahbord*, September 30, 2005, pp. 7-38.

35 Dr. Hasan Rouhani, *National Security and Nuclear Diplomacy*, (Tehran: Center for Strategic Research), 2011, pp. 24-28. The Supreme Council on New Technologies, which Iran formed in 1998 to focus on the nuclear program, "rarely met" after the June 2003 IAEA board meeting, according to Rouhani.

36 Rouhani 2011, p. 245.

37 The text of the agreement is available at http://www.iaea.org/NewsCenter/Focus/IaeaIran/statement_iran21102003.shtml. Iran signed its Additional Protocol in December 2003, but has not ratified it.

38 "Ex-chief Negotiator Says Iran Leaders Decided to Suspend Nuclear Enrichment," *Aftab-e Yazd*, April 7, 2009; John Bolton, *Surrender Is Not an Option: Defending America at the United Nations and Abroad*, (New York: Threshold Editions), 2008, p. 139; Christopher Ford, "A New Paradigm: Shattering Obsolete Thinking on Arms Control and Nonproliferation," *Arms Control Today*, November 2008. For more details about noncompliance with IAEA safeguards agreements and Security Council referral, see CRS Report R40094, *Iran's Nuclear Program: Tehran's Compliance with International Obligations*, by Paul K. Kerr.

39 *Aftab-e Yazd*, April 7, 2009; *Keyhan*, July 23, 2005; David Patrikarakos, *Nuclear Iran: The Birth of an Atomic State*, (New York: I.B. Tauris), 2012, p. 181; Seyed Hossein Mousavian, *The Iranian Nuclear Crisis: A Memoir*, (Washington, DC: Carnegie Endowment for International Peace), 2012, p. 76.

February 2005 that the United States would not take such action as long as Iran was cooperating with the IAEA and negotiating with the E3.[40]

After October 2003, Iran continued some of its enrichment-related activities, but Tehran and the E3 agreed in November 2004 to a more detailed suspension agreement. During negotiations between fall 2003 and summer 2005, both Iran and the E3 offered a number of proposals, although the two sides never reached agreement.[41] The IAEA's investigation, as well as information Tehran provided after the October 2003 agreement, ultimately revealed that Iran had engaged in a variety of clandestine nuclear-related activities, some of which violated Iran's safeguards agreement. These activities included plutonium separation experiments, uranium enrichment and conversion experiments, and importing various uranium compounds.

Current and former Iranian officials have depicted a government deeply divided during this time over diplomatic approaches regarding its nuclear program. For example, Seyed Hossein Mousavian, who was Iran's spokesperson during the government's 2003-2005 negotiations with France, Germany, and the United Kingdom (collectively known as the "E3"), explained that in 2003 "there were two schools of thought in Iran. One group advocated engagement with the West, while others were proponents of resistance."[42] President Rouhani, who headed the 2003-2005 negotiations, explained during a July 2005 interview that certain parts of the Iranian government opposed the diplomatic track, adding that "[t]he problems included both disharmony and sabotage."[43] Indeed, Rouhani later argued that Iran's Supreme National Security Council took charge of the diplomacy concerning the nuclear program because

> the Foreign Ministry was not able to be responsible for this task in a good way because some organizations did not pay sufficient attention to this ministry's decisions, especially since there had been disagreements for months between the Foreign Ministry and the Atomic Energy Organization.[44]

In a 2005 article, an Iranian Foreign Ministry official explained that the decision to delegate responsibility for the nuclear issue to the Supreme National Security Council was

> aimed at creating domestic consensus and preventing any possible discrepancies in the decision making process and its implementation at the national level. It was

[40] "Iranian Official Rowhani Gives Interview, Discusses Talks with EU, Criticizes U.S.," *Tehran Vision of the Islamic Republic of Iran Network 2*, February 7, 2005.

[41] These proposals are available at http://www.armscontrol.org/factsheets/Iran_Nuclear_Proposals.

[42] Ali Vaez, "Seyed Hossein Mousavian: The West is Pushing Iran in the Wrong Direction," *Bulletin of the Atomic Scientists*, November 18, 2011.

[43] Mehdi Mohammadi, "Nuclear Case From Beginning to End in Interview with Dr. Hasan Rowhani (Part 1): We Are Testing Europe," *Keyhan*, July 23, 2005.

[44] Rouhani 2011, p. 71.

> demonstrated in practice that this decision was crucial in preventing the friction between the government, parliament and all other relevant agencies.[45]

Iran resumed uranium conversion in August 2005 under the leadership of then-President Ahmadinejad, who had been elected two months earlier. On September 24, 2005, the IAEA Board of Governors adopted a resolution that, for the first time, found Iran to be in noncompliance with its IAEA safeguards agreement. The board, however, did not refer Iran to the Security Council, choosing instead to give Tehran additional time to comply with the board's demands. Iran announced in January 2006 that it would resume research and development on its centrifuges at Natanz. In response, the IAEA board adopted a resolution on February 4, 2006, that referred Iran's case to the Security Council. Two days later, Tehran announced that it would stop implementing its Additional Protocol.

In March 2006, the U.N. Security Council President issued a statement, which was not legally binding, that called on Iran to "take the steps required" by the February IAEA board resolution. The council subsequently adopted six resolutions concerning Iran's nuclear program: 1696 (July 2006), 1737 (December 2006), 1747 (March 2007), 1803 (March 2008), 1835 (September 2008), and 1929 (June 2010). The second, third, fourth, and sixth resolutions imposed a variety of restrictions on Iran. In addition, these resolutions required Iran to cooperate fully with an ongoing IAEA investigation of its nuclear activities, suspend its uranium enrichment program, suspend its construction of a heavy water reactor and related projects, and ratify the Additional Protocol to Iran's IAEA safeguards agreement. Resolution 1929 also required Tehran to refrain from "any activity related to ballistic missiles capable of delivering nuclear weapons" and to comply with a modified provision (called code 3.1) of Iran's subsidiary arrangement to its IAEA safeguards agreement. Beginning in June 2006, Iran later held multiple rounds of talks with China, France, Germany, Russia, the United Kingdom, and the United States, collectively known as the "P5+1," concerning various proposals for resolving the nuclear dispute. Saeed Jalili, then-head of Iran's Supreme National Security Council, conducted Iran's nuclear negotiations.

Following his June 2013 election, Iranian President Rouhani delegated the "nuclear negotiations portfolio" to the Foreign Ministry, he explained in a September 2013 interview.[46] The AEOI continued to be responsible for Tehran's negotiations with the IAEA. Supreme Leader Khamene'i was the ultimate decisionmaker regarding Iran's diplomacy concerning the Joint Cooperative Plan of Action; then-Under Secretary of

---

[45] Hamid Baeidi-Nejad, "Khatami's Nuclear Policy," *Iranian Journal of International Affairs,* vol. 18, No. 1 (Spring 2005), p. 61. An Iranian Foreign Ministry official with the same name was a participant in Iran's negotiations regarding its nuclear program.

[46] "Iranian President Hassan Rouhani Speaks with NBC News' Ann Curry in Tehran," September 18, 2013. A Foreign Ministry spokesperson told an Iranian news agency that the Supreme National Security Council would continue coordinating the talks, but the foreign ministry would have the lead. ("FM: Iran Restructuring Team of Negotiators in Upcoming N. Talks with World Powers," *FARS News Agency*, September 9, 2013).

State for Political Affairs Wendy Sherman explained during a December 2013 hearing that Khamene'i "is the only one who really holds the nuclear file—makes the final decisions about whether Iran will reach a comprehensive agreement to forego much of what it has created in return for the economic relief it seeks."

The Supreme Leader remained in charge of decisions regarding the nuclear program following Rouhani's 2013 election. Deputy Foreign Minister Seyed Abbas Araqchi explained in July 2016 that the nuclear issue was "under the senior management" of Khamene'i, adding that

> With regards the major foreign policy issues the more the decision making progresses and enters important levels the higher the level of engagement; it moves up from the ministry to the administration level and from the administration to the level of Supreme National Security Council and at the end to the supreme leader.[47]

Iran and the P5+1 met three times before concluding the Joint Plan of Action (JPA) on November 24, 2013. This agreement placed certain limitations on Iran's nuclear program and also set out an approach toward reaching a long-term comprehensive solution to international concerns regarding Iran's nuclear program. The two sides began implementing the JPA on January 20, 2014. The P5+1 and Iran reached a framework of a Joint Comprehensive Plan of Action (JCPOA) on April 2, 2015, and finalized the JCPOA on July 14, 2015. The parties began implementing the JCPOA on January 16, 2016. On that day, all of the previous Security Council resolutions' requirements were terminated. The NPT and U.N. Security Council Resolution 2231 comprise the current legal framework governing Iran's nuclear program.[48] For more information about multilateral diplomacy concerning Iran's nuclear program, see Appendix C.

Iran's Cooperation with the IAEA

Possible Military Dimensions

As noted, the IAEA investigation of Iran's nuclear program began in 2002. Iran and the IAEA agreed in August 2007 on a work plan to clarify the outstanding questions regarding Tehran's nuclear program.[49] Most of these issues,[50] which had contributed to suspicions that Iran had been pursuing a nuclear weapons program, were essentially

---

[47] "The Current Restrictions Have Nothing to do with the JCPOA," *Iran Newspaper*, July 13, 2016.

[48] "Joint Statement by EU High Representative Federica Mogherini and Iranian Foreign Minister Javad Zarif," January 16, 2016.

[49] The text of the work plan is available at http://www.iaea.org/Publications/Documents/Infcircs/2007/infcirc711.pdf.

[50] These issues included plutonium experiments, research and procurement efforts associated with two types of centrifuges, operations of a uranium mine, and experiments with polonium-210, which (in conjunction with beryllium) is used as a neutron initiator in certain types of nuclear weapons.

resolved by June 2008, but then-IAEA Director-General ElBaradei told the IAEA Board of Governors on June 2, 2008, that there is "one remaining major [unresolved] issue," which concerns questions regarding "possible military dimensions to Iran's nuclear programme."

Iran and the IAEA subsequently held a series of discussions regarding these issues. The agency provided Iran with documents or, in some cases, descriptions of documents which had been provided to the IAEA by several governments. The documents indicated that Iranian entities may have conducted studies related to nuclear weapons development. The subjects of these studies included uranium conversion, missile reentry vehicles for delivering nuclear warheads, and conventional explosives used in nuclear weapons. Iranian officials have claimed that the documents are not authentic,[51] but ElBaradei told the IAEA board on June 17, 2009, that there was "enough in these alleged studies to create concern in the minds of our professional inspectors." Iranian officials acknowledged that some of the information in the documents is accurate, but argued that the activities described were exclusively for nonnuclear purposes.[52] Tehran has provided some relevant information about these matters to the IAEA, but ElBaradei reported in August 2009 that the government should "provide more substantive responses" to the IAEA, as well as "the opportunity to have detailed discussions with a view to moving forward on these issues, including granting the agency access to persons, information and locations identified in the documents."[53]

IAEA Director-General Amano issued a report to the IAEA board in November 2011 which stated that Iran had not "engaged with the agency in any substantive way" on the alleged studies since August 2008.[54] According to this report, which provided the most detailed account to date of the IAEA's evidence regarding Iran's suspected nuclear weapons-related activities, the agency has "credible" information that Iran has carried out activities "relevant to the development of a nuclear explosive device." These activities include acquisition of "nuclear weapons development information and documentation,"

---

[51] In a September 28, 2008, letter to the IAEA, Iran described some characteristics of the documents discussed above. The letter stated that some of the information from the United States was shown to Iranian officials as PowerPoint presentations. Additionally, some of the documents are "in contradiction with typical standard Iranian documentation" and lack "classification seals," the letter said. See, Permanent Mission of the Islamic Republic of Iran, *Explanatory Comments by the Islamic Republic of Iran on the Report of the IAEA Director General to the September 2008 Board of Governors* (GOV/2008/38), September 28, 2008. INFCIRC/737. Iran also complained that the IAEA has not provided Tehran with original versions of some documentation related to the alleged "military dimensions" of Iran's nuclear program. Several reports from ElBaradei have stated that the agency has not had permission to provide this documentation from the governments which provided it. In his November 2009 report, ElBaradei again called on such governments to authorize the IAEA to share additional information with Iran.

[52] *Implementation of the NPT Safeguards Agreement and Relevant Provisions of Security Council Resolutions 1737 (2006), 1747 (2007) and 1803 (2008) in the Islamic Republic of Iran*, Report by the Director General, GOV/2008/15, May 26, 2008.

[53] *Implementation of the NPT Safeguards Agreement and Relevant Provisions of Security Council Resolutions 1737 (2006), 1747 (2007), 1803 (2008) and 1835 (2008) in the Islamic Republic of Iran*, Report by the Director General, GOV/2009/55, August 28, 2009.

[54] *Implementation of the NPT Safeguards Agreement and Relevant Provisions of Security Council Resolutions in the Islamic Republic of Iran*, GOV/2011/65, November 8, 2011.

work to develop "an indigenous design of a nuclear weapon including the testing of components," efforts "to procure nuclear related and dual use equipment and materials by military related individuals and entities," and work to "develop undeclared pathways for the production of nuclear material." Although some of these activities have civilian applications, "others are specific to nuclear weapons," the report notes. Most of these activities were conducted before the end of 2003, though some may have continued. (See Appendix D and "Nuclear Weapon Development Capabilities" for more details.)

The IAEA Board of Governors adopted a resolution on November 18, 2011, stating that "it is essential" for Iran and the IAEA "to intensify their dialogue aiming at the urgent resolution of all outstanding substantive issues." IAEA and Iranian officials met 10 times between January 2012 and May 2013 to discuss what the agency termed a "structured approach to the clarification of all outstanding issues related to Iran's nuclear programme."[55] However, during an October 2013 meeting, IAEA officials and their Iranian counterparts decided to adopt a "new approach" to resolving these issues. Iran signed a joint statement with the IAEA on November 11, 2013, describing a "Framework for Cooperation." According to the statement, Iran and the IAEA agreed to "strengthen their cooperation and dialogue aimed at ensuring the exclusively peaceful nature of Iran's nuclear programme through the resolution of all outstanding issues that have not already been resolved by the IAEA." Tehran subsequently provided the IAEA with information about several of the outstanding issues and later agreed in May 2014 to provide information to the agency by August 25, 2014, about five additional issues, including alleged Iranian research on high explosives and "studies made and/or papers published in Iran in relation to neutron transport and associated modelling and calculations and their alleged application to compressed materials." Iran subsequently provided information about four of these issues.[56]

The July 2015 JCPOA states that Tehran was to "complete" a series of steps set out in an IranIAEA "Roadmap for Clarification of Past and Present Outstanding Issues." According to IAEA Director-General Amano, this road map, which the two sides concluded in July 2015, set out "a process" under the November 2013 JPA "to enable the Agency, with the cooperation of Iran, to make an assessment of issues relating to possible military dimensions to Iran's nuclear programme."[57] According to a December 2, 2015, report to the IAEA Board of Governors from Amano, "[a]ll the activities contained in the

[55] A September 2012 IAEA Board of Governors resolution reiterated the board's support for the Agency's negotiations with Tehran, and stated that "Iranian cooperation with IAEA requests aimed at the resolution of all outstanding issues is essential and urgent in order to restore international confidence in the exclusively peaceful nature of Iran's nuclear programme."

[56] *Implementation of the NPT Safeguards Agreement and Relevant Provisions of Security Council Resolutions in the Islamic Republic of Iran*, Report by the Director General, GOV/2015/34, May 29, 2015.

[57] For more information about the Joint Plan of Action and the JCPOA, see CRS Report R43333, *Iran Nuclear Agreement*, by Kenneth Katzman and Paul K. Kerr.

road-map were implemented in accordance with the agreed schedule."[58] The road map required Amano to present this report, which contains the agency's "final assessment on the resolution" of the aforementioned outstanding issues.

In response, the board adopted a resolution on December 15, 2015, that notes Iran's cooperation with the road map and "further notes that this closes the Board's consideration" of the "outstanding issues regarding Iran's nuclear programme."[59] Since the IAEA has verified that Iran has taken the steps required for Implementation Day to take effect, the board is no longer focused on either Iran's compliance with past Security Council resolutions or past issues concerning Iran's safeguards agreement. Instead, the board is focused on monitoring and verifying Iran's JCPOA implementation "in light of" United Nations Security Council Resolution 2231, which the Council adopted on July 20, 2015. The December 2015 IAEA resolution requests the Director General to issue quarterly reports to the board regarding Iran's "implementation of its relevant commitments under the JCPOA for the full duration of those commitments." The Director General is also to report to the IAEA Board of Governors and the Security Council "at any time if the Director General has reasonable grounds to believe there is an issue of concern" regarding Tehran's compliance with its JCPOA or safeguards obligations.[60]

Parchin

Parchin is an Iranian military site. As part of its investigation into "possible military dimensions" of Iran's nuclear program, the IAEA wanted Tehran to respond to information which the agency obtained from unnamed governments indicating that in 2000 "Iran constructed a large explosives containment vessel" at Parchin in which to conduct experiments related to the development of nuclear weapons, according to Amano's November 2011 report,[61] which did not say whether Iran actually built the vessel or conducted these experiments at Parchin. IAEA inspectors visited the site twice in 2005, but did not visit the location "believed to contain the building which houses the explosives chamber."[62] The agency requested access to this latter building in February 2012, but Iran did not provide such access until September 2015 as part of the road map described above. At that time, IAEA officials conducted and supervised verification

---

58 *Final Assessment on Past and Present Outstanding Issues Regarding Iran's Nuclear Programme*, GOV/2015/68, December 2, 2015.

59 *Joint Comprehensive Plan of Action Implementation and Verification and Monitoring in the Islamic Republic of Iran in Light of United Nations Security Council Resolution 2231 (2015)*, Resolution Adopted by the Board of Governors, GOV/2015/72, December 15, 2015.

60 The JCPOA and U.N. Security Council Resolution 2231 contain a variety of reporting provisions for the IAEA. For example, the resolution requests the agency's Director General to provide regular updates to the IAEA Board of Governors and, as appropriate, in parallel to the Security Council on Iran's implementation of its commitments under the JCPOA and also to report to the IAEA Board of Governors and in parallel to the Security Council at any time if the Director General has reasonable grounds to believe there is an issue of concern directly affecting fulfilment of JCPOA commitments.

61 GOV/2011/65.

62 Ibid.

activities, including "visual observation and environmental sampling," but they "did not observe a chamber or any associated equipment inside the building."[63] Iranian officials told their IAEA counterparts in October 2015 that the building in question "had always been used for the storage of chemical material for the production of explosives," but the "information available" to the IAEA, "does not support Iran's statements on the purpose of the building."[64] Beginning in February 2012, Iran apparently undertook efforts to remove evidence of past nuclear-related activities at the site. These efforts, which included landscaping, refurbishing buildings, demolishing buildings, and removing and replacing external wall structures, "seriously undermined the Agency's ability to conduct effective verification," according to Amano's December 2, 2015, report.

Iranian officials have implied that the government's refusal to allow IAEA post-2005 access to Parchin was due to Defense Ministry resistance. Fereydoun Abbasi-Davani, then-AEOI President, indicated in 2012 that allowing inspectors to the site was the Iranian military's decision.[65] Rouhani in 2011 described a contentious internal debate regarding access to Parchin:

> In the area of Agency inspections and especially the inspections of military centers such as Parchin, this was debated for months inside the country and this issue was therefore raised in various meetings over the circumstances in which these inspections would take place. There was serious opposition to the Agency's request to inspect Parchin; the nation's domestic political climate was vigorously opposed to inspectors inspecting Parchin and military centers in general.[66]

For more information about the Parchin site, see Appendix D.

Other Issues

Iran did cooperate with the IAEA in other respects, albeit with varying consistency. The IAEA was (and still is) able to verify that Iran's declared nuclear facilities and materials have not been diverted for military purposes. Moreover, Tehran provided the agency with "information similar to that which Iran had previously provided pursuant to the Additional Protocol," ElBaradei reported to the IAEA board in February 2008, adding that this information clarified the agency's "knowledge about Iran's current declared nuclear programme."[67] Iran, however, provided this information "on an ad hoc basis and not in a consistent and complete manner," the report said. Indeed, the IAEA requested in April 2008 that Iran provide "as a transparency measure, access to additional locations related ... to the manufacturing of centrifuges, research and development (R&D) on

---

[63] GOV/2015/68.
[64] Ibid.
[65] "Iran: Military Decides if IAEA Can Visit Parchin," *Reuters*, February 29, 2012.
[66] Rouhani 2011, p. 244.
[67] GOV/2008/4.

uranium enrichment, and uranium mining."[68] Tehran provided such access pursuant to the 2013 JPA.

ElBaradei's February 2008 report underscored the importance of full Iranian cooperation with the IAEA investigation, as well as Tehran's implementation of its Additional Protocol:

> Confidence in the exclusively peaceful nature of Iran's nuclear programme requires that the Agency be able to provide assurances not only regarding declared nuclear material, but, equally importantly, regarding the absence of undeclared nuclear material and activities in Iran.... Although Iran has provided some additional detailed information about its current activities on an ad hoc basis, the Agency will not be in a position to make progress towards providing credible assurances about the absence of undeclared nuclear material and activities in Iran before reaching some clarity about the nature of the alleged studies, and without implementation of the Additional Protocol.[69]

The IAEA also asked Iran to "reconsider" its March 2007 decision to stop complying with a portion of the subsidiary arrangements for its IAEA safeguards agreement.[70] That provision (called code 3.1), to which Iran agreed in February 2003, requires Tehran to provide design information for new nuclear facilities "as soon as the decision to construct, or to authorize construction, of such a facility has been taken, whichever is earlier." Previously, Iran was required to provide design information for a new facility 180 days before introducing nuclear material into it.[71] Iran invoked the March 2007 decision when it withheld from the IAEA until September 2009 "preliminary design information" for the planned Darkhovin reactor; the agency first requested the information in December 2007. Although Iran provided the agency with preliminary design information about the Darkhovin reactor in a September 22, 2009, letter, the IAEA requested Tehran to "provide additional clarifications" of the information.[72] Amano reported in September 2010 that Iran had "provided only limited design information with respect to" the reactor.[73]

---

[68] GOV/2008/15.

[69] *Implementation of the NPT Safeguards Agreement and Relevant Provisions of Security Council Resolutions 1737 (2006) and 1747(2007) in the Islamic Republic of Iran*, Report by the Director General, GOV/2008/4, February 22, 2008.

[70] According to the 2001 IAEA Safeguards Glossary, subsidiary arrangements describe the "technical and administrative procedures for specifying how the provisions laid down in a safeguards agreement are to be applied."

[71] For more detail about Iran's safeguards obligations and reporting requirements, see CRS Report R40094, *Iran's Nuclear Program: Tehran's Compliance with International Obligations*, by Paul K. Kerr.

[72] *Implementation of the NPT Safeguards Agreement and Relevant Provisions of Security Council Resolutions 1737 (2006), 1747 (2007), 1803 (2008) and 1835 (2008) in the Islamic Republic of Iran,* Report by the Director General, GOV/2008/59, November 19, 2008.

[73] *Implementation of the NPT Safeguards Agreement in Relevant Provisions of Security Council Resolutions in the Islamic Republic of Iran*, Report by the Director General, GOV/2010/46, September 6, 2010. IAEA reports since 2012 do not appear to address this issue.

Tehran also refused to provide updated design information for the Arak reactor—a decision which, according to a May 2013 report from Amano, had "an adverse impact on the Agency's ability to effectively verify the design of the facility."[74] As part of the JPA, Iran submitted this information to the IAEA on February 12, 2014.[75] Pursuant to the JCPOA, Iran has committed to redesign and rebuild the Arak reactor based on a design agreed to by the P5+1 so that it will not produce weapons-grade plutonium. Iran has rendered the reactor's original core inoperable.

Iran had also refused to allow IAEA officials to conduct an inspection of the Arak reactor in order to verify design information that Tehran provided to the agency. ElBaradei argued in a June 2009 report to the IAEA board that this continued refusal "could adversely impact the Agency's ability to carry out effective safeguards at that facility," adding that satellite imagery is insufficient because Iran has completed the "containment structure over the reactor building, and the roofing for the other buildings on the site."[76] However, IAEA inspectors visited the reactor facility in August 2009 to verify design information, according to ElBaradei's report issued the same month; IAEA inspectors had last visited the reactor in August 2008. Inspectors have visited the facility several more times, according to reports from Amano.

In addition, Iran failed to notify the IAEA until September 2009 that it was constructing a uranium enrichment facility, called the Fordow Fuel Enrichment Plant, near the city of Qom. Iran revealed in September 2009 that it had been constructing the facility and provided some details about it to the IAEA in a September 21, 2009, letter. Four days after the IAEA received the letter, British, French, and U.S. officials revealed that they had previously developed intelligence on the facility. The three governments provided a detailed intelligence briefing to the IAEA after the agency received Iran's letter. U.S. officials have said that, despite its letter to the agency, Iran intended for the facility to be kept secret. Tehran placed the facility under IAEA safeguards after its September 2009 letter. (For more details, see the "Fordow Enrichment Facility" section below.) Pursuant to the JCPOA, Iran has begun to convert its Fordow enrichment facility into "a nuclear, physics, and technology centre" in which no nuclear material will be present.

In a letter published on October 1, 2009, the IAEA asked Iran to provide additional information about the facility, including "further information with respect to the name and location of the pilot enrichment facility, the current status of its construction and plans for the introduction of nuclear material into the facility." The letter also requested that Tehran provide IAEA inspectors with access to the facility "as soon as possible."

---

[74] *Implementation of the NPT Safeguards Agreement and Relevant Provisions of Security Council Resolutions in the Islamic Republic of Iran, Report by the Director General*, GOV/2013/27, May 22, 2013.

[75] *Implementation of the NPT Safeguards Agreement and Relevant Provisions of Security Council Resolutions 1737 (2006), 1747 (2007), 1803 (2008) and 1835 (2008) in the Islamic Republic of Iran*, Report by the Director General, GOV/2009/35, June 5, 2009.

[76] *Implementation of the NPT Safeguards Agreement and Relevant Provisions of Security Council Resolutions in the Islamic Republic of Iran,* Report by the Director General, GOV/2014/10, February 20, 2014.

IAEA officials inspected the facility and met with Iranian officials in late October 2009. According to a November 2009 report from ElBaradei to the IAEA board, Tehran "provided access to all areas of the facility," which "corresponded with the design information provided by Iran" a week before the visit. IAEA officials have since conducted regular inspections of the facility. Although Iran provided additional design information about the facility to the IAEA, the agency still had questions about the facility's "purpose and chronology" and wished to interview other Iranian officials and review additional documentation, according to ElBaradei's report. Amano reported in May 2012 that Iran has provided the IAEA with some requested information regarding the Fordow construction decision, but the agency still wanted more information from Tehran.[77] Tehran, according to Amano's November 2015 report, has not yet provided all of this information.[78] Subsequent reports from Amano have not addressed the issue.

The IAEA has also requested additional information about Iran's production of heavy water. As noted, Iran is constructing a heavy-water nuclear reactor. ElBaradei's November 2009 report states that, during an inspection of Iran's uranium conversion facility the previous month, IAEA inspectors "observed 600 50-litre drums said by Iran to contain heavy water."[79] The inspectors visited the facility in order to verify updated design information submitted by Iran in August 2009 and observed the drums after gaining access to an area of the facility which agency inspectors had not previously visited.[80] Tehran has told the IAEA that the water originated in Iran and has permitted agency inspectors to count the number of drums and to weigh a "small number of randomly selected drums."[81] For a time, Tehran did not permit the agency to take samples of the heavy water, but did allow such access in February 2014.[82] Similarly, Iran for some time did not grant repeated IAEA requests for "further access" to the country's heavy-water production plant since agency inspectors visited the facility in August 2011.[83] However, Iran granted such access in December 2013.[84]

The IAEA apparently resolved a discrepancy discovered during an August 2011 inspection of an Iranian research laboratory that had been used to conduct uranium conversion experiments. IAEA measurements revealed that Iran had overstated the

---

[77] *Implementation of the NPT Safeguards Agreement and Relevant Provisions of Security Council Resolutions in the Islamic Republic of Iran,* Report by the Director General, GOV/2012/23, May 25, 2012.

[78] *Implementation of the NPT Safeguards Agreement and Relevant Provisions of Security Council Resolutions in the Islamic Republic of Iran*, GOV/2015/65, Report by the Director General, November 18, 2015.

[79] *Implementation of the NPT Safeguards Agreement and Relevant Provisions of Security Council Resolutions 1737 (2006), 1747 (2007), 1803 (2008) and 1835 (2008) in the Islamic Republic of Iran*, Report by the Director General, GOV/2009/74, November 16, 2009.

[80] CRS analyst interview with a U.S. official, December 17, 2009.

[81] *Implementation of the NPT Safeguards Agreement and Relevant Provisions of Security Council Resolutions 1737 (2006), 1747 (2007), 1803 (2008) and 1835 (2008) in the Islamic Republic of Iran*, Report by the Director General, GOV/2010/10, February 18, 2010.

[82] *Implementation of the NPT Safeguards Agreement and Relevant Provisions of Security Council Resolutions in the Islamic Republic of Iran, Report by the Director General*, GOV/2015/15, February 19, 2015.

[83] Ibid.

[84] GOV/2015/65.

amount of material in the facility, described in Amano's November 2011 report as "natural uranium metal and process waste," by almost 20 kilograms.[85] Iran and the IAEA appear to have resolved the issue in 2013.[86]

STATUS OF IRAN'S NUCLEAR FACILITIES

Some nongovernmental experts and former U.S. officials have argued that, rather than producing fissile material for nuclear weapons indigenously, Iran could obtain such material from foreign sources.[87] A November 2007 National Intelligence Estimate (NIE) states that the intelligence community "cannot rule out that Iran has acquired from abroad—or will acquire in the future—a nuclear weapon or enough fissile material for a weapon."[88] A senior intelligence official characterized such acquisition as "an inherent option" for Iran.[89] However, Tehran's potential ability to produce its own fissile material highly is a greater cause of concern; the official explained that "getting bits and pieces of fissile material from overseas is not going to be sufficient" to produce a nuclear arsenal.[90] As noted, uranium enrichment facilities can produce highly enriched uranium (HEU), which is one of the two types of fissile material used in nuclear weapons. The other type is plutonium, which is separated from spent nuclear reactor fuel.

According to a November 14, 2013, IAEA report, Iran had generally stopped expanding its enrichment and heavy water reactor programs during the negotiations leading up to the JPA, which the parties finalized later that month.[91] That agreement essentially froze most aspects of Iran's nuclear program to allow time to negotiate the July 2015 JCPOA. When the JPA went into effect in January 2014, Iran had enough uranium hexafluoride containing up to 5% uranium-235, which, if further enriched, would have yielded enough weapons-grade HEU for as many as eight nuclear weapons.[92] The total amount of Iranian uranium hexafluoride containing 20% uranium-235 would, if it had been further enriched, have been sufficient for a nuclear weapon. Pursuant to the JCPOA, Iran has restricted and/or dismantled various portions of its nuclear program;

[85] Ibid.

[86] GOV/2013/27.

[87] See, for example, then-Under Secretary of State for U.S. Arms Control and International Security Robert Joseph's testimony before the Senate Committee on Foreign Relations, February 9, 2006, and then-Director of Research Institute for National Strategic Studies National Defense University Stephen Cambone's testimony before the Senate Committee on Governmental Affairs, September 21, 2000.

[88] *Iran: Nuclear Intentions and Capabilities*, National Intelligence Estimate, November 2007.

[89] "Unclassified Key Judgments of the National Intelligence Estimate: Iran: Nuclear Intentions and Capabilities," Background Briefing with Senior Intelligence Officials, December 3, 2007.

[90] Ibid.

[91] *Implementation of the NPT Safeguards Agreement and Relevant Provisions of Security Council Resolutions in the Islamic Republic of Iran*, Report by the Director General, GOV/2013/56, November 14, 2013.

[92] Colin Kahl, Deputy Assistant to the President and National Security Adviser to the Vice President, "Arms Control Association Annual Meeting: Unprecedented Challenges for Nonproliferation and Disarmament," May 14, 2015.

Iran currently lacks enough low-enriched uranium hexafluoride to produce a nuclear weapon.

Uranium Enrichment Facilities

Iran has used three centrifuge facilities to enrich uranium: a pilot centrifuge facility and a larger commercial facility, both located at Natanz, and the Fordow centrifuge facility located near the city of Qom. Iran also has a variety of facilities and workshops involved in the production of centrifuges and related components. During a July 31, 2015, press briefing about possible Iranian undeclared nuclear facilities, U.S. Secretary of Energy Ernest Moniz stated that "we feel pretty confident that we know their current configuration."[93]

Natanz Commercial Facility

This facility was to have held approximately 50,000 centrifuges.[94] Former Vice President Gholamreza Aghazadeh, who also headed the AEOI until July 2009, explained in February 2009 that Iran intended to install all of the centrifuges by 2015.[95] Iran began enriching uranium in the facility after mid-April 2007; as of November 5, 2013, the facility had produced 10,357 kilograms of low-enriched uranium hexafluoride containing up to 5% uranium-235. This quantity of LEU, if it had been further enriched, would have yielded enough weapons-grade HEU for as many as eight nuclear weapons.[96,97] As of

---

[93] See also Colin H. Kahl, "Not Time to Attack Iran: Why War Should Be a Last Resort," *Foreign Affairs*, January 17, 2012.

[94] A 2008 IAEA report states that Iran was planning to install 16 cascade units, each containing 18 164-centrifuge cascades. The total number of centrifuges would be 47,232. Iran, however, installed some cascades containing 174 centrifuges (*Implementation of the NPT Safeguards Agreement and Relevant Provisions of Security Council Resolutions 1737 (2006), 1747 (2007) and 1803 (2008) in the Islamic Republic of Iran*, Report by the Director General, GOV/2008/15, May 26, 2008). According to September 25, 2009, Obama Administration talking points, the facility "is designed to house 54,000 centrifuges." Gholamreza Aghazadeh, who headed Iran's Atomic Energy Organization (AEOI), said in February 2009 that Iran would install 50,000 centrifuges ("Iran to Follow Nuclear Timetable Regardless of IAEA Reports—Official," *Islamic Republic of Iran News Network*, February 25, 2009). A 2012 AEOI report gives the facility's "overall capacity" as 48,000 centrifuges (*Nuclear Industry in Iran: An Overview on Iran's Activities and Achievements in Nuclear Technology*, Atomic Energy Organization of Iran, 2012, p. 16).

[95] *Islamic Republic of Iran News Network*, February 25, 2009.

[96] Colin Kahl, Deputy Assistant to the President and National Security Adviser to the Vice President, "Arms Control Association Annual Meeting: Unprecedented Challenges for Nonproliferation and Disarmament," May 14, 2015.See also calculations from *Iran's Nuclear, Chemical, and Biological Capabilities: A Net Assessment,* International Institute for Strategic Studies, 2011, p.72. The latter report points out that Iran would likely need to produce more uranium-235 in order to produce its first nuclear weapon because "the fabrication of an initial bomb would involve an amount of unavoidable wastage" (p. 69).

[97] This number of nuclear weapons assumes that 25 kilograms of uranium-235 (approximately 27.8 kilograms of uranium containing 90% uranium-235) would be necessary for one HEU-based nuclear weapon. The IAEA term for this amount of uranium is "significant quantity," defined as the "approximate amount of nuclear material for which the possibility of manufacturing a nuclear explosive device cannot be excluded." A 2011 International Institute for Strategic Studies report points out that Iran would likely need to produce more than this amount in order to produce its first nuclear weapon because "the fabrication of an initial bomb would

October 31, 2015, the facility had produced 15,525 kilograms of uranium hexafluoride containing up to 5% uranium-235. However, Iran only had approximately 8,305 kilograms of this material because the rest was converted into various other chemical forms.[98]

Individual centrifuges are linked together in cascades; each cascade in the commercial facility contained either 164 or 174 centrifuges. As of May 17, 2015, Tehran had installed about 15,400 first generation (IR-1) centrifuges, approximately 9,150 of which were enriching uranium. Iran had also installed about 1,000 centrifuges of greater efficiency, called IR-2m centrifuges, in the facility. The IR-2m centrifuges were not enriching uranium.[99] Amano reported in February 2017 that, pursuant to its JCPOA commitments, Iran had 5,060 IR-1 centrifuges installed in the facility and had removed all other centrifuges.[100] Iran has been producing enriched uranium hexafluoride continuing no more than 3.67% uranium-235 but also shipped out most of its LEU to Russia on December 28, 2015, to reduce its stockpile to the required levels.[101] Iran's total stockpile of this material has not exceeded 300 kilograms.[102]

Natanz Pilot Facility

Iran began enriching uranium up to 20% uranium-235 in the Natanz pilot facility in February 2010. Iranian officials stated that this enriched uranium was to serve as fuel in Iran's Tehran Research Reactor (TRR), as well as future such research reactors.[103] Construction of the U.S. – supplied TRR began in 1960, and it went critical in 1967.

involve an amount of unavoidable wastage" (*Nuclear, Chemical, and Biological Capabilities*, p. 69). Some types of weapons could be developed using less uranium-235.

The term "significant quantity" should be understood in the context of IAEA safeguards objectives. One such objective, according to the agency, is the "timely detection of diversion of significant quantities of nuclear material from peaceful nuclear activities to the manufacture of nuclear weapons or of other nuclear explosive devices or for purposes unknown."

[98] GOV/2015/65. Iran's Fordow centrifuge facility also produced low-enriched uranium hexafluoride containing up to 5% uranium-235 (see "Fordow Enrichment Facility.") Additionally, Iran produced uranium hexafluoride of a similar isotopic composition by converting low-enriched uranium hexafluoride containing nearly 20% uranium-235.

[99] *Implementation of the NPT Safeguards Agreement and Relevant Provisions of Security Council Resolutions in the Islamic Republic of Iran*, GOV/2015/34, Report by the Director General, May 29, 2015.

[100] *Verification and Monitoring in the Islamic Republic of Iran in Light of United Nations Security Council Resolution 2231 (2015),* GOV/2017/10, Report by the Director General, February 24, 2017.

[101] "Press Release on the Export of Enriched Uranium from Iran Assisted by Russia as Part of Preparation for JCPOA Implementation," Ministry of Foreign Affairs of the Russian Federation, December 29, 2015. Daily Press Briefing, Department of State, December 28, 2015." Ambassador Stephen Mull, Coordinator for Implementation of the JCPOA, told the Senate Foreign Relations Committee on December 17, 2015, that the exported material "will end up at a safeguarded facility" in Russia.

[102] *Verification and Monitoring in the Islamic Republic of Iran in Light of United Nations Security Council Resolution 2231 (2015),* Report by the Director General, International Atomic Energy Agency, GOV/2018/33, August 30, 2018.

[103] GOV/2012/23. Iran will need to provide fuel for "at least 4 other research reactors," according to the text of a June Iranian proposal to the P5+1 ("Full Text of Iran's Proposals to Six World Powers in Moscow Talks," *Fars News Agency*, July 7, 2012). Abbasi stated in an April 2012 interview that Iran plans to design and build another 10 megawatt "strong pool reactor." He indicated that the reactor would also use fuel enriched to the level of the TRR fuel, but provided no additional details ("Nuclear Chief: Iran Sees No Reason For Suspending Fordo Activities," *Iranian Students News Agency*, April 8, 2012).

Initially fueled by U.S.-supplied HEU, the reactor was converted to use LEU fuel in 1994 after Argentina agreed to supply the reactor with such fuel in 1987.[104] Fereydun Abbasi-Davani, then-President of the Atomic Energy Organization of Iran, stated in a 2012 interview that, once Iran had "enough" uranium enriched to this level, the country would use its enrichment facilities to produce enriched uranium containing 3.5% uranium-235.[105]

Centrifuge Research and Development

Iran has also tested several types of more-advanced centrifuges in the pilot facility; these centrifuges could increase the other enrichment facilities' capacity.[106] Iran has altered this facility to comply with the JCPOA's limits on Iranian centrifuge research and development.[107] Iran's development of new centrifuges has apparently been less successful than development of the IR-1 centrifuge;[108] past estimates from Iranian officials regarding the deployment of more-advanced centrifuges have been excessively optimistic.[109] According to a 2012 report from a U.N. Panel of Experts, the advanced centrifuge program's lack of success may have been "the result of sanctions limiting" Tehran's "ability to procure items necessary for its centrifuge programme," as well as "[o]ther variables, including design and manufacturing limitations, or a shortage of other necessary materials."[110]

The JCPOA contains a detailed description of centrifuge Research and Development (R&D) that Iran is permitted to conduct under the agreement. Iran is to conduct centrifuge R&D with uranium only at the Natanz pilot facility and will conduct mechanical testing of centrifuges only at the pilot facility and the Tehran Research Centre. Iran submitted an "enrichment R&D plan" in January 2016 to the IAEA as part of

---

[104] This information is contained in a February 18, 2010, letter from Iran to the IAEA (GOV/INF/2010/5). An undated paper from an AEOI official places the conversion date at November 1993 (Mohammad Zaker, "Conversion and Start Up of Tehran Research Reactor with LEU Fuel," no date given. Available at http://www.iaea.org/inis/collection/ NCLCollectionStore/_Public/35/044/35044382.pdf).

[105] *Iranian Students News Agency*, April 8, 2012.

[106] Iran has experimented with a variety of advanced centrifuges. A June 2009 report from ElBaradei states that Iran was testing four other more-advanced centrifuges; Iran informed the IAEA in February 2012 that it intended to install three new types of centrifuges, according to a 2012 IAEA report (*Implementation of the NPT Safeguards Agreement and Relevant Provisions of Security Council Resolutions in the Islamic Republic of Iran*, Report by the Director General, GOV/2012/9, February 24, 2012). Iran's IR-2m could "improve the enrichment of the Iranian centrifuges threefold," according to a 2012 Israeli intelligence report (Report 9342, Iran/Nuclear/Program Status, October 22, 2012. Available at http://www.aljazeera.com/news/2015/02/leaks-netanyahu-misled-iran-nuclear-programme-guardianiran-nuclear-speech-2012-150218165622065.html).

[107] *Verification and Monitoring in the Islamic Republic of Iran in Light of United Nations Security Council Resolution 2231 (2015),* Report by the Director General, GOV/INF/2016/1, January 16, 2016.

[108] Analyst interview with U.S. official, June 25, 2009; "Iran May Be 'Struggling' with New Nuclear Machines," *Reuters*, February 28, 2012.

[109] For example, then-Atomic Energy Organization President Aghazadeh indicated in February 2009 that at least one new type of centrifuge would be installed in the "near future" (*Islamic Republic of Iran News Network*, February 25, 2009). Then-Atomic Energy Organization President Ali Akbar Salehi stated in a December 2009 interview that Iran hoped to have the new types of centrifuges operational by early 2011 ("Iran to Produce New Generation of Centrifuges—Nuclear Chief," *Fars News Agency*, December 18, 2009).

[110] *Final Report of the Panel of Experts Established Pursuant to Resolution 1929 (2010)*, June 12, 2012.

Tehran's initial declaration for its Additional Protocol.[111] Iranian adherence to that plan is a JCPOA requirement.

Fordow Enrichment Facilitym[112]

In December 2011, Iran began enriching uranium up to 20% uranium-235 in the Fordow Fuel Enrichment Plant, according to IAEA reports. As of November 1, 2013, Iran was feeding uranium hexafluoride into four cascades (696 centrifuges) of IR-1 centrifuges[113] and had installed a total of 2,710 IR-1 centrifuges in the facility. Tehran had planned to install a total of 16 cascades containing approximately 3,000 centrifuges. Tehran told the IAEA that the facility would be configured to produce both uranium enriched to 5% uranium-235 and 20% uranium-235. Iran also told the IAEA that "the facility could be reconfigured to contain centrifuges of more advanced types should Iran take a decision to use such centrifuges in the future."[114] Iran agreed under the JCPOA to convert the facility into "a nuclear, physics, and technology centre." The facility will not contain any nuclear material. Pursuant to this commitment, Iran has decreased the number of IR-1 centrifuges to 1,044 and also removed all nuclear material from the facility. In addition, Iran has modified two cascades "for the production of stable isotopes" for medical and industrial uses.[115]

As noted, Iran revealed in September 2009 that it had been constructing the facility; Tehran provided some details that month about the facility to the IAEA. The United States had been "observing and analyzing the facility for several years," according to September 25, 2009, Obama Administration talking points, which added that "there was an accumulation of evidence" earlier in 2009 that the facility was intended for enriching uranium.[116] Some of this evidence apparently indicated that "Iran was installing the infrastructure required for centrifuges earlier" in 2009.[117] U.S. officials have not said exactly when Iran began work on the facility, which is "located in an underground tunnel complex on the grounds of an Islamic Revolutionary Guard Corps" base near the Iranian city of Qom. Nevertheless, the AEOI, rather than the Iranian military, is responsible for the development and management of the facility, according to the September 2009 U.S.

---

[111] *Verification and Monitoring in the Islamic Republic of Iran in Light of United Nations Security Council Resolution 2231 (2015),* Report by the Director General, GOV/2016/8, February 26, 2016.

[112] Unless otherwise noted, this section is based on a September 21, 2009, letter from Iran to the IAEA and September 25, 2009, background briefings from U.S. officials, along with associated Obama Administration talking points. See also CRS Report R43333, *Iran Nuclear Agreement*.

[113] GOV/2012/23.

[114] GOV/2009/74.

[115] GOV/INF/2016/1. An AEOI official announced in late August 2016 that Iran had opened a "semi-industrial unit" at its uranium conversion facility in order to "produce raw materials for stable isotopes" ("Iran Opens Stable Isotope Materials Production Unit," *Mehr News Agency*, August 29, 2016).

[116] "Q&A on the Qom Enrichment Facility," September 25, 2009. Available at https://www.iranwatch.org/sites/default/files/us-wh-qomqandas-0909.pdf.

[117] A 2011 Fact Sheet from the State Department indicates that construction on the facility began as early as 2006 (U.S. Department of the Treasury, "Fact Sheet: E.O. 13382 Designations on Iran," November 21, 2011).

talking points described above.[118] According to a November 2009 report from then-IAEA Director-General ElBaradei, Iran informed the IAEA that construction on the site began in the second half of 2007.[119] However, citing information in its possession that appears to contradict Tehran's claim, the IAEA asked Iran to provide more information about the facility's chronology.[120]

U.S. officials suggested that the facility may have been part of a nuclear weapons program. President Obama stated on September 25, 2009, that "the size and configuration of this facility is inconsistent with a peaceful program." But the Administration's talking points were somewhat more vague, stating that the facility "is too small to be viable for production of fuel for a nuclear power reactor," although it "could be used" for centrifuge research and development or "configured to produce weapons-grade uranium."[121] The facility "would be capable of producing approximately one weapon's worth" of HEU per year, according to the talking points.[122]

Iran's failure to inform the IAEA of the Fordow plant's existence until well after Tehran had begun constructing it raised concerns that the country may have had other covert nuclear facilities. A November 2009 IAEA Board of Governors resolution stated that Iran's declaration of the Fordow facility "reduces the level of confidence in the absence of other nuclear facilities and gives rise to questions about whether there are any other [undeclared] nuclear facilities under construction in Iran." Furthermore, then-UK Foreign Office Minister Alistair Burt told Parliament in February 2012 that the Fordow facility "which Iran initially kept secret from the IAEA, also raises our concerns that there may also be other, undeclared sites in Iran that could be engaged in work" related to nuclear weapons.[123]

Tehran's shifting explanations regarding the facility's purpose also raised concerns that Iran would use it in the future to produce fissile material for nuclear weapons. Iran's 2009 letter to the IAEA described the Fordow facility as a "new pilot fuel enrichment plant" that would produce uranium enriched to no higher than 5% uranium-235. Tehran subsequently changed the plant's stated purpose several times. For example, Tehran, as noted, later told the IAEA that the facility would be configured to produce both uranium enriched to 5% uranium-235 and 20% uranium- 235. Apparently suggesting that Iran might later produce uranium containing higher levels of uranium-235, a U.S. official told

---

[118] "Q&A on the Qom Enrichment Facility," September 25, 2009.

[119] GOV/2009/74.

[120] Majlis speaker Ali Larijani, who was formerly Iran's lead nuclear negotiator, indicated September 27, 2009, that Iran had been constructing the facility for approximately three years. ("Iran Speaker Says Country has Fully Mastered Nuclear Technology," *Islamic Republic News Agency*, September 27, 2009).

[121] "Q&A on the Qom Enrichment Facility," September 25, 2009.

[122] Ibid. Such estimates depend on several variables, including the number and type of centrifuges used, as well as the degree to which the uranium hexafluoride feedstock is enriched. This particular estimate appears to assume the use of 3,000 IR-1 centrifuges; the other assumed parameters are unclear. For more information on the facility's potential weapons-grade HEU production capability, see *Iran's Nuclear, Chemical and Biological Capabilities: A Net Assessment*, February 2011, p. 67.

[123] "Written Answers to Questions," *Daily Hansard*, February 7, 2012.

the IAEA Board of Governors on March 8, 2012, that "[w]e cannot help but wonder ... whether Iran has finally informed us of the ultimate purpose of this facility."[124]

For its part, Iran has asserted that the facility is for peaceful purposes and that the government has acted in accordance with its international obligations. As noted, Tehran argued that it was producing enriched uranium containing up to 20% uranium-235 for use as fuel in research reactors, which will be used to produce isotopes for medical purposes. Regarding the facility's secret nature, Iranian officials argued that Tehran was not previously obligated to disclose it to the IAEA[125] and stated on several occasions that the facility was concealed in order to protect it from military attacks;[126] Iran told the IAEA in 2009 that the Fordow facility was to serve as a "contingency enrichment plant, so that the enrichment activities shall not be suspended in the case of any military attack"[127] The Natanz commercial facility "was among the targets threatened with military attacks," Iran explained.[128] Iranian officials stated during a June 2012 meeting with the P5+1 that the Fordow facility is "not a military base" and is "not located on a military base."[129]

Enriched Uranium Containing Up To 20 Percent Uranium-235

As noted, Iran argued that it was producing LEU containing nearly 20% uranium-235 for use in research reactors; as of January 20, 2014, when the JPA went into effect, Tehran had used the Natanz pilot facility and the Fordow facility to produce a total of 447.8 kilograms of uranium hexafluoride containing up to 20% uranium-235.[130] Iran's production of uranium enriched to this level has caused concern because such production requires approximately 90% of the effort necessary to produce weapons-grade HEU, which contains about 90% uranium-235.[131] This amount of material would, if it had been further enriched, have been sufficient for a nuclear weapon. Iran would need approximately 215 kilograms of uranium hexafluoride containing 20% uranium-235 in order to produce approximately 27.8 kilograms of uranium containing 90% uranium-235—a sufficient amount of weapons-grade HEU for a nuclear weapon.[132] This is a

---

124 "U.S. Statement to the Board of Governors on Iran," March 8, 2012.

125 For more information, see CRS Report R40094, *Iran's Nuclear Program: Tehran's Compliance with International Obligations*, by Paul K. Kerr.

126 See, for example, "Iranian Nuclear Negotiator Says 5+1 Talks 'Positive'," *Islamic Republic of Iran News Network*, October 1, 2009.

127 GOV/2009/74.

128 Ibid.

129 "Full Text of Iran's Proposals to Six World Powers in Moscow Talks," *Fars News Agency*, July 7, 2012. Rouhani argued in February 2005 that Iran could enrich uranium "under mountains," explaining that "[i]f we go there, no American bomb or missile can be effective." "Iranian Official Rowhani Gives Interview, Discusses Talks with EU, Criticizes U.S.," *Tehran Vision of the Islamic Republic of Iran Network 2*, February 7, 2005.

130 GOV/2014/10.

131 Former IAEA Deputy Director General Olli Heinonen, "Dealing with a Nuclear Iran: Redlines and Deadlines," Center for Strategic and International Studies, February 6, 2013; U.S. Secretary of Energy Ernest Moniz, Senate Committee on Armed Services, "Impacts of the Joint Comprehensive Plan of Action (JPCOA) on U.S. Interests and the Military Balance in the Middle East," July 29, 2015.

132 This number of nuclear weapons assumes that 25 kilograms of uranium-235 (approximately 27.8 kilograms of uranium containing 90% uranium-235) would be necessary for one HEU-based nuclear weapon. The IAEA

conservative estimate; the specific characteristics of Iran's enrichment facilities may necessitate using more than 215 kilograms of such material. Then-Director of National Intelligence James Clapper suggested during a February 16, 2012, Senate Armed Services Committee hearing that "a number of factors" could impede Tehran's ability to produce weapons-grade HEU from uranium enriched to 20% uranium-235.[133]

As of January 20, 2014, approximately 160 kilograms of the LEU described above was in the form of uranium hexafluoride and, therefore, available to be further enriched in the near term.[134] Since that date, Iran has either converted much of that material for use as fuel in the Tehran Research Reactor, or prepared it for that purpose.[135] Iran diluted the rest of that stockpile so that it contained no more than 5% uranium-235. AEOI spokesperson Behrouz Kamalvandi said in February 2014 that Iran had "the necessary reservoirs of fuel for 5 years for the Tehran research reactor."[136]

Future Centrifuge Facilities

Iranian officials indicated in the past that Tehran intended to construct 10 additional centrifuge plants—a goal that many analysts argued was virtually unachievable. Then-President of Iran's Atomic Energy Organization Ali Akbar Salehi stated in 2009 that Iran is investigating locations for the sites (Salehi was President of the Organization from 2009 to 2010. He became President again in August 2013).[137] In 2012, then-Atomic Energy Organization President Abbasi argued that "mastering" centrifuge enrichment technology would enable Iran to "develop [centrifuge] sites in various locations to avoid any threat by foreign enemies." According to the JCPOA, Iran is to enrich uranium only at the Natanz commercial facility for 15 years.[138] Expiration of the JCPOA enrichment restrictions will be "followed by gradual evolution, at a reasonable pace" of Iran's enrichment program. According to the JCPOA, Iran's centrifuge-testing program may proceed under strict limits, which begin to ease approximately eight years after the beginning of the agreement's implementation. An AEOI spokesperson stated in January 2016 that Iran's nuclear program "will begin to accelerate from the 13th or 14th year

---

term for this amount of uranium is "significant quantity," defined as the "approximate amount of nuclear material for which the possibility of manufacturing a nuclear explosive device cannot be excluded." Some types of weapons could be developed using less uranium-235.

[133] "Current and Future Worldwide Threats to the National Security of the United States," Senate Armed Services Committee, February 16, 2012.

[134] GOV/2014/10. In addition to the 43 kilograms of this material which is being prepared for use as fuel, Iran has altered another 1.6 kilograms of the material, which now contains less than 5% uranium-235.

[135] This process has generated scrap which contains LEU with up to 20% uranium-235. Iran also retains .6 kilograms of uranium hexafluoride containing up to 20% uranium-235, which "had been used as reference material for mass spectrometry" (*Implementation of the NPT Safeguards Agreement and Relevant Provisions of Security Council resolutions in the Islamic Republic of Iran*, Report of the Director General, International Atomic Energy Agency, GOV/2015/34, May 29, 2015).

[136] Sara Massoumi, Hamed Shafiei, "20% Enrichment Is Not Iran's Need Today," *Iranian Diplomacy*, February 8th, 2014.

[137] *Fars News Agency*, December 18, 2009.

[138] After 10 years Iran may produce enriched uranium at the pilot centrifuge facility as part of R&D work.

onwards,"[139] adding that Tehran plans to increase its enrichment capacity by approximately "20-fold" by the end of the 15th year.[140] Iran plans to produce enough enriched uranium to fuel five or six nuclear reactors, Deputy Foreign Minister Araqchi stated in August 2015.[141]

AEOI spokesperson Kamalvandi explained in June 2018 that Iran would begin the process of "manufacturing and assembly of centrifuge rotors," which are critical components of such machines.[142] Iran "will begin building a centrifuge rotor plant," he noted.[143] In addition, Salehi announced in June that Iran has completed building a centrifuge assembly center in the Natanz facility; Tehran had not previously disclosed this facility publicly.[144] The facility's completion "does not mean that we are going to produce these centrifuges now," Salehi said in September 2018, adding that the facility provides Iran with the capability to mass-produce such centrifuges, should the government decide to do so.[145]

Inconsistent Progress

A senior U.S. intelligence official said in 2007 that a country needs to be able to "operate large numbers of centrifuges for long periods of time with very small failure rates" in order to be able to "make industrial quantities of enriched uranium."[146] Iran's record indicates that the country has not always met this standard. The 2007 National Intelligence Estimate stated that Iran still faced "significant technical problems operating" its centrifuges. Although a 2008 report to Congress submitted by the Deputy Director for National Intelligence described the amount of LEU that Iran produced in 2008 as a "significant improvement" over the amount it had produced during the previous year,[147] data from an August 2015 Institute for Science and International Security report indicates that the average per-centrifuge performance at that facility peaked in 2010 and subsequently fluctuated.[148]

---

[139] Specifically, the JCPOA states that "Iran will commence, upon start of implementation of the JCPOA," testing of Iran's IR-6 and IR- 8 centrifuges "on single centrifuge machines and its intermediate cascades and will commence the testing of up to 30 centrifuges machines from one and a half years before the end of year 10. Iran will proceed from single centrifuges to small cascades to intermediate cascades in a logical sequence."

[140] Interview with Behruz Kamalvandi, January 11, 2016.

[141] "AEOI: Iran Starts Injecting UF6 into IR-8 Centrifuges," *Fars News Agency*, January 28, 2017.

[142] "Nuclear Chief: Iran To Start New Centrifuge Production In Natanz Tomorrow," *Fars News Agency, June 5, 2018.*

[143] "Iran to Inform IAEA of Plan to Boost Enrichment - Fuller Report," *Iranian Students News Agency*, June 4, 2018.

[144] "Iran Completes Facility to Build Advanced Centrifuge," *Islamic Republic of Iran Broadcasting*, July 18, 2018.

[145] Jon Gambrell and Nasser Karimi, "AP Interview: Iran Nuclear Chief Hopes Deal Will Survive," *The Associated Press*, September 11, 2018.

[146] Background Briefing with Senior Intelligence Officials, December 3, 2007.

[147] *Unclassified Report to Congress on the Acquisition of Technology Relating to Weapons of Mass Destruction and Advanced Conventional Munitions, Covering 1 January to 31 December 2008.*

[148] David Albright, Serena Kelleher-Vergantini, Andrea Stricker, and Daniel Schnur, *ISIS Analysis of the IAEA Iran Safeguards Report*, Institute for Science and International Security, August 27, 2015. Calculating the average performance of Iran's centrifuges became more difficult after November 2010, when the IAEA stopped reporting information about the Natanz commercial facility's average product enrichment level.

The extent to which Iran's progress is sustainable is open to question. Former Pakistani nuclear official Abdul Qadeer Khan described Pakistan's first-generation centrifuges as "unsuccessful" in a 1998 interview.[149] Furthermore, Mark Fitzpatrick of the International Institute for Strategic Studies observed that "[i]t can be years before it is clear whether an enrichment programme is working well," observing that centrifuges at a Japanese enrichment facility "started to crash seven years after installation."[150] And, as noted, Iran has had difficulty in developing and deploying more-advanced centrifuges. Nevertheless, historical experience indicates that sustained operation of gas centrifuges appears to be a manageable task for governments with even modest technical capabilities.[151] According to a U.S. Nuclear Regulatory Commission document, some centrifuges of simple design "have operated 30 years with a failure rate of less than one percent."[152] (See also "Effects of Sanctions and Sabotage on Iran's Enrichment Program").

Uranium Conversion

As noted, uranium conversion is a process whereby uranium ore concentrate is converted into several compounds, including uranium hexafluoride—the feedstock for Iran's centrifuges. Iran produced approximately 541 metric tons of uranium hexafluoride between March 2004 and August 10, 2009, using both imported uranium ore concentrate and domestically produced uranium ore concentrate.[153] Iran has not produced any uranium hexafluoride since August 2009, according to IAEA reports, although Tehran has transferred domestically produced uranium ore concentrate to the uranium conversion facility. The 2012 U.N. Panel of Experts report concluded that, based on data from Amano's February 2012 report, Iran had "an ample supply of uranium hexafluoride to maintain current levels of enrichment for the foreseeable future."[154] On June 27, 2018, Iran's official news agency announced that Iran has resumed operations at the conversion facility.[155]

---

[149] "A Talk with A.Q. Khan: Pakistan's Top Nuclear Scientist Talks About Nuclear Weapons," *Jane's Foreign Report*, July 24, 1998.

[150] Mark Fitzpatrick, *The Iranian Nuclear Crisis: Avoiding Worst-Case Outcomes*, Adelphi Paper 398, International Institute for Strategic Studies, May 2008, p. 50.

[151] R. Scott Kemp, "The Nonproliferation Emperor Has No Clothes: The Gas Centrifuge, Supply-Side Controls, and the Future of Nuclear Proliferation," *International Security*, Spring 2014, vol. 38, no. 4, pp. 39-78.

[152] USNRC Technical Training Center: Uranium Enrichment Processes, Module 4.0 of the Uranium Enrichment Processes Directed Self-Study Course 9/08 (Rev 3), Directed Self Study. The document appears to have been published in 2008.

[153] Based on data from GOV/2009/74. Iran imported 531 metric tons of uranium ore concentrate in 1982, according to *Implementation of the NPT Safeguards Agreement in the Islamic Republic of Iran*, Report by the Director General, GOV/2003/75, November 10, 2003.

[154] *Panel of Experts*, 2012.

[155] "Iran UF6 Factory Resumes Work," *Islamic Republic News Agency*, June 27, 2018.

According to a report from the Director of National Intelligence to Congress covering 2011, Iran had "almost exhausted" its supply of imported uranium ore concentrate.[156] Tehran apparently did not import any more such material prior to December 2015. According to the 2012 U.N. Panel of Experts report, "a number" of governments believed that Tehran was "seeking new sources of uranium ore to supply its enrichment efforts"; the report added that "the Panel is not aware of any confirmed cases of actual transfers."[157] British Foreign and Commonwealth Office official Tobias Ellwood informed Parliament in June 2015 that the British government was "not aware of" any recent reports that Iran had attempted to purchase foreign uranium.[158] Former State Department official Richard Nephew wrote in September 2015 that there had "not been any verified transfer of uranium to Iran aside from fuel for the Bushehr power reactor."[159] In late December 2015, Iran imported between 200 and 220 metric tons of uranium ore concentrate in exchange for LEU that Iran shipped to Russia in order to reduce its stockpile to JCPOA-required levels.[160] The IAEA verified Iran's receipt in February 2017 of approximately 125 metric tons of uranium ore concentrate.[161] During March 2017, Iranian officials stated that the country had imported between 382 and 384 metric tons of this material since concluding the JCPOA.[162] The imported uranium ore concentrate is to serve as fuel for the Bushehr reactors, according to Iranian officials.[163]

Prior to 2009, Tehran apparently improved its ability to produce centrifuge feedstock of sufficient purity for light-water reactor fuel; information in a 2010 IAEA report indicated that Iran was purifying its centrifuge feedstock.[164,165] Whether Iran is currently able to produce feedstock pure enough for weapons-grade HEU is unclear, however.

---

156 *Unclassified Report to Congress on the Acquisition of Technology Relating to Weapons of Mass Destruction and Advanced Conventional Munitions, Covering 1 January to 31 December 2011*.

157 *Panel of Experts*, 2012.

158 Iran: Nuclear Weapons: Written Question-1913. Answered by Mr Tobias Ellwood on June 15, 2015.

159 Richard Nephew, "How the Iran Deal Prevents a Covert Nuclear Weapons Program," *Arms Control Today*, September 2015.

160 Interview with Behruz Kamalvandi, January 11, 2016. "Atomic Chief: Iran Completes Swap of Surplus Enriched Uranium with Russia," *Vision of the Islamic Republic of Iran Network*," December 29, 2015; Secretary of State John Kerry," Arms Control and International Security: An Update on Progress Toward Implementation Day of the JCPOA," December 28, 2015.

161 GOV/2017/10.

162 "Iran Plans to Buy 950 Tonnes of Yellowcake from Kazakhstan: Salehi," *IRIB News Agency*, March 7, 2017; "Iran's Atomic Chief Calls Critics of Nuclear Deal 'Unfair,'" *IRIB News Agency*, March 10, 2017.

163 "Iran to Use Russian Yellow Cake at Esfahan, Bushehr Sites—Official," *Iranian Young Journalists' Club Website*, February 26, 2017.

164 IISS Strategic Comments, "Nuclear Iran: How Close Is It?," September 2007; Paul Kerr, "Iran Continues Security Council Defiance," *Arms Control Today*, June 2007; analyst interview with State Department official October 28, 2008.

165 *Implementation of the NPT Safeguards Agreement and Relevant Provisions of Security Council Resolutions 1737 (2006), 1747 (2007), 1803 (2008) and 1835 (2008) in the Islamic Republic of Iran*, Report by the Director General, GOV/2010/28, May 31, 2010. A footnote in the report states that some enriched uranium hexafluoride "was present in the feed purification cylinder."

Plutonium

Iran acknowledged to the IAEA in 2003 that it had conducted plutonium-separation experiments—an admission which contributed to suspicions that Iran could have a program to produce plutonium for nuclear weapons. The IAEA, however, continued to investigate the matter; then-IAEA Director-General ElBaradei reported in August 2007 that the agency had resolved its questions about Iran's plutonium activities.[166] As noted above, Iran has said that it does not plan to engage in reprocessing, and IAEA Director-General Amano's November 2011 report described an "absence of any indicators that Iran is currently considering reprocessing irradiated nuclear fuel to extract plutonium."[167] Amano's November 2015 report states that the agency could "confirm that there are no ongoing reprocessing related activities" at the Iranian facilities to which the Agency has access.[168]

The JCPOA prohibits Iran from reprocessing spent reactor fuel, except to produce "radio-isotopes for medical and peaceful industrial purposes." The JCPOA text states that Iran "does not intend" to engage in reprocessing after the 15-year period expires and specifies Iran's intention to "ship out all spent fuel for all future and present nuclear power and research reactors, for further treatment or disposition as provided for in relevant contracts to be concluded consistent with national laws with the recipient party." According to the IAEA, Iran has adhered to this requirement.

Arak Reactor[169]

Iran says that its reactor under construction at Arak, is intended for the production of medical isotopes and various other purposes. According to a 2008 presentation by Ambassador Soltanieh, the reactor, which was originally designed to be moderated by heavy water, is to substitute for the "outdated" Tehran Research Reactor (TRR), which has been in operation since 1967.[170] As noted, Iran subsequently decided to re-fuel the TRR. According to a 2012 AEOI report, the reactor has several objectives

- "A suitable replacement for the aging Tehran Research Reactor using local engineers and scientist [sic] with the least dependency to foreign countries;
- Medical, industrial and research radioisotope production of [sic] the country;

---

[166] *Implementation of the NPT Safeguards Agreement in the Islamic Republic of Iran*, Report by the Director General, GOV/2007/48, August 30, 2007.

[167] GOV/2011/65.

[168] Ibid.

[169] Iran informed the IAEA in April 2017 that Tehran was renaming the facility the "Khondab Heavy Water Research Reactor." (*Verification and Monitoring in the Islamic Republic of Iran in Light of United Nations Security Council Resolution* 2231 [2015], Report by the Director General, International Atomic Energy Agency, GOV/2017/24, June 2, 2017).

[170] "Iran's Exclusively Peaceful Nuclear Programs and Activities," *Briefing for NGOs*, May 5, 2008.

- Performing research in the fields of neutron physics, reactor chemistry, thermal-hydraulics, and health physics;
- Obtaining technological and scientific experience in design and construction of nuclear reactors using local experts within the country;
- Training of specialists in the nuclear field; and
- Enhancing the technological levels of the local industries in design and manufacturing of various components such as reactor vessels, heat exchangers, pumps, etc. using nuclear standards."[171]

Iran told the IAEA in 2012 that the reactor was scheduled to begin operating during the second half of 2013.[172] The project was about 75% complete as of July 2011.[173] Iran suspended several aspects of the reactor's construction pursuant to the 2013 Joint Plan of Action.[174]

The originally designed Arak reactor was a proliferation concern because its spent fuel would have contained plutonium better suited for nuclear weapons than the plutonium produced by light-water moderated reactors, such as the TRR and Bushehr reactor. The original Arak reactor, if it had been completed, could have produced enough plutonium for between one and two nuclear weapons per year.[175] In addition, Iran would have been able to operate the reactor with natural uranium and, therefore, would not have been dependent on supplies of enriched uranium.

The JCPOA requires Tehran to render the Arak reactor's original core inoperable; Iran has met this requirement.[176] The agreement also commits Tehran to redesign and rebuild the Arak reactor based on a design agreed to by the P5+1 so that the reactor will not produce weapons-grade plutonium. Tehran is "trying to complete the project in five years," an AEOI spokesperson said in January 2016.[177] AEOI President Salehi stated in September 2016 that China will supply the reactor's first fuel load "in the next five-year time."[178] Iran will subsequently produce the reactor fuel, he said. Iran is to export the spent fuel from this reactor and all other nuclear reactors. In addition, the JCPOA requires Iran to refrain from building heavy water-moderated reactors for 15 years, and Tehran has pledged to refrain from constructing any such reactors indefinitely.

---

171 *Nuclear Industry in Iran: An Overview on Iran's Activities and Achievements in Nuclear Technology*, Atomic Energy Organization of Iran, 2012, p. 29.

172 GOV/2012/23.

173 *Nuclear Industry in Iran*, p. 29.

174 Iran pledged to refrain from commissioning the reactor, transferring fuel or heavy water to the reactor site, testing and producing additional reactor fuel, and installing remaining reactor components.

175 Colin Kahl, Deputy Assistant to the President and National Security Adviser to the Vice President, "Arms Control Association Annual Meeting: Unprecedented Challenges for Nonproliferation and Disarmament," May 14, 2015.

176 GOV/INF/2016/1.

177 Interview with Behruz Kamalvandi, January 11, 2016.

178 *IRTV2*, September 10, 2016.

According to IAEA reports and Iranian officials, Iran began to operate its heavy-water production plant located near Arak in August 2006.[179] Reports from Amano since the start of JCPOA implementation indicate that the plant, which is to produce heavy water for the reactor and deuterated solvents, is operating.[180] Pursuant to the JCPOA, Tehran has committed to refrain from accumulating heavy water "beyond Iran's needs"; Iran is to "sell any remaining heavy water on the international market for 15 years."[181] According to the agreement, these "needs" are 130 metric tons of "nuclear grade heavy water or its equivalent in different enrichments" prior to commissioning the redesigned Arak reactor and 90 metric tons after the reactor is commissioned.

Iran's stock of heavy water has exceeded 130 metric tons on two occasions since the JCPOA began implementation. On February 17, 2016, the IAEA verified that Tehran's heavy water stock had exceeded 130 metric tons; on November 8, 2016, the IAEA verified that Iran's stock of heavy water had again exceeded the JCPOA limit. Iran resolved the issue on both occasions by exporting the excess heavy water. Tehran has sent this material to Russia and the United States, shipping at least some of it via Oman.[182] Iran told the IAEA on June 18, 2017, that it had transferred 19.1 metric tons of heavy water to a destination outside the country.[183] According to an April 2018 State Department report covering 2017, "[m]ost Iranian excess heavy water has been sold and delivered to international buyers; the remainder is awaiting sale and is stored in a location outside Iran, under IAEA seal, though it remains Iranian property."[184] Tehrna has continued to ship heavy water outside Iran, the IAEA reported in August 2018.[185] The IAEA verified on August 25, 2018, that Iran had 122.9 metric tons of heavy water.[186]

Bushehr Reactor

Iran is also operating a 1,000-megawatt nuclear power reactor located near the city of Bushehr moderated by light water. The original German contractor, which began constructing the reactor in 1975, abandoned the project following Iran's 1979

---

179 "'Peaceful'" Iran Has a Transparent Nuclear Program: Ahmadinejad; Arak Heavy Water Plant Launched," *Mehr News Agency*, August 26, 2006; "Iran's Heavy Water Research Reactor Project on Track, Says Official," *Fars News Agency*, August 26, 2006. A 2005 IAEA report (GOV/2005/67) describes the plant as "currently being commissioned"; a 2007 IAEA report (GOV/2007/8) states that the plant is operational.

180 *Nuclear Industry in Iran*, p. 27.

181 According to the agreement, these "needs" are 130 metric tons of "nuclear grade heavy water or its equivalent in different enrichments" prior to commissioning the redesigned Arak reactor and 90 metric tons after the reactor is.

182 Iran has also shipped "a smaller amount to other countries," a spokesperson for Iran's Atomic Energy Organization said in March 2018 ("Iran to Unveil 'Heavy Water Achievements' on 9 April," *Fars News Agency*, March 26, 2018).

183 *Verification and Monitoring in the Islamic Republic of Iran in Light of United Nations Security Council Resolution 2231 (2015),* Report by the Director General, International Atomic Energy Agency, GOV/2017/35, August 31, 2017. The report does not name the heavy water's destination.

184 *Adherence to and Compliance with Arms Control, Nonproliferation, and Disarmament Agreements and Commitments*, Department of State, April 2018.

185 GOV/2018/3.

186 Ibid.

revolution.[187] Russia agreed in 1995 to complete the reactor, but the project subsequently encountered repeated delays; both Russian and Iranian officials attributed those delays to technical issues. In February 2005, Moscow and Tehran concluded an agreement stating that Russia would supply fuel for the reactor for 10 years. Atomstroyexport sent the first shipment of LEU fuel to Iran on December 16, 2007, and the reactor received the last shipment near the end of January 2008. The fuel, which is under IAEA seal, will contain no more than 3.62% uranium-235, according to an Atomstroyexport spokesperson.[188] An August 2014 IAEA inspection revealed that the reactor "was operating at 100% of its nominal power."[189]

Before 2002, the United States had previously urged Moscow to end the project, citing concerns that it could aid an Iranian nuclear weapons program by providing the country with access to nuclear technology and expertise.[190] However, U.S. officials said in 2002 that Washington would drop these public objections if Russia took steps to mitigate the project's proliferation risks; the 2005 deal requires Iran to return the spent nuclear fuel to Russia.[191] This measure is designed to ensure that Tehran will not separate plutonium from the spent fuel. Moscow also argues that the reactor will not pose a proliferation risk because it will operate under IAEA safeguards. It is worth noting that light-water reactors are generally regarded as more proliferation-resistant than other types of reactors. Although the U.N. Security Council resolutions restricted the supply of nuclear-related goods to Iran, they did permit the export of nuclear equipment and fuel related to light-water reactors.

Experts have expressed strong doubts regarding Iran's ability to produce fuel for the reactor.[192] According to a July 2014 Iranian government report, Russia and Iran may renew the fuel supply agreement, but are also "engaged in negotiations ... to engage in cooperative arrangements for the domestic manufacturing of fuel for the facility after the

---

[187] The contractor, Kraftwerk Union, completed about 85% of the first reactor and 55% of the second ("Iran's Nuclear Ambitions: Persistence Despite Manpower Problems," Central Intelligence Agency Directorate of Intelligence, October 1986).

[188] "Atomstroyexport Completes Latest Shipment of Fuel to Bushehr Nuclear Plant," *Interfax*, December 28, 2007.

[189] *Implementation of the NPT Safeguards Agreement and Relevant Provisions of Security Council Resolutions in the Islamic Republic of Iran*, Report by the Director General, GOV/2014/43, September 5, 2014.

[190] For example, then-Deputy Assistant Secretary of Defense Marshall Billingslea testified before the Senate on July 29, 2002, that the United States was "concerned that the Bushehr nuclear power project is, in reality, a pretext for the creation of an infrastructure designed to help Tehran acquire atomic weapons." Similar concerns are expressed in a 2005 State Department report (Adherence to and Compliance with Arms Control, Nonproliferation, and Disarmament Agreements and Commitments, U.S. Department of State, August 2005, p.77.) Then-Under Secretary of State for International Security and Arms Control John Bolton told the House International Relations Committee in June 2003 that Iran could build "over 80 nuclear weapons" if it had access to sufficient fuel, operated the reactor for five to six years, and chose to withdraw from the NPT. During a June 12, 2008, House Foreign Affairs Committee hearing, then-Acting under Secretary of State for Arms Control and International Security John Rood agreed with a Department of Energy assessment that the reactor's spent fuel would contain enough plutonium for between 50 and 60 nuclear weapons. These estimates assume that Iran possesses a reprocessing facility, which the country does not possess.

[191] Estimates for the length of time the spent fuel must stay in Iran to cool range from two to five years. See Paul Kerr, "Iran, Russia Reach Nuclear Agreement," *Arms Control Today*, April 2005.

[192] See, for example, Robert Einhorn, "Will Iran Play Ball in Nuke Talks?," *The National Interest*, January 14, 2015.

expiration of the current contract."[193] According to an interview published in April 2017, AEOI Deputy Director Pezhman Rahimian stated that the two governments had almost completed a "road map" for such manufacturing.[194] AEOI President Salehi expressed "hope" in September 2018 that a second power reactor at Bushehr plant "will become operational in the next six years."[195]

Possible Future Reactors

Iran and Russia signed a contract in November 2014 for the construction of two additional light water nuclear power reactors in Bushehr, according to Rosatom, the Russian company.[196] The project's construction began in September 2016 and is to take 10 years to complete.[197] Iran was "negotiating with China for building two 100 megawatt power plants," Salehi stated in a July 2015 speech.[198] Iran informed the IAEA in an October 2017 letter that Tehran had decided to "design and construct a critical facility (Light Water Critical Reactor) ... for research purposes in near future." Iran "provided preliminary design information for the facility," which indicates that the reactor fuel is to contain "up to 3.67%" uranium 235.[199]

Fuel Manufacturing Facilities

Iran's fuel manufacturing plant was to produce fuel for the Arak and Darkhovin reactors.[200] The plant started the process of producing fuel for the pre-JCPOA Arak reactor.[201] Iran's Fuel Plate Fabrication Plant has produced fuel for the Tehran Research Reactor.[202]

Uranium Mines

Iran has a uranium mill and a uranium mine located at a site called Bandar Abbas, which is also sometimes referred to as Gchine. Iran also has a uranium mine at a site

---

193 *What Are Iran's "Practical Needs"?*, NuclearEnergy.ir, July 2014.

194 Hadi Mohammadi: "Tehran Reactor's Fuel Is Entirely Made in Iran; Country's Yellow Cake Stockpile Has Doubled," *Khorasan*, April 8, 2017.

195 "Nuclear Chief: Iran Replaces US with UK in Redesigning Arak Heavy Reactor," *FARS News Agency*, August 22, 2018.

196 "The Foundation Stone Ceremony Held on the Bushehr Phase II Construction Site (Iran)," Communications Department of ROSATOM, September 13, 2016. Available at http://tinyurl.com/jsc9z89.

197 Ibid. "Inauguration of Two New Power Plant Units Construction in Bushehr," Atomic Energy Organization of Iran, September 18, 2016. Available at http://tinyurl.com/h7bl7jl.

198 "Excerpts of the Speech Presented by H.E Dr. A.A.Salehi, President's Deputy and Head of AEOI in the Presence of Organization's Personnel," July 20, 2015. Available at http://tinyurl.com/gllptz5.

199 GOV/2007/48.

200 "Aqazadeh: Iran Heralds Peaceful Nuclear Program," *Islamic Republic News Agency*, April 8, 2008.

201 GOV/2015/65.

202 Ibid.

called Saghand and an associated uranium mill called the Ardakan Yellowcake Production Plant. Iranian officials acknowledge that the country's uranium deposits are insufficient for its planned nuclear power program.[203] These reserves are sufficient, however, to produce 250-300 nuclear weapons, according to a past U.S. estimate.[204]

Effects of Sanctions and Sabotage on Iran's Enrichment Program

A number of governments employed sanctions and, apparently, sabotage to impede Iran's nuclear program.

Sanctions

Iran has tried to improve its capabilities to produce materials and components for its centrifuge program, according to former IAEA Deputy Director General Olli Heinonen.[205] Some Iranian officials have claimed that the country can manufacture centrifuges on its own. For example, then-Iranian Ambassador to the IAEA Ali Asghar Soltanieh said in 2012 that Iran "has 'fully mastered' the nuclear energy technology and can produce all the 90 pieces of a centrifuge machine on its own and without foreign assistance."[206] However, a 2014 U.N. Panel of Experts report observed that the "quality of such [Iranian-produced] equipment is not known."[207] Furthermore, other Iranian officials have suggested that Tehran is not yet able to produce all of the necessary centrifuge components. Then-President of Iran's Atomic Energy Organization Abbasi stated during a 2012 television broadcast that "Iran could not claim that it did not need other countries" for its enrichment program, adding that "domestic production of all items was not economically viable."[208] AEOI Director Salehi stated in 2014 that Iran was purchasing some items for its nuclear program "from some developing and growing Eastern countries."[209] Moreover, then-Principal Deputy Assistant Secretary of State for

---

[203] Installation of Centrifuges Continues in Natanz—Iran Nuclear Official," *Iranian Students News Agency*, April 17, 2007; Thomas W. Wood, Matthew D. Milazzo, Barbara A. Reichmuth, and Jeffrey Bedell, "The Economics Of Energy Independence For Iran," *Nonproliferation Review*, vol. 14, No. 1, March 2007.

[204] Paul Kerr, "Iran Nuclear Abilities Limited," *Arms Control Today*, September 2005.

[205] Analyst interview, January 18, 2012.

[206] "Nuclear Official Stresses Iran's Domestic Capability to Produce Centrifuge Machines," *FARS News Agency*, December 3, 2012.

[207] *Final Report of the Panel of Experts Established Pursuant to Resolution 1929 (2010)*, June 11, 2014.

[208] "Nuclear Chief Says West Aware of Significance of Iran Achievements," *Vision of the Islamic Republic of Iran Network 2*, February 15, 2012.

[209] "Some in East Colluding with West in Iran Nuclear Sabotage: AEOI," *Press TV*, August 25, 2014.

International Security and Nonproliferation Vann Van Diepen said that Iran in 2014 was still attempting to "procure items" for the nuclear program.[210]

Nevertheless, according to the 2014 Panel of Experts report, several governments told the panel that, since mid-2013, there had been a "been a decrease in the number of detected [Iranian] attempts ... to procure items for prohibited programmes, and related seizures."[211] A 2015 Panel report states that the experts had not "identified cases of procurement for activities prohibited" by Security Council resolutions in force at the time.[212] No governments reported any such cases, the report adds.

According to various sources, international sanctions made it difficult for Iran to obtain components and materials for its centrifuge program. For example, the U.N. Panel of Experts 2011 report stated that "sanctions are constraining Iran's procurement of items related to prohibited nuclear and ballistic missile activity and thus slowing development of these programmes."[213] Similarly, the 2012 U.N. Panel of Experts report observed that "[s]anctions are slowing the procurement by the Islamic Republic of Iran of some critical items required for its prohibited nuclear programme."[214] A June 2013 Panel report suggested that this condition still existed, arguing that "Iran's reliance on procurement abroad continues to provide the international community with opportunities to limit Iran's ability to maintain and expand certain activities."[215] Then-UK Foreign Secretary William Hague wrote in 2013 that "[w]e judge that sanctions have been effective in slowing the nuclear programme to some degree."[216]

U.S. officials have also argued that the sanctions have impeded Iran's ability to acquire technology for its nuclear programs. Then-State Department Special Advisor for Nonproliferation and Arms Control Robert Einhorn told a Washington audience in 2011 that "[w]e believe Iran has had difficulty in acquiring some key technologies and we judge this has had an effect of slowing some of its programs."[217] Similarly, then-National Security Adviser Tom Donilon argued in 2011 that "[s]anctions and export control efforts have made it more difficult and costly for Iran to acquire key materials and equipment for its enrichment program, including items that Iran can't produce itself."[218]

However, the extent to which sanctions slowed Tehran's program is unclear. Donilon also cited "mistakes and difficulties in Iran," as obstacles to the program's progress. Former IAEA Deputy Director General Heinonen stated that "[w]e do not know" whether

---

[210] William Maclean, "Iran Pursuing Banned Items for Nuclear, Missile Work: U.S. Official," *Reuters*, March 16, 2014.

[211] *Panel of Experts,* 2014.

[212] *Final Report of the Panel of Experts Established Pursuant to Resolution 1929 (2010)*, June 2, 2015.

[213] *Panel of Experts Established Pursuant to Resolution 1929 (2010): Final Report*, June 2011.

[214] *Panel of Experts,* 2012.

[215] *Final report of the Panel of Experts Established Pursuant to Resolution 1929 (2010)*, June 5, 2013.

[216] Letter to Richard M. Ottaway MP, May 14, 2013.

[217] Robert J. Einhorn, "The Impact of Sanctions on Iran's Nuclear Program," Arms Control Association, March 9, 2011.

[218] Tom Donilon, "Iran and International Pressure: an Assessment of Multilateral Effort to Impede Iran's Nuclear Program," The Brookings Institution, November 22, 2011.

Iran's delays in deploying advanced centrifuges are attributable to "lack of raw materials or design problems," according to a 2012 press report.[219] Furthermore, reports from the Office of the Director of National Intelligence covering 2009, 2010, and 2011 stated that "some obstacles slowed" the progress of Iran's nuclear program during those years, but the report did not name those obstacles.[220]

Sabotage

There have been allegations of efforts by the United States and other governments, including Israel's, to sabotage Iran's centrifuge program, but the extent to which any of these efforts have affected Tehran's nuclear program is unclear. The *New York Times* reported in 2009 that such efforts have included "undermin[ing] electrical systems, computer systems and other networks on which Iran relies," according to unnamed senior U.S. and foreign government officials.[221] One effort involved foreign intelligence services sabotaging "individual power units that Iran bought in Turkey" for Tehran's centrifuge program. "A number of centrifuges blew up," according to the *Times*.[222] Western governments have reportedly made other efforts to sabotage centrifuge components destined for Iran, according to some nongovernmental experts.[223] Iranian officials have asserted that Western countries have tampered with components in transit to Iran's enrichment facilities, directly sabotaged those facilities, and conducted espionage in the country.[224] Additionally, *New York Times* reporter James Risen wrote in 2006 that, according to unnamed U.S. officials, the United States engaged in a covert operation to provide Iran with flawed blueprints for a device designed to trigger a nuclear explosion.[225]

The United States and Israel have also reportedly executed cyberattacks on Iran's nuclear facilities. Perhaps the best known of these utilized the Stuxnet computer worm,

---

219 "Iran May Be 'Struggling' with New Nuclear Machines," *Reuters*, February 28, 2012.

220 *Unclassified Report to Congress on the Acquisition of Technology Relating to Weapons of Mass Destruction and Advanced Conventional Munitions, Covering 1 January to 31 December 2009; Unclassified Report to Congress on the Acquisition of Technology Relating to Weapons of Mass Destruction and Advanced Conventional Munitions, Covering 1 January to 31 December 2010; Unclassified Report to Congress on the Acquisition of Technology Relating to Weapons of Mass Destruction and Advanced Conventional Munitions, Covering 1 January to 31 December 2011.*

221 David E. Sanger, "U.S. Rejected Aid for Israeli Raid on Nuclear Site," *New York Times*, January 11, 2009.

222 David E. Sanger and William J. Broad, "U.S. Sees an Opportunity to Press Iran on Nuclear Fuel," *New York Times*, January 3, 2010. Iranian officials alluded to this incident, according to a January 2007 Iranian press report (*Ayande-ye Now*, January 6, 2007).

223 James Blitz, Roula Khalaf, and Daniel Dombey, "Suggestions of Iran Nuclear Sabotage," *Financial Times*, July 22, 2010.

224 "Iran Atomic Energy Officials Discuss 'Thwarted' Nuclear 'Sabotage' Attempts," *Tehran Hamshahri Online*, September 6, 2014. Foreign Minister Zarif stated that there had been no such sabotage since concluding the JCPOA ("Zarif Series: On the Nuclear Deal, US Relations," July 19, 2017. Available at http://iranprimer.usip.org/blog/2017/jul/19/zarif-series-nuclear-deal-us-relations).

225 James Risen, *State of War: The Secret History of the CIA and the Bush Administration* (New York: Free Press), 2006.

which was discovered in 2010 and probably developed by a government to attack Iran's enrichment facilities.[226] Some governments have reportedly assassinated Iranians associated with Iran's nuclear program.[227] The United States also may have obtained information from Iranian officials who defected as part of a CIA program to induce them to do so.[228]

NUCLEAR WEAPON DEVELOPMENT CAPABILITIES

Statements from the U.S. intelligence community indicate that Iran has the technical capability to produce nuclear weapons. For example, the 2007 NIE assessed that "Iran has the scientific, technical and industrial capacity eventually to produce nuclear weapons if it decides to do so."[229] More recently, then-Director of National Intelligence Clapper stated during a February 2016 Senate Armed Services Committee hearing that Iran "does not face any insurmountable technical barriers to producing a nuclear weapon."[230]

Obtaining fissile material is widely regarded as the most difficult task in building nuclear weapons. As noted, Iran is enriching uranium, but whether and to what extent Tehran has taken the other steps necessary for producing a nuclear weapon is unclear. A 2008 report from former IAEA Director-General ElBaradei points out that the IAEA, with the exception of a document related to uranium metal, has "no information ... on the actual design or manufacture by Iran" of components, nuclear or otherwise, for nuclear weapons.[231] However, according to IAEA Director-General Amano's November 2011 report, the IAEA has "credible" information that Iran has carried out activities "relevant to the development of a nuclear explosive device."[232] These include acquisition of "nuclear weapons development information and documentation" and work to develop "an

---

[226] David Albright, Paul Brannan, Andrea Stricker, Christina Walrond, and Houston Wood, *Preventing Iran From Getting Nuclear Weapons: Constraining Its Future Nuclear Options*, Institute for Science and International Security, March 5, 2012; R Scott Kemp, "Worm Holes—Virus Attacks Iran's Enrichment Operation," *Jane's Intelligence Review*, September 15, 2011; David E. Sanger, "Obama Order Sped Up Wave of Cyberattacks Against Iran," *New York Times*, June 1, 2012; Ellen Nakashima, Greg Miller, Julie Tate, "U.S. and Israel Created 'Flame'," *Washington Post*, June 20, 2012. For more information about Stuxnet, see CRS Report R41524, *The Stuxnet Computer Worm: Harbinger of an Emerging Warfare Capability*, by Paul K. Kerr, John W. Rollins, and Catherine A. Theohary. See also, Geoff McDonald, Liam O. Murchu, Stephen Doherty, Eric Chien, *Stuxnet 0.5: The Missing Link*, Symantec Security Response, February 26, 2013; and Ralph Langner, *To Kill a Centrifuge: A Technical Analysis of What Stuxnet's Creators Tried to Achieve*, The Langner Group, November 2013.

[227] See, for example, Ulrike Putz, "Sabotaging Iran's Nuclear Program," *Der Spiegel*, August 2, 2011; Artin Afkhami, "Tehran Abuzz as Book Says Israel Killed 5 Scientists," *New York Times*, July 11, 2012.

[228] Greg Miller, "CIA Has Recruited Iranians to Defect; The Secret Effort Aims to Undermine Tehran's Nuclear Program," *Los Angeles Times*, December 9, 2007.

[229] *Iran: Nuclear Intentions and Capabilities*, November 2007.

[230] *Statement for the Record Worldwide Threat Assessment of the US Intelligence Community*, Senate Armed Services Committee, February 9, 2016.

[231] *Implementation of the NPT Safeguards Agreement and Relevant Provisions of Security Council Resolutions 1737 (2006), 1747 (2007),1803 (2008) and 1835 (2008) in the Islamic Republic of Iran*, Report by the Director General, GOV/2008/59, November 19, 2008.

[232] GOV/2011/65.

indigenous design of a nuclear weapon including the testing of components." Although some of these activities have civilian applications, "others are specific to nuclear weapons," the report notes.[233] Most of the report provides additional details about Iranian activities applicable to nuclear weapons development that were described in previous IAEA reports, although it does contain some previously unreported material.[234] The program's purpose was "to develop a nuclear warhead for the Shahab-3 missile," a senior Administration official stated during a November 8, 2011, briefing about Amano's November 2011 report.[235] A 2012 Department of Defense report described Amano's report as containing "extensive evidence of past and possibly ongoing Iranian nuclear weapons-related research and development work."[236] (See Appendix D for more details about the IAEA's information regarding suspected military aspects of Iran's nuclear program).

Amano's November 2011 report states that, according to information available to the IAEA, Iranian activities related to building a nuclear explosive device "took place under a structured programme" prior to the end of 2003. That program, however, "was stopped rather abruptly pursuant to a 'halt order' instruction issued in late 2003 by senior Iranian officials," the report says. The weapons-related activities were consolidated under the "AMAD Plan" and "appear to have been conducted during 2002 and 2003." Nevertheless, "[t]here are also indications that some activities relevant to the development of a nuclear explosive device continued after 2003, and that some may still be ongoing," according to the report. According to an August 2014 State Department announcement, Iran established the Organization of Defensive Innovation and Research (SPND), which "is primarily responsible for research in the field of nuclear weapons development," in 2011. The SPND "took over some of the activities related to Iran's undeclared nuclear program," the announcement said.[237] According to a 2012 Israeli intelligence report, the SPND

> was established for the purposes of preserving the technological ability and the joint organizational framework of Iranian scientists in the area of R&D of nuclear weapons, and for the purposes of retaining the skills of the scientists. This is [to] allow renewal of

---

[233] An annex to the report details these activities and provides a detailed explanation of the suspected weapons program's organizational structure.

[234] For example, the IAEA had previously reported documentation of an undisclosed Iranian uranium conversion project and an undisclosed missile reentry vehicle program. However, the November report describes documents obtained by the IAEA after May 2008 which "established a connection" between the two programs. Similarly, the annex also describes information provided by an unnamed government which contains additional details about Iranian experiments with high explosives.

[235] "Press Briefing by Senior Administration Officials on IAEA Report on Iran's Nuclear Activities," November 8, 2011.

[236] Department of Defense, *Annual Report on Military Power of Iran*, April 2012.

[237] "Additional Sanctions Imposed by the Department of State Targeting Iranian Proliferators," August 29, 2014. Amano's November 2011 report also mentioned the SPND.

> the activity necessary to produce weapon immediately when the Iranian leadership decides to do so.[238]

The report also indicates that Iran had not restarted the nuclear weapons program.

Amano's December 2, 2015, report assesses that Iran conducted "a range of activities relevant to the development of a nuclear explosive device ... prior to the end of 2003 as a coordinated effort," the report says, adding that "some [nuclear weapons-related] activities took place after 2003," but "were not part of a coordinated effort." The report concludes that "these activities did not advance beyond feasibility and scientific studies, and the acquisition of certain relevant technical competencies and capabilities." The IAEA "has no credible indications of activities in Iran relevant to the development of a nuclear explosive device after 2009," the report explains.[239]

According to some nongovernmental organization reports, the IAEA has assessed that Iran "has sufficient information to be able to design and produce a workable implosion nuclear device based upon HEU as the fission fuel."[240] However, these reports cite information from an internal 2009 IAEA document that ElBaradei has described as

> a rolling text complied by the Agency's Department of Safeguards that included all the various pieces of information that had come in from different intelligence organizations, most of which IAEA inspectors had been unable to verify or authenticate ... by definition, it was a series of best guesses.[241]

The IAEA Deputy Director General for Safeguards at the time had neither "assessed" nor "signed off on" the document, ElBaradei added.

For its part, the U.S. government assesses that Iran has not mastered "all the necessary technologies" for building a nuclear weapon, a senior Administration official stated in November 2011.[242] During the same briefing, a senior Administration official explained that "the fact that some activities have apparently continued after the full-scale program was shut down in 2003 suggests that there's been some advancement" in Iran's ability to develop nuclear weapons, but "since it appears to be relatively uncoordinated and sporadic activity ... the advancement probably hasn't been that dramatic." Perhaps reinforcing this point, Director Clapper stated during the February 2012 Senate Armed Services Committee hearing that "there are certain things" that Iran has not yet done to develop a nuclear weapon, but he did not elaborate. Ambassador Stephen D. Mull,

---

[238] Report 9342, Iran/Nuclear/Program Status, October 22, 2012.

[239] GOV/2015/68.

[240] *Excerpts from Internal IAEA Document on Alleged Iranian Nuclear Weaponization*, Institute for Science and International Security, October 2, 2009. Colin H. Kahl, Melissa G. Dalton, and Matthew Irvine, *Risk and Rivalry Iran, Israel and the Bomb*, Center for a New American Security, June 2012.

[241] Mohamed ElBaradei, *The Age of Deception: Nuclear Diplomacy in Treacherous Times*, (New York: Metropolitan Books, Henry Holt and Company), 2011, pp. 290.

[242] "Press Briefing by Senior Administration Officials," November 8, 2011.

Coordinator for Implementation of the JCPOA, told a Washington audience on January 21, 2016, that "there was a portion of the Iranian Government working in a very organized, systematic way to develop the capability to build a nuclear weapon. We don't know to the extent to which that knowledge has been tested or even survived."[243]

Amano's November 2011 report states that, according to a member of a "clandestine nuclear supply network" run by former Pakistani nuclear official Abdul Qadeer Khan, Iran "had been provided with nuclear explosive design information." However, this information may not be sufficient to produce a nuclear weapon. Although Khan's network supplied Libya with "documents related to the design and fabrication of a nuclear explosive device," according to the IAEA,[244] these documents lacked "important parts" for making a nuclear weapon, according to ElBaradei.[245] In addition to the documents supplied to Tripoli, members of the Khan network also had computer files containing "drawings for the components of two smaller, more advanced nuclear weapons."[246] However, according to former IAEA Deputy Director-General Olli Heinonen, these "detailed designs" were not "complete sets" of weapons design information.

Other members of the network could have possessed more complete nuclear weapons designs, he said.[247]

Timelines

A senior intelligence official explained during a December 2007 press briefing that the "acquisition of fissile material ... remains the governing element in any timelines" regarding Iran's production of a "nuclear device."[248] The 2007 NIE argued that "centrifuge enrichment is how Iran probably could first produce enough fissile material for a weapon" and added that "the earliest possible date Iran would be technically capable

243 "Implementation of the Joint Comprehensive Plan of Action," Washington Foreign Press Center, January 21, 2016.

244 *Implementation of the NPT Safeguards Agreement in the Socialist People's Libyan Arab Jamahiriya*, GOV/2008/39, September 12, 2008.

245 Mohamed ElBaradei, *The Age of Deception*, p.155. The International Institute for Strategic Studies described the design as "95% complete" (*Nuclear Black Markets: Pakistan, A.Q. Khan and the Rise of Proliferation Networks*, (London: The International Institute for Strategic Studies), 2007, p. 79). Khan told a former member of his network that the plans that he had provided to Libya were "for a non-working nuclear device" (Extract from the Statement of Sayed Abu Tahir Bin Bukhary, June 7, 2006, *Annexure L in Plea and Sentence Agreement, State vs. Geiges, Wisser, and Krisch Engineering*, September 2007). A report from Pakistan's Inter-Services Intelligence organization published in September 2011 argued that neither the technical assistance nor centrifuge components provided by the Khan network were sufficient "for the establishment of a small pilot [centrifuge] plant or to produce nuclear weapons." ("The A.Q. Khan Report by Pakistan ISI," September 15, 2011).

246 David Albright, *Peddling Peril: How the Secret Nuclear Trade Arms America's Enemies*, The Institute for Science and International Security, 2010. p. 151.

247 Interview with CRS analyst, August 4, 2011.

248 "Unclassified Key Judgments of the National Intelligence Estimate: Iran: Nuclear Intentions and Capabilities," Background Briefing with Senior Intelligence Officials, December 3, 2007.

of producing enough HEU for a weapon is late 2009."[249] However, it was "very unlikely" that Iran would attain such a capability by that date, the estimate says, adding that "Iran probably would be technically capable of producing enough HEU for a weapon sometime during the 2010-2015 time frame." But the State Department Bureau for Intelligence and Research, the estimate says, judged that Tehran "is unlikely to achieve this capability before 2013"[250] and all intelligence agencies recognized "the possibility that this capability may not be attained until *after* 2015."[251]

27.8 kilograms of uranium containing 90% uranium-235 is a frequently cited benchmark for determining the minimum sufficient amount of weapons-grade HEU for a nuclear weapon, but the amount assumed by U.S. government estimates is unclear. Tehran would likely need to produce more uranium-235 in order to produce its first nuclear weapon; according to a 2011 International Institute for Strategic Studies report, "the fabrication of an initial bomb would involve an amount of unavoidable wastage." Then-Deputy Assistant Secretary of Defense Colin Kahl explained during a November 15, 2011, hearing that "the time to actually complete a testable [Iranian nuclear] device could shrink over time."

Then-Secretary of Defense Leon Panetta told *60 Minutes* in 2012 that, if Iran were to decide to build a nuclear weapon, "it would probably take them about a year to be able to produce a bomb and then possibly another one to two years in order to put it on a deliverable vehicle of some sort in order to deliver that weapon."[252] Although, as noted, the United States estimated that Iran's Fordow enrichment facility "would be capable of producing approximately one weapon's worth" of HEU per year, whether and how that assessment factored into the U.S. timelines for Iranian nuclear weapons development is unclear.[253] Then-Under Secretary of State for Political Affairs Wendy Sherman explained during an October 3, 2013, Senate Foreign Relations Committee hearing that Iran would need as much as one year to produce a nuclear weapon if the government made the decision to do so.[254] At the time, Tehran would have needed two to three months to produce enough weapons-grade HEU for a nuclear weapon.[255] Iran's December 28, 2015, JCPOA-mandated shipment of LEU to Russia lengthened this time to one year, according to February 9, 2016, congressional testimony from Director of National Intelligence

---

[249] This time frame describes the point at which Iran could have enough HEU for a weapon, rather than when Iran could start producing HEU.

[250] In responses to Questions for the Record from the Senate Select Committee on Intelligence, which were made public in August 2009, the Director for National Intelligence stated that the Bureau continues to stand by this estimate.

[251] The time frame described in the 2007 NIE is the same as one described in a 2005 NIE.

[252] Transcript of remarks by Secretary Panetta from CBS's *60 Minutes* interview, January 29, 2012.

[253] See "Fordow Enrichment Facility" section.

[254] This estimate assumes the necessary time to produce a sufficient amount of weapons-grade HEU and complete the remaining steps necessary for an implosion-style nuclear explosive device suitable for explosive testing (conversation with U.S. official, July 21, 2015); "Reversing Iran's Nuclear Program," Senate Foreign Relations Committee, October 3, 2013.

[255] The White House. "Parameters for a Joint Comprehensive Plan of Action Regarding the Islamic Republic of Iran's Nuclear Program." April 2, 2015.

Clapper.[256] Then-UK Secretary of State for Foreign and Commonwealth Affairs Boris Johnson reiterated this assessment in a May 9, 2018, statement to Parliament.[257]

Declared versus Undeclared Nuclear Facilities

The U.S. estimates described above apparently assume that Iran would use its declared nuclear facilities to produce fissile material for a weapon. However, the 2007 NIE states that Iran "probably would use covert facilities—rather than its declared nuclear sites—for the production of highly enriched uranium for a weapon." Similarly, a CIA report covering 2004 concluded that "inspections and safeguards will most likely prevent Tehran from using facilities declared to the IAEA directly for its weapons program as long as Iran remains a party to the NPT."[258] Director Clapper echoed this assessment in a March 2015 interview.[259]

Iran would probably prefer to avoid using its safeguarded facilities partly because the IAEA would likely detect an Iranian attempt to use them for producing weapons-grade HEU. According to former Deputy Assistant Secretary Kahl, Tehran "is unlikely to dash for a bomb in the near future because IAEA inspectors would probably detect Iranian efforts to divert low-enriched uranium and enrich it to weapons-grade level at declared facilities."[260] Similarly, then-Deputy Assistant Secretary of Defense for Media Operations John Kirby told reporters on December 21, 2011, that, were Iran to begin producing a nuclear weapon, IAEA inspectors would likely give sufficient warning for the United States to take action. Former IAEA Deputy Director-General Heinonen observed in 2010 that Iran would probably be caught if it attempted to divert more than "small quantities" of nuclear material from its safeguarded nuclear facilities.[261] It would be extremely

---

[256] *Statement for the Record Worldwide Threat Assessment of the US Intelligence Community*, Senate Armed Services Committee, February 9, 2016.

[257] "Iran Nuclear Deal," *Hansard Online*, May 9, 2018, Volume 640.

[258] *Unclassified Report to Congress on the Acquisition of Technology Relating to Weapons of Mass Destruction and Advanced Conventional Munitions*, January 1-December 31, 2004.

[259] PBS "Charlie Rose" Interview with James Clapper, Director of National Security, March 3, 2015.

[260] Colin Kahl, "Before Attacking Iran, Israel Should Learn From Its 1981 Strike On Iraq," *The Washington Post*, March 2, 2012.

[261] Heinonen described "small quantities" as "one gram or a hundred grams"—far less than the amount necessary for a nuclear weapon. Arms Control Association, "The Status of Iran's Nuclear and Missile Programs," Transcript, November 22, 2010. The Verification Research, Training, and Information Centre assessed in 2009 that "any diversion of more than 48 grams of low enriched uranium would raise the alarm and trigger an in-depth [IAEA] investigation" (Andreas Persbo, *Safeguards in Iran: Prospects and Challenges*, presentation given to "Prospects for Dialogue in the Middle East," British Pugwash, April 30, 2009). See also "Senior Administration Official Holds A Background Briefing Previewing Iran P5+1 Talks," November 6, 2013; and Colin H. Kahl, "Not Time to Attack Iran: Why War Should Be a Last Resort," *Foreign Affairs*, January 17, 2012. Then-IAEA Deputy Director General for Safeguards Herman Nackaerts stated in July 2013 that the IAEA "would know within a week," if Iran were to use its safeguarded facilities to produce weapons-grade HEU (Barbara Slavin, "Tight IAEA Inspection Regime Hampers Iran's Nuclear Breakout," *Al-Monitor*, July 22, 2013).

difficult to reconfigure the cascades in the Natanz facility without detection[262] and, in any case, IAEA inspectors measure the isotopic content of enriched uranium and would thereby detect Iranian production of weapons-grade HEU. More recently, Clapper testified that the JCPOA

> has also enhanced the transparency of Iran's nuclear activities ... [a]s a result, the international community is well postured to quickly detect changes to Iran's declared nuclear facilities designed to shorten the time Iran would need to produce fissile material.[263]

Although Iran could eject IAEA inspectors and/or withdraw from the NPT, such a move would be "an incredibly provocative action and very risky for Iran to undertake," then-Department of State Special Advisor Einhorn argued in 2011, adding that Iran was unlikely to take such a risk because its operating first-generation centrifuges are inefficient.[264] It is worth noting that such an action would be virtually unprecedented.[265]

A senior intelligence official explained in December 2007[266] that Iran could use knowledge gained from its Natanz facilities at covert enrichment facilities; according to the NIE, a "growing amount of intelligence indicates Iran was engaged in covert uranium conversion and uranium enrichment activity," but Tehran probably stopped those efforts in 2003. U.S. officials have argued that Iran currently does not appear to have any nuclear facilities of which the United States is unaware. CIA Director John Brennan stated during a March 2015 interview that the United States has "a good understanding of what the Iranian nuclear program entails."[267] During a July 31, 2015, press briefing about possible Iranian undeclared nuclear facilities, U.S. Secretary of Energy Ernest Moniz stated that "we feel pretty confident that we know their current configuration." U.S. officials have expressed confidence in the ability of U.S. intelligence to detect Iranian covert nuclear facilities.[268]

---

[262] For more details about cascade configuration, see Houston G. Wood, Alexander Glaser, and R. Scott Kemp, "The Gas Centrifuge and Nuclear Weapons Proliferation," *Physics Today*, September 2008; International Institute for Strategic Studies, *Iran's Strategic Weapons Programmes: A Net Assessment*, (UK: Routledge, 2005), pp. 53-54.

[263] *Statement for the Record Worldwide Threat Assessment of the US Intelligence Community*, February 9, 2016.

[264] Einhorn, March 9, 2011.

[265] No state that has been found in good standing with the IAEA has ever used this tactic. North Korea restarted its nuclear weapons program, which includes previously monitored facilities, after announcing its withdrawal from the NPT in 2003, but the IAEA has never completed an assessment of that country's nuclear activities.

[266] Background Briefing with Senior Intelligence Officials, December 3, 2007.

[267] "Exclusive: CIA Director John Brennan Provides Insight into Agency Overhaul to Face Modern Threats," *Fox News Sunday*, March 22, 2015.

[268] "Exclusive: CIA Director John Brennan Provides Insight into Agency Overhaul to Face Modern Threats," Fox News Sunday, March 22, 2015. Conversation with U.S. official, October 25, 2013. Tom Donilon, Former National Security Adviser, "Iran and International Pressure: An Assessment of Multilateral Effort to Impede Iran's Nuclear Program," The Brookings Institution, November 22, 2011.

Does Iran Have a Nuclear Weapons Program?

In addition to the possible nuclear weapons-related activities discussed above, Iran has continued to develop ballistic missiles, which could potentially be used to deliver nuclear weapons. It is worth noting, however, that then-Director of National Intelligence Dennis Blair indicated during a 2009 Senate Armed Services Committee hearing that Iran's missile developments do not necessarily indicate that the government is also pursuing nuclear weapons, explaining that "I don't think those missile developments ... prejudice the nuclear weapons decision one way or another. I believe those are separate decisions."[269] Iran is developing missiles and space launch vehicles "for multiple purposes," he added. Similarly, in a June 2015 statement to Parliament, British Foreign and Commonwealth Office official Tobias Ellwood stated that "we are not aware of any current links between Iran's ballistic missile programme and nuclear programme."[270]

In any case, Tehran's nuclear program raised concerns for various other reasons. First, Iran was secretive about the program. For example, Tehran hindered the IAEA investigation by failing to disclose numerous nuclear activities, destroying evidence, and making false statements to the agency.[271] Moreover, although Iran's cooperation with the agency improved, the IAEA still repeatedly criticized Tehran for failing to cooperate fully with the agency's investigation of certain issues concerning Iran's nuclear program.[272]

Second, many observers have questioned Iran's need for nuclear power, given the country's extensive oil and gas reserves. The fact that Tehran resumed its nuclear program during its 1980 1988 war with Iraq has also cast doubt on the energy rationale.[273] Furthermore, many countries with nuclear power reactors purchase nuclear fuel from foreign suppliers—indeed, Russia has provided fuel for the Bushehr reactor—a fact that calls into question Iran's need for an indigenous enrichment capability. Moreover, Iranian officials acknowledge that Iran lacks sufficient uranium deposits for its planned nuclear power program.[274]

---

[269] "The Current and Future Worldwide Threats to the National Security of the United States," Senate Armed Services Committee Hearing, March 10, 2009.

[270] Iran: Nuclear Weapons: Written Question-1860. Answered by Mr. Tobias Ellwood on June 16, 2015. Available at http://www.parliament.uk/business/publications/written-questions-answers-statements/written-question/ Commons/2015-06-10/1860/.

[271] For example, Iran sanitized a facility where Iranian scientists had enriched uranium, falsely told the IAEA that it had not enriched uranium, and falsely claimed that it had not procured any foreign components for one of its centrifuge programs.

[272] As noted, the IAEA has concluded its investigation of the outstanding issues concerning Iran's nuclear program.

[273] During a September 2013 interview, former Iran Atomic Energy Organization President Amrollahi explained Tehran's decision to proceed with its nuclear power program during the war:

At that time 80 percent of the Bushehr Nuclear Power Plant's Unit One had been completed and we had spent $4 billion on the second unit, which was about 60-percent complete. What reasonable person would let go of his $4 billion? Then a nuclear power plant or a nuclear industry is a meeting ground for various technologies and this means improving knowledge and technology in the country. If we were to give that up we would lose a lot scientifically. (*Sharq*, September 7, 2013).

[274] *Iranian Students News Agency*, April 17, 2007. Wood et al., *Nonproliferation Review*, March 2007.

Iran's stated rationale for its Arak reactor has also been met with some skepticism. Tehran says it needs the reactor to produce medical isotopes and to replace the Tehran Research Reactor (TRR). However, that reactor is capable of producing such isotopes and has unused capacity. Furthermore, as noted, Iran expressed the desire to obtain more fuel for the TRR. In addition, nonproliferation experts have argued that a new heavy-water reactor would be unnecessary for producing such isotopes.[275]

However, Iran maintains that its nuclear program has always been exclusively for peaceful purposes; as noted, the Iranian government says that it plans to expand its reliance on nuclear power in order to generate electricity. Some experts have documented Tehran's projected difficulty in exporting oil and natural gas without additional foreign investment in its energy infrastructure.[276] Iran has explained its covert nuclear procurement efforts by arguing that it has been forced to conceal these efforts in order to counter Western efforts to deny it nuclear technology—a claim that appears to be supported by a 1997 CIA report.[277]

Tehran argues that it cannot depend on foreign suppliers for such fuel because such suppliers have been unreliable in the past.[278] At least one expert has described Iran's inability to obtain nuclear fuel from an international enrichment consortium called Eurodif; during the 1970s, Iran had reached an agreement with Eurodif that entitled Iran to enriched uranium from the consortium in exchange for a loan.[279] Former Atomic Energy Organization President Aghazadeh also argued that, although Iran does not need to produce fuel for the Bushehr reactor, the Natanz facility needed to be completed to provide fuel for the planned Darkhovin reactor.[280]

Other factors also suggest that Iran may not have had an active nuclear weapons program after 2003. First, as noted, the IAEA has resolved the outstanding issues described in the August 2007 Iran-IAEA work plan, and the agency has not discovered

---

[275] Robert J. Einhorn, "Iran's Heavy-Water Reactor: A Plutonium Bomb Factory," November 9, 2006, available at http://www.armscontrol.org/pressroom/2006/20061109_Einhorn.asp?print.

[276] See, for example, *U.S.-Iranian Engagement: The View from Tehran*, International Crisis Group, June 2, 2009; Roger Stern, "The Iranian Petroleum Crisis and United States National Security," *Proceedings of the National Academy of Sciences of America*, January 2007; and George Perkovich and Silvia Manzanero, "Plan B: Using Sanctions to End Iran's Nuclear Program," *Arms Control Today*, May 2004. A 1975 U.S. government report stated that "Iran has decided now to introduce nuclear power to prepare against the time—about 15 years in the future—when Iranian oil production is expected to begin to decline sharply." ("Report of the NSSM 219 Working Group Nuclear Cooperation Agreement with Iran," April 1975).

[277] CIA, *Report of Proliferation-Related Acquisition in 1997.* The report says that Iran had responded to "Western counterproliferation efforts by relying more on legitimate commercial firms as procurement fronts and by developing more convoluted procurement networks." Javad Zarif, than-Iran's Permanent Representative to the United Nations, wrote in a 2007 article that, because of these efforts, "Iran was left with no option but to be discrete in its peaceful activities." ("Tackling the Iran-U.S. Crisis: The Need for a Paradigm Shift," *Journal of International Affairs*, Spring/Summer 2007, vol. 60, no. 2. p. 81).

[278] For an official Iranian perspective on the issue, see *The Root Cause of Iran's Confidence Deficit vis a vis Some Western Countries on Assurances of Nuclear Fuel Supply*, INFCIRC/785, March 2, 2010. Iranian officials argued for an independent fuel production capability during the 1970s; see U.S. Embassy Tehran Airgram A-76 to State Department, 1976.

[279] Oliver Meier, "Iran and Foreign Enrichment: A Troubled Model," *Arms Control Today*, January/February 2006.

[280] "Iran to Follow Nuclear Timetable Regardless of IAEA Reports—Official," *Islamic Republic of Iran News Network*, February 25, 2009.

significant undeclared Iranian nuclear activities for a number of years. Second, Tehran, beginning in 2003, has been willing to disclose previously undeclared nuclear activities to the IAEA. Third, Iran made important changes to the administration of its nuclear program in the second half of 2003—changes that produced greater openness with the IAEA and may have indicated a decision to stop a nuclear weapons program.[281]

Fourth, as noted above, Iranian officials have stated numerous times that Tehran is not seeking nuclear weapons, partly for religious reasons—indeed, Khamene'i has issued a fatwa declaring that "the production, stockpiling, and use of nuclear weapons are forbidden under Islam," according to Iranian officials.[282] A change in this stance could damage Iranian religious leaders' credibility. In 2013, an Iranian Foreign Ministry spokesperson described the fatwa as the "operational instruction" for Iran's government.[283] Mark Fitzpatrick of the International Institute for Strategic Studies has argued that "given the pervasive religiosity of the regime, it is unlikely that Iran's supreme leader would be secretly endorsing military activity in explicit contradiction of his own religious edict."[284]

Fifth, Iranian officials argued that nuclear weapons would not improve the country's security. They argue that Iran would not be able to compete with the nuclear arsenals of larger countries, such as the United States.[285] Moreover, the Iranian government has asserted that "Iran today is the strongest country in its immediate neighborhood. It does not need nuclear weapons to protect its regional interests."[286] The U.S.-led spring 2003 invasion of Iraq, which overthrew Iraqi leader Saddam Hussein and thereby eliminated a key rival of Iran, may also have induced Tehran to decide that it did not need nuclear weapons. The government has also argued that a nuclear weapons program "would be prohibitively expensive, draining the limited economic resources of the country."[287]

In any case, since Iran has implemented its JCPOA commitments, which, as noted, include significant limits on Iran's nuclear program and transparency requirements with respect to that program, U.S. officials have argued that the Iranian nuclear program poses a less-severe proliferation threat. For example, then-Secretary of Defense Ashton Carter

---

[281] For an in-depth discussion, see Appendix B and Appendix D.

[282] "Iran's Statement at IAEA Emergency Meeting," *Mehr News Agency*, August 10, 2005. See also Statement by H.E. Dr. M. Javad Zarif, Permanent Representative of the Islamic Republic of Iran Before the Security Council, December 23, 2006. Khamene'i issued a fatwa as early as 2003 against nuclear weapons, according to Iranian officials ("Iran: Rowhani Says Khamene'i Considers Attempts to Access Nuclear Weapons 'Religiously Illegal'," *Islamic Republic News Agency*, October 25, 2003).

[283] "Leader's Fatwa on Nuclear Weapons Binding for Iran: Foreign Ministry," *Islamic Republic of Iran Broadcasting*, January 16, 2013. Iran's current Foreign Minister Zarif indicated in a 1999 journal article that Iran had produced chemical weapons, but the country's "religious leadership found it very difficult to condone the use of these weapons, even as reprisal." Iran later ceased producing the weapons, he wrote (Mohammad Javad Zarif and Mohammad Reza Alborzi, "Weapons of Mass Destruction in Iran's Security Paradigm: The Case of Chemical Weapons," *The Iranian Journal of International Affairs*, vol. XI, no. 4, Winter 1999).

[284] Fitzpatrick, 2008, p. 13.

[285] "Interview with Iran's Ambassador to IAEA," June 29, 2008.

[286] Iran's Permanent Mission to United Nations in New York, "An Unnecessary Crisis: Setting the Record Straight about Iran's Nuclear Program," published as advertisement in *New York Times*, November 18, 2005.

[287] Ibid.

testified in March 2016 that the agreement "places significant limitations on Iran that will effectively cut off its pathways to the fissile material for a nuclear bomb."[288]

Government Estimates

Since at least 2007, the U.S. intelligence community has issued unclassified assessments that Iran has not decided whether to develop nuclear weapons. According to the 2007 NIE, "Iranian military entities were working under government direction to develop nuclear weapons" until fall 2003, after which Iran halted its nuclear weapons program "primarily in response to international pressure." The NIE defines "nuclear weapons program" as "Iran's nuclear weapon design and weaponization work and covert uranium conversion-related and uranium enrichment-related work." The NIE adds that the intelligence community also assessed "with moderate-to-high confidence that Tehran at a minimum is keeping open the option to develop nuclear weapons." The NIE also states that, because of "intelligence gaps," the Department of Energy and the National Intelligence Council assessed "with only moderate confidence that the halt to those activities represents a halt to Iran's entire nuclear weapons program." The NIE added that "[s]ince fall 2003, Iran has been conducting research and development projects with commercial and conventional military applications—some of which would also be of limited use for nuclear weapons."

The NIE also states that "Tehran's decision to halt its nuclear weapons program suggests it is less determined to develop nuclear weapons than we have been judging since 2005."[289] The change in assessments, a senior intelligence official said in December 2007, was the result of "new information which caused us to challenge our assessments in their own right, and illuminated previous information for us to be able to see it perhaps differently than we saw before, or to make sense of other data points that didn't seem to self-connect previously."[290] According to press accounts, this information included various written and oral communications among Iranian officials which indicated that the

[288] Statement before Senate Committee on Armed Services, March 17, 2016.

[289] Although the 2005 NIE stated that "Iran currently is determined to develop nuclear weapons despite its international obligations and international pressure," that assessment was somewhat qualified. Titled "Iran's Nuclear Program: At A Crossroads," the estimate stated that Iran was not "immovable" on the question of pursuing a nuclear weapons program and also addressed the possibility that Tehran may not have had such a program. Moreover, the word "determined" was used in lieu of "pursuing" a nuclear weapon because the authors believed the latter to be a stronger term. The NIE was issued as a Memorandum to Holders of NIE 2001-15HC, "Iran's Nuclear Weapons Program: Multifaceted and Poised to Succeed, But When?"

[290] Background Briefing with Senior Intelligence Officials, December 3, 2007. Former National Intelligence Council official Thomas Fingar explained that this judgment was "based on ... double-checked new intelligence streams" that the intelligence community had begun to acquire during the first half of 2007. (Thomas Fingar, *Reducing Uncertainty: Intelligence Analysis and National Security*, (Stanford: Stanford University Press), 2011, p. 120).

program had been halted.[291] As noted, the United States may also have obtained information from Iranian officials who defected as part of a CIA program to induce them to do so,[292] as well as from penetration of Iran's computer networks.[293] Additionally, the NIE also incorporated open-source information, such as photographs of the Natanz facility that became available after members of the press toured the facility.

According to the 2007 NIE, the intelligence community assessed "with moderate-to-high confidence that Iran [did] not have a nuclear weapon." The community assessed "with low confidence that Iran probably [had] imported at least some weapons-usable fissile material," but still judged "with moderate-to-high confidence" that Tehran still lacked sufficient fissile material for a nuclear weapon.

On several occasions, the U.S. intelligence community has reaffirmed the 2007 NIE's assessment that Iran halted its nuclear weapons program but is keeping its options open.[294] The late-September 2009 revelation of the Fordow facility increased suspicions that Iran may have restarted its nuclear weapons program; as noted, some U.S. officials indicated that the facility was likely intended for a nuclear weapons program. Nevertheless, Administration talking points made public September 25, 2009, stated that the intelligence community still assessed that "Iran halted its nuclear weapons program in 2003." More recently, then-Director of National Intelligence Clapper testified in February 2016 that

> [w]e continue to assess that Iran's overarching strategic goals of enhancing its security, prestige, and regional influence have led it to pursue capabilities to meet its nuclear energy and technology goals and give it the ability to build missile-deliverable nuclear weapons, if it chooses to do so. Its pursuit of these goals will dictate its level of adherence to the CPOA over time. We do not know whether Iran will eventually decide to build nuclear weapons."[295]

Any decision to produce nuclear weapons "will be made by the Supreme Leader," Clapper stated in April 2013.[296]

---

[291] Dafna Linzer and Joby Warrick, "U.S. Finds that Iran Halted Nuclear Arms Bid in 2003," *Washington Post,* December 4, 2007; Greg Miller, "Iran's Nuclear Ambitions on Hold, U.S. Agencies Conclude," *Los Angeles Times*, December 4, 2007; David E. Sanger and Steven Lee Myers, "Details in Military Notes Led to Shift on Iran, U.S. Says," *New York Times*, December 6, 2007; Peter Baker and Dafna Linzer, "Diving Deep, Unearthing a Surprise; How a Search for Iran's Nuclear Arms Program Turned Up an Unexpected Conclusion," *Washington Post*, December 8, 2007.

[292] Miller, *Los Angeles Times*, December 9, 2007.

[293] David Sanger and William Broad, "U.S. and Allies Press Iran over Nuclear Plant 'Deception'," *The New York Times*, September 26, 2009.

[294] See, for example, February 12, 2009, testimony before the Senate Intelligence Committee by Director of National Intelligence Dennis Blair; "Annual Threat Assessment of the Intelligence Community for the Senate Intelligence Committee," February 12, 2009; and March 10, 2009, testimony before the Senate Armed Services Committee by Director of the Defense Intelligence Agency Michael Maples.

[295] *Statement for the Record Worldwide Threat Assessment of the US Intelligence Community*, Senate Armed Services Committee, February 9, 2016.

[296] "Hearing on Current and Future Worldwide Threats," Senate Committee on Armed Services, April 18, 2013.

The November 2011 report from IAEA Director-General Amano appears to support the U.S. assessment.[297] As noted, the report states that Iranian activities related to building a nuclear explosive device "took place under a structured programme," but senior Iranian officials ordered a halt to the program in late 2003. Echoing the judgment of the 2007 NIE, Amano's report mentions "indications that some activities relevant to the development of a nuclear explosive device continued after 2003," adding that some such activities "may still be ongoing." Most of the activities listed in the report occurred before the end of 2003. During a briefing about Amano's report, a senior Administration official described Iran's post-2003 weapons-related work as "a much less coordinated ... more sporadic set of research activities," some of which "are sort of related to nuclear weapons development."[298] As noted, an April 2012 Department of Defense report described Amano's report as containing "extensive evidence of past and possibly ongoing Iranian nuclear weapons-related research and development work."[299] Amano's December 2, 2015, report assesses that "before the end of 2003, an organizational structure was in place in Iran suitable for the coordination of a range of activities relevant to the development of a nuclear explosive device." Some Iranian nuclear weapons-related activities "took place after 2003," the report adds, noting that these activities "were not part of a coordinated effort." The IAEA "has no credible indications of activities in Iran relevant to the development of a nuclear explosive device after 2009," the report explains.[300] (See also "Nuclear Weapon Development Capabilities").

Some foreign intelligence agencies have apparently concurred with the U.S. assessment that Iran has not yet decided to build nuclear weapons. Director of the French General Directorate of External Security Erard Corbin de Mangoux stated in an interview published in 2010 that "[w]e do not yet know whether Tehran's objective is to enable itself to acquire such a capability (so-called 'threshold status') or actually to possess it."[301] In 2012, Israeli Foreign Minister Avigdor Lieberman appeared to confirm reports that Israeli intelligence shares this U.S. assessment.[302] Moreover, according to a 2012 Israeli intelligence report, "until 2003," Iran had a "set nuclear program ... for R&D of nuclear weapons."[303] However, the report indicates that Iran had not restarted the nuclear weapons program. German intelligence assessments have also reportedly concurred with this assessment.[304]

---

[297] GOV/2011/65.

[298] "Press Briefing by Senior Administration Officials," November 8, 2011.

[299] *Annual Report on Military Power of Iran*, April 2012.

[300] GOV/2015/68.

[301] Isabelle Lasserre, "Intelligence and the New Threats," *Politique Internationale*, January 1-March 31, 2010.

[302] "Israeli Foreign Minister Says Iran Nuclear Programme 'of Military Nature,'" *Voice of Israel*, March 19, 2012. The reports appeared in James Risen, "U.S. Faces a Tricky Task in Assessment of Data on Iran," *New York Times*, March 17, 2012, and Amy Teibel, "Israelis Agree Iran Hasn't Decided on Atom Bomb," *The Associated Press*, March 18, 2012.

[303] Report 9342, Iran/Nuclear/Program Status, October 22, 2012.

[304] "'Iran Striving for Nuclear Bomb'—Security Sources: Political Decision Still Pending," *Main Frankfurter Allgemeine*, July 1, 2011.

It is worth noting that the February 2018 Nuclear Posture Review asserts that "Iran's development of increasingly long-range ballistic missile capabilities, and its aggressive strategy and activities to destabilize neighboring governments, raises questions about its long-term commitment to foregoing nuclear weapons capability."[305]

Living with Risk

Other findings of the NIE indicate that the international community may, for the foreseeable future, have to accept some risk that Iran will develop nuclear weapons. According to the 2007 NIE, "only an Iranian political decision to abandon a nuclear weapons objective would plausibly keep Iran from eventually producing nuclear weapons—and such a decision is inherently reversible." As noted, the U.S. intelligence community assesses that Iran has the capacity to produce nuclear weapons at some point. This is not to say that an Iranian nuclear weapons capability is inevitable; as noted above, Iran does not yet have such a capability. But Tehran adherence to the JCPOA is probably necessary to provide the international community with confidence that it is not pursuing a nuclear weapon.

Other Constraints on Nuclear Weapons Ambitions[306]

Although the production of fissile material is widely considered to be the most difficult step in nuclear weapons development, Iran would, even with the ability to produce weapons-grade HEU, still face challenges in producing nuclear weapons, such as developing a workable physics package and effective delivery vehicles. A 1978 CIA report points out that there is a

> great difference between the development and testing of a simple nuclear device and the development of a nuclear weapons system, which would include both relatively sophisticated nuclear designs and an appropriate delivery system.[307]

Moreover, Iran would face significant challenges if it were to attempt developing and producing HEU-based nuclear weapons covertly, although, as noted, covert production

---

[305] *Nuclear Posture Review*, Office of the Secretary of Defense, February 2018.

[306] For more detail about nuclear weapons development, see "Appendix B. Nuclear Weapons Development" in CRS Report R43333, *Iran Nuclear Agreement*.

[307] "RE: Pakistan Strong Motivation to Develop Their Nuclear Capability," Central Intelligence Agency, April 26, 1978. For a more detailed discussion, see Office of Technology Assessment, *Technologies Underlying Weapons of Mass Destruction* (OTA-BP-ISC-115), December 1993.

would probably be Tehran's preferred option. Covert centrifuge facilities are notoriously difficult for intelligence agencies to detect,[308] but Iran may well not be able to complete a covert centrifuge facility without detection. A 2005 International Institute for Strategic Studies report concluded that "an Iranian planner would have little basis for confidence that significant nuclear facilities could be kept hidden."[309] Tehran would need to hide a number of activities, including uranium conversion, the movement of uranium from mines, and the movement of centrifuge feedstock.[310]

Alternatively, Iran could import uranium ore or centrifuge feedstock, but would also need to do so covertly. Iran's implementation of the JCOA has further decreased the probability that the government could successfully conceal a nuclear weapons program.

The difficulty of the above task becomes clearer when one considers that foreign intelligence agencies apparently possess a significant amount of information about the Iran's enrichment program. First, both the Natanz and Fordow facilities were discovered by foreign governments before they became operational. Second, the development of the Stuxnet computer worm, discussed above, indicates that at least one foreign government possesses a large amount of information about Iran's centrifuge program which could not have been obtained via IAEA reporting, according to some experts.[311] As noted, U.S. officials have expressed confidence in the ability of U.S. intelligence to detect Iranian covert nuclear facilities.

It is also worth noting that Iran could produce only fairly simple nuclear weapons, which are not deliverable by longer-range missiles, without conducting explosive nuclear tests. Such tests, many analysts argue, would likely be detected.[312] It is also worth noting that moving from the production of a simple nuclear weapon to more sophisticated nuclear weapons could take several additional years.[313]

---

[308] International Institute for Strategic Studies, February 2011, p.68. See also, David Albright, Paul Brannan, and Jacqueline Shire, *Can Military Strikes Destroy Iran's Gas Centrifuge Program? Probably Not*, Institute for Science and International Security, August 7, 2008; and Kemp, *International Security*, Spring 2014.

[309] International Institute for Strategic Studies, *Iran's Strategic Weapons Programmes: A Net Assessment*, (UK: Routledge, 2005).

[310] The 2005 IISS report also explains that concealing a plutonium-based nuclear weapons program would be even more difficult (pp. 62-63).

[311] David Albright, Paul Brannan, Andrea Stricker, Christina Walrond, and Houston Wood, *Preventing Iran From Getting Nuclear Weapons: Constraining Its Future Nuclear Options*, Institute for Science and International Security, March 5, 2012; R Scott Kemp, "Worm Holes—Virus Attacks Iran's Enrichment Operation," *Jane's Intelligence Review*, September 15, 2011.

[312] For a detailed discussion of this issue, see Steven A. Hildreth, statement before the House Committee on Oversight and Government Reform, Subcommittee on National Security and Foreign Affairs, March 5, 2008. Iran is a party to the Treaty Banning Nuclear Weapon Tests in the Atmosphere, in Outer Space and Under Water, also known as the Limited Test Ban Treaty. Iran has signed, but not ratified, the Comprehensive Nuclear-Test-Ban Treaty, which has not entered into force.

[313] *Iran's Nuclear and Missile Potential: A Joint Threat Assessment by U.S. and Russian Technical Experts*, EastWest Institute, May 2009. pp. 5-6.

Appendix A. Iranian Statements on Nuclear Weapons

Iranian officials have repeatedly asserted that the country's nuclear program is exclusively for peaceful purposes. For example, Supreme Leader Ayatollah Ali Khamene'i declared during a June 3, 2008, speech that Iran is opposed to nuclear weapons "based on religious and Islamic beliefs as well as based on logic and wisdom." He added, "[n]uclear weapons have no benefit but high costs to manufacture and keep them. Nuclear weapons do not bring power to a nation because they are not applicable. Nuclear weapons cannot be used." Similarly, then-Iranian Foreign Ministry spokesperson Hassan Qashqavi stated on November 10, 2008, that "pursuance of nuclear weapons has no place in the country's defense doctrine." Khamene'i stated in 2012 that

> Ideologically and religiously speaking, we believe that it is not right [to have nuclear weapons]. We believe that this move [making nuclear weapons] and the use of such weapons are a great sin. We also believe that stockpiling such weapons is futile, expensive and harmful; and we would never seek this.[314]

Asked in 2012 if Iran is trying to develop the capability to produce a nuclear weapon, Ambassador Mohammad Khazaee, Iran's Permanent Representative to the United Nations, stated that "[w]e are not going to develop the capacity to be able to make any weapon of mass destruction."[315] Iranian Foreign Minister Javad Zarif argued in 2014 that Khamene'i "has explicitly declared his opposition with regard to the manufacture, stockpile and use of nuclear weapons," and observed that "nuclear weapons have no place in Iran's defense doctrine."[316] More recently, President Hassan Rouhani stated that "we are not thinking about developing nuclear weapons, nor will we think about it. The Supreme Leader [Ali Khamenei] has banned it and said that it is not appropriate."[317]

Appendix B. Organization of Iran's Nuclear Program

The Atomic Energy Organization of Iran (AEOI), which the government established in 1974, operates Iran's declared nuclear program and has a variety of peaceful programs in areas such as agriculture, medicine, and basic nuclear research and development.[318]

---

[314] "Leader Says West Knows Iran Not Seeking 'Nuclear Weapons,'" *Vision of the Islamic Republic of Iran Network 1*, February 22, 2012.

[315] *The Charlie Rose Show*, January 18, 2012.

[316] "Iran Foreign Minister Calls for Building Mutual Trust with West," *Islamic Republic News Agency*, January 7, 2014.

[317] "Iran President Labels Trump's Threats 'Empty,'" *Islamic Republic of Iran News Network*, April 25, 2018.

[318] Atomic Energy Organization of Iran, "Nuclear Industry in Iran: An Overview on Iran's Activities and Achievements in Nuclear Technology," 2012. Although a 2012 EU regulation (Council Implementing Regulation (EU) No 1264/2012 Implementing Regulation (EU) No 267/2012 Concerning Restrictive Measures

According to the U.S. Department of the Treasury, the AEOI "reports directly to the Iranian President"[319] and is the "main Iranian organization responsible for research and development activities in the field of nuclear technology."[320] The AEOI has been Tehran's main interlocutor with the IAEA. According to an August 2008 Institute for Science and International Security (ISIS) report, the AEOI controls the country's centrifuge program, but that program is operated by an AEOI entity called the Kalaye Electric Company.[321] AEOI officials told the IAEA in 2003 that Iran decided to begin its centrifuge enrichment program in 1985. The program

> consisted of three phases: activities during the first phase, from 1985 until 1997, had been located mainly at the AEOI premises in Tehran; during the second phase, between 1997 and 2002, the activities had been concentrated at the Kalaye Electric Company in Tehran; during the third phase, 2002 to the present, the R&D and assembly activities were moved to Natanz.[322]

Gholamreza Aghazadeh's term as AEOI president, which began in 1997, marked an acceleration of Iran's enrichment program.[323] According to President Hassan Rouhani, who headed the 2003 2005 negotiations concerning the nuclear program, the government in 1998 formed the Supreme Council for New Technologies, chaired by then-President Mohammad Khatami, which focused on the nuclear program.[324] Beginning around 1999, Iran's central government gave the AEOI "authorities that it did not have before," Rouhani stated in a 2004 speech, explaining that

> we gave the agency a freer hand with new credits and a more liberal spending procedure, new facilities, and special regulations. This allowed them to become more active, without being forced to go through bureaucratic and regulatory labyrinths.[325]

Against Iran, December 21, 2012) described the Islamic Revolutionary Guard Corps (IRGC) as "[r]esponsible for Iran's nuclear programme," a State Department official indicated in an October 25, 2016, email to the author that this description is inaccurate.

[319] U.S. Department of the Treasury, "United States Increases Sanctions Against Iranian Proliferation Networks," December 13, 2012.

[320] U.S. Department of the Treasury, "Fact Sheet: E.O. 13382 Designations on Iran," November 21, 2011.

[321] David Albright, Paul Brannan, and Jacqueline Shire, *Can Military Strikes Destroy Iran's Gas Centrifuge Program? Probably Not*, Institute for Science and International Security, August 7, 2008. For entities associated with the centrifuge program, see Appendix E.

[322] *Implementation of the NPT Safeguards Agreement in the Islamic Republic of Iran*, Report by the Director General, GOV/2003/63, August 26, 2003.

[323] Dr. Hasan Rouhani, *National Security and Nuclear Diplomacy*, (Tehran: Center for Strategic Research), 2011, p. 25; David Patrikarakos, *Nuclear Iran: The Birth of an Atomic State*, (New York: I.B. Tauris), 2012, pp.163-171.

[324] Rouhani, 2011, pp. 24-28.

[325] "Beyond the Challenges Facing Iran and the IAEA Concerning the Nuclear Dossier," *Rahbord*, September 30, 2005, pp. 7-38.

Nuclear Weapons Program

Beginning in the late 1980s, Iran's nuclear weapons program was coordinated by entities connected with Iran's Ministry of Defense Armed Forces Logistics (MODAFL).[326,327] The AMAD Plan took over these activities several years later; the projects were "allegedly managed through the 'Orchid Office.'"[328] After Iran ended the nuclear weapons program in 2003, "staff remained in place to record and document the achievements of their respective projects," according to information provided to the IAEA by unnamed governments. Later, "equipment and work places were either cleaned or disposed of so that there would be little to identify the sensitive nature of the work which had been undertaken."[329] Tehran established an organization called the Organization of Defensive Innovation and Research (SPND) in 2011 by an individual who had "managed activities useful in the development of a nuclear explosive device" as part of the Amad Plan and associated entities.[330]

According to a 2012 Israeli intelligence document, Iran established the SPND "for the purposes of preserving the technological ability and the joint organizational framework of Iranian scientists in the area of R&D in nuclear weapons, and for the purposes of retaining the skills of the scientists."[331] These activities were to "allow renewal of the activity necessary to produce weapons immediately when the Iranian leadership decides to do so."[332] Nevertheless, the IAEA reported in December 2015 that, despite the SPND's establishment in 2011, the post-2003 activities "were not part of a coordinated effort" and the agency "has no credible indications of activities in Iran relevant to the development of a nuclear explosive device after 2009."[333] (For more details, see Appendix D).

---

[326] According to a November 2011 report from IAEA Director-General Yukiya Amano, "organizational structures and administrative arrangements for an undeclared nuclear programme were established and managed through the Physics Research Centre (PHRC), and were overseen, through a Scientific Committee, by the Defence Industries Education Research Institute (ERI), established to coordinate defence R&D for the Ministry of Defence Armed Forces Logistics (MODAFL)." (*Implementation of the NPT Safeguards Agreement and Relevant Provisions of Security Council Resolutions in the Islamic Republic of Iran*, GOV/2011/65, November 8, 2011).

[327] Although some IRGC entities are associated with MODAFL (see Council Implementing Regulation (EU) No 1264/2012), the Guard Corps was not part of the nuclear weapons program, a State Department official indicated in an October 25, 2016, email to the author.

[328] GOV/2011/65.

[329] Ibid.

[330] "Additional Sanctions Imposed by the Department of State Targeting Iranian Proliferators," August 29, 2014.

[331] Report 9342, Iran/Nuclear/Program Status, October 22, 2012. Available at http://tinyurl.com/h2syl8q. Former State Department Special Advisor for Nonproliferation and Arms Control Robert Einhorn wrote in May 2018 that "the weapons development materials were archived at the direction of then-Defense Minister Ali Shamkhani."(Robert Einhorn, "Israeli Intelligence Coup Could Help Trump "Fix" the Iran Deal," Order from Chaos, Brookings Institution, May 4, 2018).

[332] Ibid.

[333] *Final Assessment on Past and Present Outstanding Issues Regarding Iran's Nuclear Programme*, GOV/2015/68, December 2, 2015.

The AEOI had links with some entities that were apparently connected to the Amad Plan. For example, a company called Kimia Maadan "was a cover company for chemical engineering operations under the AMAD Plan while also being used to help with procurement for the [AEOI]."[334] The organization contracted with the same company to design and build the Gchine mill.[335] Furthermore, Tehran's AEOI-run centrifuge program had connections to entities controlled by Iran's MODAFL, which controlled the Amad Plan.[336] For example, Iran fabricated some components for its second-generation centrifuge in a workshop located on a site belonging to Iran's Defence Industries Organization, which was part of MODAFL.[337]

Nevertheless, there are several indications that the AEOI's illicit nuclear activities were not necessarily part of the nuclear weapons program. First, the NIE appeared to exclude the AEOIrun enrichment program. Explaining that the U.S. intelligence community defined the weapons activities as "nuclear weapon design and weaponization work and covert uranium conversion-related and uranium enrichment-related work," the estimate added that "Iran's declared civil work related to uranium conversion and enrichment" was not part of the weapons program.[338] Moreover, a November 2011 IAEA description of the suspected past nuclear weapons program's management structure omits the AEOI.[339] Lastly, September 2009 U.S. intelligence community talking points regarding the September 2009 joint British, French, and U.S. revelation of Iran's Fordow centrifuge facility state that the plant's existence did "not contradict" the 2007 NIE's conclusions regarding Iran's nuclear weapons program.[340] One reason for this assessment, the talking points suggest, was that the Fordow facility was developed by the AEOI.

U.S. and British officials have stated that Iranian missile development is not currently linked to the nuclear program. Iran's MODAFL oversees Iran's ballistic missile program; the Aerospace Industries Organization, a MODAFL subsidiary, oversees the country's missile production.[341] Although some Islamic Revolutionary Guard Corps (IRGC) entities are associated with MODAFL and the IRGC Air Force operates Iran's ballistic missiles, these entities do not appear to be associated with the AEOI. A State Department

---

[334] GOV/2011/65.

[335] *Implementation of the NPT Safeguards Agreement and Relevant Provisions of Security Council Resolutions 1737 (2006) and 1747(2007) in the Islamic Republic of Iran, Report by the Director General*, GOV/2008/4, February 22, 2008.

[336] GOV/2011/65.

[337] U.S. Department of the Treasury, "Treasury Designates Iranian Proliferation Network and Identifies New Aliases," April 7, 2009; Implementation of the NPT Safeguards Agreement in the Islamic Republic of Iran, Report by the Director General, GOV/2004/34, June 1, 2004.

[338] "Iran: Nuclear Intentions and Capabilities," November 2007.

[339] GOV/2011/65.

[340] "Q&A on the Qom Enrichment Facility," September 25, 2009. Available at https://www.iranwatch.org/sites/default/files/us-wh-qomqandas-0909.pdf.

[341] Unless otherwise noted, this paragraph is based on "Fact Sheet: Increasing Sanctions Against Iran," U.S. Department of the Treasury, July 12, 2012; and Council Implementing Regulation (EU) No 1264/2012. Also see CRS Report R42849, *Iran's Ballistic Missile and Space Launch Programs*, by Steven A. Hildreth; and CRS Report R44017, *Iran's Foreign and Defense Policies*, by Kenneth Katzman.

official explained in October 2016 that the IRGC "was not responsible for" activities related to the Possible Military Dimensions of Iran's nuclear program.[342]

Appendix C. Multilateral Diplomacy Concerning Iran's Nuclear Program

In fall 2002, the IAEA began to investigate Iran's nuclear activities at Natanz and Arak; inspectors visited the sites the following February. The IAEA board adopted its first resolution, which called on Tehran to increase its cooperation with the agency's investigation and to suspend its uranium enrichment activities, in September 2003. The next month, Iran concluded an agreement with France, Germany, and the United Kingdom, collectively known as the "E3," to suspend its enrichment activities, sign and implement an Additional Protocol to its IAEA safeguards agreement, and comply fully with the IAEA's investigation.[343] As a result, the IAEA board decided to refrain from referring the matter to the U.N. Security Council, despite U.S. advocacy for such a referral.[344] Statements from current and former Iranian officials indicate that, during fall 2003, Tehran feared that the United States might use Security Council referral as a means to undertake military action or other coercive measures against Iran.[345]

The IAEA's investigation, as well as information Tehran provided after the October 2003 agreement, ultimately revealed that Iran had engaged in a variety of clandestine nuclear-related activities, some of which violated Iran's safeguards agreement. These included plutonium separation experiments, uranium enrichment and conversion experiments, and importing various uranium compounds.

---

[342] Email to CRS analyst, October 25, 2016.

[343] The text of the agreement is available at http://www.iaea.org/NewsCenter/Focus/IaeaIran/statement_iran21102003.shtml. Iran signed its Additional Protocol in December 2003 but has not ratified it. An August 2003 letter from the E3 to the Iran asked the government "to stop the construction of installations that give Iran the ability to produce fissionable material, including any sort of enrichment or reprocessing" (Letter of the Ministers of Foreign Affairs of Germany, France, and England to the Minister of Foreign Affairs of the Islamic Republic of Iran, Dated 15/05/1382 [6 August 2003], Dr. Hasan Rouhani, *National Security and Nuclear Diplomacy*, [Tehran: Center for Strategic Research], 2011, pp. 595-96). According to a French official involved in drafting the letter, the Bush Administration gave a "yellow light," rather than a "green light " or "red light," to the letter (Kelsey Davenport and Elizabeth Philipp, "A French View on the Iran Deal: An Interview With Ambassador Gérard Araud," *Arms Control Today*, July/August 2016).

[344] "Ex-chief Negotiator Says Iran Leaders Decided to Suspend Nuclear Enrichment," *Aftab-e Yazd*, April 7, 2009; John Bolton, *Surrender Is Not an Option: Defending America at the United Nations and Abroad*, (New York: Threshold Editions), 2008, p. 139; Christopher Ford, "A New Paradigm: Shattering Obsolete Thinking on Arms Control and Nonproliferation," *Arms Control Today*, November 2008. For more details about noncompliance with IAEA safeguards agreements and Security Council referral, see CRS Report R40094, *Iran's Nuclear Program: Tehran's Compliance with International Obligations*, by Paul K. Kerr.

[345] *Aftab-e Yazd*, April 7, 2009; Mehdi Mohammadi,"Nuclear Case From Beginning to End in Interview with Dr. Hasan Rowhani (Part 1): We Are Testing Europe," *Keyhan*, July 23, 2005; David Patrikarakos, *Nuclear Iran: The Birth of an Atomic State*, (New York: I.B. Tauris), 2012, p. 181; Seyed Hossein Mousavian, *The Iranian Nuclear Crisis: A Memoir*, (Washington, DC: Carnegie Endowment for International Peace), 2012, p. 76.

After October 2003, Iran continued some of its enrichment-related activities, but Tehran and the E3 agreed in November 2004 to a more detailed suspension agreement. During negotiations between fall 2003 and summer 2005, both Iran and the E3 offered a number of proposals, although the two sides never reached agreement.[346] According to one former British official involved in the negotiations, a chief obstacle was E3 opposition to a 2005 Iranian proposal that would have included a limited Iranian enrichment program.[347] A former Iranian official argued that the perceived lack of success of Iranian officials who had participated in negotiations with the E3 discredited those officials in the eyes of other Iranian officials.[348]

The United States influenced several aspects of the E3 negotiations during this time. For example, the Bush Administration opposed an E3 request to ease sanctions on certain U.S. goods.[349] The United States also persuaded the E3 to refrain from agreeing to any arrangement with Iran which included even a limited Iranian enrichment program, according to accounts from E3 officials directly involved in the diplomacy.[350] Former President George W. Bush has written that the United States' "ultimate goal" was "stopping Iranian enrichment."[351]

Iran resumed uranium conversion in August 2005 under the leadership of President Ahmadinejad, who had been elected two months earlier. On September 24, 2005, the IAEA Board of Governors adopted a resolution that, for the first time, found Iran to be in noncompliance with its IAEA safeguards agreement. The board, however, did not refer Iran to the Security Council, choosing instead to give Tehran additional time to comply with the board's demands. Iran announced in January 2006 that it would resume research and development on its centrifuges at Natanz. In response, the IAEA board adopted a resolution on February 4, 2006, that referred the matter to the Security Council. Two days later, Tehran announced that it would stop implementing its Additional Protocol.

In June 2006, China, France, Germany, Russia, the United Kingdom, and the United States, collectively known as the "P5+1," presented a proposal to Iran that offered a variety of incentives in return for Tehran taking several steps to assuage international concerns about its enrichment and heavy-water programs.[352] The proposal called on the

---

[346] These proposals are available at http://www.armscontrol.org/factsheets/Iran_Nuclear_Proposals.

[347] Peter Jenkins, "Did Hassan Rouhani Dupe Europe in 2003?," *LobeLog*, June 25, 2013.

[348] Mousavian, 2012, pp. 200, 209, 267, 280.

[349] Jack Straw, *Last Man Standing: Memoirs of a Political Survivor*, (London: MacMillan), 2012, p. 453.

[350] Richard Dalton, "Iran Is not in Breach of International Law," *The Guardian*, June 9, 2011; Francois Nicoullaud, former French Ambassador to Iran, quoted in Patrikarakos 2012, p. 194.

[351] George W. Bush, *Decision Points*, (New York: Crown Publishing), 2010, p. 416. U.S. officials decided during the first Obama Administration to leave open the possibility of reaching an agreement with Iran that would include an Iranian enrichment program. (Trita Parsi, *Losing an Enemy: Obama, Iran, and the Triumph of Diplomacy*, [New Haven, Yale University Press], 2017, p. 217).

[352] The proposal text is available at http://armscontrol.org/pdf/20060606_Iran_P5+1_Proposal.pdf. Prior to late May 2006, the United States refused to participate in direct talks with Iran about its nuclear program. In March 2005, Washington had offered some limited incentives for Iran to cooperate with the E3. (See Kerr, *Arms Control Today*, June 2006). For more information about the state of international diplomacy with Iran, see CRS Report RL32048, *Iran: Politics, Human Rights, and U.S. Policy*, by Kenneth Katzman.

government to address the IAEA's "outstanding concerns ... through full cooperation" with the agency's ongoing investigation of Tehran's nuclear programs, "suspend all enrichment-related and reprocessing activities," and resume implementing its Additional Protocol.

Then-European Union High Representative for Common Foreign and Security Policy Javier Solana presented a revised version of the 2006 offer to Iran in June 2008.[353] Representatives from the P5+1 discussed the new proposal with Iranian officials the next month. Iran provided a follow-up response in August 2008, but the six countries deemed it unsatisfactory.[354] Tehran told the IAEA that it would implement its Additional Protocol "if the nuclear file" were "returned from the Security Council" to the agency.[355] It is not clear that the council could have met this condition. The 2006 offer's requirements were also included in several U.N. Security Council resolutions, including Resolution 1929, which was adopted on June 9, 2010.[356] Iran issued another proposal in early September 2009 which described a number of economic and security issues as potential topics for discussion but only obliquely mentioned nuclear issues and did not explicitly mention Iran's nuclear program.[357]

Tehran Research Reactor Discussions[358]

After an October 1, 2009, meeting in Geneva with the P5+1 and High Representative Solana, Iranian officials repeatedly stated that Tehran wanted future discussions about its September 2009 proposal. Nevertheless, during that meeting, Iranian officials agreed in principle to a proposal that would provide LEU fuel containing about 20% uranium-235 for Iran's U.S.-supplied Tehran Research Reactor (TRR), which produces medical isotopes and operates under IAEA safeguards. Iran asked the IAEA in a June 2, 2009, letter to provide fresh fuel for its U.S-supplied TRR. Initially fueled by U.S.-supplied HEU, the reactor was converted to use LEU fuel in 1994 after Argentina agreed to supply

---

[353] The revised proposal text is available at http://www.auswaertiges-amt.de/diplo/de/Aussenpolitik/Themen/Abruestung/IranNukes/Angebot-e33-080614.pdf.

[354] Iran had also presented a proposal to the P5+1 in May 2008. See Peter Crail, "Proposals Offered on Iranian Nuclear Program," *Arms Control Today*, May 2008. The proposal text is available at http://www.iaea.org/Publications/ Documents/Infcircs/2008/infcirc729.pdf.

[355] *Implementation of the NPT Safeguards Agreement and Relevant Provisions of Security Council Resolutions 1737 (2006), 1747 (2007) and 1803 (2008) in the Islamic Republic of Iran*, Report by the Director General, GOV/2008/4, February 22, 2008.

[356] The resolution text is available at http://www.iaea.org/newscenter/focus/iaeairan/unsc_res1929-2010.pdf. The resolutions also required Iran to suspend work on its heavy water-related projects.

[357] The proposal text may be found at http://documents.propublica.org/iran-nuclear-program-proposal#p=1.

[358] Unless otherwise noted, this section is based on an October 1, 2009, background briefing by senior U.S. officials; ElBaradei's remarks during an October 4, 2009, press conference; an October 13, 2009, French Foreign Ministry briefing; an analyst interview with a U.S. official; Mark Hibbs, "Six Nations Might Place Conditions on Reactor Fuel Supply to Iran," *Nuclear Fuel*, October 5, 2009; "Iran to Provide 20% Fuel if Probable Deal with West Fails: AEOI," *Iranian Students News Agency*, October 10, 2009; and "Iran Foreign Ministry Spokesman's Weekly News Conference," *Iranian News Network Channel*, October 12, 2009.

the reactor with such fuel, which contained about 20% uranium-235, in 1987.[359] Subsequent to Iran's June 2009 request, the United States and Russia presented a proposal to the IAEA (which the agency conveyed to Iran) for providing fuel for the reactor.

According to the proposal, Iran would have transferred approximately 1,200 kilograms of its low-enriched uranium hexafluoride to Russia, which would have either enriched the uranium to about 20% uranium-235 or produced such LEU from Russian-origin uranium. Russia would then have transferred the low-enriched uranium hexafluoride to France for fabrication into fuel assemblies. Finally, Paris would have transferred the assemblies to Russia for shipment to Iran. France would have delivered the fuel within about one year.[360] Iran had, as of October 30, 2009, produced 1,763 kilograms of low-enriched uranium hexafluoride containing less than 5% uranium-235.[361]

Beginning on October 19, 2009, Iranian officials met with officials from the IAEA, France, Russia, and the United States to discuss details of implementing the proposal, such as the fuel price, contract elements, and a timetable for shipping the fuel. Two days later, then-IAEA Director-General ElBaradei announced the conclusion of a "draft agreement," which was drafted by the IAEA. Although Iran, France, Russia, and the United States held further discussions regarding the proposal's implementation, they did not reach agreement with Tehran. Iran resisted transferring all 1,200 kilograms of low-enriched uranium hexafluoride out of the country before receiving the reactor fuel, arguing that the proposal needed more credible assurances that the fuel would actually be delivered. During the last few months of 2009, Iranian officials did suggest different compromises, such as shipping its low-enriched uranium hexafluoride out of the country in phases or simultaneously exchanging that material for the TRR fuel on an Iranian island or in a third country, but these proposals were not accepted by the United States, France, and Russia.[362]

Further details about the French, Russian, and U.S. proposals later became public.[363] For example, the IAEA had agreed to take formal custody of any Iranian low-enriched uranium hexafluoride transferred pursuant to a TRR agreement. Additionally, France, Russia, and the United States had agreed to a "legally binding Project and Supply Agreement"; agreed to "support technical assistance through the IAEA to ensure" that the TRR would operate safely; and expressed support for allowing Iran to transfer its low-

---

359 This information is contained in a February 18, 2010, letter from Iran to the IAEA (GOV/INF/2010/5).

360 These details appeared in a June 2010 letter from France, Russia, and the United States to the IAEA ("Text: Powers Dismiss Iran Fuel Offer before U.N. Vote," *Reuters*, June 9, 2010).

361 *Implementation of the NPT Safeguards Agreement and Relevant Provisions of Security Council Resolutions 1737 (2006), 1747 (2007), 1803 (2008) and 1835 (2008) in the Islamic Republic of Iran*, Report by the Director General, GOV/2009/74, November 16, 2009.

362 See, for example, "Iran Says It Would Swap Nuclear Material with West in Turkey," *The Associated Press*, December 26, 2009; "Mottaki: Iran Ready for Simultaneous N. Fuel Swap," *Fars News Agency*, December 26, 2009.

363 These details are contained in an official February 12, 2010, letter from those three governments to IAEA Director-General Amano.

enriched uranium hexafluoride to a third country, which would hold that material in escrow until the TRR fuel was fabricated. The United States also offered "substantial political assurances that the agreement would be fulfilled." An April 20, 2010, letter from President Obama to then-President Brazilian President Luis Inácio Lula da Silva stated that the United States had expressed its willingness to "potentially even play a more direct role in the fuel production process," but did not elaborate.

Notably, the October 2009 IAEA draft did not include an explicit prohibition on Iranian production of uranium enriched to about 20% uranium-235. Instead, the agreement's proponents thought that the supply of fuel for the TRR would obviate the need for Tehran to produce the fuel on its own.[364] The escrow proposal described in the previous paragraph was not contained in the October 2009 IAEA draft.[365] Whether the other provisions described above were explicitly contained in that draft is unclear because there is no public official copy of it.

Following a November 20, 2009, meeting, the P5+1 issued a joint statement expressing disappointment with Tehran's failure to respond positively to the TRR proposal. "We have agreed to remain in contact and expect a further meeting soon to complete our assessment of the situation and to decide on our next steps," the statement said. Although some subsequent Iranian statements suggested that Iran was still open to some version of the IAEA proposal,[366] Tehran never officially accepted it. Although, as discussed below, Iran has manufactured fuel for the reactor, whether Iran can produce sufficient amounts of acceptable-quality fuel is unclear.[367]

Following a May 17, 2010, meeting of Iranian President Ahmadinejad, Turkish Prime Minister Recep Tayyip Erdogan, and Brazilian President Lula, Iran did accept a proposal, known as the Tehran Declaration, for supplying the TRR with fuel.[368] Iran conveyed its acceptance of the declaration in a May 24, 2010, letter to the IAEA. The Tehran Declaration contained some of the same elements as the October 2009 IAEA draft proposal and other elements described in a February 12, 2010, letter to the IAEA. For example, the declaration stated that Iran would be willing to "deposit" 1,200 kilograms of LEU in Turkey. Iran would deposit the fuel, which would be subject to IAEA monitoring in Turkey, "not later than one month" after reaching an agreement regarding the details of the exchange with France, Russia, the United States, and the IAEA. However, unlike the IAEA draft proposal, the declaration did not mention an ultimate destination for the LEU to be deposited in Turkey. As noted, Tehran had resisted transferring all 1,200 kilograms of LEU out of the country before receiving fuel for the TRR.

---

[364] Ibid.

[365] Analyst interview with knowledgeable U.S. official, June 16, 2010.

[366] See, for example, Iran's February 18, 2010, letter to the IAEA.

[367] David Albright and Jacqueline Shire, *Iran's Recent Statements about Production of Fuel for the Tehran Research Reactor: A Quick Review*, Institute for Science and International Security, February 8, 2010.

[368] The text is available at http://www.brasil.gov.br/news/history/2010/05/17/joint-declaration-by-iran-turkey-and-brazil?set_language=en.

IAEA Director-General Amano told the agency's Board of Governors on June 7, 2010, that he had "immediately conveyed Iran's letter" to France, Russia, and the United States "and asked for their views." Those three governments responded to the IAEA two days later with letters and a joint paper titled "Concerns about the Joint Declaration Conveyed by Iran to the IAEA."[369] The paper conveyed several reservations about the Tehran Declaration, but did not reject it outright. One reason for the U.S. refusal to accept the proposal was fear that the proposal would disrupt efforts to persuade the Security Council to adopt a resolution imposing additional sanctions on Iran (the council adopted Resolution 1929 in June 2010).[370]

Further Talks

Iran and the P5+1 met in December 2010 and January 2011, but the two meetings, held in Geneva and Istanbul, respectively, produced no results. In April 2012, the two sides resumed talks in Istanbul. Iran and the P5+1 subsequently have held two rounds of talks—a May meeting in Baghdad and a June meeting in Moscow. Additionally, the two sides held expert-level discussions in Istanbul in July 2012.[371]

Following the April 2012 talks, the P5+1 stated that the process of inducing Iranian compliance with "all its international obligations" would be "guided by the principle of the step-by-step approach and reciprocity."[372] The P5+1 presented their proposal the next month during the Baghdad meeting. The six governments demanded that Tehran end its production of enriched uranium containing approximately 20% uranium-235; ship to a third country Iran's stockpile of uranium enriched to this level (this uranium would be

---

[369] The text appears in "Text: Powers Dismiss Iran Fuel Offer Before U.N. Vote," *Reuters*, June 9, 2010.

[370] Hillary Rodham Clinton, *Hard Choices*, (New York: Simon & Shuster), 2014, pp. 361-363.

[371] Iranian and U.S. officials began holding secret bilateral discussions in July 2012 that were brokered by the Sultan of Oman (Clinton 2014, pp. 368-69). Former White House and State Department official Jake Sullivan explained in January 2015 that the two parties formulated the "outlines of a first-step agreement," which informed the later P5+1 negotiations with Iran ("President Obama's 'Fourth Quarter' Foreign Policy: A Conversation with Jake Sullivan about 2015-2016," YouTube video, 33:20, posted by DukeSanfordSchool, January 23, 2015, https://www.youtube.com/ watch?v=un_l53E4hiI).

Obama had sent two secret letters to Supreme Leader Ayatollah Ali Khamene'i in 2009 (Clinton 2014, p. 352). A senior U.S. official told reporters in January 2016 that, following Rouhani's 2013 election, President Obama sent him a letter "indicating that we wanted to open up diplomatic discussions around the nuclear deal." ("Senior Administration Officials Hold a Background Briefing via Teleconference on Iran," January 17, 2016).

[372] This paragraph is based on the following sources: Kelsey Davenport, "Iran, P5+1 Move to Technical Talks," *Arms Control Today*, July/August 2012; Kelsey Davenport, "P5+1 and Iran Claim Progress in Talks," *Arms Control Today*, June 2012; Kelsey Davenport, *History of Official Proposals on the Iranian Nuclear Issue*, Arms Control Association, August 2012; *The P5+1, Iran and the Perils of Nuclear Brinkmanship*, International Crisis Group Middle East Briefing, June 15, 2012; "Text of statement by EU's Ashton After Iran Talks," *Reuters*, May 24, 2012; Jay Solomon, "Iran, U.S. Agree Only to Resume Their Talks Next Month," *Wall Street Journal*, May 24, 2012; Paul Richter, "Iran, World Powers Clash At Latest Talks; Tehran Says The Six Nations Haven't Given It A 'Balanced' Offer On Its Nuclear Program," *Los Angeles Times*, May 24, 2012; "Full Text of Iran's Proposals to Six World Powers in Moscow Talks," *Fars News Agency*, July 7, 2012.

under IAEA monitoring); halt enriching uranium, as well as installing centrifuges and centrifuge components, at the Fordow facility; and cooperate fully with the IAEA's investigation. Then-European Union High Representative Catherine Ashton for Common Foreign and Security Policy stated on May 24, 2012, that the P5+1 "put ideas on the table on reciprocal steps we would be prepared to take." These included

- refraining from imposing new sanctions on Iran;
- facilitating Iranian access to spare aircraft parts, as well as safety and repair inspections;
- providing fuel for the TRR;
- supporting IAEA technical cooperation regarding the TRR's safety;
- providing medical isotopes to Tehran;
- potentially reviewing suspended IAEA technical cooperation projects with Iran;[373] and
- cooperating on Tehran's acquisition of a light-water reactor for producing radioisotopes.

The two sides again held talks in February 2013. Technical experts from the P5+1 and Iran met the next month, and another round of talks at the political director level took place in April 2013. Following the June 2013 election of Iranian President Hassan Rouhani, many observers expressed optimism that these negotiations would produce an agreement. After Rouhani took office in August 2013, Iran and the P5+1 met twice later that year (once in October and once in November). The two sides met again on November 20, 2013, and agreed to an accord called the Joint Plan of Action (JPA) on November 24. This agreement set out an approach toward reaching a long-term comprehensive solution to international concerns regarding Iran's nuclear program. The two sides began implementing the JPA on January 20, 2014. The P5+1 and Iran reached a framework of a Joint Comprehensive Plan of Action (JCPOA) on April 2, 2015, and finalized the JCPOA on July 14, 2015.

Appendix D. Possible Military Dimensions of Iran's Nuclear Program

Then-International Atomic Energy Agency (IAEA) Director-General Mohamed ElBaradei told the agency's Board of Governors on June 2, 2008, that questions

[373] These are apparently the same technical cooperation projects which the IAEA Board of Governors suspended in 2007.

regarding "possible military dimensions" to Iran's nuclear program constituted the "one remaining major issue" concerning the IAEA's investigation of the program. A November 2011 report by current IAEA Director-General Yukiya Amano to the IAEA board contains the most detailed account to date of the IAEA's evidence regarding Iran's suspected nuclear weapons-related activities.[374] Unless otherwise noted, this appendix is based on Amano's November 2011 report.

The IAEA has "credible" information that Iran has carried out activities "relevant to the development of a nuclear explosive device." Although some of these activities have civilian applications, "others are specific to nuclear weapons," the report notes. Most of these activities were conducted before the end of 2003, though some may have continued. The Iranian government managed these activities via a program structure which included "senior Iranian figures." Amano's report contains a detailed description of the program's structure, which was set up in the late 1980s. The program's activities were managed via an institution called the Physics Research Center and overseen by an Iranian Ministry of Defense entity. About a decade later, the center's activities were consolidated under a new entity called the AMAD Plan. After the Iranian regime halted the AMAD Plan's work in 2003, "staff remained in place to record and document the achievements of their respective projects," according to information provided to the IAEA by unnamed governments. Later, "equipment and work places were either cleaned or disposed of so that there would be little to identify the sensitive nature of the work which had been undertaken."

The IAEA has "other information" from governments which "indicates that some activities previously carried out under the AMAD Plan were resumed later." Some of these activities "would be highly relevant to a nuclear weapon programme." A December 2015 report from Amano assesses that, although some Iranian nuclear weapons-related activities "took place after 2003," these activities "were not part of a coordinated effort."[375] The IAEA "has no credible indications of activities in Iran relevant to the development of a nuclear explosive device after 2009,"the report explains.[376]

The IAEA has information that the AMAD Plan either obtained or attempted to obtain dual-use "equipment, materials and services which ... would be useful in the development of a nuclear explosive device." Additionally, the program may have conducted studies on uranium conversion, missile reentry vehicles for delivering nuclear warheads, and conventional explosives used in nuclear weapons.

---

[374] *Implementation of the NPT Safeguards Agreement and Relevant Provisions of Security Council Resolutions in the Islamic Republic of Iran*, GOV/2011/65, November 8, 2011.

[375] GOV/2015/68.

[376] Ibid.

Nuclear Explosive Device Components

The IAEA has information indicating that Iran may have conducted work on components for nuclear weapons. Iran possesses a document "describing the procedures" for reducing uranium hexafluoride to uranium metal, as well as "machining ... enriched uranium metal into hemispheres," which are "components of nuclear weapons."[377] Tehran has previously told the IAEA that it was offered equipment for casting uranium but never actually received it.[378] Moreover, a member of a clandestine nuclear supply network run by former Pakistani nuclear official Abdul Qadeer Khan told the IAEA that Iran "had been provided with nuclear explosive design information." However, this information may not be sufficient to produce a nuclear weapon. (See "Nuclear Weapon Development Capabilities.") The IAEA has also received information from an unnamed government that Iran carried out "preparatory work, not involving nuclear material, for the fabrication of natural and high enriched uranium metal components for a nuclear explosive device."

As noted, the AMAD Plan may have conducted studies on conventional explosives used in nuclear weapons. Implosion-type nuclear explosive devices use conventional explosives to compress a core of highly enriched uranium or plutonium in order to start a nuclear chain reaction. Specifically, Iran developed detonators which have limited nonnuclear applications, but also could be used in a nuclear explosive device. Tehran also may have experimented with a multipoint initiation system which could be used in conjunction with the detonators. Additionally, Iran may have conducted high explosive testing, possibly in association with nuclear materials, at a military site (see "Parchin" below). Iran also may have worked on neutron initiators, which are used in implosion-type nuclear weapons.

Reentry Vehicle

As noted, the IAEA suspects that the AMAD Plan conducted studies on missile reentry vehicles for delivering nuclear warheads. Iran may have conducted "engineering studies to examine" integrating a payload into the reentry vehicle of Iran's Shahab-3 ballistic missile. Although these activities "may be relevant to the development of a non-nuclear payload, they are highly relevant to a nuclear weapon programme." Iran also may have conducted work on a "prototype firing system" that would enable a missile's

---

[377] *Implementation of the NPT Safeguards Agreement and Relevant Provisions of Security Council Resolutions 1737 (2006), 1747 (2007), and 1803 (2008) in the Islamic Republic of Iran*, Report by the Director General, GOV/2008/15, May 26, 2008.

[378] According to Iran, its nuclear suppliers, many of whom were affiliated with the Khan network, provided the document in 1987 at their own initiative, rather than at Tehran's request. Islamabad has confirmed to the IAEA that "an identical document exists" in Pakistan.

nuclear payload "to explode both in the air above a target, or upon impact of the re-entry vehicle with the ground."

Parchin

Parchin is an Iranian military site.[379] The Institute for Science and International Security described the complex in a 2004 report as "a huge site dedicated to the research, development, and production of ammunition, rockets, and high explosives," adding that the site "is owned by Iran's military industry and has hundreds of buildings and test sites."[380] IAEA inspectors investigated the Parchin site in 2005 after receiving "information ... from a Member State in the early 2000s alleging that Iran was conducting high explosive testing, possibly in association with nuclear materials."[381] Such testing could contribute to the development of implosion-type nuclear explosive devices. IAEA inspectors visited the site twice in 2005, but "did not uncover anything of relevance."

Parchin was not under IAEA safeguards. However, the IAEA wanted Tehran to respond to information which the agency obtained from unnamed governments indicating that "Iran constructed a large explosives containment vessel" in 2000 at Parchin "in which to conduct hydrodynamic experiments."[382] Such experiments are conducted to validate the design of an implosion-type nuclear weapon and are "strong indicators of possible weapon development." The report does not say whether Iran actually conducted these experiments at Parchin. The inspectors in 2005 did not visit the location that the IAEA currently assessed to contain the building housing the containment vessel.[383] The agency requested access to this latter building in February 2012, but Iran did not provide such access until September 2015. At that time, IAEA officials "did not observe a chamber or any associated equipment inside the building." Iranian officials told their IAEA counterparts in October 2015 that the building in question "had always been used for the storage of chemical material for the production of explosives," but the "information available" to the IAEA, "does not support Iran's statements on the purpose of the building."[384]

---

[379] Then-Iranian Ambassador to the IAEA Ali Asghar Soltanieh described Parchin as "a military site" in a March 2012 statement. (Statement by H.E. Ambassador Soltanieh Resident Representative of the Islamic Republic of Iran to the IAEA Before the IAEA Board of Governors, March 8, 2012). Similarly, the IAEA described Parchin as a "military complex" (GOV/2011/65).

[380] David Albright and Corey Hinderstein, *Parchin: Possible Nuclear Weapons-Related Site in Iran*, Institute for Science and International Security, September 15, 2004.

[381] GOV/2011/65.

[382] Ibid. The report also notes that the IAEA "has obtained commercial satellite images that are consistent with this information. From independent evidence ... the Agency has been able to confirm the date of construction of the cylinder and some of its design features."

[383] GOV/2011/65.

[384] *Final Assessment on Past and Present Outstanding Issues Regarding Iran's Nuclear Programme*, GOV/2015/68, December 2, 2015.

Other Issues[385]

The IAEA also asked Tehran about other indications, some of which do not appear in Amano's November 2011 report, suggesting that the country may have pursued nuclear weapons.[386] These include

- "information about a high level meeting in 1984 on reviving Iran's pre-revolution nuclear programme";
- "the scope of a visit by officials" associated with Iran's Atomic Energy Organization "to a nuclear installation in Pakistan in 1987";
- information on 1993 meetings between Iranian officials and members of a clandestine procurement network run by former Pakistani nuclear official Abdul Qadeer Khan;
- information about work done in 2000 which apparently related to reprocessing;
- Iranian scientists' mathematical research with nuclear weapons applications; and
- information indicating that Iran "may have planned and undertaken preparatory experimentation which would be useful were Iran to carry out a test of a nuclear explosive device."

APPENDIX E. IRANIAN CENTRIFUGE WORKSHOPS AND RELATED ENTITIES

This appendix lists Iranian entities which appear to have manufactured centrifuges or related components. It also includes some entities which appear to have conducted work closely related to these activities. The appendix excludes entities which have only been identified as involved in procuring materials or components for Iran's centrifuge program. This list is probably not exhaustive and at least some of the publicly available information about Iran's centrifuge workshops may be outdated. International Atomic Energy Agency (IAEA) inspectors had access to Iranian centrifuge workshops until early 2006 in order to verify the October 2003 agreement under which Iran suspended its enrichment program. However, the agency's knowledge of Iran's workshops deteriorated after Tehran ended this access in early 2006. Iran may subsequently have moved centrifuge-related work to other locations[387] and likely built more such workshops.[388]

---

[385] Officials from the Departments of State and Energy described these matters as "historic" during a July 1, 2016, interview.

[386] The first four items are discussed in GOV/2008/15. The last two items are in GOV/2011/65.

[387] A former top Middle East intelligence analyst at the Department of State expressed concern in 2006 that Tehran could be moving some components related to its nuclear program. See Paul Kerr, "News Analysis: IAEA Limits Leave Iran Intel Gaps," *Arms Control Today*, October 2006.

Tehran has provided the IAEA with access to some centrifuge workshops pursuant to the Joint Plan of Action and the Joint Comprehensive Plan of Action. The latter agreement requires Iran to declare specific types of equipment for producing certain centrifuge components, as well as the locations where such production takes place.

Kalaye Electric

U.N. Security Council Resolution 1737 describes Kalaye Electric, which is located in Tehran, as a "provider" to Iran's pilot centrifuge facility located at Natanz. According to an August 2008 Institute for Science and International Security (ISIS) report, the Atomic Energy Organization of Iran (AEOI) controls the country's centrifuge program, but the program is operated by Kalaye Electric, which is an AEOI entity.[389] A December 2011 European Union Council regulation describes several entities as current suppliers to Kalaye Electric, suggesting that the company was involved in Iran's centrifuge program at that time.[390]

7th of Tir

Resolution 1737 describes this entity, which is located in Esfahan, as "directly involved" in Iran's nuclear program. 7th of Tir was involved in manufacturing centrifuge components, according to the ISIS report, which added that Iran moved "the key centrifuge manufacturing equipment and components to Natanz and other AEOI sites" when the IAEA began monitoring the 2003 suspension agreement. Whether and to what extent the facility is still involved in manufacturing centrifuge components is unknown, the report says.

Farayand Technique

Resolution 1737 describes this entity, which is located in Esfahan, as "involved in" Iran's centrifuge program. The facility was involved in "making and assembling"

---

[388] A U.S. official told CRS in April 2011 that there "could be lots of workshops" in Iran. And a former U.S. government official with direct experience on the issue told CRS in February 2012 that Iran's centrifuge production is widely distributed and that the number of workshops probably multiplied "many times" since 2005 because of an increase in Iranian contractors and subcontractors working on the program.

[389] David Albright, Paul Brannan, and Jacqueline Shire, *Can Military Strikes Destroy Iran's Gas Centrifuge Program? Probably Not*, Institute for Science and International Security, August 7, 2008. The description of Kalaye Electric as "AEOI entity" is found in a November 2011 Fact Sheet by the Department of the Treasury (*Fact Sheet: E.O. 13382 Designations on Iran*, November 21, 2011).

[390] *Council Implementing Regulation (EU) No 503/2011 Implementing Regulation (EU) No 961/2010 on Restrictive Measures Against Iran*, May 23, 2011.

centrifuge components, according to the 2008 ISIS report. According to a 2010 European Council regulation, another entity, called the Iran Centrifuge Technology Company, "has taken over the activities of Farayand Technique," which include "manufactur[ing] uranium enrichment centrifuge parts."[391]

Iran Centrifuge Technology Company

As noted, this entity, which is apparently located in Esfahan, took over "the activities of Farayand Technique," which have included "manufactur[ing] uranium enrichment centrifuge parts," according to the 2010 European Council regulation.[392]

Pars Trash

Resolution 1737 describes this Tehran-based entity as "involved in" Iran's centrifuge program. According to the ISIS report, the company manufactured centrifuge components. The report does not say whether Pars Trash is still involved in Iran's centrifuge program.

Kaveh Cutting Tools Company

This entity, according to the 2008 ISIS report, manufactured centrifuge components. The company is "part of" Khorasan Metallurgy Industries, the ISIS report says. Both of these entities are located in Mashad. Khorasan Metallurgy Industries is "involved in the production of centrifuge components," according to the 2010 European Council regulation.

Khorasan Metallurgy Industries

This entity, which is located in Mashad, has been "involved in the production of centrifuge components," according to the 2010 European Council regulation.

---

[391] *Council Regulation (EU) No 961/2010 on Restrictive Measures Against Iran and Repealing Regulation (EC) No 423/2007*, October 25, 2010.

[392] Ibid.

Sanam Electronic Industry Group

Located in Tehran, this entity was, according to ISIS, "involved in making centrifuge components."

Abzar Boresh Kaveh Company

U.N. Security Council Resolution 1803 describes this company as "[i]nvolved in the production of centrifuge components."

Parto Sanat Company

The 2010 European Council regulation describes this company, which is located in Tehran, as a "[m]anufacturer of frequency changers ... capable of developing/modifying imported foreign frequency changers in a way that makes them usable in gas centrifuge enrichment."

Eyvaz Technic

The 2011 European Council regulation states that, as recently as 2011, this Tehran-based company supplied equipment relevant to centrifuge operations to Iran's Natanz and Fordow centrifuge facilities.

Ghani Sazi Uranium Company

According to the 2011 European Council regulation, this company, which is located in Tehran, had "production contracts" with Kalaye Electric and Iran Centrifuge Technology Company.

Iran Pooya

The 2011 European Council regulation describes this Tehran-based entity as "a major manufacturer of aluminium cylinders for centrifuges whose customers" included the AEOI and Iran Centrifuge Technology Company.

Mohandesi Toseh Sokht Atomi Company

The 2011 European Council regulation describes this company, which is located in Tehran, as "contracted to" Kalaye Electric "to provide design and engineering services across the nuclear fuel cycle."

Saman Nasb Zayendeh Rood

The 2011 European Council regulation describes this company, which is located in Esfahan, as a "[c]onstruction contractor that has installed piping and associated support equipment at the uranium enrichment site at Natanz." The company "has dealt specifically with centrifuge piping," according to the regulation.

Jelvesazan Company

This company, located in Esfahan, was a possible supplier of vacuum pumps to the Iran Centrifuge Technology Company, according to a December 2012 European Council regulation.[393]

Iran Aluminium Company

According to the December 2012 European Council regulation, this company, located in Arak, was a supplier to the Iran Centrifuge Technology Company as of mid-2012.

Simatec Development Company

The December 2012 European Council regulation identified this company, apparently located in Tehran, as a supplier of inverters for centrifuges to the Kalaye Electric Company.

---

[393] *Council Implementing Regulation (EU) No 1264/2012 Implementing Regulation (EU) No 267/2012 Concerning Restrictive Measures Against Iran*, December 21, 2012.

Sharif University of Technology

This university, located in Tehran, has provided laboratories for use by the entity Kalaye Electric Company and the Iran Centrifuge Technology Company, according to the December 2012 European Council regulation.

Zirconium Production Plant

A 2012 report from the AEOI identified this plant, located in Esfahan, as a "provider of pipes and aluminum sheets used in different parts of centrifuge machines."[394]

Aluminat

This Tehran-based company had a contract in 2012 to supply aluminum to the Iran Centrifuge Technology Company, according to the December 2012 European Council regulation.

Pishro Systems Research Company

This company, according to a 2013 State Department announcement, was "responsible for research and development efforts across the breadth of Iran's nuclear program," including Iran's enrichment program.[395] The company "likely has or will have a facility" in Tehran, the State Department said.

Fulmen Group

This company "was involved in procuring goods" and installing "electrical equipment" for Iran's Fordow enrichment facility prior to 2009, according to the State Department and the European Union.[396] The company also worked with Kalaye Electric "on the construction of elements of the Natanz Uranium Enrichment Plant."[397]

---

[394] *Nuclear Industry in Iran: An Overview on Iran's Activities and Achievements in Nuclear Technology*, Atomic Energy Organization of Iran, 2012, p. 19.

[395] Patrick Ventrell, "State Department Actions Targeting Iran's Nuclear Enrichment and Proliferation Program," May 9, 2013.

[396] *Fact Sheet: E.O. 13382 Designations on Iran*, November 21, 2011; *Council Regulation (EU) No 267/2012 Concerning Restrictive Measures Against Iran and Repealing Regulation (EU) No 961/2010*, March 23, 2012.

[397] *Fact Sheet: E.O. 13382 Designations on Iran*, November 21, 2011.

Appendix F. Post-2003 Suppliers to Iran's Uranium Enrichment Program

Iran has obtained components, expertise, and material for its nuclear program from a variety of foreign sources. Tehran sought assistance for the program from the Russian and Chinese governments,[398] but also obtained relevant components, expertise, and material via deceptive procurement techniques.[399] Perhaps Iran's best-known source was a clandestine procurement network run by former Pakistani nuclear official Abdul Qadeer Khan. This network began supplying Iran's centrifuge program in 1987,[400] but U.S. and Pakistani officials have characterized the network as defunct since Pakistan publicly revealed the network in early 2004.[401] It is worth noting that, according to former Deputy Director General of the International Atomic Energy Agency (IAEA) Olli Heinonen,[402] the IAEA has not determined the source of material that Iran obtained for its advanced centrifuges.

Methodology

Because the original Khan network appears to be defunct, this appendix focuses on post-2003 suppliers to Iran's enrichment program. To obtain the information for this appendix, official U.S. government reports,[403] were reviewed, as well as lists of entities sanctioned by the United States and the European Union since early 2004.[404] Also reviewed were public information from the Department of Justice, reports from a U.N.

[398] A Russian entity agreed during the 1990s to provide Iran with a centrifuge facility but later canceled the transaction. See Robert J. Einhorn and Gary Samore, "Ending Russian Assistance to Iran's Nuclear Bomb," *Survival*, Summer 2002. The United States dissuaded China in 1997 from supplying Iran with a uranium conversion facility, although Iran did receive blueprints for the facility. See *Report of Proliferation-Related Acquisition in 1997,* and *Implementation of the NPT Safeguards Agreement and Relevant Provisions of Security Council Resolutions 1737 (2006) and 1747 (2007) in the Islamic Republic of Iran*, Report by the Director General, GOV 2007/58, November 15, 2007.

[399] According to *Report of Proliferation-Related Acquisition in 1997*, "Tehran is attempting to acquire fissile material and technology for weapons development and has set up an elaborate system of military and civilian organizations to support its effort."

[400] Iran began obtaining centrifuge-related technology from non-Khan network sources in 1985. See David Albright, *Peddling Peril: How the Secret Nuclear Trade Arms America's Enemies* (New York: Free Press), 2010, pp. 70-73.

[401] For more information, see CRS Report RL34248, *Pakistan's Nuclear Weapons*, by Paul K. Kerr and Mary Beth D. Nikitin.

[402] Analyst interview January 18, 2012.

[403] State Department reports to Congress covering 2004 through 2008 (submitted pursuant to Section 1308 of the Foreign Relations Authorization Act for Fiscal Year 2003; CRS does not have the report covering 2006); State Department reports reviewing countries' compliance with international arms control and nonproliferation agreements covering between 2004-2010 and December 31, 2008; and intelligence community reports mandated by Section 721 of the Intelligence Authorization Act for Fiscal Year 1997 covering 2004-2010.

[404] Specially Designated Nationals List and lists of entities sanctioned pursuant to several nonproliferation laws (available at http://www.state.gov/t/isn/c15231.htm).

Panel of Experts, and selected nongovernmental reports.[405] In order to identify suppliers germane to this appendix, Iranian entities or nationals, Iranian ships under foreign flags, and entities associated with the Khan network were excluded. This methodology has limitations. Official reports generally do not provide enough information to identify specific suppliers to Iran's enrichment program and Federal Register announcements of the imposition of sanctions generally do not explain the specific transactions which warranted the sanctions.[406] Even if official reports do identify suppliers to Iran's *nuclear* program, they often do not say whether the entities were supplying Iran's *enrichment* program. For example, an October 2008 Justice Department fact sheet stated that the sales director of a California-based corporation attempted to export illegally to Iran "machinery and software to measure the tensile strength of steel," explaining that these items "can make a contribution to nuclear activities of concern." The fact sheet, however, did not provide additional information and neither 2007 testimony from a Department of Commerce official nor a 2008 Commerce Department announcement explained whether the exports were intended for Iran's enrichment program.[407] Similarly, a 2008 report from the Czech Republic's Security Information Service stated that an Iranian company "subject to sanctions because of its involvement in the Iranian nuclear program" attempted to acquire "specific machinery" from a Czech supplier, but the report did not specify further.[408]

Suppliers to Iran's Enrichment Program

The information reviewed for this appendix indicates that Iranian-owned entities were using deceptive means in attempts to acquire enrichment technology from foreign entities.[409] However, the sources described above contain no evidence that foreign governments are currently supplying Iran's enrichment program. According to a 2009 State Department report, "all major suppliers, apart from Russia which is providing assistance to Iran's Bushehr Nuclear Power Plant, have agreed not to provide nuclear technology to Iran."[410] Additionally, State Department reports covering countries'

---

[405] *Panel of Experts Established Pursuant to Resolution 1929 (2010): Final Report*, June 2011; *Final Report of the Panel of Experts Established Pursuant to Resolution 1929 (2010)*, June 12, 2012.

[406] CRS checked the lists of sanctioned entities against news reports and other sources in order to obtain additional information.

[407] Statement of Mark Foulon, Acting Under Secretary of Commerce for Industry and Security, Before Committee on Banking, Housing, and Urban Affairs, March 21, 2007; Order Denying Export Privileges, Bureau of Industry and Security, January 25, 2008.

[408] Annual Report of the Security Information Service (BIS) for 2008.

[409] The extent to which these attempts have been successful is unclear.

[410] *Report on the Proliferation of Missiles and Essential Components of Nuclear, Biological, Chemical and Radiological Weapons. Report Submitted to the Congress Pursuant to Section 1308 of the Foreign Relations Act for Fiscal Year 2003*. January 2008-December 2008. Previous official statements from the United States and the United Kingdom appear to support this statement with respect to Russia. John Rood, then-Acting Under Secretary of State for Arms Control and International Security, stated during a June 12, 2008, House Committee on Foreign Affairs hearing that the Bush Administration did not believe there was "ongoing

compliance with international nonproliferation agreements between 2004 and 2010 indicate that the Chinese government is not involved in supplying Iran's suspected nuclear weapons program.[411]

Chinese Entities

Robert J. Einhorn, then-State Department Special Advisor for Nonproliferation and Arms Control, stated in March 2011 that the United States continued "to have concerns about the transfer of proliferation-sensitive equipment and materials to Iran by Chinese companies."[412] Similarly, the State Department compliance reports mentioned above indicate that unspecified non-Chinese entities have attempted to acquire "nuclear-related" materials and equipment from Chinese entities. Furthermore, a CIA report covering 2007 stated that "private Chinese businesses continue to sell materials, manufacturing equipment, and components suitable for use in ballistic missile, chemical weapon and nuclear weapon programs to North Korea, Iran and Pakistan."[413] The report did not specify further.[414] It is worth noting that Chinese entities may have supplied Iran with enrichment-related equipment obtained from Western suppliers. According to court documents made public in July 2012, an Iranian national attempted to obtain U.S.-origin components for Iran's enrichment program using entities in China and the Philippines.[415] More recently, a Chinese citizen pleaded guilty in December 2015 to exporting U.S.-origin components used for uranium enrichment to Iranian entities via China.[416]

Russian nuclear assistance [to Iran] outside of the Bushehr project" that would cause concern. Similarly, the UK Foreign and Commonwealth Office stated in August 2007 that the "Russian relationship with Iran in connection with Bushehr is now the only significant foreign relationship Iran has in the nuclear field," adding that "[e]arlier plans for a wider Russian relationship with Iran on nuclear matters ... have been shelved."

[411] The reports covering 2011-15 do not address this issue.

[412] Robert J. Einhorn, "The Impact of Sanctions on Iran's Nuclear Program," Arms Control Association, March 9, 2011.

[413] Director of Central Intelligence, *Unclassified Report to Congress on the Acquisition of Technology Relating to Weapons of Mass Destruction and Advanced Conventional Munitions, 1 January through 30 June 2007*, Washington, DC.

[414] For nonofficial reports on Chinese suppliers to Iran's enrichment program, see also, John Pomfret, "Chinese Firms Bypass Sanctions on Iran, U.S. Says," *The Washington Post*, October 18, 2010; and *Chinese Firms Continue to Evade Iran Sanctions*, Institute for Science and International Security, October 19, 2010.

[415] United States District Court for the District of Columbia, Grand Jury Indictment: *United States of America v. Parviz Khaki and Zongcheng Yi*, May 7, 2012, unsealed July 12, 2012.

[416] U.S. Department of Justice, *Summary of Major U.S. Export Enforcement, Economic Espionage, Trade Secret and Embargo-Related Criminal Cases*, (January 2010 to the present: updated June 27, 2016).

Other Suppliers

Iran has reportedly established front companies in Turkey in order to obtain nuclear-related items. Notably, Turkish entities were involved with the Khan network.[417] Iranian entities have also attempted to obtain nuclear-related items from companies in the Czech Republic, according to reports from that government's Security Information Service.[418]

Iran has also attempted to obtain enrichment-related equipment from U.S. suppliers. For example, according to a January 2012 Justice Department fact sheet, a man was sentenced in 2010 for attempting in March 2009 to export pressure transducers to Iran via Canada and the United Arab Emirates; he had purchased the items in the United States.[419] "Pressure transducers have applications in the production of enriched uranium," according to the fact sheet. Also, the Justice Department announced in January 2016 that a Chinese citizen was sentenced in the United States for exporting U.S.-origin pressure transducers to Iran from 2009 to 2012.[420] Additionally, a California-based firm exported "vacuum pumps and pump-related equipment to Iran through a free trade zone located in the United Arab Emirates [UAE]" between December 2007 and November 2008. This equipment has "a number of applications, including in the enrichment of uranium," according to the Justice Department fact sheet. In July 2013, an Iranian national pleaded guilty to arranging the illegal export of carbon fiber in 2008 to an Iranian entity. The individuals obtained the material from a U.S. supplier and shipped it to Iran via Europe and the United Arab Emirates. Carbon fiber "has nuclear applications in uranium enrichment as well applications in missiles," according to an October 2014 Justice Department fact sheet.[421]

Furthermore, declassified documents from the Canada Services Border Agency state that Iranian entities were attempting to acquire items from Canada for Iran's nuclear program, though the documents do not specifically mention Tehran's enrichment program.[422] The documents also state that "Iranian procurement agents have ... been able to export items [from Canada]," international sanctions notwithstanding. The documents, however, do not specify whether exported items were destined for Iran's nuclear program. Moreover, as noted, court documents made public in July 2012 state that an

---

[417] Aaron Stein, "Front Companies Use Turkey for Iran's Nuclear Programme," *Southeast European Times*, November 6, 2011; Andrea Stricker, *United States Indicts Man behind Alleged Multi-Million Dollar Iranian Smuggling Network*, Institute for Science and International Security, February 11, 2011.

[418] Annual Reports of the Security Information Service (BIS) for 2004 and 2008. Available at http://www.bis.cz/annual-report.html.

[419] U.S. Department of Justice, *Summary of Major U.S. Export Enforcement and Embargo-Related Criminal Prosecutions: 2007 to the Present*.

[420] "Extradited Chinese National Sentenced to Nine Years for Providing U.S. Goods to Iran to Support its Nuclear Program," Department of Justice January 27, 2016.

[421] U.S. Department of Justice, *Summary of Major U.S. Export Enforcement, Economic Espionage, Trade Secret and Embargo-Related Criminal Cases* (January 2008 to the present: updated October 22, 2014).

[422] The Canadian press reported on the documents in August 2012 (Lee Berthiaume, "Canadian Goods Destined for Iran's Nuclear Program Slip Through: Documents," *Postmedia News*, August 22, 2012). One document is dated October 28, 2011. The other document is undated, but appears to have been created in 2011 or 2012.

Iranian national attempted to obtain U.S.-origin components via Canada for Iran's enrichment program.

Entities in the UAE were part of the Khan network and have been cited as shippers for enrichment-related technology to Iran. Einhorn described the UAE in March 2011 as a "transshipment hub for Iran," but added that the UAE "has also taken strong steps in recent months to curtail illicit Iranian activities."[423] A 2011 European Council regulation identified two UAE entities, Modern Technologies FZC and Qualitest FZE, as "[i]nvolved in procurement of components for [the] Iranian nuclear programme," although the regulation did not specify whether the components were for uranium enrichment.[424]

---

[423] Einhorn, March 9, 2011. For more information, see CRS Report R40344, *The United Arab Emirates Nuclear Program and Proposed U.S. Nuclear Cooperation*, by Christopher M. Blanchard and Paul K. Kerr.

[424] *Council Implementing Regulation (EU) No 503/2011 of 23 May 2011 implementing Regulation (EU) No 961/2010 on restrictive measures against Iran.*

In: Iran: Economic, Political and Nuclear Policies
Editor: Everett Fowler
ISBN: 978-1-53614-827-5

Chapter 9

IRAN NUCLEAR AGREEMENT AND U.S. EXIT*

Paul K. Kerr and Kenneth Katzman

ABSTRACT

On July 14, 2015, Iran and the six powers that had negotiated with Tehran about its nuclear program since 2006 (the United States, the United Kingdom, France, Russia, China, and Germany—collectively known as the P5+1) finalized a Joint Comprehensive Plan of Action (JCPOA). The JCPOA required constraints that seek to ensure that Iran's nuclear program can be used for purely peaceful purposes in exchange for a broad lifting of U.S., European Union (EU), and United Nations (U.N.) sanctions on Iran. The agreement replaced the Joint Plan of Action (JPA), an interim nuclear accord in effect from 2014 to 2016. Congress did not enact a resolution of disapproval of the JCPOA by the deadline of September 17, 2015, which was set by the Iran Nuclear Agreement Review Act (P.L. 114-17); the JCPOA formally took effect on "Adoption Day" (October 18, 2015). "Implementation Day" was declared by the P5+1 on January 16, 2016, representing the completion of Iran's nuclear requirements; entry into effect of U.N. Security Council Resolution 2231, which endorsed the JCPOA; and the start of sanctions relief stipulated in the agreement. Officials from both the Barack Obama and Donald Trump Administrations have certified that Iran has abided by its JCPOA commitments.

The Obama Administration and other P5+1 leaders asserted that the JCPOA is the most effective means to ensure that Iran cannot obtain a nuclear weapon and that all U.S. options to prevent Iran from developing a nuclear weapon are available indefinitely. The agreement contains provisions for U.N. sanctions to be reimposed if Iran violates its commitments.

Top Trump Administration officials have argued that the JCPOA does not adequately serve U.S. interests because the extensive sanctions relief provided under the accord gives Iran additional resources to conduct "malign activities" in the region, and does not restrict Iran's development of ballistic missiles. Resolution 2231, which was

* This is an edited, reformatted and augmented version of Congressional Research Service, Publication No. R43333, dated July 20, 2018.

adopted in July 2015, prohibits arms transfers to or from Iran, but only for five years, and contains a voluntary restriction on Iran's development of nuclear-capable ballistic missiles for only up to eight years.

On May 8, President Trump announced that the United States would no longer participate in the JCPOA and would reimpose sanctions that had been suspended pursuant to the agreement. The other powers that negotiated the accord with Iran—Russia, China, France, Britain, and Germany—opposed the U.S. decision and have been meeting with Iranian officials to continue implementing the JCPOA. Iran's President Hassan Rouhani has pledged to continue implementing the accord, provided Iran continues to receive the economic benefits of the agreement.

In the 114th and 115th Congresses, legislation has been introduced with the stated purpose of redressing asserted weaknesses of the deal or preventing any U.S. sanctions relief beyond that explicitly promised in the JCPOA. The Countering America's Adversaries through Sanctions Act (P.L. 115-44) mandates sanctions on Iranian proliferation, human rights abuses, and support for terrorist activities. For details on the sanctions relief aspects of the JCPOA.

INTRODUCTION

Multilateral negotiations regarding Iran's nuclear program date back to 2003 after the International Atomic Energy Agency (IAEA) reported on the existence of clandestine nuclear facilities at Natanz. In October of that year, Iran concluded an agreement with France, Germany, and the United Kingdom under which Iran temporarily suspended aspects of its nuclear program, including enrichment of uranium, and signed an Additional Protocol to its IAEA safeguards agreement, but also asserted its right to develop nuclear technology. In January 2006, Tehran announced that it would resume research and development on its centrifuges at Natanz. After that time, Iran held multiple rounds of talks with China, France, Germany, Russia, the United Kingdom, and the United States (collectively known as the P5+1).

The U.N. Security Council meanwhile adopted several resolutions, the most recent and sweeping of which (Resolution 1929) was adopted in June 2010. These resolutions required Iran to cooperate fully with an ongoing IAEA investigation of its nuclear activities, suspend its uranium enrichment program, suspend its construction of a heavy water reactor and related projects, and ratify the Additional Protocol to its IAEA safeguards agreement. Resolution 1929 also required Tehran to refrain from "any activity related to ballistic missiles capable of delivering nuclear weapons" and to comply with a modified provision (called code 3.1) of Iran's subsidiary arrangement to its IAEA safeguards agreement.[1] The resolutions also imposed sanctions on Iran.

[1] Iran is a party to the nuclear Non Proliferation Treaty (NPT) and has concluded a comprehensive safeguards agreement with the IAEA. Such agreements are designed to enable the IAEA to detect the diversion of nuclear material from peaceful purposes to nuclear weapons uses, as well as to detect undeclared nuclear activities and material. For more information, see CRS Report R40094, ***Iran's Nuclear Program: Tehran's Compliance with International Obligations***, by Paul K. Kerr.

Diplomacy bore fruit after the June 2013 election of Iranian President Hassan Rouhani with the achievement, on November 24, 2013, of an interim nuclear accord—the Joint Plan of Action (JPA; referred to in international documents as JPOA). The JPA set out an approach toward reaching a long-term comprehensive solution to international concerns regarding Iran's nuclear program. The two sides began implementing the JPA on January 20, 2014. The P5+1 and Iran reached a framework of a Joint Comprehensive Plan of Action (JCPOA) on April 2, 2015, and the JCPOA was finalized on July 14, 2015. With the JPA remaining in effect until the JCPOA entered into implementation, the IAEA certified on January 16, 2016, that Iran had completed its required JCPOA nuclear-related tasks for Implementation Day. The United States, the U.N., and the EU ceased application of most sanctions that day. Since Implementation Day, the agency has "verified and monitored Iran's implementation of its [JCPOA] nuclear-related commitments."[2]

On November 11, 2013, coinciding with concluding the JPA, Iran and the IAEA signed a joint statement that included a "Framework for Cooperation"[3] to "strengthen their cooperation and dialogue aimed at ensuring the exclusively peaceful nature of Iran's nuclear programme through the resolution of all outstanding issues that have not already been resolved by the IAEA." The agency had long sought to resolve some outstanding questions regarding Tehran's nuclear program, some of which concern possible Iranian research on nuclear weapons development.

Amano issued the IAEA's "Final Assessment on Past and Present Outstanding Issues Regarding Iran's Nuclear Programme" on December 2, 2015.[4]

BACKGROUND ON IRAN'S NUCLEAR PROGRAM[5]

Iran has nuclear programs that could potentially provide Tehran with the capability to produce both weapons-grade highly enriched uranium (HEU) and plutonium—the two types of fissile material used in nuclear weapons. (In addition to the production of weapons-grade nuclear material, a nuclear weapons program requires other key elements, such as warhead design and reliable delivery systems [see *Appendix B*].) Statements from the U.S. intelligence community indicate that Iran has the technological and industrial

---

[2] *Verification and Monitoring in the Islamic Republic of Iran in Light of United Nations Security Council Resolution 2231 (2015),* Report by the Director General, International Atomic Energy Agency, GOV/2018/24, May 24, 2018.

[3] Available at http://www.iaea.org/press/?p=4018.

[4] Final Assessment on Past and Present Outstanding Issues Regarding Iran's Nuclear Programme, GOV/2015/68, December 2, 2015.

[5] For more information, see CRS Report RL34544, Iran's Nuclear Program: Status, by Paul K. Kerr.

capacity to produce nuclear weapons at some point, but the U.S. government assesses that Tehran has not mastered all of the necessary technologies for building a nuclear weapon.[6]

A November 2007 National Intelligence Estimate[7] assessed that Iran "halted its nuclear weapons program" in 2003,[8] but the estimate and subsequent statements by the intelligence community also assessed that Tehran was keeping open the "option" to develop nuclear weapons.[9] Then-Under Secretary of State for Political Affairs Wendy Sherman explained during an October 3, 2013, Senate Foreign Relations Committee hearing that Iran would need as much as one year to produce a nuclear weapon if the government made the decision to do so.[10] Tehran would have needed two to three months of this time to produce enough weapons-grade HEU for a nuclear weapon.[11] Iran's implementation of the JCPOA lengthened the latter timeline to one year, according to February 9, 2016, congressional testimony from then-Director of National Intelligence James Clapper.[12] (See "Major Nuclear Provisions of the JCPOA.")

U.S. officials argue that the IAEA and/or U.S. intelligence would likely detect an Iranian attempt to produce weapons-grade HEU with either its safeguarded facilities or clandestine facilities.[13] Regarding the former, Clapper testified that the JCPOA has

> enhanced the transparency of Iran's nuclear activities ... [a]s a result, the international community is well postured to quickly detect changes to Iran's declared

---

[6] "Press Briefing by Senior Administration Officials on IAEA Report on Iran's Nuclear Activities," November 8, 2011. Ambassador Stephen D. Mull, Coordinator for Implementation of the JCPOA, told a Washington audience on January 21, 2016, that "there was a portion of the Iranian Government working in a very organized, systematic way to develop the capability to build a nuclear weapon. We don't know to the extent to which that knowledge has been tested or even survived." ("Implementation of the Joint Comprehensive Plan of Action," Washington Foreign Press Center, January 21, 2016.)

[7] "Iran: Nuclear Intentions and Capabilities," National Intelligence Estimate, November 2007.

[8] The estimate defined "nuclear weapons program" as "nuclear weapon design and weaponization work and covert uranium conversion-related and uranium enrichment related work."

[9] See, for example, Director of National Intelligence James Clapper's February 26, 2015, testimony before the Senate Armed Services Committee (Statement for the Record, *Worldwide Threat Assessment of the U.S. Intelligence Community*, February 26, 2015).

[10] This estimate assumes the necessary time to produce a sufficient amount of weapons-grade HEU and complete the remaining steps necessary for an implosion-style nuclear explosive device suitable for explosive testing. (Conversation with U.S. official, July 21, 2015.) "Reversing Iran's Nuclear Program," Senate Foreign Relations Committee, October 3, 2013.

[11] The White House. "Parameters for a Joint Comprehensive Plan of Action Regarding the Islamic Republic of Iran's Nuclear Program." April 2, 2015.

[12] *Statement for the Record Worldwide Threat Assessment of the US Intelligence Community*, Senate Armed Services Committee, February 9, 2016. Director of National Intelligence Daniel Coats reiterated this assessment in May 2017 (*Statement for the Record Worldwide Threat Assessment of the Intelligence Community,* Senate Select Committee on Intelligence, May 11, 2017) and February 2018 (*Statement for the Record Worldwide Threat Assessment of the Intelligence Community*, February 13, 2018). Then-UK Secretary of State for Foreign and Commonwealth Affairs Boris Johnson also reiterated this assessment in a May 9, 2018, statement to Parliament ("Iran Nuclear Deal," *Hansard Online*, May 9, 2018, Volume 640. Available at: https://hansard.parliament.uk/commons/2018-05-09/debates/A90A082B-BAB0-445E-BAB1-DBBCDA9BCCE9/IranNuclear Deal 1/17.

[13] "Hearing on Security Threats to the United States," Senate Select Committee on Intelligence, March 12, 2013. Then- IAEA Deputy Director General for Safeguards Herman Nackaerts stated in July 2013 that the IAEA "would know within a week" if Iran were to use its safeguarded facilities to produce weapons-grade HEU. (Barbara Slavin, "Tight IAEA Inspection Regime Hampers Iran's Nuclear Breakout," *Al-Monitor*, July 22, 2013.)

nuclear facilities designed to shorten the time Iran would need to produce fissile material.[14]

The intelligence community assesses that Iran is more likely to use clandestine facilities to produce weapons-grade HEU, Director Clapper stated in a March 2015 interview.[15] U.S. officials have expressed confidence in the ability of U.S. intelligence to detect Iranian covert nuclear facilities[16] and have indicated that Iran currently does not appear to have any nuclear facilities of which the United States is unaware.

IAEA Safeguards

The IAEA's ability to inspect and monitor nuclear facilities in, as well as to obtain information from, a particular country pursuant to that government's comprehensive safeguards agreement has been limited to facilities and activities that have been declared by the government. Additional Protocols to IAEA comprehensive safeguards agreements increase the agency's ability to investigate undeclared nuclear facilities and activities by increasing the IAEA's authority to inspect certain nuclear-related facilities and demand information from member states. Iran signed such a protocol in December 2003 and agreed to implement the agreement pending ratification. However, following the 2005 breakdown of limited agreements with the European countries to suspend uranium enrichment, Tehran stopped adhering to its Additional Protocol in 2006.[17] Subsidiary arrangements to IAEA safeguards agreements describe the "technical and administrative procedures for specifying how the provisions laid down in a safeguards agreement are to be applied."[18] Code 3.1 of Iran's subsidiary arrangement to its IAEA safeguards agreement requires Tehran to provide design information for new nuclear facilities "as soon as the decision to construct, or to authorize construction, of such a facility has been taken, whichever is earlier."

[14] Statement for the Record Worldwide Threat Assessment of the US Intelligence Community, February 9, 2016.

[15] PBS "Charlie Rose" Interview with James Clapper, Director of National Security, March 3, 2015.

[16] "Senior Administration Official Holds A Background Briefing Previewing Iran P5+1 Talks," November 6, 2013; Colin H. Kahl, "Not Time to Attack Iran: Why War Should Be a Last Resort," Foreign Affairs, January 17, 2012. However, Director of National Intelligence Clapper stated in a February 2015 hearing that, although the United States has "a reasonably capable intelligence capability," IAEA safeguards would be an "important aspect of any sort of agreement we might reach with the Iranians" (Worldwide Threat Assessment of the U.S. Intelligence Community, February 26, 2015).

[17] Iran announced that it would stop implementing the protocol two days after the IAEA Board of governors adopted a resolution in February 2006 which referred Iran's noncompliance with its IAEA safeguards agreement to the U.N. Security Council.

[18] 2001 IAEA Safeguards Glossary. Available at http://www-pub.iaea.org/books/IAEABooks/6570/IAEA-SafeguardsGlossary-2001-Edition.

Declared Iranian Nuclear Facilities[19]

Iran did not build any new nuclear facilities or expand the existing facilities since the JPA went into effect in January 2014. Iran operates a Russian-built nuclear power reactor, for which Russia is providing fuel until 2021. The JCPOA focuses on Iran's enrichment program and its heavy water reactor due to their potential for nuclear weapons material production.

Iran has two gas centrifuge enrichment facilities: the Natanz Fuel Enrichment Plant and the Natanz Pilot Fuel Enrichment Plant. Gas centrifuges enrich uranium by spinning uranium hexafluoride gas at high speeds to increase the concentration of the uranium-235 isotope. Such centrifuges can produce low-enriched uranium (LEU), which can be used for fuel in nuclear power reactors or research reactors, and weapons-grade highly enriched uranium (HEU). LEU used in nuclear power reactors typically contains less than 5% uranium-235; research reactor fuel can be made using 20% uranium-235; HEU used in nuclear weapons typically contains about 90% uranium-235. Tehran argues that it is enriching uranium for use as fuel in nuclear power reactors and nuclear research reactors.

- *Natanz Commercial-Scale Fuel Enrichment Plant.* In this facility, Iran is using first-generation centrifuges, called IR-1 centrifuges, to produce LEU containing up to 5% uranium-235. As of November 2013, Iran had installed about 15,400 of these centrifuges, approximately 8,800 of which are enriching uranium. Iran had also installed about 1,000 centrifuges with a greater enrichment efficiency, called IR-2m centrifuges, in the facility, but they are not enriching uranium.
- *Natanz Pilot Fuel Enrichment Plant.* Iran had been using IR-1 centrifuges in this facility to produce LEU containing approximately 20% uranium-235 until halting this work pursuant to the JPA. Tehran's production of LEU enriched to the 20% level has caused concern because such production requires approximately 90% of the effort necessary to produce weapons-grade HEU, which, as noted, contains approximately 90% uranium-235.[20] Iran is testing other centrifuge models in this facility under IAEA supervision, but such work was monitored by the IAEA, even before the JPA (see below) limited this testing.

---

[19] Unless otherwise noted, this section is based on CRS Report RL34544, *Iran's Nuclear Program: Status*, by Paul K. Kerr, and reports from IAEA Director-General Yukiya Amano to the IAEA Board of Governors: GOV/2013/27 (May 2013), GOV/2013/40 (August 2013), GOV/2013/56 (November 2013, and GOV/2015/34 (May 2015).

[20] Former IAEA Deputy Director General Olli Heinonen, "Dealing with a Nuclear Iran: Redlines and Deadlines," Center for Strategic and International Studies, February 6, 2013; U.S. Secretary of Energy Ernest Moniz, Senate Committee on Armed Services, "Impacts of the Joint Comprehensive Plan of Action (JPCOA) on U.S. Interests and the Military Balance in the Middle East," July 29, 2015.

Iran has been constructing a nuclear reactor moderated by heavy water at Arak,[21] a type of reactor that produces spent fuel containing plutonium that is better suited for nuclear weapons than plutonium produced by light water-moderated reactors.[22] Tehran has asserted that the reactor is intended to produce radioisotopes for medical use and to replace the Tehran Research Reactor. Heavy water production requires a separate production plant, which Iran possesses. Prior to JCPOA implementation, the Arak reactor, if it had been completed, could have produced enough plutonium for between one and two nuclear weapons per year.[23] However, plutonium must be separated from the used fuel—a procedure called "reprocessing." Iran has always maintained that it would not engage in reprocessing. Prior to the JPA, Tehran notified the IAEA that it had produced enough heavy water to commission the reactor.

The "Joint Plan of Action" (JPA)

The JPA, also widely known as the JPOA, essentially froze most aspects of Iran's nuclear program to allow time to negotiate the JCPOA. When the JPA went into effect in January 2014, Iran had enough uranium hexafluoride containing up to 5% uranium-235, which, if further enriched, would have yielded enough weapons-grade HEU for as many as eight nuclear weapons.[24] The total amount of Iranian LEU containing 20% uranium-235 would, if it had been further enriched, have been sufficient for a nuclear weapon. After the JPA went into effect, Iran either converted much of that material for use as fuel in a research reactor located in Tehran (called the Tehran Research Reactor), or prepared it for that purpose.[25] Iran diluted the rest of that stockpile so that it contained no more than 5% uranium-235. Tehran's uranium conversion facility is not set up to reconvert the reactor fuel to uranium hexafluoride.[26] According to a November 14, 2013, IAEA report,

---

[21] Iran informed the IAEA in April 2017 that Tehran was renaming the facility, which Iran had called the "Arak Heavy Water Research Reactor," the "Khondab Heavy Water Research Reactor." Verification and Monitoring in the Islamic Republic of Iran in Light of United Nations Security Council Resolution 2231 (2015), Report by the Director General, International Atomic Energy Agency, GOV/2017/24, June 2, 2017.

[22] Both the Tehran Research Reactor and the Bushehr reactor are light-water reactors.

[23] Kahl, May 14, 2015.

[24] Colin Kahl, Deputy Assistant to the President and National Security Adviser to the Vice President, "Arms Control Association Annual Meeting: Unprecedented Challenges for Nonproliferation and Disarmament," May 14, 2015.

[25] This process has generated scrap which contains LEU with 20% uranium-235. Iran also retains .6 kilograms of uranium hexafluoride containing 20% uranium-235, which "had been used as reference material for mass spectrometry" (*Implementation of the NPT Safeguards Agreement and relevant provisions of Security Council resolutions in the Islamic Republic of Iran*, Report of the Director General, International Atomic Energy Agency, GOV/2015/34, May 29, 2015).

[26] *Nuclear Industry in Iran: An Overview on Iran's Activities and Achievements in Nuclear Technology*, Atomic Energy Organization of Iran, 2012, p. 13. Also see GOV/2015/34.

Iran had generally stopped expanding its enrichment and heavy water reactor programs during the negotiations leading up to the JPA.[27]

Nuclear Program Provisions under the JPA[28]

Under the JPA, Iran agreed to refrain from "any further advances of its activities" at the Natanz commercial-scale facility, Fordow facility, and Arak reactor. Tehran was also required to provide the IAEA with additional information about its nuclear program, as well as access to some nuclear-related facilities to which Iran's IAEA safeguards agreement does not require access. The JPA required Iran:

- *Centrifuge Limits.* To refrain from feeding uranium hexafluoride into its installed centrifuges that were not previously enriching uranium, to replace existing centrifuges only with "centrifuges of the same type," and to produce centrifuges only to replace damaged centrifuges. Tehran was also required to refrain from installing additional centrifuges at the Natanz facility. Iran was permitted to use its previously operating centrifuges in the Natanz commercial facility and the Fordow facility to produce enriched uranium containing as much as 5% uranium-235.
- *Level of Enrichment Limits.* To only enrich uranium up to 5% uranium-235. Tehran was also to dilute half of its stockpile of uranium hexafluoride containing 20% uranium-235 to no more than 5% uranium-235. The rest of the uranium hexafluoride containing 20% uranium-235 was to be converted to uranium oxide for use as fuel for the Tehran Research Reactor.[29] Iran also agreed to refrain from building a line in its uranium conversion facility for reconverting the uranium oxide back to uranium hexafluoride.
- *EU Stockpile Limits.* To, in effect, freeze the amount of stocks of enriched uranium hexafluoride containing up to 5% uranium-235.[30]
- *Centrifuge R&D.* To continue its "current enrichment R&D Practices" under IAEA safeguards, "which are not designed for accumulation of the enriched uranium." This provision prohibited Tehran from producing enriched uranium hexafluoride containing more than 5% uranium-235.

---

[27] Implementation of the NPT Safeguards Agreement and Relevant Provisions of Security Council Resolutions in the Islamic Republic of Iran, GOV/2013/56, November 14, 2013.

[28] Unless otherwise noted, this section is based on the agreement text (available at http://eeas.europa.eu/statements/docs/2013/131124_03_en.pdf), "Background Briefing by Senior Administration Officials on First Step Agreement on Iran's Nuclear Program," November 24, 2013, and GOV/2013/56.

[29] This material is unsuitable for further enrichment. Uranium hexafluoride is the form of uranium used as feedstock for centrifuge enrichment.

[30] Iran began operating a conversion plant for this purpose in July 2014.

- *Additional Monitoring***.** The JPA provided for additional IAEA monitoring of the enrichment facilities by allowing IAEA inspectors to access video records from those facilities on a daily basis. Previously, inspectors did not access such records daily (and the video is not streamed in real time to the agency).[31]
- *Arak Reactor.* Iran pledged to refrain from commissioning the reactor, transferring fuel or heavy water to the reactor site, testing and producing additional reactor fuel, and installing remaining reactor components. Tehran was permitted to continue some construction at the reactor site and to produce some reactor components off-site. Iran also agreed to refrain from reprocessing spent nuclear material and building a reprocessing facility.[32]
- *Additional Pledges/Information***.** The JPA reiterated previous Iranian statements "reaffirm[ing] that under no circumstances will Iran ever seek or develop any nuclear weapons." In addition, Iran was to provide the IAEA with other information, such as plans for future nuclear facilities, even though Iran was already required to provide some of this information by code 3.1 of Iran's subsidiary arrangement to its IAEA safeguards agreement. Iran also provided IAEA inspectors with "managed access" to its centrifuge assembly workshops, centrifuge rotor production workshops, centrifuge storage facilities, and uranium mines and mills.[33]

"Right to Enrichment"

The JPA acknowledged that Iran's right to the peaceful use of nuclear energy under the nuclear Non-Proliferation Treaty (NPT) would be part of a comprehensive solution, but shied away from stating that uranium enrichment is part of this right. The JPA stipulated that an enrichment program in Iran would have defined limits and transparency measures.[34] The Obama Administration applied to Iran its interpretation that the NPT does not contain an explicit right to enrichment. A senior Administration official

---

[31] Then-deputy National Security Adviser Anthony Blinken stated in a November 25, 2013, television interview that such access would enable IAEA inspectors to detect Iranian efforts to produce weapons-grade HEU at its declared enrichment facilities "almost instantaneously." However, as noted, U.S. officials have previously expressed confidence in the IAEA's ability to detect such Iranian efforts; the extent to which the November 24, 2013, agreement improved this ability is unclear.

[32] There is no public official evidence that Iran has a reprocessing facility.

[33] According to the IAEA, "managed access" to nuclear-related facilities is "arranged in such a way as 'to prevent the dissemination of proliferation sensitive information, to meet safety or physical protection requirements, or to protect proprietary or commercially sensitive information. Such arrangements shall not preclude the Agency from conducting activities necessary to provide credible assurance of the absence of undeclared nuclear material and activities at the location in question." (*2001 IAEA Safeguards Glossary*.)

[34] Tehran has long argued that it has the right to enrich uranium pursuant to the NPT, Article IV of which states, in part, that nothing in the treaty "shall be interpreted as affecting the inalienable right of all the Parties to the Treaty to develop research, production and use of nuclear energy for peaceful purposes without discrimination and in conformity" with the NPT's nonproliferation provisions. For example, Iran demanded in a 2012 proposal to the P5+1 that those countries recognize and announce "Iran's nuclear rights, particularly its enrichment activities, based on NPT Article IV." Available at http://www.armscontrol.org/factsheets/Iran_Nuclear_Proposals.

explained on November 24, 2013, that "the United States has not recognized a right to enrich for the Iranian government, nor do we intend to. The document does not say anything about recognizing a right to enrich uranium."[35]

Sanctions Easing Under the JPA

The JPA provided for some modest sanctions relief for Iran.[36] Its provisions, which remained in force until "Implementation Day" (January 16, 2016), included the following:

- *Access to Hard Currency.* Iran was able to repatriate $700 million per month in hard currency from oil sales, and to access an additional $65 million per month of its foreign exchange reserves for tuition for Iranian students abroad.
- *Oil Exports Capped.* Iran's oil exports were required to remain at their December 2013 level of about 1.1 million barrels per day (mbd).
- *Resumption of Trade in Selected Sectors.* International sanctions were suspended on Iran's sales of petrochemicals, trading in gold and other precious metals, and transactions involving Iran's auto production sector.

THE JOINT COMPREHENSIVE PLAN OF ACTION (JCPOA)

The JPA stated that a JCPOA would include a "mutually defined [Iranian] enrichment programme with practical limits and transparency measures to ensure the peaceful nature of the programme." Specifically, Iran and the P5+1 would, in a JCPOA, reach agreement on permanent, comprehensive sanctions relief in exchange for restrictions—"for a period to be agreed upon"— on the "scope and level" of Iran's enrichment activities, the capacity and location of Iranian enrichment facilities, and the size and composition of Tehran's enriched uranium stocks.

P5+1-Iran negotiations on a comprehensive settlement began in February 2014 but did not meet July 20 or November 24 deadlines in 2014. On November 24, 2014, Iran and the P5+1 announced their intent to finalize a detailed agreement by June 30, 2015, after first attempting to reach an overarching framework and roadmap for the agreement within four months. The framework accord was agreed on April 2, 2015, in Lausanne, Switzerland.[37] The parties strived to meet the June 30 deadline because the Iran Nuclear

---

[35] "Background Briefing By Senior Administration Officials On First Step Agreement On Iran's Nuclear Program," November 24, 2013.

[36] White House Office of the Press Secretary. "Fact Sheet: First Step Understandings Regarding the Islamic Republic of Iran's Nuclear Program." November 23, 2013.

[37] The text of the framework accord is at The White House. "Parameters for a Joint Comprehensive Plan of Action Regarding the Islamic Republic of Iran's Nuclear Program." April 2, 2015. U.S. Secretary of Energy Ernest

Agreement Review Act (P.L. 114-17) mandated a 30- day congressional review period for an agreement completed by that date. However, the JCPOA was not finalized until July 14, 2015; the failure to meet the June 30 deadline triggered a 60-day review period under that act. The provisions of the JPA remained in effect until the JCPOA was formally "adopted," as discussed below.

Timeline for Implementing the JCPOA

The JCPOA outlines steps, as follows:

- *Finalization Day: July 14, 2015***.** Iran and the P5+1 countries, along with the High Representative of the European Union for Foreign Affairs and Security Policy (Frederica Mogherini), endorsed the JCPOA. A U.N. Security Council Resolution to endorse the JCPOA was submitted for adoption.
- *Adoption Day/New U.N. Security Council Resolution.* The JCPOA formally came into effect 90 days after endorsement of JCPOA by U.N. Security Council, (or earlier by mutual consent). Resolution 2231 was adopted for that purpose on July 20, 2015, placing Adoption Day at October 18, 2015. The Administration asserted that the 90-day time frame allowed for review of the JCPOA by the U.S. Congress and by any legislature of any party to the JCPOA. On Adoption Day, the United States issued the provisional presidential waivers required to implement U.S. sanctions relief, with the waivers to take effect on Implementation Day.
- *Implementation Day.* This day was defined in the JCPOA as the day the IAEA verified that Iran has completed the several stipulated nuclear related measures (e.g., reducing centrifuges, removing the core of the Arak reactor) and the United States, the U.N., and the EU cease application of specific sanctions (see text below). The U.N. Security Council terminated the provisions of its resolutions on Iran: 1696 (2006), 1737 (2006), 1747 (2007), 1803 (2008), 1835 (2008), 1929 (2010), and 2224 (2015); and Resolution 2231 became the sole operative U.N. Security Council resolution on Iran's nuclear program. Implementation Day was declared on January 16, 2016, after the IAEA made the required certification of Iran's completion of the stipulated tasks.[38]
- *Transition Day.* Represents initial stages of Iran's emergence from U.N. Security Council scrutiny. Transition Day is eight years from Adoption Day (October 18,

---

Moniz described this timeline as "very, very conservative" in an April 2015 interview (Michael Crowley, "Ernest Moniz: Iran Deal Closes Enrichment Loophole," *Politico,* April 7, 2015).

[38] Verification and Monitoring in the Islamic Republic of Iran in Light of United Nations Security Council Resolution 2231 (2015), GOV/INF/2016/1, January 16, 2016.

2023)—or upon "Broader Conclusion" report from the IAEA Director General to the IAEA Board of Governors and U.N. Security Council—whichever is earlier.[39] As of Transition Day, additional EU entities are to be removed from sanctions, the United States is required to remove from designation specified additional Iranian entities subjected to sanctions, and the Administration is required to seek legislative termination of sanctions that were suspended on Implementation Day.

- *UNSCR Termination Day***.** Ten years from Adoption Day (October 18, 2025). Provisions and measures imposed in U.N. Security Council Resolution endorsing JCPOA would terminate and the Security Council would not be involved in the Iran nuclear issue. However, the JCPOA itself and its remaining provisions do not terminate on this day: the accord states that, following successful implementation of the final steps of the JCPOA, Iran's nuclear program "will be treated in the same manner as that of any non-nuclear weapon state party to the NPT." Iran's IAEA safeguards obligations, as well as some JCPOA obligations, last for an indefinite duration. Potential nuclear-related exports to Iran remain subject to the Nuclear Suppliers Group's export guidelines.[40]

Resolution 2231 also ended the role of the U.N. panel of experts, which Resolution 1929 had created to work with a committee (established in Resolution 1737) that monitored states' compliance with the resolutions discussed above. The Security Council decided on January 16, 2016, to "select on an annual basis one member to serve as its facilitator" for implementing certain provisions of Resolution 2231, including Security Council approval of various Iranian exports and imports described in Annex B of the resolution.[41]

Major Nuclear Provisions of the JCPOA

The JCPOA places constraints on Iran's enrichment and heavy water reactor programs and includes monitoring provisions designed to detect Iranian efforts to produce nuclear weapons using either declared or covert facilities. The nuclear-related provisions of the agreement, according to U.S. officials, extend the amount of time that Iran would need to produce enough weapons-grade HEU for one nuclear weapon to a

---

[39] See "Broader Conclusion" below.

[40] For information about the Nuclear Suppliers Group, see CRS Report RL33865, *Arms Control and Nonproliferation: A Catalog of Treaties and Agreements*, by Amy F. Woolf, Paul K. Kerr, and Mary Beth D. Nikitin.

[41] *Note by the President of the Security Council, Security Council Tasks under Security Council Resolution 2231 (2015)*, S/2016/44, January 16, 2016.

minimum of one year, for a duration of at least 10 years.[42] In addition to the restrictions on activities related to fissile material production, the JCPOA indefinitely prohibits Iranian "activities which could contribute to the design and development of a nuclear explosive device," including research and diagnostic activities. An IAEA report on January 16, 2016, certified that Iran had met the requirements for Implementation Day stipulated below.[43]

Enrichment Program

The JCPOA limits Iran's enrichment of uranium for fixed durations. The agreement required the IAEA to certify that Iran had completed most of the tasks described below in order for Tehran to qualify for Implementation Day sanctions relief. According to the JCPOA, expiration of the JCPOA enrichment restrictions will be "followed by gradual evolution, at a reasonable pace" of Iran's enrichment program. Iran has submitted an "enrichment R&D plan" to the IAEA as part of Tehran's initial declaration for its Additional Protocol. (See "Verification" section below.) Iranian adherence to that plan is a JCPOA requirement.

- *Centrifuge Limitation (10 years).* For 10 years, Tehran is to use no more than 5,060 IR-1 centrifuges to enrich uranium, and to install only IR-1 centrifuges in the facility. All excess centrifuges are to be used only as replacements for operating centrifuges and equipment.
- *Level of Enrichment Limitation (15 years).* For at least 15 years, Iran is to refrain from producing enriched uranium containing more than 3.67% uranium-235.
- *Facility Limitation (15 years).* For 15 years, Iran is to enrich uranium only at the Natanz commercial facility and is not to build any new enrichment facilities.[44]

  LEU Stockpile Limitation (15 years). For 15 years, Iran is to maintain its LEU stockpile at no more than 300 kilograms of LEU containing 3.67% uranium-235.[45] Tehran's three options for disposing of the remaining portion of its LEU

[42] "Background Conference Call by Senior Administration Officials on Iran," July 14, 2015. U.S. Secretary of Energy Ernest Moniz described this timeline as "very, very conservative" in an April 2015 interview (Michael Crowley, "Ernest Moniz: Iran Deal Closes Enrichment Loophole," *Politico,* April 7, 2015). British Foreign and Commonwealth Office official Tobias Ellwood echoed this statement in a July 20, 2015, statement to Parliament, explaining that, under the JCPOA provisions, "Iran's breakout period will be over 12 months for 10 years, and is not expected to fall to zero afterwards." (Iran: Nuclear Power: Written question-6891. Answered by Mr. Tobias Ellwood on July 20, 2015.)

[43] GOV/INF/2016/1.

[44] After 10 years, Iran may produce enriched uranium at the pilot centrifuge facility as part of R&D work.

[45] Secretary Moniz explained in September 2016 that this stockpile only includes nuclear material determined by a Technical Working Group set up by the JCPOA-established Joint Commission to be "usable" as potential fissile material for a nuclear weapon. (A Conversation With Ernest J. Moniz, Paul C. Warnke Lecture on International Security, September 19, 2016.)

stockpile were (1) diluting the material so that it contains the same levels of uranium-235 found in natural uranium; (2) selling the LEU to another country; or (3) selling it to an IAEA-established international LEU bank. Iran's LEU containing between 5% and 20% uranium-235 is to be "fabricated into fuel plates for the Tehran Research Reactor or transferred, based on a commercial transaction, outside of Iran or diluted" so that it contains a maximum of 3.67% uranium-235. Iran is to export LEU that cannot be fabricated into fuel for the Tehran Research Reactor or dilute that LEU to at most 3.67% uranium-235. On December 28, 2015, Iran shipped out LEU to Russia to reduce its stockpile to the required levels.[46] All fuel plates for the Tehran Research Reactor were irradiated, according to the January 2016 IAEA report.

The JCPOA-established Joint Commission has deemed some enriched uranium in Iran as "unrecoverable"—and therefore not counted against the JCPOA limits on Iran's enriched uranium stockpiles. Such exempted material includes LEU contained in low-level solid waste and LEU containing as much as 3.67% uranium-235 in low-level liquid and sludge waste "provided that Iran does not build or operate any facility or part of a facility capable of recovering" this material for 15 years. Tehran will store this waste under IAEA safeguards. The commission has similarly deemed enriched uranium containing 20% uranium-235 described as "laboratory contamination."

The commission announced on January 10, 2017, that it had approved an Iranian plan to flush enriched uranium from the process lines of an Iranian facility designed to produce uranium dioxide powder from LEU containing up to 5% uranium-235.[47] Iran had approximately 100 kilograms of this material when Tehran and the P5+1 agreed to the JCPOA.[48] Any LEU remaining after Iran completes the specified process, which the government started on January 31, 2017, will be deemed "unrecoverable" and will not count against the 300 kilogram limit described above.[49]

- *Fordow Conversion (15 years).* For 15 years, Iran is to maintain no more than 1,044 IR-1 centrifuges at the Fordow enrichment facility. Iran is not to conduct uranium enrichment or related research and development (R&D) there and the facility will not contain any nuclear material. Iran agreed to convert Fordow into

---

46 "Press Release on the Export of Enriched Uranium from Iran Assisted by Russia as Part of Preparation for JCPOA Implementation," Ministry of Foreign Affairs of the Russian Federation, December 29, 2015. Daily Press Briefing, Department of State, December 28, 2015." Ambassador Stephen Mull, Coordinator for Implementation of the JCPOA, told the Senate Foreign Relations Committee on December 17, 2015, that the exported material "will end up at a safeguarded facility" in Russia.

47 Decision of the Joint Commission Established by the Joint Comprehensive Plan of Action, January 10, 2017, https://eeas.europa.eu/sites/eeas/files/jc_paper_of_10_01_2017_-_eupp.pdf.

48 *Verification and Monitoring in the Islamic Republic of Iran in Light of United Nations Security Council Resolution 2231 (2015),* Report by the Director General, International Atomic Energy Agency, GOV/2017/10, February 24, 2017.

49 Ibid. Decision of the Joint Commission, January 10, 2017.

"a nuclear, physics, and technology centre." 348 of the IR-1 centrifuges may be used to produce stable isotopes for medical and industrial uses.[50]

- *Centrifuge Production (8, 10 years).* With regard to centrifuge manufacturing, Iran for 10 years is to use the excess IR-1 centrifuges from the Natanz and Fordow facilities "for the replacement of failed or damaged machines." Tehran may resume producing IR-1 centrifuges if its stock of replacement centrifuges "falls to 500 or below." After 8 years, Iran will be permitted to begin to manufacture 2 types of advanced centrifuges; after 10 years, Iran will be permitted to produce complete versions of those centrifuges and store them under IAEA monitoring "until they are needed for final assembly."
- *Centrifuge R&D (10 years).* For 10 years, Iran is to refrain from pursuing R&D on any technologies other than gas centrifuge enrichment.

Arak Reactor

The JCPOA commits Iran to redesign and rebuild the Arak reactor based on a design agreed to by the P5+1 so that it will not produce weapons-grade plutonium. Iran is to export the spent fuel from this reactor and all other nuclear reactors. The JCPOA also requires Tehran to render the Arak reactor's original core inoperable; the IAEA report of January 16, 2016, said that Iran had met this requirement. Tehran is managing an international project to redesign and construct the replacement reactor; P5+1 participants established a working group "to support and facilitate the redesigning and rebuilding of the reactor." The group was to "conclude an official document" before Implementation Day which would "define the responsibilities" assumed by the P5+1 participants. China's Atomic Energy Authority and the U.S. Department of Energy "affirmed their readiness to convene and co-chair" the working group, according to an October 18, 2015, joint statement from China, Iran, and the United States, which added that the three parties "intend to work together to conclude expeditiously" the document described above.[51] The parties issued the document on November 22, 2015. The United States is no longer participating in the project and the United Kingdom has taken the U.S. role.[52]

Chinese and Iranian companies signed the first consultancy services contract" for this project on April 23, 2017,[53] and the "conceptual redesigning" of the reactor was completed thereafter, according to an April 2018 official Iranian news report.[54]

---

[50] Iran and Russia have been discussing cooperation on the production of such isotopes (Russian statement to the IAEA General Conference, September 26, 2016; "Iran Launches Building of Two Power Units in Bushehr," *BBC Worldwide Monitoring*, September 10, 2016).

[51] "Joint Statement of Intent Concerning the Arak Heavy Water Reactor Research Reactor Modernization Project under the Joint Comprehensive Plan of Action," October 18, 2015.

[52] See "U.S. Exit from the JCPOA." "Statement from the Joint Commission on the Joint Comprehensive Plan of Action," European External Action Service. July 6, 2018.

[53] Chair's Statement Following the 25 April 2017 Meeting of the JCPOA Joint Commission, April 25, 2017.

[54] "Salehi: Designing of Arak Reactor Platform Ends," *Islamic Republic News Agency*, April 14, 2018.

The JCPOA prohibits Iran from reprocessing spent reactor fuel, except to produce "radio-isotopes for medical and peaceful industrial purposes." The JCPOA text states that Iran "does not intend" to engage in reprocessing after the 15-year period expires. Furthermore, Tehran has also committed to refrain from accumulating heavy water "beyond Iran's needs"; Iran is to "sell any remaining heavy water on the international market for 15 years."[55] The JCPOA requires Iran to refrain from building heavy water-moderated reactors for 15 years, and Iran pledges to refrain from constructing any such reactors indefinitely.

Iran's stock of heavy water has exceeded 130 metric tons on 2 occasions since the JCPOA began implementation. On February 17, 2016, the IAEA verified that Tehran's heavy water stock had exceeded 130 metric tons; on November 8, 2016, the IAEA verified that Iran's stock of heavy water had again exceeded the JCPOA limit. Iran resolved the issue on both occasions by exporting the excess heavy water. Tehran has sent this material to Russia and the United States, shipping at least some of it via Oman.[56] Iran told the IAEA on June 18, 2017, letter that it had transferred 19.1 metric tons of heavy water to a destination outside the country.[57] According to an April 2018 report covering 2017, "[m]ost Iranian excess heavy water has been sold and delivered to international buyers; the remainder is awaiting sale and is stored in a location outside Iran, under IAEA seal, though it remains Iranian property."[58] The IAEA verified on May 6, 2018, that Iran had 120.3 metric tons of heavy water.[59]

Other Provisions Verification

The IAEA monitors Iranian compliance with the JCPOA provisions concerning its enrichment program and the Arak program, as well as dual-use nuclear weapon-related activities. To do so, the agency has increased the number of its inspectors in Iran and begun using more-advanced modern verification technologies, such as the Online Enrichment Monitor. Iran pledged to allow a "long-term IAEA presence in Iran" and "has agreed to implement" the Additional Protocol to its safeguards agreement.[60] Iran is also

---

[55] According to the agreement, these "needs" are 130 metric tons of "nuclear grade heavy water or its equivalent in different enrichments" prior to commissioning the redesigned Arak reactor and 90 metric tons after the reactor is commissioned.

[56] Iran has also shipped "a smaller amount to other countries" a spokesperson for Iran's Atomic Energy Organization said in March 2018 ("Iran to Unveil 'Heavy Water Achievements' on 9 April," *Fars News Agency*, March 26, 2018).

[57] *Verification and Monitoring in the Islamic Republic of Iran in Light of United Nations Security Council Resolution 2231 (2015),* Report by the Director General, International Atomic Energy Agency, GOV/2017/35, August 31, 2017. The report does not name the heavy water's destination.

[58] *Adherence to and Compliance with Arms Control, Nonproliferation, and Disarmament Agreements and Commitments*, Department of State, April 2018.

[59] GOV/2018/24.

[60] Article 17 of the Model Additional Protocol says that a state may, before the Protocol enters into force, "declare that it will apply this Protocol provisionally." In July 2016, as required by its Additional Protocol, Iran submitted its declarations of various nuclear activities to the IAEA. (For more information about declaration requirements, see Selected Provisions of the IAEA Model Additional Protocol in CRS Report R44142, *Iran Nuclear Agreement: Selected Issues for Congress*, coordinated by Kenneth Katzman and Paul K. Kerr.)

to implement the modified code 3.1 of the subsidiary arrangements to its IAEA safeguards agreement. According to IAEA reports, the government has taken these steps since it began implementing the JCPOA in January 2016. Iran submitted its declarations pursuant to its Additional Protocol in July 2016.[61] It is worth noting that Iran's IAEA safeguards obligations last for an indefinite duration. Potential nuclear-related exports to Iran would remain subject to the Nuclear Suppliers Group's (NSG) export guidelines.[62] The April 2018 State Department report noted that "Tehran's adherence" to its JCPOA commitments "will hinder its ability to produce a nuclear weapon even after the time-bound provisions of the deal expire, helping to ensure that its nuclear program remains exclusively peaceful in nature."[63]

The JCPOA also describes other monitoring and inspections. For 15 years, the IAEA will monitor the stored Iranian centrifuges and related infrastructure. During this time, Iran will also permit the IAEA "daily access" to "relevant buildings" at the Natanz facilities. For 20 years, Tehran will allow the agency to verify Iran's inventory of certain centrifuge components and the manufacturing facilities for such components. Additionally, Iran is to allow the IAEA to monitor the country's uranium mills for 25 years and to monitor Iran's plant for producing heavy water.[64] As noted, Amano also reported that, since Implementation Day, the IAEA "verified and monitored Iran's implementation of its nuclear-related commitments under the JCPOA."[65]

IAEA Director-General Yukiya Amano told reporters on July 14, 2015, that the agency's workload would increase under the JCPOA. On August 25, 2015, the IAEA Board of Governors authorized Amano "to undertake the verification and monitoring" of Iran's nuclear-related JCPOA commitments "subject to the availability of funds and consistent with our standard safeguards practices. "[66] The IAEA has integrated these costs into its regular budget.[67]

The Obama Administration argued that these provisions will prevent Iran from developing a nuclear weapon covertly. Then-Secretary of State John Kerry explained in a September 2, 2015, speech that Iran "would have to come up with a complete ... and completely secret nuclear supply chain," adding that "our intelligence community and our Energy Department ... both agree Iran could never get away with such a deception."[68]

---

[61] GOV/2016/46.

[62] For information about the Nuclear Suppliers Group, see CRS Report RL33865, *Arms Control and Nonproliferation: A Catalog of Treaties and Agreements*, by Amy F. Woolf, Paul K. Kerr, and Mary Beth D. Nikitin.

[63] Department of State, April 2018.

[64] This plant was not under IAEA safeguards prior to the JCPOA.

[65] GOV/2016/55.

[66] "IAEA Director General Yukiya Amano's Statement to the Board of Governors," September 7, 2015.

[67] Ambassador Henry S. Ensher, IAEA Board of Governors Meeting June 6-10, 2016. Conversation with U.S. officials, July 1, 2016.

[68] "Remarks on Nuclear Agreement With Iran," September 2, 2015. For a detailed explanation, see Richard Nephew, "How the Iran Deal Prevents a Covert Nuclear Weapons Program," *Arms Control Today*, September 2015.

The JCPOA and U.N. Security Council Resolution 2231 contain a variety of reporting provisions for the IAEA. For example, the resolution requests the agency's Director General

> to provide regular updates to the IAEA Board of Governors and, as appropriate, in parallel to the Security Council on Iran's implementation of its commitments under the JCPOA and also to report to the IAEA Board of Governors and in parallel to the Security Council at any time if the Director General has reasonable grounds to believe there is an issue of concern directly affecting fulfillment of JCPOA commitments.

It is worth noting that, although the IAEA reports findings of its inspection and monitoring activities and the JCPOA-established Joint Commission monitors the parties' implementation of the agreement, compliance determinations are national decisions.

Access to Undeclared Sites

The JCPOA describes arrangements for the IAEA to gain access to Iranian sites other than those Tehran declares to the agency "if the IAEA has concerns regarding undeclared nuclear materials or activities, or activities inconsistent with" the JCPOA. If the IAEA has such concerns at one of these sites, the agency "will provide Iran the basis for such concerns and request clarification." The IAEA could request access to the site if Iran's explanation did not provide sufficient clarification, and Tehran may respond by proposing alternative means of resolving the IAEA's concerns. If such means did not resolve the IAEA's concerns or the two sides did not "reach satisfactory arrangements ... within 14 days of the IAEA's original request for access," Iran "would resolve the IAEA's concerns through necessary means agreed between Iran and the IAEA." Tehran would make such a decision "in consultation with the members of the Joint Commission" established by the JCPOA.[69] If the two sides cannot reach agreement, the commission "would advise on the necessary means to resolve the IAEA's concerns" if at least a majority of commission members agreed to do so. The Joint Commission would have seven days to reach a decision, and Iran is required to implement the necessary means within three additional days. (*The total time for the stipulated procedures would be 24 days.*)

The JCPOA contains several provisions that address Iranian concerns that IAEA inspectors may try to obtain information unrelated to the country's nuclear program. For example, the IAEA may only request access to the types of facilities described above "for the sole reason to verify the absence of undeclared nuclear materials and activities or

[69] Even in the absence of compliance issues, the commission is to meet every three months. (Ambassador Stephen D. Mull, "Implementation of the Joint Comprehensive Plan of Action," Washington Foreign Press Center, January 21, 2016.) According to the agreement, the work of the Joint Commission, which makes decisions by consensus, is "is confidential and may be shared only among JCPOA participants and observers as appropriate, unless the Joint Commission decides otherwise."

activities inconsistent with the JCPOA." In addition, the agency would provide Iran with written reasons for access and "make available relevant information."

Procurement Channel

The JCPOA established a "procurement channel" for Iran's nuclear program.[70] The Joint Commission established by the JCPOA is to monitor and approve transfers made via the channel for 10 years. The agreement requires Iran to provide the IAEA with "access to the locations of intended use of all items, materials, equipment, goods and technology" listed in the NSG's "Guidelines for Nuclear Transfers."[71] Moreover, Tehran is to permit exporting governments to "verify the end-use of all items, materials, equipment, goods and technology" listed in the NSG's "Guidelines for Transfers of Nuclear-Related Dual-Use Equipment, Materials, Software, and Related Technology."[72]

IAEA officials will have access to information about and may participate in meetings regarding such transfers when they are proposed. According to a June 2016 GAO report, IAEA officials asserted that "there is additional work to be done in informing exporting countries of their obligations and standardizing the data that the countries would report to IAEA so that they are usable to the agency."[73]

According to a December 8, 2017, report by U.N. Secretary-General António Guterres, the Security Council had received 37 nuclear-related export proposals since Implementation Day; the council approved 24 of those proposals and disapproved three. Five proposals were withdrawn by the submitting states and three were under review.[74]

Broader Conclusion

The JCPOA also indicates that the IAEA will pursue drawing a "Broader Conclusion that all nuclear material in Iran remains in peaceful activities." According to the IAEA, the agency can draw such a conclusion for states with comprehensive safeguards agreements and additional protocols in force. According to the IAEA,

> The conclusion of the absence of undeclared nuclear material and activities is drawn when the activities performed under an additional protocol have been completed, when relevant questions and inconsistencies have been addressed, and when no indications have been found by the IAEA that, in its judgement, would constitute a safeguards concern.[75]

---

[70] Information about the channel is available at http://www.un.org/en/sc/2231/pdf/160113-Information-on-the-procurement-channel.pdf.

[71] INFCIRC/254/Rev.12/Part 1.

[72] INFCIRC/254/Rev.9/Part 2.

[73] *Iran Nuclear Agreement: The International Atomic Energy Agency's Authorities, Resources, and Challenges*, U.S. Government Accountability Office, GAO-16-565, June 2016.

[74] *Fifth Report of the Secretary-General on the Implementation of Security Council Resolution 2231 (2015)*, S/2018/602, June 12, 2018.

[75] *2001 IAEA Safeguards Glossary.*

The average time for the IAEA to draw the broader conclusion for states with complex nuclear programs has been five to seven years.[76] Former IAEA Deputy Director General Heinonen wrote that "it has taken up to five years for the IAEA to reach a 'broader conclusion' for other countries with large nuclear programs that are in good standing under the Non-Proliferation Treaty."[77] Amano explained on March 20, 2017, that "I cannot tell how many years it will take" to draw such a conclusion for Iran, adding that "it depends very much on the level of cooperation from Iran."[78] In October 2017, Amano stated that the process is "likely to take many years," and there are no recent public indications that the IAEA is close to issuing that conclusion.[79]

International Cooperation

The JCPOA discusses a variety of nuclear projects in Iran that would include other countries. These include the Arak reactor project; research at the Fordow facility; other nuclear reactor projects; nuclear medicine; nuclear safety; and the supply of nuclear fuel. This latter form of cooperation is presumably designed to obviate the need for Iran to produce its own nuclear fuel. Some, but not necessarily all, of the P5+1 countries, will participate in these projects. The JCPOA also envisions forms of technical cooperation between Iran and the IAEA.[80] The Obama Administration argued that international nuclear cooperation would provide additional transparency into Iran's nuclear program.[81]

The United States does not have a civil nuclear cooperation agreement with Iran, and U.S. sanctions laws prohibit the United States from engaging in most forms of nuclear cooperation with Iran. Section 129b.(1) of the Atomic Energy Act (AEA) of 1954, as amended, forbids the export of "nuclear materials and equipment or sensitive nuclear technology" to any country designated as a state sponsor of terrorism.[82] Section 129b.(3) allows the President to waive this provision. Section 57b.(2) of the AEA allows for limited forms of nuclear cooperation related to the "development or production of any special nuclear material outside of the United States" without a nuclear cooperation agreement if

---

[76] Conversation with U.S. official, July 31, 2015.

[77] Olli Heinonen, *Concerns about a Reduction of Transparency in IAEA Reporting on Iran's Nuclear Program*, Foundation for Defense of Olli Heinonen, *Concerns about a Reduction of Transparency in IAEA Reporting on Iran's Nuclear Program*, Foundation for Defense of Democracies, November 28, 2016.

[78] Yukiya Amano, "The Iran Deal: International Perspectives," Carnegie International Nuclear Policy Conference 2017, March 20, 2017.

[79] Yukiya Amano, "International Cooperation for Enhancing Nuclear Safety, Security, Safeguards and Non-Proliferation - 60 Years Atoms for Peace and Development," October 9, 2017.

[80] Implementing a provision of U.N. Security Council Resolution 1737, the IAEA halted some technical cooperation with Iran in 2007. Tehran had seven technical cooperation projects with the agency in 2017.

[81] "Background Conference Call by Senior Administration Officials on Iran," July 14, 2015.

[82] Section 129b. (2) of the AEA states that the prohibitions described in the previous section "shall not apply to exports, reexports, transfers, or retransfers of radiation monitoring technologies, surveillance equipment, seals, cameras, tamper-indication devices, nuclear detectors, monitoring systems, or equipment necessary to safely store, transport, or remove hazardous materials ... except to the extent that such technologies, equipment, seals, cameras, devices, detectors, or systems are available for use in the design or construction of nuclear reactors or nuclear weapons." For more information, see CRS Report RS22937, *Nuclear Cooperation with Other Countries: A Primer*, by Paul K. Kerr and Mary Beth D. Nikitin.

that activity has been authorized by the Secretary of Energy following a determination that it "will not be inimical to the interest of the United States."

Nuclear Weapons Research and Development

In addition to addressing Iran's ability to produce fissile material, the JCPOA contains other provisions intended to render Iran unable to produce a nuclear weapon. For example, the agreement indefinitely prohibits specific activities "which could contribute to the design and development of a nuclear explosive device."[83] Neither Iran's comprehensive safeguards agreement nor its additional protocol explicitly prohibit these activities. As noted, the U.S. government assesses that Tehran has not mastered all of the necessary technologies for building a nuclear weapon. In addition, for 15 years Iran is to refrain from "producing or acquiring plutonium or uranium metals or their alloys" and "conducting R&D on plutonium or uranium (or their alloys) metallurgy, or casting, forming, or machining plutonium or uranium metal." Producing uranium or plutonium metals is a key step in producing nuclear weapons.

Resolving Questions of Past Nuclear Weapons-Related Research

The IAEA has concluded its investigation of the outstanding issues concerning Iran's nuclear program. According to IAEA reports, the agency has evidence that Iran may have conducted work relevant to nuclear weapons, such as research about a nuclear payload for missiles. U.N. Security Council resolutions required Iran to resolve these questions by providing full information to the IAEA, and the agency has held regular talks with Iran to chart a path forward. But past reports from Amano to the agency's Board of Governors said that, although the IAEA could verify that there was no diversion of nuclear material from Iran's declared nuclear facilities, it could not conclude that no nuclear weapons-related activity was taking place in the country.

According to the JCPOA, Tehran would "complete" a series of steps set out in an Iran-IAEA "Roadmap for Clarification of Past and Present Outstanding Issues." According to Amano, this road map set out "a process, under the November 2013 Framework for Cooperation, to enable the Agency, with the cooperation of Iran, to make an assessment of issues relating to possible military dimensions to Iran's nuclear programme."[84] "All the activities contained in the road-map were implemented in

[83] Listed in Annex I of the JCPOA, these activities are designing, developing, acquiring, or using computer models to simulate nuclear explosive devices; designing, developing, fabricating, acquiring, or using multi-point explosive detonation systems suitable for a nuclear explosive device; designing, developing, fabricating, acquiring, or using explosive diagnostic systems(streak cameras, framing cameras and flash x-ray cameras) suitable for the development of a nuclear explosive device; and designing, developing, fabricating, acquiring, or using explosively driven neutron sources or specialized materials for explosively driven neutron sources. Iran may conduct some of these activities for non-nuclear purposes if Tehran receives permission from the Joint Commission established by the JCPOA. Such permitted activities would be "subject to monitoring."

[84] "IAEA Director General Amano's Remarks to the Press on Agreements with Iran," July 14, 2015.

accordance with the agreed schedule," according to a December 2, 2015, report from Amano.[85]

On December 2, 2015, in advance of the December 15 deadline in the road map, Amano presented the stipulated report, as a final assessment on all past and present outstanding [Iranian nuclear] issues described in a November 2011 report.[86] It indicated that the information provided by Iran did not allow the IAEA to resolve some outstanding issues and also casts doubt on some of the information's accuracy. Nevertheless, the report assesses that "before the end of 2003, an organizational structure was in place in Iran suitable for the coordination of a range of activities relevant to the development of a nuclear explosive device." Iran conducted "a range of activities relevant to the development of a nuclear explosive device ... prior to the end of 2003 as a coordinated effort," the report says, adding that "some [nuclear weapons-related] activities took place after 2003," but "were not part of a coordinated effort." The report concludes that "these activities did not advance beyond feasibility and scientific studies, and the acquisition of certain relevant technical competencies and capabilities" and notes that the IAEA "has no credible indications of activities in Iran relevant to the development of a nuclear explosive device after 2009." Amano told the IAEA board on December 15 that, although "it was not possible for the Agency to reconstruct all the details of activities conducted by Iran in the past, we were able to clarify enough elements to provide an assessment of the whole picture."[87] The IAEA reiterated this conclusion on May 1, 2018, following Israeli Prime Minister Benjamin Netanyahu's disclosure of documents concerning Iran's past nuclear weapons program, though the agency did not comment on the documents specifically.[88] On June 5, 2018, Nicole Shampaine, the Chargé d'Affaires at the U.S. Mission to International Organizations in Vienna, stated that Israeli Prime Minister Benjamin Netanyahu's April 2018 disclosure of documents concerning Iran's past nuclear weapons program "further reaffirms" the IAEA's December 2015 conclusion that Iran had conducted such research in the past.[89] In accordance with the road map, Iran presented, in writing, its "comprehensive assessment to the IAEA" on Amano's report, on January 7, 2016. The document apparently acknowledges Iranian "scientific studies of dual-use technologies" for "peaceful civilian or conventional military uses."[90] But the statement reiterated previous Iranian claims that the country has done no work on nuclear weapons and that some of the evidence underlying the agency's concerns is inauthentic.

---

[85] *Final Assessment on Past and Present Outstanding Issues Regarding Iran's Nuclear Programme*, GOV/2015/68, December 2, 2015.

[86] GOV/2015/68; *Implementation of the NPT Safeguards Agreement and Relevant Provisions of Security Council Resolutions in the Islamic Republic of Iran*, Report by the Director General, GOV/2011/65, November 8, 2011.

[87] IAEA Director General Amano's Introductory Statement to the Board of Governors, December 15, 2015.

[88] "Statement on Iran by the IAEA Spokesperson," 22/2018, May 1, 2018.

[89] U.S. Statement as Delivered by U.S. Chargé d'Affaires Nicole Shampaine, IAEA Board of Governors Meeting: Agenda Item 5: Verification and Monitoring in Iran, June 5, 2018.

[90] *Communication Dated 7 January 2016 Received from the Permanent Mission of the Islamic Republic of Iran to the Agency Regarding the Report of the Director General on the Final Assessment on Past and Present Outstanding Issues Regarding Iran's Nuclear Programme*, INFCIRC/893, January 8, 2016.

Virtual Closure of the Issue

The JCPOA states that, following Amano's report, the P5+1 "in their capacity as members of the [IAEA] Board of Governors, will submit a resolution to the Board of Governors for taking necessary action, with a view to closing the issue." The board adopted a resolution on December 15 which closed "the Board's consideration" of the "outstanding issues regarding Iran's nuclear programme."[91]

The Board is no longer focused on Iran's compliance with past Security Council resolutions and past issues concerning Iran's safeguards agreement, but is instead focused on JCPOA implementation and verification and monitoring in Iran in light of Security Council Resolution 2231. The resolution requests the Director General to issue quarterly reports to the board regarding Iran's "implementation of its relevant commitments under the JCPOA for the full duration of those commitments." The Director General is also to report to the Board of Governors and the Security Council "at any time if the Director General has reasonable grounds to believe there is an issue of concern" regarding Tehran's compliance with its JCPOA or safeguards obligations. It is worth noting that the IAEA will not be able to draw the "Broader Conclusion that all nuclear material in Iran remains in peaceful activities" without addressing these issues. The April 2018 State Department report notes that closing the agenda item concerning Iran's past military-related nuclear activities "does not preclude the IAEA from investigating if there is reason to believe Iran is pursuing any covert nuclear activities, including nuclear weapons work."[92]

Issue Significance

The significance of resolving these issues for ensuring that Iran's current program is for purely peaceful purposes is unclear. Former IAEA Deputy Director General Olli Heinonen argued during a July 2014 Senate hearing that gaining full understanding of Iran's past suspected nuclear weapons program is important for determining that Iran is not reconstituting that program and also for determining the probability that Iran will use a future centrifuge program to produce nuclear weapons.[93] However, in April 2015, Jofi Joseph, a former Obama Administration official whose portfolio included the Iran nuclear issue, commented

> Some argue that it will be very difficult to identify future covert Iranian nuclear weapons efforts without a detailed understanding of what happened before. I'm not so sure. It is not clear if the individuals involved with the previous [nuclear weapons

---

[91] GOV/2015/72.

[92] Department of State, April 2018.

[93] *Iran: Status of the P-5+1, Panel 2*, Senate Committee on Foreign Relations Hearing, July 29, 2014.

program] would be the ones tapped again for a future covert program or whether a clear understanding of their previous actions would help identify future efforts.[94]

Former State Department official Robert Einhorn argued that

It is sometimes argued that full Iranian disclosure is essential to designing an effective JCPOA monitoring system. But the provisions of an agreement that could be most effective in monitoring small-scale weaponization activities would be more intrusive than any sovereign state would be willing to accept (e.g., keeping close track of all scientists with the necessary expertise, on-site verification of all equipment in the country that could be used in nuclear weapons design and diagnostics). With or without full knowledge of past Iranian activities, it would have been nearly impossible to reach agreement on such intrusive arrangements.[95]

Einhorn also explained that

the United States already has considerable knowledge of past Iranian nuclear weapons work. And in any event, in calculating how much time it would have to thwart an Iranian breakout, the United States would have to make the conservative assumption that Iran had made substantial headway in weaponization and would not require much time to proceed from the production of fissile material to the fabrication of a weapon. It is unlikely that anything the Iranians might say about past weaponization efforts would affect U.S. planning to stop an Iranian breakout, especially because whatever they said would hardly be taken at face value.[96]

Iranian Compliance with the JCPOA Nuclear Requirements

Regarding Iranian compliance with the JCPOA, the Iran Nuclear Agreement Review Act of 2015 (INARA, P.L. 114-17)[97] requires the President[98] to "determine whether the President is able to certify" that Iran

- "is transparently, verifiably, and fully implementing the agreement, including all related technical or additional agreements";
- "has not committed a material breach" of the agreement or cured any material breaches that Iran has committed; and

---

[94] "Jofi Joseph on the Iran Deal," Arms Control Wonk, April 7, 2015. Available at http://lewis.armscontrolwonk.com/ archive/7623/jofi-joseph-on-the-iran-deal.

[95] Robert Einhorn, "A Verdict on Iranian Military Nukes Won't Kill the Deal," *The National Interest*, November 30, 2015. November 30, 2015.

[96] Ibid.

[97] For greater detail on all the provisions of that law, see CRS Report RS20871, *Iran Sanctions*, by Kenneth Katzman.

[98] President Obama delegated to the Secretary of State the authority to issue this certification.

- "has not taken any action, including covert activities, that could significantly advance its nuclear weapons program."[99]

Then-Secretary of State Rex Tillerson issued this certification on July 17, 2017., All official reports and statements from the United Nations, European Union, the IAEA, and the P5+1 indicate that Iran has complied with the JCPOA. The most recent report from IAEA Director General Amano states that the IAEA has continued verification and monitoring of the restrictions described in Section T of the JCPOA, which prohibits a number of nuclear weapons-related activities.[100] Secretary of State Michael Pompeo stated during an April 12, 2018, Senate Foreign Relations Committee hearing that he had seen no evidence of Iranian noncompliance with the agreement. High Representative of the European Union for Foreign Affairs and Security Policy Mogherini stated on April 16 that "Iran is fully compliant with its nuclear commitments."[101]

The agreement, as noted, describes arrangements for agency inspectors to gain access to Iranian sites, including military sites, other than those that Tehran has declared to the agency, "if the IAEA has concerns regarding undeclared nuclear materials or activities, or activities inconsistent with" the JCPOA. The agreement also provides for alternative means to clarify the matter. The IAEA has not reported whether it has requested access to any Iranian military facilities, but the agency has a number of methods other than inspections, such as analyzing open source information and receiving intelligence briefings from governments, to monitor Iranian compliance with these and other JCPOA commitments. According to the April 2018 State Department report,

> [t]he IAEA continues to exercise its full authorities in pursuing any new safeguards-relevant or JCPOA-related information in Iran, including any new concerns regarding weaponization should they arise, through implementation of Iran's Safeguards Agreement, Additional Protocol, and the enhanced transparency and verification measures contained in the JCPOA.[102]

In a June 4, 2018, statement to the IAEA board Amano noted that the IAEA has been able to access "all the sites and locations in Iran which" agency inspectors "needed to visit."

---

[99] INARA defines "material breach" as "any failure to perform those commitments, that substantially (A) benefits Iran's nuclear program; (B) decreases the amount of time required by Iran to achieve a nuclear weapon; or (C) deviates from or undermines the purposes of" the JCPOA.

[100] GOV/2018/24.

[101] "Remarks by HR/VP Federica Mogherini upon Arrival at the Foreign Affairs Council," *European External Action Service*, April 16, 2018.

[102] Department of State, April 2018.

Sanctions Relief under the JCPOA and Reimposition

Under the JCPOA, the overwhelming bulk of sanctions relief occurred at Implementation Day.[103]

Iran remains subject to its obligations pursuant to the JCPOA and Resolution 2231. A "snap back" mechanism was incorporated into the JCPOA to account for the possibility that Iran might not satisfactorily resolve a P5+1 inquiry about possible JCPOA noncompliance. According to the JCPOA, the United States (or any veto-wielding member of the U.N. Security Council) would be able to block a U.N. Security Council resolution that would continue the lifting of U.N. sanctions despite Iran's refusal to resolve the dispute. In that case, "... the provisions of the old U.N. Security Council resolutions would be reimposed, unless the U.N. Security Council decides otherwise." These provisions are included in U.N. Security Council Resolution 2231.[104] The wording implies that the Council has the option to reimpose some, but not all, sanctions that existed prior to the JCPOA. *The total time for this "dispute resolution" mechanism—between the time of the complaint of Iranian noncompliance and the reimposition of U.N. sanctions—is 65 days.*

The other P5+1 states are able to invoke this mechanism, if they choose. But whether the United States may do so is unclear because the resolution provides that only a "JCPOA participant state" may bring a noncompliance finding to the Security Council; U.S. officials have stated that the United States is no longer participating in the agreement.

Formal Congressional Review and Oversight[105]

Legislation providing for U.S. congressional review was enacted as the Iran Nuclear Agreement Review Act of 2015 (INARA, P.L. 114-17).[106] Because the agreement was reached after July 10, the congressional review period was 60 days from the date of submission to Congress, which is to be within 5 days of finalization of the accord. The transmission of all required materials, according to the Administration, took place on July 19, 2015. No statutory sanctions could be waived during the review period, which concluded on September 17.

---

[103] http://www.politico.com/story/2015/07/full-text-iran-deal-120080.html.

[104] http://www.scribd.com/doc/271711382/Iran-Deal-Draft-UNSC-Resolution-as-Uploaded-by-Inner-City-Press.

[105] For more information on the potential use of legislative mechanisms to cease implementing the JCPOA, see CRS Report R44942, *U.S. Decision to Cease Implementing the Iran Nuclear Agreement*, by Kenneth Katzman, Paul K. Kerr, and Valerie Heitshusen.

[106] For greater detail on all the provisions of that law, see CRS Report RS20871, *Iran Sanctions*, by Kenneth Katzman.

Joint resolutions of disapproval were introduced in each chamber: H.J.Res. 64 in the House, and S.Amdt. 2640 to H.J.Res. 61 in the Senate. However, the House acted on three bills: H.R. 3461 to *approve* the deal was voted down 162-269. Another bill, H.Res. 411, asserting that the President did not comply with P.L. 114-17 because the IAEA-Iran agreements were not submitted to Congress, passed the House 245-186. A third bill, H.R. 3460, denying the President the ability to waive any sanctions laws until January 2017, passed 247-186. None of the bills was taken up by the Senate. In that body, several cloture motions on the disapproval resolution (H.J.Res. 61) were defeated and the review process under P.L. 114-17 ended on September 17, 2015, with no resolution either approving or disapproving the JCPOA being enacted.

Iranian Parliamentary Review

In August 2015, the Iranian *Majles* (parliament) set up a 15- person committee to review the JCPOA. The committee asserted that the JCPOA had "flaws," but stopped well short of saying it should not be adopted.[107] Acting just before the deadline for Adoption Day, the *Majles* formally voted to approve the agreement, and Council of Guardians concurred. On October 21, 2015, Supreme Leader Khamene'i formally accepting the *Majles* and Council of Guardians decisions, while stressing stipulations, reservations, and distrust of the U.S. intent to fully implement its JCPOA commitments.[108]

Ongoing Oversight under INARA

INARA provides for Administration reporting to Congress under several scenarios and at differing intervals:

- *Material Breach Report.* INARA requires that the President report to Congress any information relating to a potentially significant Iranian breach of the JCPOA, within 10 days of receiving information on such a possible breach. Within 30 calendar days after submitting such a report, the Administration is to make a determination whether there has been a material breach of the JCPOA by Iran. This reporting requirement is largely mooted by the U.S. exit from the JCPOA.
- *Compliance Certification.* Under INARA, the Administration is required to certify, within 90 days or less of the end of the INARA congressional review period (first report by December 16, 2015), and each 90 days thereafter, that Iran is fulfilling its commitments under the JCPOA. If the President does not make the required certification of Iranian compliance, or reports a material breach by Iran, Congress "may" initiate within 60 days "expedited consideration" of legislation that would reimpose any Iran sanctions that the President had

---

107 http://news.yahoo.com/iran-nuclear-review-panel-says-deal-flawed-103101551.html.

108 Open Source Center. "Leader Issues Important Order to Ruhani on JCPOA." October 21, 2015.

suspended through use of waiver or other authority. As is any legislation, such "snap back" sanctions legislation would be subject to potential presidential veto. This certification requirement is mooted by the U.S. exit from the JCPOA.

- *Semi-Annual Report.* INARA requires an Administration report every 180 days on Iran's nuclear program and Iran's compliance with the agreement during the period covered in the report. The report is also to include whether Iranian banks are involved in terrorism financing; Iran's ballistic missile advances; and whether Iran continues to support terrorism. (First report was due by March 12, 2016.) It is unclear whether this reporting requirement remains active in light of the U.S. exit from the JCPOA.

U.S. Implementation of and Exit from the JCPOA

The Obama Administration and the IAEA asserted that they put in place measures to vigorously enforce the terms of the agreement. On September 17, 2015, then-Secretary of State Kerry announced the appointment of Ambassador Stephen Mull as Lead Coordinator for Iran Nuclear Implementation, leading an interagency effort to ensure that the nuclear steps Iran committed to in the JCPOA are fully implemented and verified. Deputy Secretary of State John Sullivan indicated during a July 17, 2017 hearing that Mull's position was "under review."[109] The position no longer exists; its functions are now handled by the State Department's Bureau of International Security and Nonproliferation.

The JCPOA in the Trump Administration

During the 2016 presidential campaign, Donald Trump was a vocal critic of the agreement. At times, he pledged to seek to renegotiate it, to strictly enforce its terms on Iran, or to abrogate it outright.[110] The JCPOA does not contain a provision for any party to end the agreement; nevertheless, the President could decide to stop implementing some or all of the U.S. commitments in the deal, but doing so leaves open the possibility for the agreement to be implemented by the remaining parties, including Iran.

Throughout some of its first year, the Trump Administration indicated support for the agreement. On February 10, 2017, following meetings with the Administration focused on the JCPOA, the EU High Representative for Foreign Policy, Frederica Mogherini, stated

---

[109] A Review of the State Department Reauthorization Bill for FY2018 and the State Department Reorganization Plans, Senate Committee on Foreign Relations, July 17, 2017.

[110] http://lobelog.com/can-the-iran-deal-survive-a-us-withdrawal/.

that Administration officials "reassured" her that the Administration intended to fully implement the JCPOA.[111]

However, by the beginning of 2018, U.S. officials expressed increasing hostility toward the JCPOA.

Then-Secretary of State Rex Tillerson told reporters on April 19, 2017, that the Administration will "review completely the JCPOA itself."[112] Asserting that "Iran's nuclear ambitions are a grave risk to international peace and security," Tillerson argued that the "JCPOA fails to achieve the objective of a non-nuclear Iran; it only delays their goal of becoming a nuclear state." Asked whether the United States should stop fulfilling its JCPOA commitments, Tillerson replied, "[w]e just don't see that that's a prudent way to be dealing with Iran, certainly not in the context of all of their other disruptive activities." Trump Administration officials argued that Iran may pursue nuclear weapons in the future. Trump Administration officials stated on July 17, 2017, that the Administration is "trying to take stronger steps to interpret the agreement more stringently against Iran" because the "existing restrictions on the JCPOA were, in our view, inadequately enforced."[113] The February 2018 Nuclear Posture Review asserts that "Iran's development of increasingly long-range ballistic missile capabilities, and its aggressive strategy and activities to destabilize neighboring governments, raises questions about its long-term commitment to foregoing nuclear weapons capability."

President Trump announced on October 13, 2017, that the Administration had completed the Iran policy review described above. With respect to the JCPOA, Trump announced that the Administration would not issue an INARA-specified compliance certification, and that he would direct his Administration to "work closely with Congress and our allies to address the deal's many serious flaws so that the Iranian regime can never threaten the world with nuclear weapons." Secretary Tillerson did not address Iranian compliance, but he wrote in a letter to Congress the same day that he was "unable to certify" that "continued suspension of [U.S.] sanctions" is "appropriate and proportionate to the specific and verifiable measures taken by Iran with respect to terminating its illicit nuclear program."[114] The withholding of the certification under INARA permitted Congress to act on legislation, under expedited procedures, reimposing those sanctions that were suspended. Congress did not take such action.

On January 12, 2018, President Trump stated that "the United States will not again waive sanctions" pursuant to the JCPOA absent "our European allies' agreement to fix the terrible flaws of the Iran nuclear deal."[115] In this statement, Trump also demanded new congressional legislation concerning the JCPOA. A senior Administration official

---

[111] http://www.reuters.com/article/us-usa-trump-eu-idUSKBN15P1XM.

[112] An April 18 letter from Tillerson to Congress stated that this NSC-led review "will evaluate whether suspension of sanctions related to Iran pursuant to the JCPOA is vital to the national security interests of the United States."

[113] "Administration Officials Background Briefing on Iran," July 17, 2017.

[114] Tillerson reiterated this finding in a January 12, 2018, letter to Congress.

[115] "Statement by the President on the Iran Nuclear Deal," January 12, 2018.

explained the same day that Trump "hopes to see an amendment to the Iran Nuclear Agreement Review Act" which must

- "demand that Iran allow timely, sufficient and immediate inspections at all sites that are requested by international inspectors from the IAEA";
- "ensure" that Iran does not become capable of producing enough fissile material for a nuclear weapon in less than one year;
- allow the United States for an indefinite period of time to reimpose U.S. nuclear sanctions if Iran does not comply with these new criteria; and
- "state explicitly ... that we view Iran's long-range missile programs and nuclear weapons as inseparable and that Iran's development and testing of missiles should be subject to severe sanctions."

Congress has not acted on such legislation. A senior Administration official stated on January 12 that the Trump Administration would "work with our European partners on some kind of follow-on agreement" to the JCPOA to address Iran's ballistic missile program, the JCPOA restrictions containing expiration dates, and improved inspections of Iran's nuclear program.[116] U.S. officials subsequently met several times with their counterparts from France, Germany, and the United Kingdom to discuss Trump's demands, but the two sides did not reach agreement on a path forward that was sufficient to satisfy President Trump's demands.

U.S. Exit from the JCPOA

On May 8, President Trump, noting that the two sides had been unable to reach an agreement, announced that the United States would no longer participate in the JCPOA and would reimpose sanctions that had been suspended pursuant to the JCPOA.[117] President Trump ordered Secretary of State Pompeo to "take all appropriate steps to cease the participation of the United States in the JCPOA," and, along with Secretary of the Treasury Steven Mnuchin, immediately "begin taking steps to reimpose all United States sanctions lifted or waived in connection" with the agreement.[118] The United States has notified the other P5+1 states that the United States will no longer attend meetings of the joint commission, the working group concerning the Arak reactor, and the procurement working group.[119]

---

[116] "Senior Administration Officials Hold A Background Briefing Via Teleconference on Iran," January 12, 2018; "Director For Policy Planning Brian Hook Holds A State Department News Briefing Via Teleconference on the JCPOA Joint Commission Meeting," March 21, 2018.

[117] "Ceasing U.S. Participation in the JCPOA and Taking Additional Action to Counter Iran's Malign Influence and Deny Iran All Paths to a Nuclear Weapon," Presidential Memoranda, May 8, 2018.

[118] Ibid.

[119] CRS analyst conversation with State Department official, May 21, 2018.

Secretary Pompeo detailed a new U.S. approach with respect to Iran during a May 21, 2018 speech as applying "unprecedented financial pressure on the Iranian regime," working "with the Department of Defense and our regional allies to deter Iranian aggression," and advocating "tirelessly for the Iranian people." He asserted that, in exchange for "major changes" in Iran's behavior, the United States is "prepared to end the principal components of every one of our sanctions against the regime ..., re-establish full diplomatic and commercial relationships with Iran ..., [a]nd support the modernization and reintegration of the Iranian economy into the international economic system."

Pompeo listed a number of essential elements for any new agreement:

- "First, Iran must declare to the IAEA a full account of the prior military dimensions of its nuclear program, and permanently and verifiably abandon such work in perpetuity.
- Second, Iran must stop enrichment and never pursue plutonium reprocessing. This includes closing its heavy water reactor.
- Third, Iran must also provide the IAEA with unqualified access to all sites throughout the entire country.
- Iran must end its proliferation of ballistic missiles and halt further launching or development of nuclear-capable missile systems.
- Iran must release all U.S. citizens, as well as citizens of our partners and allies, each of them detained on spurious charges.
- Iran must end support to Middle East terrorist groups, including Lebanese Hizballah, Hamas, and the Palestinian Islamic Jihad.
- Iran must respect the sovereignty of the Iraqi Government and permit the disarming, demobilization, and reintegration of Shia militias.
- Iran must also end its military support for the Houthi militia and work toward a peaceful political settlement in Yemen.
- Iran must withdraw all forces under Iranian command throughout the entirety of Syria.
- Iran, too, must end support for the Taliban and other terrorists in Afghanistan and the region, and cease harboring senior al-Qaida leaders.
- Iran, too, must end the IRGC [Islamic Revolutionary Guard Corps] Qods Force's support for terrorists and militant partners around the world.
- And too, Iran must end its threatening behavior against its neighbors—many of whom are U.S. allies. This certainly includes its threats to destroy Israel, and its firing of missiles into Saudi Arabia and the United Arab Emirates. It also includes threats to international shipping and destructive ... cyberattacks."

On May 21, 2018, State Department Director for Policy Planning Hook stated that "the plan is to continue working with our allies, as we have been over the last few months, to create a new security architecture." During a July 2, 2018, press briefing Hook explained that, following Trump's May 8, 2018, announcement, Secretaries Pompeo and Mnuchin "decided to create joint teams of senior officials to visit every region of the world. These teams were launched on June 4." The United States is "bringing severe economic pressure on Iran until the regime changes its destabilizing policies," Hook stated. Although Hook explained that the administration's policy "is not about changing the regime, it is about changing the behavior of the leadership in Iran," most observers assert that it would be inconceivable for the current regime in Iran to change its behavior to comport with the requirements outlined by Secretary Pompeo. Pompeo himself stated during a June 22 television interview that, if Iran were to "ramp up" work on its nuclear program, "the wrath of the entire world will fall upon" the government, explaining that "wrath" referred to "moral opprobrium and economic power," rather than military action.

Reaction to the U.S. Exit

The U.S. exit from the JCPOA attracted broad criticism among the other parties to the JCPOA. The other JCPOA parties assert that unilateral U.S. reimposition of sanctions appears to violate the JCPOA. The agreement requires that a noncompliance notification to the U.N. Security Council, which would be necessary to trigger the reimposition of U.N. sanctions, be accompanied by "a description of the good-faith efforts the participant made to exhaust the dispute resolution process specified in this JCPOA." The agreement also states that the P5+1 and Iran "commit to implement this JCPOA in good faith and in a constructive atmosphere, based on mutual respect, and to refrain from any action inconsistent with the letter, spirit and intent of this JCPOA that would undermine its successful implementation." Whether this course of action violates UNSCR 2231 is unclear. U.S. officials have argued that the JCPOA is not legally binding.[120] But a European Union official told CRS in a November 30, 2016, email that "the commitments under the JCPOA have been given legally binding effect through UNSC Resolution 2231 (2015)."

Other P5+1 countries immediately reiterated their support for the JCPOA and announced that they intend to fulfill their JCPOA commitments and protect their companies from the effects of any U.S.-imposed sanctions. In a joint statement, France, Germany, and the United Kingdom declared their intention to remain party to the JCPOA and to "work with all the remaining parties" to the deal to ensure that Iran continues to receive "the continuing economic benefits ... linked to the agreement."[121] EU High Representative Mogherini stated that, if "Iran continues to implement its nuclear related

---

[120] See, for example, remarks by Colin Kahl to the Center for Strategic and International Studies, August 13, 2015.

[121] "Joint Statement from Prime Minister Theresa May, Chancellor Angela Merkel and President Emmanuel Macron Following President Trump's Statement on Iran," May 8, 2018.

commitments ... the European Union will remain committed to the continued full and effective implementation" of the agreement.

Iranian Reaction

Iranian officials have repeatedly stated that Tehran would fulfill its JCPOA commitments, as long as the United States did, and repeatedly have rejected renegotiating the JCPOA or negotiating a new agreement such as the sort described by U.S. officials.[122] However, Zarif has asserted that Iran "is fully prepared to return to the pre-JCPOA situation or even [to conditions] more robust than that if the US reneges on its promises to the extent that the JCPOA's continuation harms our national interests," Iranian Foreign Minister Javad Zarif asserted the previous month.[123] Deputy Foreign Minister Seyed Abbas Araqchi claimed that Iran "will be able to reach the industrial enrichment phase in less than two years";[124] other Iranian officials have asserted that the country can rapidly reconstitute its fissile material production capability.[125]

Iranian officials have described a number of possible responses to a U.S. decision to reimpose U.S. sanctions, including resuming uranium enrichment, referring the matter to the Joint Commission, decreasing cooperation with the IAEA, and withdrawing from the NPT.[126] These responses do not include the possible Iranian development of nuclear weapons, Iranian officials have said.[127] Asked on April 21 if Iran will continue to meet its JCPOA obligations if all P5+1 parties except for the United States continue to uphold their obligations, Zarif replied, "I believe that's highly unlikely," adding that

> it is important for Iran receive the benefits of the agreement. And there is no way that Iran would do a one-sided implementation of the agreement. And it would require a major effort because right now, with the United States ostensibly in the agreement, a lot has been lacking in terms of Iran benefiting from the deal.[128]

Following Trump's May 8 announcement, Iranian officials rejected negotiating any new agreements. In a May 10, 2018, letter to U.N. Secretary General António Guterres,

---

[122] See, for example, "Countries that Undermine Nuclear Deal to Pay Dearly, says Iran," *Iranian Students News Agency*, April 18, 2018; and "Iran FM Says USA Will 'Regret' Dropping Nuclear Deal," *Press TV*, April 20, 2018.

[123] "Iranian FM Warns U.S. Against Violation of Nuclear Deal," *PressTV*, March 21, 2017.

[124] "Iran Major Power in Mideast Region – Official," *Tasnim News Agency*, February 22, 2017.

[125] See, for example, "Iran Can Resume 20 Per Cent Uranium Enrichment Only in 5 Days: Salehi," *Iranian Students News Agency (ISNA),* August 22, 2017; "AEOI Chief: Iran Able to Resume 20% Enrichment in Maximum 5 Days," *FARS News Agency*, August 22, 2017; "Nuclear Chief: Iran Able to Immediately Return to Pre-JCPOA Conditions," *FARS News Agency*, April 10, 2018.

[126] "Iran to Reconsider Cooperation with IAEA if U.S. Violates Deal - Nuclear Chief," *Mehr News Agency*, January 8, 2018; Robin Wright, "The Scramble to Salvage the Iran Nuclear Deal," *The New Yorker*, April 22, 2018; "Zarif in New York: Interview on Nuclear Deal, Regional Issues," *Iran Primer*, U.S. Institute for Peace, April 23, 2018, available at http://iranprimer.usip.org/blog/2018/apr/23/zarif-new-york-interview-nuclear-deal-regional-issues.

[127] "Zarif in New York," April 23, 2018.

[128] Ibid.

Foreign Minister Zarif wrote that "[i]f JCPOA is to survive, the remaining JCPOA Participants and the international community need to fully ensure that Iran is compensated unconditionally through appropriate national, regional and global measures," adding that

> Iran has decided to resort to the JCPOA mechanism in good faith to find solutions in order to rectify the United States' multiple cases of significant non-performance and its unlawful withdrawal, and to determine whether and how the remaining JCPOA Participants and other economic partners can ensure the full benefits that the Iranian people are entitled to derive from this global diplomatic achievement.[129]

Supreme Leader Khamene'i stated on May 23 that Iran will only continue to participate in the JCPOA if Europe provides "concrete guarantees" that it maintains Iran's existing revenue stream from oil sales to the EU countries. He also demanded that Europe not to raise the issues of Iran's missiles programs or regional influence, and added that "Iran has the right to resume its nuclear activities."[130] President Rouhani expressed a similar view in a July 4 speech.[131]

According to Iranian officials, Tehran has begun preparations for expanding its uranium enrichment program, albeit within the parameters of the JCPOA for the time being. Spokesman of the Atomic Energy Organization of Iran (AEOI) Behrouz Kamalvandi stated on June 5 that the organization "will start the process of boosting the capacity of the country's uranium enrichment," by increasing Iran's capacity to produce uranium hexafluoride.[132] On June 27, 2018, Iran's official news agency announced that Iran has resumed operations[133] at its uranium conversion facility, which Iran has used to produce this material.[134] Kamalvandi also explained that Iran would begin the process of "manufacturing and assembly of centrifuge rotors," which are critical components of such machines.[135] Iran "will begin building a centrifuge rotor plant," he noted.[136] In addition, AEOI head Ali Akbar Salehi stated that Tehran will begin using an "advanced centrifuge assembly centre in the Natanz nuclear facility," which Iran had not disclosed

---

[129] Available at http://en.mfa.ir/index.aspx?siteid=3&fkeyid=&siteid=3&pageid=36409&newsview=514551.

[130] "To Remain in JCPOA, Imam Khamenei Announces Conditions to be Met by Europe," May 23, 2018, available at http://english.khamenei.ir/print/5696/To-remain-in-JCPOA-Imam-Khamenei-announces-conditions-to-be.

[131] "JCPOA A Key Deal for Iran, EU, World/Iran to Stay in JCPOA without US if Its Interests Met/Time of Unilateralism Over; A Country Can't Decide for World, Other People," July 4, 2018. Available at: http://www.president.ir/en/105171.

[132] Nuclear Chief: Iran To Start New Centrifuge Production In Natanz Tomorrow," *Fars News Agency*, June 5, 2018. The IAEA had received a letter on June 4 informing the agency of "a tentative schedule to start production" of this material. ("Iran Tells IAEA It Plans to Produce Feedstock for Centrifuges," *Reuters*, June 5, 2018).

[133] Iran has not produced any uranium hexafluoride since August 2009.

[134] "Iran UF6 Factory Resumes Work," *Islamic Republic News Agency*, June 27, 2018.

[135] *Fars News Agency*, June 5, 2018.

[136] "Iran to Inform IAEA of Plan to Boost Enrichment - Fuller Report," *Iranian Students News Agency*, June 4, 2018.

publicly.[137] Kamalvandi noted that Iran would continue to operate within the constraints of its JCPOA commitments, but added that, should the JCPOA collapse, Iran would produce centrifuges beyond those constraints.[138]

As noted, Iran remains subject to its obligations pursuant to the JCPOA and Resolution 2231 and could be subject to the reimposition of multilateral sanctions if Tehran violates these obligations.

Efforts to Preserve the Accord

Following the initial reactions to the U.S. exit from the accord, Iran and the other parties began negotiations on concrete steps that would continue to provide Iran with the economic benefits of the JCPOA. On May 16, 2018, in an apparent effort to meet Iran's demands for remaining in the agreement, the EU announced "practical measures" for continued implementation of the JCPOA, including:

- maintaining and deepening economic relations with Iran;
- the continued sale of Iran's oil and gas condensate petroleum products and petrochemicals and related transfers;
- effective banking transactions with Iran;
- continued sea, land, air, and rail transportation relations with Iran;
- provision of export credit and special provisions in financial banking to facilitate economic and financial cooperation and trade and investment;
- further memoranda of understanding and contracts between European companies and Iranian counterparts;
- further investments in Iran; and
- the protection of European Union economic operators and ensuring legal certainty; and finally further development of a transparent, rules-based business environment in Iran.[139]

Several multilateral meetings since the U.S. exit have not produced a firm Iranian commitment to the JCPOA. At Iran's request, the Joint Commission held meetings, attended by all of the JCPOA parties except for the United States, on May 25 and July 6. At the conclusion of the July 6 meeting, the Joint Commission participants reaffirmed their commitment to the EU "practical measures" enumerated above.[140] However, President Rouhani reacted to the pledges by saying that "Unfortunately, the EU's

---

[137] "Iran to Begin Using Advanced Centrifuge Assembly Centre," *Islamic Republic of Iran News Network*, June 5, 2018. AEOI head Salehi stated on July 18 that Iran has completed constructing this facility ("Iran Completes Facility to Build Advanced Centrifuge," Islamic Republic of Iran Broadcasting, July 18, 2018).

[138] *Iranian Students News Agency*, June 4, 2018.

[139] "Iran Nuclear Deal: EU, France, Germany, UK and Iran Meet to Discuss Way Forward," *European External Action Service*, May 16, 2018.

[140] "Statement from the Joint Commission on the Joint Comprehensive Plan of Action." *European External Action Service*, July 6, 2018.

package of proposals lacked an operational solution and a specific method for cooperation."[141] Rouhani's reaction likely reflected a lack of confidence that EU and other countries can counter the effects of a steady stream of announcements by EU, Japanese, South Korean, and Indian companies that they are leaving the Iran market rather than face the risk of reimposed U.S. sanctions. The corporate announcements are the result, at least in part, of Trump Administration official statements that the Administration plans to fully enforce reimposed sanctions and will likely deny requests by companies and their governments for waivers or exemptions to the U.S. sanctions.

Appendix A. Chart on the JCPOA[142]

Table A-1. Summary of Timeline

Implementation	Components	Date/Expected
Finalization Day	• Date on which JCPOA announced. • Joint Commission established comprised of representatives of Iran and the P5+1, with the EU High Representative. • Coordination led by EU High Representative. • Meet on quarterly basis or at request of any JCPOA participant. • Decision and work subject to U.N. rules of confidentiality. • Among other things, in charge of dispute resolution and establishing procurement channel.	July 14, 2015
JCPOA submitted to U.N. Security Council	• P5+1will "promptly" send JCPOA to U.N. Security Council (UNSC) for review and adoption "without delay."	Resolution 2231 submitted on July 15 and adopted on Monday, July 20, 2015
Adoption Day	• 90 days (or earlier if agreed by P5+1and Iran) after endorsement of JCPOA by the UNSC. From this date, participants start making preparations for implementing commitments. • EU to adopt regulation terminating nuclear-related sanctions with effect from Implementation Day. • U.S. President to issue sanctions waivers to take effect on Implementation Day.	October 18, 2015

[141] "Rouhani: EU's Incentive Package Disappointing." *Fars News*, July 6, 2018.

[142] Appendix prepared by Christopher Mann, Research Assistant, CRS; adapted from European Council on Foreign Relations.

Implementation	Components	Date/Expected
Implementation Day	• Iran to prepare nuclear related commitments and notify IAEA that it will apply Additional Protocol provisionally with effect from Implementation Day. • Simultaneously with IAEA report verifying implementation by Iran of the nuclear-related measures, U.N. sanctions terminate, EU sanctions terminate (in some cases only suspended), U.S. "ceases" application of nuclear related sanctions.	Not tied to any date, but expected to occur within 4-6 months from Adoption Day. Roughly in the first half of 2016. Occurred on January 16, 2016
Transition Day	• 8 years after Adoption Day or the date when IAEA submits a report that all nuclear material in Iran remains in peaceful activities (whichever is earlier). EU terminates remaining sanctions. U.S. terminates or modifies remaining sanctions. Iran ratifies Additional Protocol.	Expected mid-October 2023
U.N. Security Council Resolution Termination Day	• 10 years from Adoption Day, the UNSC resolution endorsing JCPOA terminates—provided no U.N. sanctions have been reimposed. UNSC "would no longer be seized of the Iran nuclear issue."	Expected mid-October 2025

Table A-2. JCPOA Commitments

Commitments	Components	Timeframe
U.N. Security Council Resolution endorsing the JCPOA	• U.S. Congress will be faced with a UNSC Resolution endorsing JCPOA before casting votes on the deal	Resolution 2231 adopted on July 20, 2015. Comes into force within 90 days.
Nuclear-Related: to be Carried Out by Iran		
Iran-IAEA Roadmap on Possible Military Dimension(PMD)	• Pursuant to Roadmap agreed between Iran and IAEA on 20 July 2015 (confidential document). • Iran will provide IAEA explanation on outstanding issues. • There will be technical and political meetings. • Arrangements in place regarding the issue of Parchin (there has been previous access to this military site). • All steps in Roadmap must be fulfilled before Implementation date.	Iran submits written answers by August 15, 2015. IAEA has one-month review. IAEA resolves remaining PMD issues/questions by October 15, 2015. IAEA presents report on PMD by December 15, 2015.
Enrichment only at Natanz—preventing "uranium path to weaponization"	• For 10 years: centrifuges reduced to 5,060 IR-1. Excess centrifuges stored under IAEA monitoring. • For 15 years: level of uranium enrichment capped at 3.67%. • For 15 years: Natanz is Iran's only enrichment facility. • Between years 11-15: Iran can replace IR-1 centrifuges at Natanz with more advanced ones.	Implementation Day

Table A-2. (Continued)

Commitments	Components	Timeframe
Enriched Uranium Stockpile—preventing "uranium path to weaponization"	• For 15 years: stockpile kept under 300 kg up to 3.67% enriched uranium hexafluoride (UF6) or the equivalent in other chemical forms (this is a 98% reduction from existing stockpiles). • Excess sold based on international prices. • Uranium oxide enriched 5%-20% fabricated into fuel for Tehran Research Reactor.	Implementation Day
Fordow—"uranium path to weaponization"	• Converted to research facility. • No more enrichment or R&D at this facility. • 1,044 IR-1 centrifuges in six cascades will remain here, but cannot enrich uranium.	Implementation Day
Research & Development	• For 10 years: R&D with uranium will only include IR-4, IR-5, IR-6,and IR-8 centrifuges. • After 8 years: Iran starts manufacturing agreed numbers of IR-6 and IR-8 centrifuges without rotors. • After 10 years: begin phasing out IR-1 centrifuges. • Manufacture advanced centrifuge machines only for the purposes specified with P5+1.	Implementation Day
Arak Heavy Water Reactor—preventing "plutonium path to weaponization"	• Iran will redesign and rebuild reactor into lower power research reactor with P5+1partnership. • Iran would take out the original core of the reactor; this will become unusable. • Permanent: Iran will not produce weapons grade plutonium. • For 15 years: no heavy water reactors in Iran. • Permanent: Iran ships out all spent fuel from Arak reactor.	Implementation Day Before Implementation date, Iran and P5+1 agree on joint venture.
Transparency—preventing "covert path to weaponization"	• By October 15, 2015: Iran clears up questions about its alleged past research on nuclear weapons (Possible Military Dimensions, or PMD) • Permanently: Additional Protocol measures—Iran will provisionally apply this and eventually its parliament will ratify it. • Permanently: full implementation of modified Code 3.1 of the Subsidiary Arrangements to its Safeguards Agreement. • For 20-25 years: IAEA has access to Iran's supply chain for its nuclear program and has continuous surveillance of centrifuge manufacturing and storage facilities. • Procurement channel created for Iran's purchase of nuclear related equipment and material.	Implementation Day PMD measures by October 15, 2015.

Commitments	**Components**	**Timeframe**
Access	• Requests for access to suspect sites will be made in good faith by IAEA. Not aimed at interfering with Iranian military/national security activities. • IAEA provides Iran reasons for concerns regarding undeclared nuclear materials or activities and request access to those locations. • Iran may propose to the IAEA alternative means of resolving the IAEA's concerns. • If cannot agree within 14 days of original IAEA request, the Joint Commission will adjudicate and if needed decision made by majority vote. • Consultation with, and voting by Joint Commission must happen within 7 days. • Iran would implement decision within 3 days (total of 24 days after original IAEA request).	Implementation Day
Sanctions Relief to be Carried Out by P5+1		
U.N.	• UNSCR Resolution 2231endorsing JCPOA goes into effect to terminate all previous resolutions targeting Iran's nuclear program—1696 (2006), 1737 (2006), 1747 (2007), 1803 (2008), 1835 (2008), 1929 (2010), and 2224 (2015). • Subject to snap-back under dispute resolution process (Preamble to agreement, paragraphs 36 and 37). • 15 days for review by the Joint Commission to assess the dispute. Time for review can be extended by mutual consent. • If unresolved, 15 days for review by Ministers of Foreign Affairs. Any participant could refer the issue to the Ministers. Time for review can be extended by mutual consent. • If unresolved, 15 days for review by Advisory Board (three members, one each appointed by the participants in the dispute and a third independent member). Will provide nonbinding decision. • Joint Commission has 5 days to review decision of Advisory Board. If no resolution and complaining party sees action as "significant non-performance"—unresolved issue can be treated as grounds to cease performing commitments in whole or part. • Complaining party will notify UNSC. • UNSC will then vote on a resolution as to continuing lifting of sanctions. If resolution not adopted by 30 days, old UNSC resolution sanctions snap back. China and Russia cannot veto. • Iran will cease to perform its obligations if sanctions snap back. • Sanctions snap-back not applicable with retroactive effect to contracts signed between any party and Iran. • After 5 years: U.N. sanctions on conventional weapons that were linked to Iran's nuclear activities terminate.	Implementation Day

Table A-2. (Continued)

Commitments	Components	Timeframe
U.N.	• After 8 years: U.N. sanctions on Iran's missile program that were linked to Iran's nuclear activities terminate. • U.S. and international sanctions on Iran's conventional weapons and missile capabilities remain.	Implementation Day
USA	• Under easing of U.S. and EU sanctions, Iran will be allowed access to roughly $100 billion revenues frozen abroad in a special escrow. • Cease the application of economic sanctions against Iran's oil and banking sector allowing Iranian banks and companies to reconnect with international systems. • Will remove designation of certain entities and individuals (Attachment III). • Allows for licensed non-U.S. persons that are owned or controlled by a U.S. person to engage in activities with Iran permitted under JCPOA. • Allows for the sale of commercial passenger aircraft to Iran. • Allows for license for importing Iranian-origin carpets and foodstuffs into U.S. U.S. takes appropriate measures to address laws at state or local level preventing full implementation of JCPOA—U.S. will actively encourage officials to adhere to JCPOA policy. • 8 years after Adoption date—if IAEA concludes that all nuclear activity in Iran remains peaceful—U.S. will seek legislative action to terminate/modify nuclear related sanctions. • U.S. sanctions on Iran targeting human rights, terrorism, and missile activities remain. • Implementation Day	Implementation Day
EU	• Terminate all provisions of the EU Regulation related to Iran's nuclear program. • Includes: financial and banking transactions; transactions in Iranian Rial; provision of U.S. banknotes to Iranian government; access to SWIFT; insurance services; efforts to reduce Iran's crude oil and petrochemical product sales; investment; transactions with Iran's energy and shipping sector; trade in gold and other precious metals; trade with Iran's automotive sector. • Removes individuals and entities designated under sanctions (Attachment 1)	Implementation Day

Commitments	Components	Timeframe
EU	• EU refrains from reintroducing sanctions terminated under JCPOA (Iran views any reintroduction as grounds to cease performing its commitments). • Refrain from policy intended to adversely affect normalization of economic relations with Iran. • For 8 years after Implementation date: EU's arms embargo and restrictions on transfer of ballistic missiles remain.	Implementation Day
Congressional Review	• 60 days: Vote to approve or disapprove agreement. • 12 days: President has 12 days to veto. • 10 Days: Congress has 10 days to override presidential veto. • Every 90 days after the review period, the Administration is required to certify Iran is fully complying with the agreement. If such certification is not made, Congress has the opportunity to enact a resolution snapping back U.S. statutory U.S. sanctions.	Thursday, September 17, 2015: Congressional approval/disapproval deadline. Tuesday, September 29, 2015: deadline for presidential veto. Friday, October 9, 2015: congressional deadline for Overriding presidential veto.

APPENDIX B. NUCLEAR WEAPONS DEVELOPMENT[143]

An effective nuclear weapons capability has three major elements: producing fissile material in sufficient quantity and quality for a nuclear explosive device; designing and weaponizing a survivable nuclear warhead; and producing an effective means for delivering the weapon, such as a ballistic missile.[144] The U.S. government assesses that, although Iran could eventually produce nuclear weapons, it has not yet decided to do so and has not mastered all of the necessary technologies for building a nuclear weapon. Tehran had a nuclear weapons program but halted it in 2003, according to U.S. government estimates.[145]

Before the JCOA took effect, then-Under Secretary of State for Political Affairs Wendy Sherman explained during an October 3, 2013, Senate Foreign Relations Committee hearing that Iran would have needed as much as one year to produce a nuclear weapon if the government made the decision to do so.[146] This estimate took into account the amount of time that Iran would have needed to produce a sufficient amount of weapons-grade highly enriched uranium (HEU), which is widely regarded as the most

[143] For more information about Iran's ballistic missile program, see CRS Report R42849, *Iran's Ballistic Missile and Space Launch Programs*, by Steven A. Hildreth.

[144] For a more detailed discussion, see Office of Technology Assessment, *Technologies Underlying Weapons of Mass Destruction* (OTA-BP-ISC-115), December 1993.

[145] A 2007 National Intelligence Estimate defined "nuclear weapons program" as "nuclear weapon design and weaponization work and covert uranium conversion-related and uranium enrichment related work."

[146] "Reversing Iran's Nuclear Program," Hearing of the Senate Foreign Relations Committee, October 3, 2013.

difficult task in building nuclear weapons, as well as to develop the other components necessary for a nuclear weapon. This estimate did not include the time that Iran would need to be able to render a nuclear weapon deliverable by a ballistic missile. Then-Secretary of Defense Leon Panetta stated in January 2012 that Iran would have needed "possibly ... one to two years in order to put [a nuclear weapon] on a deliverable vehicle of some sort."[147]

A senior intelligence official explained during a December 2007 press briefing that the "acquisition of fissile material" was the "governing element in any timelines" regarding Iran's production of a "nuclear device."[148] However, the estimate articulated by Sherman assumed that Iran would need two to three months to produce enough weapons-grade HEU for a nuclear weapon.[149] This estimate also apparently assumed that Iran would use its declared nuclear facilities to produce fissile material for a weapon.[150] The other assumptions behind the estimate are not clear.[151]

Tehran would probably use covert enrichment facilities to produce fissile material for nuclear weapons—a tactic that would require a longer period of time, according to testimony from then-Director of National Intelligence James Clapper during an April 18, 2013, Senate Armed Services Committee hearing. In his February 2016 testimony to Congress, Director Clapper said that

> We continue to assess that Iran's overarching strategic goals of enhancing its security, prestige, and regional influence have led it to pursue capabilities to meet its nuclear energy and technology goals and give it the ability to build missile-deliverable nuclear weapons, if it chooses to do so. Its pursuit of these goals will dictate its level of adherence to the JCPOA over time. We do not know whether Iran will eventually decide to build nuclear weapons.[152]

As noted in the body of this report, U.S. officials have argued that the International Atomic Energy Agency would likely detect an Iranian attempt to use its safeguarded facilities to produce weapons-grade HEU. They have also expressed confidence in the United States' ability to detect covert Iranian enrichment plants.

---

[147] Transcript of remarks by Secretary Panetta from CBS's 60 Minutes interview, January 29, 2012.

[148] "Unclassified Key Judgments of the National Intelligence Estimate: Iran: Nuclear Intentions and Capabilities," Background Briefing with Senior Intelligence Officials, December 3, 2007.

[149] The White House. "Parameters for a Joint Comprehensive Plan of Action Regarding the Islamic Republic of Iran's Nuclear Program." April 2, 2015.

[150] It is worth noting that no country has ever used a centrifuge facility designed and built for low-enriched uranium production to produce weapons-grade HEU. Therefore, Iran may need a trial-and-error period to determine the proper modifications for its own centrifuge facilities, were Tehran to adapt them for such a purpose.

[151] For a detailed discussion of the variables such estimates must take into account, see *Iran's Nuclear, Chemical, and Biological Capabilities: A Net Assessment*, International Institute for Strategic Studies, 2011, pp. 69-70 and William C. Witt, Christina Walrond, David Albright, and Houston Wood, *Iran's Evolving Breakout Potential*, Institute for Science and International Security, October 8, 2012.

[152] *Statement for the Record Worldwide Threat Assessment of the US Intelligence Community*, Senate Armed Services Committee, February 9, 2016.

In: Iran: Economic, Political and Nuclear Policies
Editor: Everett Fowler
ISBN: 978-1-53614-827-5

Chapter 10

U.S. DECISION TO CEASE IMPLEMENTING THE IRAN NUCLEAR AGREEMENT*

Kenneth Katzman, Paul K. Kerr and Valerie Heitshusen

ABSTRACT

On May 8, 2018, President Donald Trump announced that his Administration would cease implementing U.S. commitments under the 2015 multilateral Joint Comprehensive Plan of Action (JCPOA) with Iran and reimpose all U.S. sanctions that were in place prior to the JCPOA. His announcement made reference to his previous statements on the issue, including an October 13, 2017, announcement of U.S. strategy on Iran and a January 12, 2018, statement pledging to leave the agreement unless Congress and U.S. allies acted to address the full range of U.S. concerns on Iran. In his May 8 and earlier statements, President Trump asserted that the agreement does not address the full range of potential threats posed by Iran, or permanently ensure that Iran cannot develop a nuclear weapon. President Trump also again asserted that the JCPOA provided Iran with additional financial resources with which to pursue its ballistic missile program and support its regional "malign activities." In his May 8 statement, President Trump indicated that reimposed U.S. sanctions would succeed in pressuring Iran to renegotiate the JCPOA to accommodate Administration demands.

President Trump's May 8 statement also implied that, based on an early May presentation by Israeli Prime Minister Benjamin Netanyahu, Iran has not abandoned an intent to ultimately develop a nuclear weapon. International nuclear inspectors, as well as senior U.S. officials, have consistently indicated in their reports that Iran is complying with the provisions of the JCPOA. The President foreshadowed his May 8 announcement with his October 2017 and January and April 2018 refusal to certify to Congress, under the Iran Nuclear Agreement Review Act (INARA, P.L. 114-17), that continued U.S. sanctions relief to Iran under the JCPOA is "appropriate and proportionate" to the measures taken by Iran to terminate its illicit nuclear program. The withholding of that

* This is an edited, reformatted and augmented version of Congressional Research Service, Publication No. R44942, dated May 9, 2018.

certification did not automatically reimpose any U.S. sanctions on Iran, but gave Congress the opportunity to use expedited procedures to do so. Congress did not act to reimpose the sanctions.

The other powers that negotiated the accord with Iran—Russia, China, France, Britain, and Germany—have consistently asserted that the JCPOA is succeeding in its core objectives and that its implementation should not be jeopardized. Several European countries have sought to address President Trump's demands in negotiations with U.S. officials. In late April 2018 visits to Washington, DC, the President of France and the Chancellor of Germany told President Trump they want to work with the United States to formulate joint action that would address his concerns, but they urged that he keep the United States in the accord as a foundation on which to build additional restrictions on Iran. The leaders of Britain, France, and Germany, as well as the European Union, expressed "regret" about the U.S. decision and pledged to work with Iran to continue implementing the JCPOA. Iran's President Hassan Rouhani immediately reacted to the May 8 U.S. decision by pledging to continue implementing the accord, provided Iran continues to receive the economic benefits of the agreement.

This chapter analyzes the U.S. pullout from the JCPOA and its potential implications.

Overview of the Issue

In October 2017 and more explicitly in January 2018, the President linked continued U.S. participation in the Joint Comprehensive Plan of Action (JCPOA) to congressional and allied action to address the deficiencies in the JCPOA that the President identified. On May 8, he announced that the United States would cease implementing the JCPOA, using the mechanism of reimposing suspended U.S. sanctions to implement the U.S. pullout. The May 8 announcement came in advance of a May 12, 2018, date when the existing waiver of a key U.S. sanctions law was to expire. The U.S. withdrawal from the JCPOA will likely have significant implications for U.S. policy in the region.

This chapter bases its analysis primarily on the text of key documents involved in the issue—the JCPOA itself;[1] U.N. Security Council Resolution 2231 of July 20, 2015,[2] which endorsed the JCPOA; and the Iran Nuclear Agreement Review Act (INARA, P.L. 114-17, of May 22, 2015).

Presidential Decision to Cease Implementing the JCPOA

The JCPOA does not specifically provide for any party to the agreement to "withdraw."[3]

---

[1] The text of the JCPOA can be found on the website of the Department of State at https://www.state.gov/e/eb/tfs/spi/iran/jcpoa/

[2] The text of Security Council Resolution 2231 is at the following link: http://www.securitycouncilreport.org/atf/cf/%7B65BFCF9B-6D27-4E9C-8CD3-CF6E4FF96FF9%7D/s_res_2231.pdf.

[3] Some of this section is taken from a legal analysis of this option provided in CRS Report R44761, *Withdrawal from International Agreements: Legal Framework, the Paris Agreement, and the Iran Nuclear Agreement*, by Stephen P. Mulligan.

Although European and other diplomats argue that Resolution 2231 makes the agreement binding on all parties under the U.N. Charter, officials in the Obama Administration asserted that the JCPOA is a nonbinding political commitment,[4] and Trump Administration officials continued that assertion. As President Trump noted in his October 2017 and January 2018 statements, he has the authority to cease U.S. implementation of the accord. He has the authority to reimpose all or some of the U.S. sanctions that were revoked or suspended to implement the deal, to reinstate those sanctions imposed by Executive Order, and to redesignate for sanctions entities that were "de-listed" from sanctions to implement the JCPOA. The President's May 8, 2018, announcement that the United States would no longer implement the JCPOA indicated that he would exercise all these options to reimpose all U.S. sanctions that were revoked or suspended to implement the JCPOA. The President apparently does not require the approval of Congress for these courses of action.

President Trump's May 8 announcement was widely foreshadowed. On August 1, 2017, then- Secretary of State Tillerson told a press briefing: "The conversation on Iran does not begin and end with the JCPOA, the nuclear agreement, and I think if there's one thing I hope I can help people understand it's that agreement dealt with a very small slice of Iran's threats, and that was their nuclear program."[5] In a speech to the U.N. General Assembly on September 19, 2017, President Trump said

> We cannot let a murderous regime continue these destabilizing activities while building dangerous missiles, and we cannot abide by an agreement if it provides cover for the eventual construction of a nuclear program. The Iran Deal was one of the worst and most one-sided transactions the United States has ever entered into. Frankly, that deal is an embarrassment to the United States, and I don't think you've heard the last of it, believe me.[6]

On October 13, 2017, President Trump announced a new U.S. strategy on Iran,[7] following a six- month policy review. The President raised the possibility that he might terminate U.S. participation in the JCPOA if certain conditions are not met, stating that

> By its own terms, the Iran Deal was supposed to contribute to "regional and international peace and security." And yet, while the United States adheres to its commitment under the deal, the Iranian regime continues to fuel conflict, terror, and turmoil throughout the Middle East and beyond. Importantly, Iran is not living up to the spirit of the deal.... That is why I am directing my administration to work closely with Congress and our allies to address the deal's many flaws so that the Iranian regime

---

[4] Letter from Julia Frifield Assistant Secretary of State for Legislative Affairs, to then-Rep. Mike Pompeo, November 19, 2015.

[5] Department of State. Remarks by Secretary of State Rex Tillerson at a Press Availability, August 1, 2017.

[6] White House Office of the Press Secretary. Remarks by President Trump to the 72nd Session of the United Nations General Assembly. September 19, 2017.

[7] White House Office of the Press Secretary. "Remarks by President Trump on Iran Strategy." October 13, 2017.

> can never again threaten the world with nuclear weapons.... However, in the event we are not able to reach a solution working with Congress and our allies then the agreement will be terminated. It is under continuous review, and our participation can be cancelled by me, as President, at any time.

On January 12, 2018, President Trump again threatened to withdraw the United States from the JCPOA unless Congress and the European allies "fix the terrible flaws of the Iran nuclear deal."[8]

He identified the "fixes" as (1) a requirement that Iran allow immediate inspections at all sites requested by international inspectors; (2) ensuring that Iran "never even comes close to possessing a nuclear weapon"; (3) the elimination of an expiration date for the JCPOA's nuclear restrictions on Iran; and (4) subjecting Iran's development and testing of missiles to "severe sanctions." The President also called on U.S. allies to "take stronger steps with us to confront Iran's other malign activities," defined as Iran's support for terrorist groups, its development of missiles and their supply to Iran's allies and proxies, Iran's cyber threats, its human rights violations, and its threats to international shipping.

After the January 12, 2018, statement, the President replaced Tillerson and National Security Adviser H.R. McMaster with officials who have been critics of the JCPOA. Secretary of State Mike Pompeo, sworn in on April 26, 2018, and National Security Adviser John Bolton, who began his appointment on April 9, 2018, both, prior to assuming their current posts, argued in favor of military action against Iran's nuclear program and for U.S. efforts to change Iran's regime.

The May 8 announcement signaled that the Administration seeks to encourage further efforts to address its concerns about the JCPOA and broader Iran issues, possibly in a revised nuclear agreement. According to the May 8 statement

> As we exit the Iran deal, we will be working with our allies to find a real, comprehensive, and lasting solution to the Iranian nuclear threat. This will include efforts to eliminate the threat of Iran's ballistic missile program, to stop its terrorist activities worldwide, and to block its menacing activity across the Middle East.... Iran's leaders will naturally say that they refuse to negotiate a new deal. They refuse, and that's fine. I'd probably say the same thing if I was in their position. But the fact is, they are going to want to make a new and lasting deal, one that benefits all of Iran and the Iranian people.[9]

REACTION TO THE ANNOUNCEMENT

Global reaction to the May 8 announcement tracked closely with the consistent positions taken by countries and leaders on the JCPOA. The decision drew statements of

---

[8] White House. Statement by the President on the Iran Nuclear Deal. January 12, 2018.

[9] White House. Remarks by President Trump on the Joint Comprehensive Plan of Action. May 8, 2018.

support from Israel, Saudi Arabia, the United Arab Emirates, and Bahrain—all countries that assert that Iran is a major threat to their security.

European Reaction and Plans

The leaders of France, Germany, and Britain (the three European countries that negotiated the JCPOA alongside the United States)—as well as the EU collectively—issued a joint statement expressing "regret" over the decision. European leaders stated that they remained committed to the JCPOA as "important for our joint security." European diplomats have consistently asserted that the JCPOA is a binding international commitment under Resolution 2231, which endorsed the accord.

The European reaction appeared to reflect disappointment in the failure of their efforts to address President Trump's concerns through a supplemental agreement or pledges of joint action. Since President Trump's October 13, 2017, speech, Britain, France, and Germany held numerous meetings with U.S. State Department officials led by senior adviser to the Secretary of State Brian Hook, to discuss potential European steps that could satisfy Mr. Trump's demands. As the May 12 deadline to again waive key sanctions laws loomed, France's President Emmanuel Macron and Germany's Chancellor Angela Merkel each met with President Trump in Washington, DC, during the week of April 23, expressing support for working with the United States on additions to the JCPOA, or other U.S.-European joint action, that would address the expiration of nuclear restrictions, Iran's regional activities, and Iran's ballistic missile programs.

President Macron's comments during his visit suggested he might be willing to try to engage Iran (and presumably also Russia and China) in new negotiations regarding these issues.[10] Yet, no firm agreements were announced in the course of the European leadership visits. The European leaders indicated that it would be unwise to risk the collapse of the accord without a clear alternative in place, and both indicated they intended to continue implementing the JCPOA even if President Trump ceases to implement it. According to a senior State Department official briefing reporters after the May 8 presidential announcement The President made clear on January 12th that he was giving a certain number of months to try to—for—try to get a supplemental agreement with the E3 (Britain, France, and Germany). We didn't get there. We got close. We made a—we had movement, a ton of good progress, which will not be wasted, but we didn't get there.... [11]

---

[10] https://www.whitehouse.gov/briefings-statements/remarks-president-trump-president-macron-france-joint-press-conference/

[11] https://www.state.gov/r/pa/prs/ps/2018/05/281959.htm./

Iranian Reaction and Plans

Iran's President Hassan Rouhani reacted to the May 8 announcement immediately, stating that Iran would work with the remaining parties to the accord to keep it intact. He indicated that Iran would continue to implement its commitments as long as Iran derives the economic benefits of the agreement, an implicit threat that Iran might leave the accord if reimposed U.S. sanctions damage its economy significantly. Paragraph 26 of the JCPOA states that "... Iran has stated that it will treat such a reintroduction or reimposition of the sanctions specified in Annex II, or such an imposition of new nuclear-related sanctions, as grounds to cease performing its commitments under this JCPOA in whole or in part."[12] At the same time, on May 8, Rouhani directed Iran's nuclear program officials to be prepared to restart suspended aspects of Iran's program if the accord collapses entirely.

Iranian officials have consistently insisted that they would not renegotiate the JCPOA under any circumstances. Iranian hardliners are likely to oppose any such renegotiation as a capitulation and Iran's leaders have argued that no amount of U.S. or international pressure will cause Iran to cede what it views as its right to have a civilian nuclear program or the ballistic missile programs Iran says are needed to defend itself. Yet, in late 2017, some Iranian military figures suggested Iran might be willing to refrain from developing missiles with ranges over the 1,200 mile ranges of Iran's existing missile arsenal. On May 9, Iranian parliamentarians burned copies of the JCPOA and chanted anti-U.S. slogans in Iran's parliament chamber to express opposition to the U.S. decision.

Possible Congressional Responses

As noted above, President Trump has called on Congress to act on new legislation that addresses the weaknesses of the JCPOA. On October 13, 2017, Senate Foreign Relations Committee Chairman (SFRC) Bob Corker and Senator Tom Cotton released an outline of legislation that would address some of the President's concerns by setting up a trigger to automatically reimpose U.S. sanctions at any time that Iran violates existing JCPOA nuclear restrictions—even after the restrictions expire under the JCPOA. The legislation was not introduced. Another version, reportedly negotiated between Senator Corker and SFRC ranking member Senator Robert Menendez, also was not introduced. Senator Corker indicated in a press interview on April 29, 2018, that Congress might act to address President Trump's concerns about the JCPOA if European leaders support joint action on the JCPOA even if doing so might appear to contradict the provisions of the

[12] Paragraph 26 of the JCPOA.

JCPOA.[13] This suggests that congressional action might hinge on whether European leaders are able to forge a new agreement with Iran or a U.S.-European agreement that would convince President Trump to resume implementing the existing JCPOA.

USE OF JCPOA PROVISIONS

The Trump Administration could have used provisions of the JCPOA itself to cease implementation of U.S. commitments under the agreement. It opted not to do so, but instead to cease implementing the JCPOA by reimposing U.S. sanctions (see below). Paragraph 36 of the JCPOA outlines a complex "Dispute Resolution Mechanism" under which any party to the agreement can assert that another party is violating the accord and seek to resolve the issue. The JCPOA mechanism outlines a process by which Iran can resolve such a dispute but provides that, "if the complaining participant deems the issue to constitute significant nonperformance, then that participant could treat the unresolved issue as grounds to cease performing its commitments under this JCPOA.... "[14] The dispute resolution mechanism provides for the United States to be able to "snap back" all sanctions.[15] The United States is a veto-wielding permanent member of the U.N. Security Council, and the dispute resolution mechanism enables any veto-wielding member to block a U.N. Security Council resolution that would continue the lifting of U.N. sanctions.

Iranian Compliance with the JCPOA

On January 16, 2016, IAEA Director General Yukiya Amano reported to the agency's Board of Governors that Iran had implemented the nuclear measures required for the JCPOA's "Implementation Day." The agency has continued to monitor Iranian compliance with the agreement's nuclear-related requirements; all subsequent reports, the most recent of which Amano issued on February 22, 2018, document Iranian compliance with these obligations.[16] Although the IAEA reports findings of its inspection and monitoring activities and the JCPOA-established Joint Commission monitors the parties' implementation of the agreement, compliance determinations are national decisions. Department of State Director of Policy Planning Brian Hook told reporters on March 21 that Iran is in "compliance with their commitments under the JCPOA"—a reiteration of past U.S. assessments.

Although these reports and U.S. official statements and certifications indicate that Iran has not engaged in any JCPOA- prohibited activities, the agreement describes arrangements for

[13] http://www.foxnews.com/transcript/2018/04/28/corker-on-what-foreign-policy-will-look-like-under-pompeo.html
[14] Paragraph 36 of the JCPOA.
[15] Paragraph 37 of the JCPOA.
[16] Verification and Monitoring in the Islamic Republic of Iran in Light of United Nations Security Council Resolution 2231 (2015), GOV/INF/2016/1, January 16, 2016, and Verification and Monitoring in the Islamic Republic of Iran in Light of United Nations Security Council Resolution 2231 (2015). Report by the Director General, International Atomic Energy Agency, GOV/2018/7, February 22, 2018.

agency inspectors to gain access to Iranian sites, including military sites, other than those that Tehran has declared to the agency, "if the IAEA has concerns regarding undeclared nuclear materials or activities, or activities inconsistent with" the JCPOA. Should such concerns arise, the IAEA is to "provide Iran the basis for such concerns and request clarification." The IAEA could request access to the site if Iran's explanation does not sufficiently clarify the matter. The JCPOA provides for a process to resolve the issue in question if Tehran initially declines to provide access to the site. Iran allowed the IAEA to visit the Parchin military site in September 2015 as part of an agreed process for resolving IAEA concerns about possible past Iranian military-related nuclear activities.

Amano's February 2018 report states that the IAEA has continued verification and monitoring of the restrictions described in Section T of the JCPOA, which prohibits a number of nuclear-weapons-related activities.[17] The IAEA has not reported whether it has requested access to any Iranian military facilities, but the agency has a number of methods other than inspections, such as analyzing open source information and receiving intelligence briefings from governments, to monitor Iranian compliance with these and other JCPOA commitments. Amano stated in a March 5 address to the IAEA board that agency inspectors "have had access to all the sites and locations which we needed to visit."

U.S. officials have expressed concern regarding Iran's accumulation of heavy water. According to the JCPOA, Iran has committed to refrain from accumulating heavy water "beyond Iran's needs"—an amount which the JCPOA specified is 130 metric tons of "nuclear grade heavy water or its equivalent in different enrichments" prior to commissioning the redesigned Arak reactor. Tehran is to "sell any remaining heavy water on the international market for 15 years." Iran's stock of heavy water has exceeded 130 metric tons on two occasions since the JCPOA began implementation. On February 17, 2016, the IAEA verified that Tehran's heavy water stock had exceeded 130 metric tons; on November 8, 2016, the IAEA verified that Iran's stock of heavy water had again exceeded the JCPOA limit. Iran resolved the issue on both occasions by exporting the excess heavy water. Iran has sent this material to Russia and the United States, shipping at least some of it via Oman. The IAEA verified on February 11, 2018, that Iran had 117.9 metric tons of heavy water.[18]

The dispute resolution mechanism generally refers to the ability of any party to complain about potential nonperformance of only those issues that are directly addressed in the JCPOA. A U.S. accusation of Iranian noncompliance, in the absence of supporting evidence from the International Atomic Energy Agency (IAEA), would undoubtedly raise questions about the use of this mechanism to leave the agreement.

[17] Ibid.

[18] Ibid.

USE OF INARA PROVISIONS

The INARA law gives the Administration options to cease U.S. implementation of the JCPOA. However, the May 8 presidential statement on the JCPOA did not invoke INARA provisions, but instead was based on presidential authority to reimpose those sanctions that were suspended.

Material Breach Report

INARA authorizes the President to provide Congress with "credible and accurate information relating to a potentially significant breach or compliance incident by Iran ..." and, within 30 days of submitting such information, to determine whether the Iranian breach "constitutes a material breach" and whether Iran has "cured such material breach."[19] Under INARA, an Administration confirmation of an uncured material breach of the JCPOA by Iran would trigger expedited procedures for congressional consideration of legislation that would reimpose those U.S. sanctions that have been waived to implement the JCPOA—and prevent further such waivers. A summary of the expedited procedures is provided in the text box, "Expedited Congressional Procedures," at the end of this chapter.

An Administration report to Congress of a material breach by Iran would almost certainly prompt other P5+1 parties to question whether U.S. assertions are corroborated by similar findings by the IAEA. The INARA material breach report does not appear to provide for the Administration to accuse Iran of an uncured breach on any grounds other than compliance with the nuclear commitments of the JCPOA. Other P5+1 parties might also question whether the United States has provided information on any potential Iranian breach to the IAEA for further investigation under the dispute resolution mechanism discussed above. If the Administration has not provided such information to the IAEA for investigation, its not doing so would likely raise questions about the credibility of the information or the motives of the Administration in reporting such accusations to Congress separately.[20]

Compliance Certification Decisions

INARA requires the Administration to certify every 90 days that all of 4 main conditions of Iranian compliance have been met. The four points are that (1) Iran is

[19] Text of INARA.

[20] Richard Nephew. "Will Trump Recertify Iran? Much Hangs in the Balance." *Bulletin of the Atomic Scientists*, August 23, 2017.

verifiably and fully implementing the JCPOA; (2) Iran has not committed an uncured material breach; (3) Iran has not taken any action that could advance a nuclear weapons program; and (4) continued suspension of sanctions (including issuance of waivers of applicable sanctions laws) is (a) appropriate and proportionate to the specific and verifiable measures taken by Iran with respect to terminating its illicit nuclear program and (b) vital to the national security interests of the United States.

A decision on INARA certification is separate from a presidential decision whether to reimpose sanctions. INARA gives Congress the option to reimpose sanctions on Iran under expedited privileges, but does not require such action. INARA contains a provision under which sanctions reimposed by the INARA process cannot be waived or otherwise not implemented by the President.

In his October 13, 2017, speech on Iran, President Trump announced that he was withholding INARA compliance certification on the grounds that he cannot certify that continued sanctions relief is "appropriate and proportionate" to the measures taken by Iran to terminate its illicit nuclear program. Explaining this decision, the President argued that the JCPOA provided "urgently needed relief from the intense domestic pressure the sanctions had created" and also allowed Iran to "sprint towards a rapid nuclear weapons breakout" after the time-bound restrictions on Iran's nuclear program end. President Trump also asserted that Iran has not complied with the "spirit" of the agreement and has violated some JCPOA nuclear-related provisions. The President used the same grounds to withhold certification at the certification deadline of January 13, 2018. The absence of certification continued at the subsequent certification decision deadline of April 13, 2018.

As discussed in the text box below, the refusal to certify Iranian compliance gave Congress the option to act under expedited procedures to reimpose sanctions on Iran. Congress has not taken such action, to date.

SANCTIONS WAIVER DECISIONS

Separately from INARA, the President has the option to reimpose sanctions by refusing to renew waivers of the various sanctions laws, reissuing Executive Orders that were revoked, or imposing new sanctions by executive order.[21] A refusal to certify Iranian compliance under INARA does not automatically cause the reimposition of any Iran sanctions. On May 8, President Trump announced that he was withdrawing from the JCPOA by using his authority to reimpose all sanctions that were suspended or revoked. The sanctions, to go fully back into effect by no later than November 6, 2018 (180 days

[21] The waivers required are for the following provisions: Sections 1244(i), 1245(g), 1246(e), and 1247(f) of the Iran Freedom and Counter Proliferation Act of 2012 (P.L. 112-239)—every 180 days; Section 1245(d) of the National Defense Authorization Act for FY2012 (P.L. 112-81)—every 120 days; Sections 212(d)(1) and 213(b)(1) of the Iran Threat Reduction and Syria Human Rights Act of 2012 (P.L. 112-158)—every 6 months; and the Iran Sanctions Act of 1996 (P.L. 104-172)—every 6 months.

from May 8). The May 8 statement was in advance of the May 12 expiration of the waiver in place for the FY2012 NDAA (120-day waiver period). The waivers of the other 3 laws that were waived were scheduled to expire in mid-July 2018 (180-day/6- month waiver periods). Prior to the May 8 announcement, the President had renewed the waivers when they have come up for renewal—most recently on January 12, 2018.

Expedited Congressional Procedures

In the absence of the required certification, or after a presidential determination of noncompliance or an uncured breach, a House or Senate party floor leader may introduce, within 60 calendar days, a bill (with stipulated text) to reinstate sanctions. The bill is subject to expedited congressional procedures (though each chamber could choose to use its existing procedures instead). Committees that are referred the bill are automatically discharged if it has not been reported after 10 legislative days (House) or session days (Senate).

In the House, on or after the third legislative day after reporting/discharge, a majority could agree to a nondebatable motion to bring up the bill. In the Senate, after reporting/discharge, a majority could agree to a nondebatable motion to bring up the bill; no cloture process, with its associated three-fifths vote threshold, is necessary for the Senate to do so.

House floor consideration is limited to two hours. The Senate limit on floor consideration is 10 hours; thus, a numerical majority could pass the bill without the need for three-fifths to first invoke cloture. (A majority could also agree to a nondebatable motion to spend less time on the bill.) Floor amendments are precluded in both chambers. Other procedures would expedite second-chamber consideration of a bill received from the other house.

A bill agreed to by both chambers is subject to presidential veto, which can be overridden by two-thirds vote in both chambers. (Senate consideration of the veto message is limited to 10 hours; no cloture process would be required to reach the override vote.)

Source: INARA congressional review provisions, 42 U.S.C. 2160(e).

As part of the process of reimposing all Iran sanctions, the Administration will be restoring the "Specially Designated National" (SDN) designation to all of the entities that were "de-listed" to implement the JCPOA. The entities that were de-listed are those that involve Iran's civilian economy, such as banks, shipping firms, insurance entities, civilian manufacturers, and energy- related entities. Redesignating such entities resumes the application of some U.S. secondary sanctions to those entities, including provisions of the Comprehensive Iran Sanctions, Accountability, and Divestment Act of 2010 (CISADA, P.L. 111-195) or the Iran Freedom and Counter-Proliferation Act (IFCA, P.L. 112-239), that largely close the U.S. economy to third- country entities that conduct transactions with Iran-related SDNs. The entities to be "re-listed" (at the 180-day mark, which is November 4, 2018) include those that are crucial to Iran's economy, such as the Central Bank of Iran, the Islamic Republic of Iran Shipping Lines (IRISL), Iran Air, and the National Iranian Oil Company (NIOC).

POSSIBLE IMPLICATIONS OF THE U.S. WITHDRAWAL[22]

The possible implications of the U.S. decision to cease implementing the JCPOA are varied and extensive. Some possible implications are as follows:

- The European Union countries as well as Russia, China, and other major Iran trading partners might attempt to shield from—or obtain exemptions from—any U.S. penalties for conducting transactions with Iran that violate reimposed U.S. sanctions. The EU might do so through such actions as blocking regulations or the World Trade Organization complaint process. EU governments might also seek from the United States exemptions from penalties As noted, should a "critical mass" of major international firms remain in the Iran market, it might be possible to sustain the JCPOA without U.S. participation.
- It is possible that the JCPOA will collapse without U.S. participation. Major international firms, now that they face the threat of being virtually shut out of the large U.S. market, might exit Iran and thereby cause Iran's economy to deteriorate sharply. Iranian leaders might argue that Iran is no longer benefitting from complying with the JCPOA and then resume those nuclear activities that are restricted under the accord. Iran could, for example, reinstall centrifuges, increase centrifuge production, or produce enriched uranium containing more than the JCPOA-permitted amount of uranium-235. Iran could also undertake new undeclared nuclear activities and/or resume its nuclear weapons program.[23]
- Whether Tehran would be able to do so undetected would depend on both the nature of the activities, whether and to what extent Iran would disallow IAEA monitoring, and the capabilities of various governments' intelligence services. Even if Iran were to stop implementing its JCPOA obligations, the government would still be bound by its IAEA comprehensive safeguards agreement and the nuclear Nonproliferation Treaty.
- There is potential for Iran to react to the U.S. pullout from the JCPOA in ways unrelated to the agreement. Iran could, for example, expand its support to regional armed factions and groups to enhance Iran's regional reach. Iran could potentially conduct cyberattacks on U.S. or other targets. Iran could also increase the pace of its missile tests, or the ranges of those missiles, both of which would, according to U.S. officials, be inconsistent with Resolution 2231.

---

[22] For arguments put forward by experts and former U.S. national security officials, see "Keep the Iran Deal–10 Good Reasons." The National Coalition to Prevent an Iranian Nuclear Weapon. March 2018. See also Dennis Ross. "Rejecting the Iran Deal Would be a Loss for the U.S." Washington Post, op-ed. April 3, 2018.

[23] Iran ended its nuclear weapons program in late 2003 and never completed some steps necessary for building such a weapon; CRS is not aware of any public official evidence of a bureaucratic apparatus for developing nuclear weapons. For more information, see CRS Report RL34544, *Iran's Nuclear Program: Status*, by Paul K. Kerr.

- The U.S. pullout from the JCPOA might cause other regional countries, such as Saudi Arabia, to try to develop nuclear weapons to counter a possible nuclear-armed Iran.
- North Korea, perceiving that the United States does not uphold its commitments, might become reluctant to negotiate a nuclear accord with the United States.
- A resumption of Iran's JCPOA-restricted nuclear activities could prompt Israel or the United States to strike Iran's nuclear facilities to prevent Iran from having the option of developing a nuclear weapon. In his May 8, 2018, statement, President Trump said, "If the regime continues its nuclear aspirations, it will have bigger problems than it has ever had before"—a statement that could potentially be interpreted as including possible military action.
- The reimposition of sanctions could cause Iranian economic deterioration to the point where substantial unrest erupts. Iran experienced significant public demonstrations, mainly on economic grounds, in late 2017 and early 2018, and a downturn in Iran's economy could cause such unrest to reemerge.
- Contrary to the forecasts of many experts, there is potential for Iran's economy to decline to the point where Iran's leaders decide to accept a renegotiation of the JCPOA along the lines President Trump has insisted upon. Alternately, severe economic deterioration could prompt Iranian officials to negotiate restrictions on Iran's missile program, such as a limitation on the ranges of such missiles.[24]

[24] https://www.reuters.com/article/us-iran-nuclear-usa-irgc/iran-hardliners-pragmatists-show-unity-in-response-to-trump-idUSKBN1CF0R0.

In: Iran: Economic, Political and Nuclear Policies
Editor: Everett Fowler
ISBN: 978-1-53614-827-5

Chapter 11

IRAN MISSILE TESTS AND SANCTIONS[1]

POLICY CONTEXT

On February 1, 2017, the Trump Administration announced that it was "officially putting Iran on notice" for recent actions that "threaten U.S. friends and allies in the region," including the January 29 test of a ballistic missile and "weapons transfers [to groups such as Houthi rebels in Yemen], support for terrorism, and other violations of international norms." The July 2015 multilateral nuclear agreement with Iran, the "Joint Comprehensive Plan of Action" (JCPOA), does not restrict Iran's ballistic missile programs. However, U.N. Security Council Resolution 2231, which endorses the JCPOA, prohibits Iran from exporting weaponry and "call[s] upon" Iran "not to undertake any activity related to ballistic missiles designed to be capable of delivering nuclear weapons, including launches." Yet, Iran has conducted several ballistic missile tests since JCPOA Implementation Day on January 16, 2016—the day Resolution 2231 formally took effect.

POST-IMPLEMENTATION DAY TESTS

In general, Iran continues to demonstrate progress in developing a variety of short- and medium-range ballistic missiles (SRBMs and MRBMs) and demonstrating their reliability. However, public details regarding Iran's ballistic missile tests and the missile program's technical progress are vague and somewhat conflicting.

On March 8, 2016, Iran test launched two MRBMs—the Qadr-H and Qadr-F (sometimes referred to as the Ghadr). Both are liquid-fueled variants of Iran's Shahab-3 MRBM. The Shahab-3 in turn is based on the North Korean Nodong-1 MRBM, which is

---

[1] This is an edited, reformatted and augmented version of CRS Insights report, dated February 8, 2017.

derived from Soviet-era SCUD missile technology. The Shahab-3 has likely been used in Iran's space launch program. Iran's Islamic Revolutionary Guards Corp (IRGC), which runs Iran's missile programs, said the two March tests were successful, adding that the Qadr-H has a range of 1,700 kilometers (km) and the Qadr-F could strike targets some 2,000 km away. A video showed the missiles were fired in quick succession during military drills, demonstrating a salvo capability that could seriously challenge the capability of missile defense systems. The Associated Press said Iran also test launched several SRBMs, including the Shahab-1 and -2 and the Qiam (which the UN Security Council mentioned as well), during those same military exercises.

There are unverified reports of other Iranian ballistic missile tests. In May 2016, an Iranian military official claimed that an MRBM test launch took place, but this was disputed by Iran's Defense Minister and not confirmed by the White House. In January 2017, Fox News reported a Shahab-3 test launch from December 6, 2016, that had not been reported previously or confirmed, but coincides with an Iranian news agency report that referenced only the earlier March 2016 test launches.

The details of the January 29, 2017, missile launch remain unclear. A National Security Council official described the launch only as a Shahab, without providing further details. A Defense Department official said that the test ended with a failed reentry into the earth's atmosphere where it reportedly exploded after about 1,000 km. Other U.S. officials said it was a failed reentry vehicle test. Some analysts said the test was a "Khorramshahr" MRBM (that some analysts speculate to be a derivative of a North Korean missile) or perhaps even a failed satellite launch. One expert argued that Iran may have attempted to launch a satellite or tested "a nuclear-capable ballistic missile, a land-attack cruise missile, or perhaps even both."

U.S. and U.N. Responses

Subsequent to the January 29 missile test, the Trump Administration stated that it was undertaking a "deliberative process" to formulate responses to such Iranian actions as missile development and "malign" activities in the Middle East—particularly weapons transfers to groups opposed to the United States and its allies. The Administration characterized the latest Iranian test in terms similar to those used by the Obama Administration in 2016 as "in defiance of" Resolution 2231 and as "destabilizing and provocative," but not a "violation" of the resolution. The post-Implementation Day tests might not be considered a violation because of the resolution's characterization of the restriction on Iranian missile development as voluntary (i.e., "calls upon") rather than mandatory. Administration officials also stated that the tests did not violate the JCPOA, which does not contain any restrictions on ballistic missile development, and that U.S.

responses to Iran's test would be separate from and not in conflict with U.S. commitments in the JCPOA.

The Administration also followed a process at the United Nations similar to that used by the Obama Administration following Iran's March 2016 missile.

INDEX

C

D

E

F

G

H

I

J

K

L

M

N

O

P

R

U

V

W

Y

Z

Iranians in the Minds of Americans

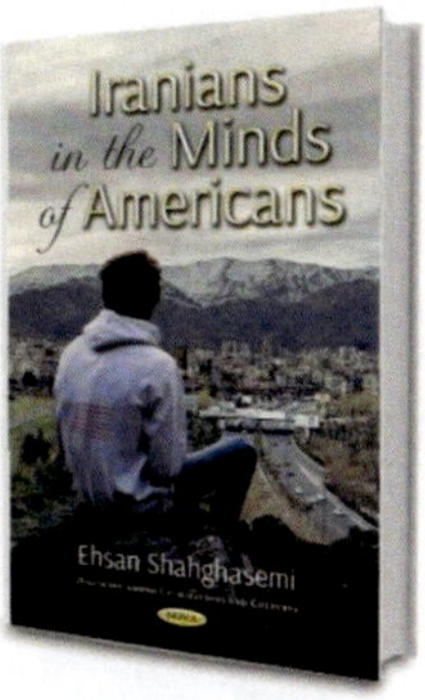

Author: Ehsan Shahghasemi (Assistant Professor, University of Tehran, Tehran, Iran)

Series: Dialogues among Civilizations and Cultures

Book Description: *Iranians in the Minds of Americans* is hitherto the most extensive study on perceptions American people have of Iranians. Also, though there are many books that study political relations between Iran and the US, this book tries to take an intercultural approach and reveal what is actually behind politics.

Hardcover ISBN: 978-1-53612-785-0
Retail Price: $195

Verification and Monitoring of the Nuclear Agreement with Iran: Resources and Challenges

Editor: Ingrid Berman

Series: Politics and Economics of the Middle East

Book Description: This book, which updates the preliminary findings from an interim report released in February 2016 (GAO-16-417), examines the JCPOA commitments that IAEA has been asked to verify and monitor and its authorities to do so; the resources IAEA has identified as necessary to verify and monitor those JCPOA commitments; and potential challenges and mitigating actions IAEA and others have identified with regard to verifying and monitoring the JCPOA.

Softcover ISBN: 978-1-53610-164-5
Retail Price: $62